Fixing A Hole

A Second Look At The Beatles'
Unauthorized Recordings

by L.R.E. King

1989

P. O. Box 77513
Tucson, AZ, USA 85703-5513

FIXING A HOLE
A SECOND LOOK AT THE BEATLES' UNAUTHORIZED RECORDINGS

Production:
John W. Blocher

Published by
Storyteller Productions
P. O. Box 77513
Tucson, AZ, USA, 85703-5513

First edition.   5 4 3 2 1

ISBN   0-944692-028

This book was prepared on an Apple Macintosh SE, using
Microsoft Word Software. Join the desktop revolution!

Printed in the United States Of America.

CONTENTS

ANOTHER FOREWORD

Looking back on it now, I think the legacy of L. R. E. King began the day my husband stuffed an envelope into Paul McCartney's mailbox.

It was late 1986. In the envelope was a tape of a song rumored to have Beatles involvement (see "AKA The Centremen?" in *Do You Want to Know A Secret?*). There was also a brief note requesting that Paul check off whether the Beatles really were on the thing (yes, no, or I don't remember), and return postage. Even then, more than a year before my husband (L. R. E. King to the public, "Larry" to no one) thought of writing a book about the Beatles, he was keenly interested in Beatles scholarship.

Paul never wrote back, the crumb, but a lot of other people have, since *Do You Want To Know A Secret?* was published. Readers have ordered extra copies for themselves and friends, collectors, scholars, and fanzine editors have sent in tapes and information, and in general Beatles-related networking has added significantly to the information presented in this book. For that, my husband and I are grateful.

Now, if you'll each get five people to buy the entire Storyteller catalog as it becomes available, we'll be even more grateful. And the five people will benefit as well.

Karen C. King
30 Jul 89

HERE WE GO AGAIN

This book is dedicated to the Fifth Beatles:

Brian Epstein, George Martin, Pete Best, Stu Sutcliffe, Mal Evans, Neil Aspinall, Tony Barrow, Geoff Emerick, Glyn Johns, Jimmy Nichol, Billy Preston, Tommy Moore, Derek Taylor, Pete Shotton, Tony Sheridan, Allan Williams, Kenny Everett, Murray The K, Ed Rudy, Phil Spector, Magic Alex Mardas, Dezo Hoffman, Allen Klein, Yoko Ono, Maharishi Mahesh Yogi, and Clarence.

Sometimes I think, as I look at a cassette label or album jacket, that if I have to listen to one more murky version of **The Long And Winding Road** or **Two Of Us**, I'm going to scream. That I never do is, I think, a tribute to the quality and freshness of the original performances rather than to my patience, since those who know me say I have none.

It has never been my intention to examine every single Beatles bootleg; not only would this involve too much mind-numbing repetition, but *You Can't Do That* listed 891 titles several years ago. Generally speaking, I prefer to look at the older titles to clear up a lot of bad information which has accumulated over years of careless scholarship, and to ferret out those all-too-few rare gems which haven't been reprinted half-a-hundred times in decreasing sound quality.

The advent of the CD format (and the corresponding high profit margin) seems to be shaking loose some excellent tapes, especially the **ULTRA RARE**s and the Pyramid titles (of course, inconsistent international copyright law is also responsible). Heaven forfend we should ever have to listen to a dull, scratchy Shea Stadium soundtrack on CD, but it will probably happen. Nevertheless, things do seem to be getting better and this has become a golden age for Beatles music collectors. But, it may also be the beginning of the end; once we have a nearly-complete issue of important studio sessions (honestly, did you ever think you would hear those?) and the major live shows in excellent sound, what remains?

Is it too early to get depressed?

WITH A LITTLE HELP FROM MY FRIENDS

The word went out and from across the globe they came to answer the call! From small fishing villages on the ocean-hewn rockbound coasts, from the soot-covered chimney forests of industrial —

...um, no; wait a minute. That was World War One. Or was it Two? Or...

Still, I asked for help, and I got it.

A tremendous amount of new information has reached me since *DYWTKAS* was published. Not only have we had *The Beatles: Recording Sessions* and *The Lost Lennon Tapes* and the **ULTRA RARE**s, but scores of readers have written to share time, tapes and knowledge (or speculation) with me. There are still many questions to be dealt with, but I believe that the collective mind of Beatles scholarship can sort them out. Meanwhile, my special thanks to the following folks:

Belmo, Walt, Captain Acetate, Budd Root and Dug for access, cooperation and understanding.

Mark Lewisohn for leading the way and setting the pace.

Arno Guzek, for a number of solid pieces of information—as well as for admitting he may have been mistaken about some of his earlier work. Also, for copies of his books.

Ian Drummond and Alison Kiddler, for the bird's eye lowdown on **The Ball Of Inverary** (Balls To Your Partner), and a number of great pieces of information!

Randy Hall, for many pages of corrections and reference material.

Todd Hawkins, for the information from *The Beatles On Record*.

Gary McCullough, for identifying Gene Vincent's **Wildcat**.

David Meile, for his memories of meeting Howard Cosell and seeing John on *Monday Night Football*.

Keith Queensen, for the Wackers info about **Oh My Love** (many had mentioned it, but only he bothered to prove it).

Richard Royston for the Donovan information, the **I Love You Too** sheet music, and a handful of typos (well, okay—errors).

For the (first) identification of **The Walk** (as well as a couple dozen points, both major and minor) as an actual song by Jimmy McCracklin, Ray Schweighardt.

John Sep, for first pointing out that **Blue Suede Shoes** on **I HAD A DREAM** was actually **Roll Over Beethoven**.

Arve Stromsether for special help with **SESSIONS**.

Doug Sulpy, for editing *Illegal Beatles* and spreading the word. Write to him and bug him about subscriptions!

For pointing out that **FIRST LIVE SHOW** was Hull, not Nottingham—well, just about everyone who wrote, especially UK Tony (he was first).

John Winn, for pointing out several things about **NOT GUILTY** and **SESSIONS** that I probably would have overlooked, and for helping out on numerous fiddley bits.

And anybody else I may have missed, especially to all of you who have bought my books and supported my efforts. Couldn't have done it withoutcha. Honest.

One last note: during 1989-90, at least, I will be editing *Belmo's Beatleg News*, the newsletter that keeps you on the cutting edge of Beatlebootlegmania. If this interests you, please write for subscription information c/o STORYTELLER. And, as always, corrections, comments and new information are encouraged and welcome, but please enclose a SASE or IRC if you need a reply.

L.R.E. King
Tucson, Jun 89

What follows is a brief explanation the various parts of the entries:

DON'T BOTHER ME
Bootleg records such as the ones discussed in this book are illegal. The author does not wish to encourage anyone to manufacture, distribute, sell or purchase such recordings.

However, he acknowledges the fact that they are available and are bought by a relatively small number of collectors. This book is intended to evaluate such recordings by examining their artistic and historical significance.

He also wishes to emphasize that he does not manufacture, distribute or sell bootleg recordings. He cannot supply you with them, nor can he advise you on how to locate them. So don't ask.

ALBUM TITLE

In most cases, this is obvious. In those instances where it is not, I have chosen what I felt was the most obvious possibility.

ARTIST

The records are listed alphabetically by title, and solo albums are inter-mixed with group albums. I did it this way because it makes the most sense to me.

MANUFACTURER

Some bootleg labels have been around for years; others exist for a single record; sometimes more than one manufacturer uses the same label name; some specialize in quality and original material; others in reprints. Many of the discs listed have been issued under more than one label.

DESCRIPTION

Many bootlegs have been reprinted, sometimes in altered form. This brief description should make it clear which pressing I'm referring to.

SONG TITLES

The listings here reflect the actual content of the records, not the listings on the jacket or sleeve. In most cases, no mention is made of inaccuracies on them (wrong titles, non-existent songs, and so forth).

Known song titles are in **boldface**, uncertain titles are in regular type (this category includes those assumed to be improvisations). Unknown instrumentals and jams are not included. Locations of the material may be found in the Index. When unknown, a significant phrase from the track is used to represent it, and is printed in regular type. Legitimate medleys or songs performed together without an obvious break have the titles separated by a "/" mark.

COMPOSER CREDITS

On the **GET BACK** material especially, it is often difficult to be sure if a brief snippet of tune is part of a real song or just a quick improvisation. In such instances, I have made my best guess.

TIMING

The timings have all been done with a digital stopwatch and are subject to a certain amount of reflex error. They are not meant to be definitive, but only used for comparison. When two identical cuts on two records have different timings, the difference is often the result of one tape being slower than the other, or one disc being mastered slower than the other. In most cases, the timing represents the actual song time. For BBC (and other similar) material, timing does not include chat. On live performances, the timing represents the length of the show (or segment of the show), and does include chat and pauses. On cuts which are excerpts from television or radio shows, or films, the timing generally represents the length of the excerpt. On **GET BACK** material, the timing tries to represent the actual time spent performing the song.

SOURCE AND DATE

In most cases, the place and date are the place and date of recording (EMI is understood to mean Abbey Road studios; **GET BACK** sessions include both Twickenham and Apple). The exception to this is for media (tv and radio—especially BBC) sources, which are typically represented by date of broadcast. Generally, if there is just one song from a source (for example, a concert), then the song title is listed first. If there is more than one song from the same source, the source is listed first.

The slate numbers of the **GET BACK** material, when known, are in the left-hand margins, in brackets. This is helpful for judging the continuity of the material, as well as its relative position within the sessions.

With regard to the release date of bootlegs, it is nearly impossible to be specific on the older titles, and even the copyright date (when present) cannot be trusted (the SAPCOR series, which came out in 88, carries an 85 date).

QUALIFICATIONS

"Probably" means I'm guessing on the basis of strong evidence. "Possibly" means I'm guessing on the basis of weak evidence. "?" means maybe.

SOUND QUALITY

This is in terms of bootleg quality, not commercial quality. Something rated poor to fair is difficult or unpleasant to listen to.

MONO/STEREO

This isn't always cut and dried. As a recording goes through many generations of copies, the separation often disappears until it's almost undetectable. In such cases, if the separation is not noticeable, I have noted the cut as mono. In some cases, a cut may have a stereo ambiance—an open, stereo "feel" to it—but no noticeable separation. These may have been run through stereo expanders, and I have generally noted them as mono. Finally, I have been told by an audio buff friend that playing a 2-track (professional) tape on a 4-track (amateur) machine can result in a loss in one of the channels which, if not compensated for, can make stereo hard to detect by having too weak a signal on one channel.

No doubt I have made some mistakes in this area but, as someone once said, "A difference is which makes no difference *is* no difference."

THE LOST LENNON TAPES

A brief note on the terms used to describe material from the *Lost Lennon Tapes*. The three-hour special does not count as an episode, so the first few programs look like this:

24 Jan 88	3-hour special
(week of) 25 Jan 88	program 1
(week of) 1 Feb 88	program 2
(week of) 8 Feb 88	program 3

and so on. The show's number and date refer to the original broadcast; the number should be universal, although broadcast dates will vary from one market to another.

"Kenwood" was John's house in Weybridge, Surrey, where he lived from Jul 64-68. "Kinfauns" was George's bungalow in Esher, Surrey, where he lived from Jul 64-Mar 70. "Tittenhurst" (Park) was John's mansion in Ascot, where he and Yoko lived from Aug 69 until they moved to NYC. "**POB**" sessions," "**W&B** sessions," and "**DF** sessions" refer to, of course, the **JOHN LENNON/PLASTIC ONO BAND**, the **WALLS AND BRIDGES**, and the **DOUBLE FANTASY** sessions, respectively. *Clock* was a film made by John and Yoko at the St. Regis hotel in NYC during the Summer of 71; it apparently consisted of a one-hour shot of the face of a clock, and had a soundtrack of John performing some of his old rock favorites on acoustic guitar.

WHAT'S THE NEW MARY JANE
UPDATES TO
DO YOU WANT TO KNOW A SECRET?

What follows is a list of major corrections from my previous book. However, there are scores of other corrections which are not discussed here but do appear in updated form throughout the book and in the cumulative index.

BACK TO MONO

Despite various listings in *Do You Want To Know A Secret*, I am now convinced that all **GET BACK** material available to date on disc (except that from the **GET BACK** LPs and acetates, and various **SESSIONS**-type material) is mono. Some cuts may have been expanded to sound like stereo (or my ears are playing tricks), but there seems to be no doubt that the source tapes (at least from the Twickenham sessions) have been single-mic mono tapes. Sorry for the confusion.

GET BACK sessions

Since the first book, the following songs and performances have been added to the **GET BACK** listing (from **CODENAME RUSSIA, BYE BYE LOVE** and **CLASSIFIED DOCUMENT, VOLUME 3**):

Across The Universe
All Things Must Pass
Another Day
(You're So Square) Baby I Don't Care
Brown-eyed Handsome Man
Bye Bye Love (brief)
Commonwealth
(There's A) Devil In Her Heart
Dig It
Dig It (another tune)
Don't Be Cruel
Don't Let Me Down
Early In The Morning (Darin-Harris; the actual song, brief)
Every Little Thing
For You Blue
Frere Jacques
Get Back
Gimme Some Lovin' (brief riff)
A Hard Rain's Gonna Fall (brief)
Hear Me Lord
Hello Dolly
Hello Mudduh, Hello Fadduh

Hi Heel Sneakers
House Of The Rising Sun
I Want You (She's So Heavy)
I've Got A Feeling
In The Middle Of An Island
It Ain't Me Babe
Jenny Jenny
Lady Madonna
Let It Be
London Bridge Is Falling Down (brief)
Low-Down Blues Machine
Oh! Darling
(Take Another) Piece Of My Heart
Please Mrs. Henry
Ramblin' Woman
Rock And Roll Music
Sabre Dance
A Shot Of Rhythm And Blues
Shout!
Slippin' And Slidin'
Suzy Parker
Take This Hammer (spoken)
Takin' A Trip To Carolina
Teddy Boy
Tennessee
That'll Be The Day
Till There Was You
Two Of Us
Under The Boardwalk (brief riff)
Well All Right
What'd I Say
You Really Got A Hold On Me (riff only)

A set of CDs (**SONGS FROM THE PAST**) has also appeared, although too late for full inclusion. They will be covered in the next volume.

If you're counting (and I am), I think this brings us up to 221 different songs or pieces of songs.

In addition:

Balls To Your Partner (GRAVE, JOURN, MAGTR)

A UK correspondent writes that this is a chorus "sung by rugby players after a game and lots of alcohol." He also includes the full chorus lyrics:

> Balls to your partner, arses to the wall,
> If you don't get f*cked on a Saturday night
> You'll never get f*cked at all!

and adds that "it runs for hundreds of verses."

Another reader writes that the song is often called "Four And Twenty Virgins," although it's usually listed as **The Ball Of Inverary** (trad.). A typical verse would run:

> Four and twenty virgins
> came down from Inverness
> and when the ball was over
> there were four and twenty less.

She included some other verses which I would love to print, but somewhere Tipper Gore is listening! Boo!

Bring It To Jerome (Green) (JOURN, Side N)

This very brief (one line) excerpt appears just after **Milk Cow Blues**, and was identified by Doug Sulpy. The influential version was probably by Bo Diddley.

C'Mon Everybody (BLACK, Side D, et. al.)

is actually **Move It** (Samwell), a 58 hit for Cliff Richard.

Domino (various)
>is confirmed as (Kaye-Ferrari) ©1951, recorded by Tony Martin.

Help!
>John recites a line of lyric on JOURN (Side L).

Hey Little Girl (In The High School Sweater) (Stevenson-Blackwell)
>is found between **Not Fade Away** and **Bo Diddley** on FILE1 and OBLA.

Jealous Guy ("Child Of Nature" version) (various)
>is now just **Child Of Nature**, since we have a complete demo of this alternate version.

Long Tall Sally (Johnson-Penniman-Blackwell)
>John recites one line of lyric on JOURN (Side L)

the **Moby Dick**
>riff from JOURN is from **Watch Your Step** (Parker-Belmonte), recorded by Bobby Parker (1961, V-Tone 223).
>
>This information appeared in an excerpt of John's WNEW interview, as broadcast on *The Lost Lennon Tapes*. John called the song "son of **What'd I Say**," because of the riff; a number of songs seems to have been derived from the Ray Charles classic, including **Love Is A Swingin' Thing** and **Some Other Guy** (Ritchie Barrett's version, anyway). The riff also appears in slightly different forms in Chuck Berry's original versions of **Around And Around** (1958) and **I Want To Be Your Driver** (1965).

Piano Boogie (various)
>is ©1970 as **Jazz Piano Song** (McCartney-Starkey) What a boring title!

(Take Another) Piece Of My Heart (Berns-Ragovoy)
>appears on SOUND on Side C, between **Let It Be** and **Little Yellow Pills**.

A Quick One While He's Away (Townshend)
>It now seems that this and Feedback Guitar (WATCH) are from the Jan 69 **GB** sessions, and not from EMI Jul 69.

"The Real Case Has Just Begun"
>Turns out to be, happily, **Vacation Time** (Berry), the uncollected B-side of Chuck Berry's **Beautiful Delilah**.

Rocker (aka Link Track & Instrumental #42)
>on the versions of the **GET BACK** album may be (or be based on) an instrumental version of **Down The Road A Piece** (Raye), covered by Chuck Berry in 60. Efforts continue to locate the original version (if one exists).
>
>This instrumental may also be based on **I'm Ready**, as the lyrics which appear here are not identical to those on JOURN (Side P). The **Rocker** title comes from Lewisohn's book on the EMI sessions, where there is an illustration of the tape box on which is written "Rocker" in what (he says) is Paul's handwroter. This may have been just a quick, off-the-cuff title, but I'm adopting it because it's obviously closer to the source.

Roll Over Beethoven (Berry)
>appears on IHAD, SHOTS and JOURN (Side P), previously listed as a version of **Blue Suede Shoes**.

Suzy Parker (various)
>is ©1971 (Lennon-McCartney-Harrison-Starkey).

Tutti Frutti (LaBostrie-Penniman)
>John recites one line of lyric on FILE1 and JOURN (Side L).

The Walk (various)
>is **The Walk** (McCracklin-Gorlic), recorded in 58 by Jimmy McCracklin.

What Do You Want To Make Those Eyes At Me For?
>is (Monaco-McCarthy-Johnson), based on the 45's label.

What'd I Say (JOURN, Side Q)
>is actually **Love Is A Swingin' Thing** (Dixon-Owens-Denson); this was the B-side of **Soldier Boy**, by the Shirelles. **What'd I Say** does appear on **CODENAME RUSSIA** (honest!).

Won't You Please Come On Home? (Dylan?) (various)
>is now "Ramblin' Woman" (Dylan?), a more concise and more likely title.

ELSEWHERE

All Of You
> as mentioned in the discussion of **ONE HAND CLAPPING**, is *not* the Cole Porter song as reported. It is probably a McCartney composition.

The studio performances for *Around The Beatles* were recorded at IBC Studios, 19 Apr 64, and not at EMI 27-28 Apr 64 as reported. The rehearsals for the filming of *ATB* were at Associated-Rediffusion's Wembley studios on 27 Apr 64, with the actual filming the following day; the first broadcast was 6 May 64.

The **BACK TO THE EGG** recording sessions were 78, with mostly mixing and dubbing in 79.

The interview segment when the group introduce themselves on **BOTH SIDES** is from the *Pop '63* interview, 24 Oct 63, *Karlaplansstudion*.

CANDLESTICK PARK
> The last song performed by the Beatles at their last concert ought to have been **I'm Down** and not **Long Tall Sally**, as that was the song they always used to close their '66 performances. However, a recent CD release of the concert confirms that **Long Tall Sally** was used just that once. The story is that tape of the last song is incomplete because Tony Barrow, who was taping the show informally at Paul's request, turned off his recorder and left early to prepare for the Beatles' departure.

Christmas Comes But Once A Year...
> While working on another project, my wife turned this up:
> > "At Christmas play and make good cheer,
> > For Christmas comes but once a year."
> > — Thomas Tusser, *Five Hundred Points Of Good Husbandry*
> > Chapter 12, *The Farmer's Daily Diet*
> Also found was:
> > "Then let us sing amid our cheer,
> > Old Christmas comes but once a year."
> > — Thomas Miller, as quoted in *All About Christmas*
> Probably the original, though, is this rhyme from Mother Goose:
> > "Bounce, buckram, velvet's dear,
> > Christmas comes but once a year;
> > And when it comes, it brings good cheer,
> > But when it's gone, it's never near."

COLD CUTS and COLD CUTS (ANOTHER)
> **Hey Diddle**, **Proud Mum** and **Wide Prairie** are ©Oct 74; **Tomorrow** (instrumental) is ©Feb 75. Exact recording dates are still uncertain.

CONFIDENTIAL DOCUMENT (which was also available as CLASSIFIED DOCUMENT)
> **For No One** is from a 14 Oct 84 *South Bank* BBC tv show documenting the making of *Give My Regards To Broad Street*. It was shown in the US as part of the *Film On Film* series on PBS. It was also shown on the Arts & Entertainment network (cable) as *The Making Of Broad Street*. (first US broadcast dates unknown, but it was repeated as recently as Aug 88) as part of the *Biography* series.
>
> **Peggy Sue** and **I'm Gonna Love You Too** are apparently from Paul's 74 unreleased film *Backyard*. Pieces of this are available on video which include **Country Dreamer** and **Blackbird** "dedicated to Edie."

A DARK HOARSE IN '74 is a reissue of **MORE FROM THE TOUR**, not **A DARK HORSE IN '74**.

DECEMBER 1963

Those four annoying "live" cuts at the end of Side B have been pinned down, thanks to Massimo Meregalli. They are not live; the screaming and "thank you" have been dubbed in. They are:

Rock And Roll Music: BBC, 26 Dec 64
Everybody's Trying To Be My Baby: BBC, 26 Nov 64
I'll Follow The Sun: BBC, 26 Nov 64
Kansas City/Hey-Hey-Hey-Hey!: BBC, 26 Dec 64

FIRST LIVE SHOW SPRING 72

The Wings concert here is from Hull University (11 Feb 62) and not Nottingham (9 Feb 62) as listed. Nottingham is around on tape, though.

George with Alan Freeman

on **BY GEORGE!** and **OHNOTHIMAGEN**. An unconfirmed (but likely) report identifies this as from *Rock Around The World*, a radio broadcast (most likely syndicated) in Toronto on 21 Dec 75; UK and US broadcast dates currently unknown. This applies to the the the cuts **Awaiting On You All**, **Far East Man**, **I Don't Care Anymore** and the brief piece of poetry, *Life Is...*

Have You Heard The Word (various)

On KHJ-AM in Oct 74, John was asked if he'd done this song. "No, no," he said. "I know there's a bootleg on it, but there's no such song. It *sounds* like us—it's a good imitation." It is indeed, but he should know.

There was a longstanding controversy about this song, which first appeared on a 1970 UK 45, **Have You Heard The Word** b/w **Futting**, by the Fut (Beacon, 160). While it was rumored to have some combination of the Beatles and Bee Gees on it (as late as 1967, the Bee Gees were managed by NEMS), Castleman and Podrazik had reasoned that it was in fact Steve Kipner (of Tin Tin) and Maurice Gibb (of the Bee Gees). But Wiener, writing in *Goldmine* (3 Jun 88) revealed that the song had been copyrighted in 1974 by Steve Kipner and Steve Groves (with two additional, unrecorded verses).

Even more remarkable, however, is that, according to Wiener, Yoko tried to copyright the song in John's name in 1985 (possibly due to a tape copy being found among his possessions)!

Hey Jude

Two different takes of the 4 Sep 68 Twickenham performances are currently available on video. On casual watching, they appear similar but a side-by-side comparison reveals not only different shots but, when the same shots are used simultaneously, different expressions, eye and body positions and so forth, indicating that they are not merely different edits of the same take.

One, which seems to be on film, is that used 8 Sep 68 on *Frost On Sunday*. This often includes the spoken intro by David Frost, the **David Frost Theme** (called "A Perfect Rendition" in *Do You Want To Know A Secret*; composer credit: George Martin) and **It's Now Or Never**, and has appeared most recently on **HEY JULIAN**. Could it be that the reports of **Tom Dooley** being performed result from a misinterpretation of **The David Frost Theme**, since they sound a bit alike?

The other, which is clearly a videotape, is that introduced by George and broadcast 6 Oct 68, on *The Smothers Brothers Comedy Hour*. It is this version which exists in stereo (although presumably the film does as well, somewhere).

The vocals were live for both versions, but the music (despite the presence of a small orchestra) was pre-recorded. The group would probably have preferred to lip-synch, but they apparently wanted to avoid the musician's union ban on miming, which difficulties were supposed to have prevented their **Hello Goodbye** video(s) from being shown in the UK. The same applies to **Revolution**, of which there is only a single version.

On the McCartney **HOME REHEARSALS** tape:
The song following **Call Me Back Again** is **Lunch Box/Odd Sox**.

The song listed as "You Know It's True" sounds a bit like, but is definitely *not*, **Death-cab For Cutie** (Stanshall-Innes), the song performed by the Bonzo Dog Band in *Magical Mystery Tour*.

In the first edition, I dated the tape (tentatively) as 78. But, at the suggestion (prodding) of others, I've reconsidered.

One sticking point in a 78 dating is the presence of **Mull Of Kintyre**, seemingly well on its way but not quite there yet. Paul shares composer credits with Denny Laine for this song, but we do not know just who contributed what. The song was supposed to have been composed during Summer 76 (after the band returned to Scotland following the world tour), but it's possible that Paul had the melody earlier than that, and that he and Denny simply finished the song in 76. If that's so (and we know that Paul often carries melodies around for a long time before recording them), then this ceases to be a difficulty.

A second problem is the apparent working version of **Letting Go**. The idea that he had merely forgotten the lyrics does not sit well, because he performed the number extensively on his 75-76 tour. If this is an accurate assumption, then the tape must pre-date (late) 75 (the tour). It is equally unlikely that he would have forgotten the lyrics between the **VENUS AND MARS** sessions (Jan-Apr 75) and the tour, especially as the band rehearsed frequently during this time (probably the *One Hand Clapping* sessions). If the song truly is still being worked on at this point, it could be no later than the end of the **VENUS AND MARS** sessions (Apr 75) and possibly as early as late 74, depending on when the song was written.

Another possibility is that the tape comes from the **TUG OF WAR** sessions (80-82), or even later. This would mean that the (released) songs which appear to be working versions, with different tunes or lyrics, might actually be just misremembered, because it had been five or six years since he had played some of them. **I'll Give You A Ring**, recorded during the **TOW** sessions and notably out of place in 74-77, is complete and very close to the released version. I am beginning to favor this dating myself.

It has been suggested that the material may be compiled from a number of different sessions. While there *are* a number of edits in the recording (sounding very much as though the machine were simply shut off; one follows a child's voice, as if one of the kids were asking a question or calling Paul to dinner), they are not placed [Mull Of Kintyre (76-77) is followed by **I'll Give You A Ring** (80-82), and later **Letting Go** (75) is followed by **Call Me Back Again** (also 75)] so that they explain the inconsistencies. This theory also does not account for the uniformity of the ambiance; these simply don't sound as if they were recorded over a number of years.

Date still unknown, but my best guess now places them circa Fall 1980. An interesting rumor claims that the original cassette was stolen from Paul's parked car somewhere in England.

Honey Don't
on **ROUGH NOTES** is not a BBC cut, as I had speculated. It may be, as some have said, a forgery.

Honey Pie
on **CONFIDENTIAL DOCUMENT** and **IT WAS TWENTY YEARS AGO TODAY**, is a bogus outtake of someone singing along with the commercial release; I was wrong when I said the lead vocals were different. Its first appearance was apparently on **FROM A WHISPER TO A SHOUT!**, covered in this book, where it is accompanied by several other equally dubious "outfakes."

I Love You Too is (Ryan-Jaques), 65, the Fourmost.
This song was performed by the Fourmost in the film *Ferry 'Cross The Mersey*; it is not on the American version of the soundtrack album, although it is on the British release (the song was co-published by Dick James Music and produced by George Martin), which has recently been reissued in stereo.

I Sat Belonely
> The tape of John reading this poem comes from Murray The K's fan club record, **As It Happened**, and probably dates from Apr 64.

The unknown **In My Life** from George's 74 tour (BOTH, 4SIDES) turns out to be from 10 Nov 74, at the Long Beach Arena.

IN THE 1970'S...

> The interview with Paul on Side B which includes a partial studio performance of **Give Ireland Back To The Irish** may be from the 21 May 75 David Frost salute to the Beatles on ABC's *Wide World Of Entertainment.*
> *Wings Over The World* is the source of the brief **Bip Bop**, **Hey Diddle**, and **Lucille** on **IN THE 1970'S**. This tv special, based on the 75-76 world tour, first aired on CBS 16 Mar 79. The **Lucille** clip may have appeared earlier still on a national news show. Although *Wings Over The World* was simulcast in stereo, these particular cuts were broadcast in mono.
> "John introduces Sergeant Pepper's Lonely Hearts Club Band" is said to have been recorded by John for Kenny Everett (?) at the **PEPPER** launch party, 19 May 67, at Brian Epstein's, and was broadcast, probably by Everett, on *Where It's At*, BBC, 20 May 67; the source of this tape would seem to be *The Beatles Story*. According to my correspondents, he also recorded an intro for **Lucy In The Sky With Diamonds**:
>> "Now we'd like to play you one that's a sad little song. Picture yourself on an old fashioned elephant. **Lucy In The Sky**. For everyone. Now."
> **Guitar Blues**—sometimes called **Talking Blues** (trad.)—is indeed from *What's Happening! The Beatles In The USA*, but the brief ad-lib is performed by George in their Miami suite in the Deauville Hotel as they are packing to leave, and is probably dated 21 Feb 64.

LAST LIVE CONCERT

is probably 15 Dec 74, Nassau Coliseum (and not MSG, 20 Dec 74)

Monday Night Football
> John's brief interview by Howard Cosell on *Monday Night Football*—traditionally dated 12 Sep 74—on **TEDDY BOY**, is probably 9 Dec 74 instead.
> The main reason for this is that between Sep and Dec 74, only one *Monday Night Football* game was broadcast from Los Angeles (where John was living then), and that was the Rams vs. the Redskins, on 9 Dec 74. On the video, Cosell gives the half-time score between Los Angeles and Washington; this is reinforced by a reader who recalls seeing John on *MNF after* he saw George in Denver (18 Nov 74) and the fact (oops) that 12 Sep 74 was a Thursday.

NOT FOR SALE

The versions of **One After 909** and **Catswalk** come from an early (probably Spring) 62 rehearsal tape, according to an Aug 88 episode of *The Lost Lennon Tapes*. This may be the same (unnamed) source that is implied in *All Together Now* as "Early/Mid 62—Various Demo Tapes."

NOT GUILTY (LP)

The title cut appears to have come from an acetate, possibly the one mentioned in *Rare Rock*.
> The first **Rain** seems to be a legitimate (if trivial) alternate mix—aside from the heavy reverb on the lead vocals, Ringo's drum fill before the backward vocals is different. The second **Rain** may lack tambourine, but the sound is so murky that it's impossible to be certain. The third **Rain** (backing vocals only) appears to be nothing more remarkable than one channel of the commercial stereo mix. **Paperback Writer** (echoless mix) seems to have been lifted directly from the *SPLHCB: AHOTBY* radio show, along with that piece of studio chat (which may belong with **Run For Your Life**). **Let It Be** may be from an acetate, or it may just be from a boot of the sound-

track. **You're Going To Lose That Girl** has a different guitar solo, aside from lacking bongos, and may also come from an acetate (a tiny fragment of the countdown remains) mentioned in *Rare Rock*. **We Love You Beatles** by the Carefrees is ©1964 (Adam-Strouse), as a rewrite of **We Love You Conrad** (from *Bye Bye Birdie*).

Now, does that put this bugger to bed?

Oh My Love (GUITAR, RARER, WORK, et al.)

Supposedly an outtake from the Jul 71 **IMAGINE** sessions, or even a Beatles version from spring 69 (?), this cut is in fact the Canadian group The Wackers performing John's song on their 72 album **HOT WACKS** (Elektra 75025), speeded up and fiddled with to make it sound rougher.

Paul In Montserrat

The listings in **TOMORROW NEVER KNOWS** should, of course, be for 81, not 71.

The Pirate Song (various)

is definitely (Harrison-Idle), as revealed in *I Me Mine*.

Quarry Men discoveries

The song listed as "Oh No, Not Me" in *DYWTKAS* is **Wildcat** (Schroeder-Gold), originally recorded by Gene Vincent (Capitol 4313), and released in the UK in Jan 60 (identification by reader Gary McCullough).

The song listed as an instrumental version of **Brown-Eyed Handsome Man** is, despite the similarity of the riffs, actually **Moovin' And Groovin'** (Eddy-Hazelwood), recorded by Duane Eddy (Jamie 904) (identification by, I believe, Allen Wiener).

John's "Rock And Roll medley" (4SIDES)

Filmed during Summer 72 in San Francisco by Geraldo Rivera and crew, John's performance of these oldies was broadcast on an unknown *Eyewitness News* (WABC-TV, NYC), probably the one during which John first announced his intention to play a benefit for the children of Willowbrook. These are not from the film *Clock*.

Say You Don't Mind

on **LIVE IN HANOVER** is (Laine), not (McCartney)

SILVER LINING (LP)

The interview on Side B (with Jimmy Nichol) was actually recorded 5 Jun 64, Treslong studios, Hillegom, The Netherlands, and broadcast 10 Jun 64, on VARA-TV as part of a tv show called *The Beatles*.

Sound Stage Of Mind (various live 74 shows) is ©1975 (Harrison).

SUNSHINE SUPERMEN!!! (and **NO. 3 ABBEY ROAD NW 8**)

Mr. Wind and **The Unicorn** are (Leitch), and **The Walrus And The Carpenter** is (Carroll-Leitch), from the 71 LP **HMS DONOVAN**.

Thank You Guru Dai

on FILE2, ROPE, SFF, and WHEN should more properly be "Thank You Guru Dev."

Too Many Cooks

may be (Holland-Dozier-Holland), Mar 74, L.A., Record Plant West

20X4 (LP)

Holding On To A Dream

In *Do You Want To Know A Secret* I repeated Wiener's assertion that this song (often called "Penny O'Dell") was not Wings but was in fact singer/songwriter Kenny O'Dell recording a song of his own. No amount of research has so far been able to produce this song, although I did turn one up by that title ©1974 (Strang), which seems not to have been recorded (or at least, released) by anyone.

Kenny O'Dell (Kenneth Gist, Jr.) is probably best known as the composer of **Behind Closed Doors**. He had a couple of singles on Kapp in 72, then changed to Capricorn in 73. His self-titled LP **KENNY O'DELL** was issued in 74, and he released another LP in 78. I have listened to both albums, and the vocals on **Holding On To A Dream** sound absolutely nothing like Kenny O'Dell (who is a country soft-rocker, with an appropriate accent); neither does the music.

But his name unquestionably appears during the playback of the song which is the source of this tape. And here's where it gets interesting, because McCartney's Jul 74 Nashville sessions (oddly, the Country Hams 45 says that both songs were recorded in England) were at the Soundshop Studios, where Kenny O'Dell's first LP was also recorded in 74. Here is also where my research hits a dead end (for the moment), because Soundshop no longer has any information from 74, and Capricorn records is defunct.

Help!

While the jacket claims that this was recorded in the studio by a reporter, many people claim it is a fake (or, as Ray Schweighardt puts it, "a forgery produced at home by a moron.").

Every Little Thing

Along the lines of the previous cut, this may be a fake of someone playing (badly) along with the commercial version.

What's The New Mary Jane

Since we now have a May 68 demo by John (with the Beatles) to compare to the Aug 68 take, it seems unlikely that, despite tradition, Magic Alex had much—if any—input into the song. Therefore, composer credits change from (Lennon-Mardas?) to (Lennon). If the song ever gets published or released, it will no doubt become (Lennon-McCartney).

When Everybody Comes To Town (Harrison?)

is more correctly **Every Time Somebody Comes To Town** (Harrison-Dylan?).

The speculation that this and **I'd Have You Any Time** were recorded 1 May 70 appears to be incorrect. George had spent some time with Dylan at Woodstock in late Nov 68 (while in the U.S. to work on Jackie Lomax's album—this is also the time at which he recorded his segment of the 68 Christmas record) and from chat and performances during the **GET BACK** sessions, it is clear that he returned with some tapes which he gave to the other Beatles. Some informal work during this period seems to have produced the two Harrison-Dylan songs.

The 1 May 70 session at CBS in Nashville may have produced the material on **CONFIDENTIAL DOCUMENT, VOLUME 3** (copied from a Dylan boot, **YESTERDAY'S BLUES**). This appears to have been mostly a Dylan session, with George sitting in, and his contributions are minimal.

WHEN IT SAYS BEATLES...

Memphis is from the 1 Jan 62 Decca audition, and not 5 Oct 63 BBC.

THE POLYDOR SESSIONS

Current thinking (although some of these are disputed) puts the Hamburg recording dates as follows:

Ain't She Sweet	May 61
Cry For A Shadow	May 61
My Bonnie	May 61
Nobody's Child	May 61
When The Saints Go Marching In	May 61
Why (Can't You Love Me Again)	May 61
If You Love Me Baby	May 61

Sweet Georgia Brown	Apr 62
Sweet Georgia Brown (new vocals, Sheridan only)	early 64

and, possibly:

Swanee River (on MGM SE 4215?)	Apr 62
or	
Skinny Minnie (on German Polydor 21485?)	Apr 62

A SECCA DECCA AUDITION?

In *The Beatles On Record*, J. P. Russell seems to claim that there was a second Decca audition on 9 Jan 62. This date appears in Grid Leek's bogus history of the Decca singles on **THE DECCA TAPES** bootleg LP as their first Decca recording session. Does anyone out there have any reason to think that Russell didn't mistake a piece of fiction for fact? [The Beatles were in Liverpool that day, playing a lunchtime set at the Cavern, but could have made it to London.]

POP GO THE BEATLES!

From Oct-Dec 88, the BBC ran *The Beeb's Lost Beatles Tapes*, 14 half-hour radio shows comprising "the very best in session music and chat recorded," including '60s material which was never broadcast. The word was that eventually they would be syndicating these to American radio. New music was minimal, with many of the tracks coming directly from bootlegs, although there were many new chat and interview pieces of some value. These shows are only now becoming available via trading circles.

NEW LIVE SHOWS?

In the last year, a couple of new live Beatles shows are said to have surfaced. One, a Detroit show from 6 Sep 64, is supposed to have been pressed as a 500-copy limited edition available only in Detroit (although I have yet to hear from anyone who actually has a copy). The other is said to be video and audio from Singapore. As the Beatles never played Singapore, the tape—if it exists at all—might be Hong Kong (9 Jun 64) or Manilla (4 Jul 66).

SHAME, SHAME: OUTFAKES

This is a category which includes cuts which (a) sound like the Beatles, or (b) have such terrible sound quality that they could be anybody, or (c) are the Beatles but consist of home-made "rarities."

The following bootleg LP cuts are dubious enough to qualify:

Birthday
EXTEN, NOT4, RED
The End
TALKS
Every Little Thing
ROPE
Help!
20X4
Hey Bulldog
RECO, ROPE
Honey Don't
ROUGH
Honey Pie
CONFI, HEAD, OFF, 1234, WHISP, YEARS
It's All Too Much
NIGHT
It's Only Love
ROPE

Rain (instrumental)
    NOTG
Savoy Truffle
    1234, ROPE, WHISP

Currently making the tape trading rounds are:

"Annie" and "Not Unknown"
    As discussed in the section **TOMORROW NEVER KNOWS**, these sound nothing like any or all of the Beatles. I have been told that these are from a single by the group Blonde (not Blondie).

"The Dream"
    Three different versions! A vocal version allegedly from 66, and instrumental and vocal versions supposedly from 68.
    The 66 version sounds like someone using a vocoder and the sound quality is so poor that the melody and lyrics are virtually indistinguishable. Doesn't sound like Lennon-McCartney at all.
    The 68 instrumental is good mono; a pleasant tune but nothing special. Lots of piano and phased guitar. Sounds like Al Stewart's **Year Of The Cat**.
    The 68 vocal sounds a little like Paul, but more like someone trying to imitate him. Probably a finished version, with sound effects (sea gulls) and lots of strings. No way is this the Beatles.

Make Love To The End
    This one has been around for a number of years, but only booted once that I know of. It's supposed to be John & Yoko & Mal (or Ringo), sometime in the early '70s. It does sound a bit like John and Yoko, but the thing is a terrible mess.

"Take Out The Hudson"
    A pleasant little tune which sounds a bit like Paul, but the sound quality is terrible, so who can be sure?

"A famous producer's (or rock star's) remixes"
    The story here is that some famous rock star or producer or somebody was allowed to take the Beatles' master tapes home for remixing practice. Uh-huh, I'm sure. There are about twenty of these remixes floating around; their quality is astonishingly good—as they should be, since they're taken from CDs. In fact, these mixes (all mono—and there's that warning buzzer) are nothing but single-channel or OOPSed versions. They are different and fun to listen to—as long as you know what they are: not rare and certainly not valuable.

"Wings' Wild Wonders"

Signs Of Love (78)	Please Come Home (77)
The Best Is Yet To Come (75)	Go For The Beer (78)
Looking Into Love (74)	Shake Your Engines (74)
Need A Guarantee Of Love (74)	Runaway Teenager (79)
Jimmy Takes A Ride (78)	Relax In Red (78)

    About half an hour of stuff along the lines of "The Dream" and "Take Out The Hudson." Some parts sound a little like Paul & co., but the sound quality is abominable and seems to be deliberately distorted, which is certainly a reason to be suspicious. Extremely dubious.

STOP PRESS

Too late to be included properly but too important to leave out is the identifcation (by reader Greg Smith) of "I Hate To See The Evening Sun Go Down" as **St. Louis Blues**, by W. C. Handy.

BBC SHOW INDEX
(VERSION 2.0)

Song titles not in boldface were recorded but not broadcast. The designation "(live)" indicates that the songs were performed in front of a live audience. Note that this index includes **THE BEATLES AT THE BEEB, VOL.S 12 & 13**, although they have not been examined in this book. Many new talk appearances have been added, and a few non-BEEB (pirate radio) appearances have been included as well in an effort to make this listing as complete as possible.

8 Mar 62, *TEENAGER'S TURN* (live)
Dream Baby
      BEEB, LBEEB, MEET, 1234, REINTRO, WOND, W/PETE
Memphis
      LBEEB, MEET, WOND, W/PETE
Please Mr. Postman
      LBEEB, MEET, W/PETE

15 Jun 62, *HERE WE GO*
Ask Me Why
      LBEEB, MEET, W/PETE
Besame Mucho
      LBEEB, MEET, W/PETE
A Picture Of You
      LBEEB, MEET, 1234, WOND, W/PETE
Shiela

26 Oct 62, *HERE WE GO*
Love Me Do
A Taste Of Honey
P.S. I Love You

4 Dec 62, *THE TALENT SPOT*
Love Me Do
P.S. I Love You
Twist And Shout

22 Jan 63, *POP INN*
interview

25 Jan 63, *HERE WE GO*
Chains
Please Please Me
Ask Me Why
Three Cool Cats

26 Jan 63, *SATURDAY CLUB*
Some Other Guy
     BEAUT, BEEB, CASTS, MEET, SHOTS, W/PETE
Love Me Do
Please Please Me
Keep Your Hands Off My Baby
     BEAUT, CASTS, MEET, PLEASE, SHOTS, WOND, W/PETE
Beautiful Dreamer
     BEAUT, MEET, REINTRO, WOND, W/PETE

29 Jan 63, *THE TALENT SPOT*
Please Please Me
Ask Me Why
Some Other Guy

20 Feb 63, *PARADE OF THE POPS* (live)
Love Me Do
Please Please Me

12 Mar 63, *HERE WE GO*
Misery
Do You Want To Know A Secret
Please Please Me
I Saw Her Standing There

16 Mar 63, *SATURDAY CLUB* (live)
I Saw Her Standing There
     MEET, W/PETE
Misery
     MEET, W/PETE
Too Much Monkey Business
     MEET, W/PETE
I'm Talking About You
     BEAUT, MEET, PLEASE, W/PETE
Please Please Me
     MEET, W/PETE
The Hippy Hippy Shake
     MEET, W/PETE

28 Mar 63, *ON THE SCENE*
Misery
Do You Want To Know A Secret
Please Please Me

7 Apr 63, *EASY BEAT*
Please Please Me
Misery
From Me To You
     MEET, W/PETE

9 Apr 63, *POP INN*
interview

18 Apr 63, *SWINGING SOUND '63* (live)
Twist And Shout
     BEEB1, MONKEY
From Me To You
     BEEB1, MONKEY

22 Apr 63, *SIDE BY SIDE*
Side By Side (theme)
>BEEB1, BEEB2, BEEBCD, MONKEY, REINTRO, YEARS

I Saw Her Standing There
Do You Want To Know A Secret
Baby It's You
Please Please Me
From Me To You
Misery

13 May 63, *SIDE BY SIDE*
Side By Side (theme)
>BEEB1, BEEB2, BEEBCD, MONKEY, REINTRO, YEARS

From Me To You
Long Tall Sally
>AUCTION, BEEB2, MONKEY

A Taste Of Honey
>BEEB2, MONKEY

Chains
>BEEB2, MONKEY

Thank You Girl
>BEEB2, MONKEY, WITHER

Boys
>BEEB2, MONKEY

25 May 63, *SATURDAY CLUB*
I Saw Her Standing There
>BEEB1, BEEBCD, MONKEY

Do You Want To Know A Secret
>BEEB1, BEEBCD, MONKEY

Boys
>BEEB1, BEEBCD, MONKEY

Long Tall Sally
>BEEB1, BEEBCD, MONKEY

From Me To You
>BEEB1, BEEBCD, MONKEY

Money (That's What I Want)
>BEEB1, BEEBCD, MONKEY

3 Jun 63, *STEPPIN' OUT*
Please Please Me
>BEEB1, MONKEY

I Saw Her Standing There
>BEEB1, MONKEY

Roll Over Beethoven
Thank You Girl
From Me To You
Twist And Shout

4 Jun 63, *POP GO THE BEATLES*
Pop Go The Beatles (theme)
>BEEB2, BEEBCD

From Me To You
Everybody's Trying To Be My Baby
>BEEB2, MONKEY

Do You Want To Know A Secret
>BEEB2, COMPL, MONKEY, STONE, STUDIO, STUD1

You Really Got A Hold On Me
>BEEB2, MONKEY, STUDIO, STUD1

Misery
        COMPL, LBEEB, RECO, STONE, STUDIO, STUD1
The Hippy Hippy Shake
        DEMO, LBEEB, STUD1, THEIR, 21

11 Jun 63, *POP GO THE BEATLES*
Pop Go The Beatles (theme)
        BEEB2, BEEBCD
Too Much Monkey Business
        BEAUT, BEEB2, MONKEY, 1234, WOND
I Got To Find My Baby
        BEEB2, BEEBCD, MONKEY, 1234, PLEASE, WOND
Young Blood
        BEAUT, BEEB2, BEEBCD, KNIGHT, MONKEY, 1234, WOND, YOUNG
Baby It's You
        BEEB2, BEEBCD, MONKEY, PLEASE
Till There Was You
        BEEB2, MONKEY
Love Me Do
        BEEB2, MONKEY

18 Jun 63, *POP GO THE BEATLES*
Pop Go The Beatles (theme)
        BEEB, BEEB2, BEEB3, BEEB4, BEEB5, BEEB6, BEEBCD, BROAD, REINTRO
A Shot Of Rhythm And Blues
        BEEB3, BEEBCD, WITHER, YOUNG
Memphis
        BEEB3, BEEBCD
A Taste Of Honey
        BEEB3, PLEASE
Sure To Fall (In Love With You)
        BEEB3, BEEBCD, YOUNG
Money (That's What I Want)
        BEEB3, WITHER
From Me To You
Happy Birthday To You
        BEEB3, BEEBCD

23 Jun 63, *EASY BEAT*
Some Other Guy
        BEEB1, BEEBCD, MONKEY, WITHER, YEARS
A Taste Of Honey
        BEEB1, BEEBCD, MONKEY
Thank You Girl
        BEEB1, BEEBCD, MONKEY
From Me To You
        BEEB1, BEEBCD, MONKEY

24 Jun 63, *SIDE BY SIDE*
Side By Side (theme)
        BEEB1, BEEB2, BEEBCD, MONKEY, REINTRO, YEARS
Too Much Monkey Business
        BEEB1, BEEBCD, KNIGHT, MONKEY
Love Me Do
Boys
        BEEB1, BEEBCD, MONKEY, PLEASE
I'll Be On My Way
        BEEB, BEEB1, BEEBCD, DIGIT, LINING, MONKEY, ROUGH, SOLDIER, 2MUCH,
        WALK, WITHER, WITHL, YEARS

From Me To You
    BEEB1, BEEBCD, MONKEY

25 Jun 63, *POP GO THE BEATLES*
Pop Go The Beatles (theme)
    BEEB, BEEB2, BEEB3, BEEB4, BEEB5, BEEB6, BEEBCD, BROAD, REINTRO
Anna (Go To Him)
    BEEB3, PLEASE
I Saw Her Standing There
    BEEB3
Boys
    BEEB3
Chains
    BEEB3
P.S. I Love You
    BEEB3, PLEASE
Twist And Shout
    BEEB3
A Taste Of Honey

29 Jun 63, *SATURDAY CLUB*
I Got To Find My Baby
    BEAUT, BEEB, BEEB2, MONKEY
Memphis
    BEEB2, MONKEY, WITHER
Money (That's What I Want)
    LBEEB, STUD1
Till There Was You
    LBEEB, STUDIO, STUD1
From Me To You
    BEEB2, MONKEY, STUDIO, STUD1
Roll Over Beethoven
    BEEB2, MONKEY, STUDIO, STUD1

29 Jun 63, *JUKE BOX JURY* (John only)

4 Jul 63, *THE BEAT SHOW*
From Me To You
A Taste Of Honey
Twist And Shout

16 Jul 63, *POP GO THE BEATLES*
Pop Go The Beatles (theme)
    BEEB, BEEB2, BEEB3, BEEB4, BEEB5, BEEB6, BEEBCD, BROAD, REINTRO
That's All Right, Mama
    BEAUT, BEEB, BEEB3, BEEBCD, DIGIT, KNIGHT, 1234
There's A Place
    BEAUT, BEEB3, BEEBCD, PLEASE
Carol
    BBC, BEEB, BEEB3, BEEBCD, BROAD, DEMO, LINING, REINTRO, SPLHCB
Soldier Of Love
    BBC, BEEB, BEEB3, BEEBCD, BROAD, SOLDIER, THEIR, WITHER, YEARS
Lend Me Your Comb
    BBC, BEEB, BEEB3, BEEBCD, BROAD, DEMO, LINING, PLEASE
Clarabella
    BBC, BEEB, BEEB3, BEEBCD, BROAD, REINTRO
Three Cool Cats
Sweet Little Sixteen
Ask Me Why

Ask Me Why

21 Jul 63, *EASY BEAT*
I Saw Her Standing There
　　　MEET, W/PETE
A Shot Of Rhythm And Blues
　　　DEMO, MEET, WOND, W/PETE
There's A Place
　　　MEET, W/PETE
Twist And Shout
　　　W/PETE

23 Jul 63, *POP GO THE BEATLES*
Pop Go The Beatles (theme)
　　　BEEB, BEEB2, BEEB3, BEEB4, BEEB5, BEEB6, BEEBCD, BROAD, REINTRO
Sweet Little Sixteen
　　　BEAUT, BEEB, BEEB4, KNIGHT, 1234, YOUNG
A Taste Of Honey
Nothin' Shakin' (But The Leaves On The Trees)
　　　BBC, BEEB, BEEB4, DEMO, DON'T, PETE, SILVER, WITHER, WITHL, YELL
Love Me Do
　　　8ARMS, LBEEB, RAREST2, RECO, STUDIO, STUD1
Lonesome Tears In My Eyes
　　　BBC, BEEB, BEEB4, DEMO, DON'T, SILVER, WITHL, YELL
So How Come (No One Loves Me)
　　　BBC, BEEB, BEEB4, DEMO, DON'T, PETE, SILVER, WITHER, YELL

30 Jul 63, *POP GO THE BEATLES*
Pop Go The Beatles (theme)
　　　BEEB, BEEB2, BEEB3, BEEB4, BEEB5, BEEB6, BEEBCD, BROAD, REINTRO
Memphis
　　　BEEB, BEEB4, BROAD
Do You Want To Know A Secret
　　　BEEB, BEEB4, BROAD, PLEASE
Till There Was You
　　　BEEB4, BROAD
Matchbox
　　　BEEB, BEEB4, BROAD
Please Mr. Postman
　　　BEEB, BEEB4, PETE, SILVER, WITHL, YEARS
The Hippy Hippy Shake
　　　BEEB, BEEB4, BROAD

6 Aug 63, *POP GO THE BEATLES*
Pop Go The Beatles (theme)
　　　BEEB, BEEB2, BEEB3, BEEB4, BEEB5, BEEB6, BEEBCD, BROAD, REINTRO
I'm Gonna Sit Right Down And Cry (Over You)
　　　BEAUT, BEEB4, DEMO, DON'T, PLEASE, THEIR, 21, YELL
Crying, Waiting, Hoping
　　　BEEB, BEEB4, DEMO, DON'T, PETE, REINTRO, SILVER, SUPER1, THEIR, 21,
　　　WITHL, YEARS, YELL, YOUNG
Kansas City/Hey-Hey-Hey-Hey!
　　　BEEB4, STUDIO, STUD1, YOUNG
To Know Her Is To Love Her
　　　BEAUT, BEEB, BEEB4, DEMO, DON'T, KNIGHT, 21, YELL
The Honeymoon Song
　　　BEAUT, BEEB, BEEB4, DEMO, DON'T, KNIGHT, THEIR, YELL
Twist And Shout
　　　BEEB4

13 Aug 63, *POP GO THE BEATLES*
Pop Go The Beatles (theme)
     BEEB, BEEB2, BEEB3, BEEB4, BEEB5, BEEB6, BEEBCD, BROAD, REINTRO
Long Tall Sally
     BEEB5, STUDIO, STUD1
Please Please Me
     BEEB5, COMPL, 8ARMS, PLEASE, RAREST2, STONE, STUDIO, STUD1
She Loves You
     BEEB5
You Really Got A Hold On Me
     BEEB5
I'll Get You
     BEAUT, BEEB5
I Got A Woman
     DEMO, DON'T, BEEB5, YELL

20 Aug 63, *POP GO THE BEATLES*
Pop Go The Beatles (theme)
     BEEB, BEEB2, BEEB3, BEEB4, BEEB5, BEEB6, BEEBCD, BROAD, REINTRO
She Loves You
     BEEB5, STUDIO, STUD2
Words Of Love
     AUCTION, BEAUT, BEEB5, RECO, STUDIO, STUD2
Glad All Over
     BEAUT, BEEB5, DEMO, DON'T, REINTRO, YELL
I Just Don't Understand
     BEEB, BEEB5, DEMO, DON'T, PLEASE, THEIR, YELL
(There's A) Devil In Her Heart
     BEEB5, STUDIO, STUD2
Slow Down
     AUCTION, BEEB5, DON'T, HOWDO, YELL

24 Aug 63, *SATURDAY CLUB*
Long Tall Sally
She Loves You
Glad All Over
Twist And Shout
You Really Got A Hold On Me
I'll Get You

27 Aug 63, *POP GO THE BEATLES*
Pop Go The Beatles (theme)
     BEEB, BEEB2, BEEB3, BEEB4, BEEB5, BEEB6, BEEBCD, BROAD, REINTRO
Ooh! My Soul
     BEAUT, BEEB5, 1234, WITHER, WOND, W/PETE
Don't Ever Change
     BBC, BEEB, BEEB5, DEMO, DON'T, REINTRO, THEIR, WITHL, YELL
Twist And Shout
     BEEB5
She Loves You
Anna (Go To Him)
     LBEEB, STUDIO, STUD2
A Shot Of Rhythm And Blues
     BBC, BEEB, DEMO, DON'T, LBEEB, 21, WITHL, WOND, YELL

30 Aug 63, *NON STOP POP*
"Pop Chat" interview by Phil Tate
     MEET

3 Sep 63, *POP GO THE BEATLES*
Pop Go The Beatles (theme)
        BEEB, BEEB2, BEEB3, BEEB4, BEEB5, BEEB6, BEEBCD, BROAD, REINTRO
From Me To You
I'll Get You
Money (That's What I Want)
        LBEEB, STUDIO, STUD2
There's A Place
        BEEB5, STUDIO, STUD2
Honey Don't
        BACK, BEEB5, BOTH, CASTS, LINING, POWER, SHOTS, SNAPS, STUDIO,
        STUD2
Roll Over Beethoven
        BEEB5
Lucille
Baby It's You
She Loves You

10 Sep 63, *POP GO THE BEATLES*
Pop Go The Beatles (theme)
        BEEB, BEEB2, BEEB3, BEEB4, BEEB5, BEEB6, BEEBCD, BROAD, REINTRO
Too Much Monkey Business
        BBC, BEEB, BEEB6, LINING, YOUNG
Till There Was You
Love Me Do
        BEEB6, PLEASE
She Loves You
        BEEB6, KNIGHT
I'll Get You
        BEEB6, KNIGHT
A Taste Of Honey
        BEEB6
The Hippy Hippy Shake
        BEEB6, YOUNG

17 Sep 63, *POP GO THE BEATLES*
Pop Go The Beatles (theme)
        BEEB, BEEB2, BEEB3, BEEB4, BEEB5, BEEB6, BEEBCD, BROAD, REINTRO
Chains
        BEEB6, PLEASE, STUDIO, STUD2
You Really Got A Hold On Me
        BEEB6, WITHER
Misery
        BEEB6, PLEASE
Lucille
        BEEB6, DEMO, KNIGHT, SOME, STUD2, THEIR
From Me To You
        BEEB6, KNIGHT
Boys
        BEEB6, SOME, STUDIO, STUD2
A Taste Of Honey

24 Sep 63, *POP GO THE BEATLES*
Pop Go The Beatles (theme)
        BEEB, BEEB2, BEEB3, BEEB4, BEEB5, BEEB6, BEEBCD, BROAD, REINTRO
She Loves You
        BEEB6
Ask Me Why
        BEEB6, PLEASE

(There's A) Devil In Her Heart
  BEEB6, WITHER, YOUNG
I Saw Her Standing There
  BEEB6, PLEASE, STUDIO, STUD2
Sure To Fall (In Love With You)
  BACK, BEEB6, DEMO, DON'T, POWER, REINTRO, STUD2, 21, YELL
Twist And Shout
  BEEB6, PLEASE

5 Oct 63, *SATURDAY CLUB*
I Saw Her Standing There
  BEEB7
Memphis
  BEAT, BEEB7, WHEN, WOND, YOUNG
Happy Birthday To You
  BEAT, BEEB, BEEB7, 1234, REINTRO, WOND
I'll Get You
She Loves You
Lucille
  BEEB7, HAVE, RECO

20 Oct 63, *EASY BEAT*
I Saw Her Standing There
  BEEB7
Love Me Do
  BEEB7
Please Please Me
  BEEB7
From Me To You
  BEEB7
She Loves You
  BEEB7

3 Nov 63, *THE KEN DODD SHOW*
She Loves You

3 Nov 63, *THE PUBLIC EAR*
chat

21 Dec 63, *SATURDAY CLUB*
All I Want For Christmas Is A Beatle
  BEEB8
Rudolph The Red-Nosed Reindeer
  BEEB8
All My Loving
This Boy
  BEEB, BEEB8, KNIGHT, WITHL
I Want To Hold Your Hand
  BEEB8
Till There Was You
  BEEB8
Roll Over Beethoven
  BEEB8
She Loves You
  BEEB8
"Crimble" medley
  BEEB8

26 Dec 63, *FROM US TO YOU*
From Us To You (theme)
  BEEB, BEEB8, BEEB9, BEEB10, BEEB11, BUG, PARL, RARE, REINTRO, ROUGH,
  SOME, WITHL
Tie Me Kangaroo Down, Sport
  BEEB8
She Loves You
  BEEB8
All My Loving
  BEEB8
Roll Over Beethoven
  BEEB8
Till There Was You
  BEEB8
Boys
  BEEB8
Money (That's What I Want)
  BEEB8
I Saw Her Standing There
  BEEB8
I Want To Hold Your Hand
  BEEB8

8 Feb 64, *SATURDAY CLUB*
phone call from New York City
  BEEB8, LBEEB, WITHER

15 Feb 64, *SATURDAY CLUB*
All My Loving
  BEEB9
Money (That's What I Want)
  BEEB9
The Hippy Hippy Shake
  BEEB9
I Want To Hold Your Hand
  BEEB9
Roll Over Beethoven
  BEEB9
Johnny B. Goode
  BEAT, BEAUT, BEEB, BEEB9
I Wanna Be Your Man
  BEEB9

22 Mar 64, *THE PUBLIC EAR*
chat from George, Ringo & John

30 Mar 64, *FROM US TO YOU*
From Us To You (theme)
  BEEB, BEEB8, BEEB9, BEEB10, BEEB11, BUG, PARL, RARE, REINTRO, ROUGH,
  SOME, WITHL
You Can't Do That
  BEEB9
Roll Over Beethoven
  BEEB, BEEB9, BUG, WITHER, WITHL
Till There Was You
  BEEB, BEEB9, WITHER
I Wanna Be Your Man
  BBC, BEEB, BEEB9, BUG, RECO, WITHER, WITHL

Please Mr. Postman
 BEEB9, ROUGH, WITHER
All My Loving
 BEEB, BEEB9, BUG, WITHER, WITHL
This Boy
 BEEB9, 1964, PETE, ROUGH, SILVER, YEARS
Can't Buy Me Love
 BEEB, BEEB9, KNIGHT, 1964, SILVER, WITHL

4 Apr 64, *SATURDAY CLUB*
Everybody's Trying To Be My Baby
 BEEB10
I Call Your Name
 BEEB10
I Got A Woman
 BEEB, BEEB10, DEMO, HOWDO, SOLDIER, SNAPS
You Can't Do That
 BEEB10
Can't Buy Me Love
 BEEB10
Sure To Fall (In Love With You)
 BBC, BEEB, BEEB10, BROAD
Long Tall Sally
 BEEB10, BROAD

2 May 64, *A SLICE OF LIFE*
John is interviewed

18 May 64, *FROM US TO YOU*
From Us To You (theme)
 BEEB, BEEB8, BEEB9, BEEB10, BEEB11, BUG, PARL, RARE, REINTRO, ROUGH,
 SOME, WITHL
I Saw Her Standing There
 BEEB10
Kansas City/Hey-Hey-Hey-Hey!
 BEEB10
Happy Birthday To You
 BEEB10
I Forgot To Remember To Forget
 DEMO, BEEB10, HEARD, MAIL, 1234, RECO, YOUNG
You Can't Do That
 BEEB10
Sure To Fall (In Love With You)
 BEEB10
Can't Buy Me Love
 BEEB10
Matchbox
 BEEB10
Honey Don't
 BEEB10

16 Jul 64, *TOP GEAR*
Long Tall Sally
 BEEB, BEEB11, LAST, LONG, LOOKING, MARY, NASSAU, POPS, ROAD, TOP
Things We Said Today
 BEEB, BEEB11, BOTH, BUG, KNIGHT, LAST, LOOKING, MARY, NASSAU, POPS,
 ROAD, TOP, 20X4, WITHL
A Hard Day's Night
 BEEB, BEEB11, BUG, KNIGHT, LAST, LONG, LOOKING, LOVE, MARY, NASSAU,
 POPS, ROAD, TOP, WITHL, YEARS,

And I Love Her
> BBC, BEEB, BEEB11, KNIGHT, WITHL

I Should Have Known Better
> BEEB11

If I Fell
> BEEB11

You Can't Do That
> BEEB11

18 Jul 64, *HIGHLIGHT*
Paul is interviewed

3 Aug 64, *FROM US TO YOU*

From Us To You (theme)
> BEEB, BEEB8, BEEB9, BEEB10, BEEB11, BUG, PARL, RARE, REINTRO, ROUGH, SOME, WITHL

Long Tall Sally
> BEEB11, PARL

If I Fell
> BEEB11, KNIGHT, PARL

I'm Happy Just To Dance With You
> BEEB11, KNIGHT, PARL

Things We Said Today
> BEEB11, PARL, RARE

I Should Have Known Better
> BEEB11, PARL, RARE

Boys
> BEEB10, PARL

A Hard Day's Night
> BEEB10, PARL

Kansas City/Hey-Hey-Hey-Hey!
> BEEB10, PARL, RARE

11 Sep 64, *A BEATLE'S EYE VIEW*
a rerun of the 18 Jul 64 *HIGHLIGHT* interview

26 Nov 64, *TOP GEAR*

I'm A Loser
> AUCTION, BEEB, BEEB12, BROAD

Honey Don't
> BEEB12

She's A Woman
> BEEB, BEEB12, BROAD

Everybody's Trying To Be My Baby
> BEEB12, DEC63

I'll Follow The Sun
> AUCTION, BBC, BEEB, BEEB12, BROAD, DEC63

I Feel Fine
> BEEB, BEEB12, BROAD

26 Dec 64, *SATURDAY CLUB*

Rock And Roll Music
> AUCTION, BEEB, BEEB12, DEC63, PETE, SILVER, WITHL

I'm A Loser
> BEEB12

Everybody's Trying To Be My Baby
> AUCTION, BEEB, BEEB12, BROAD, LINING, WHEN

I Feel Fine
> BEEB12

Kansas City/Hey-Hey-Hey-Hey!
AUCTION, BEEB, BEEB12, DEC64, 1964, PETE, SILVER, WITHL
She's A Woman
BEEB12

13 Apr 65, *POP INN*
a live interview from Twickenham

7 Jun 65, *THE BEATLES INVITE YOU TO TAKE A TICKET TO RIDE*
Ticket To Ride (short)
BEEB13, PETE, SILVER
Everybody's Trying To Be My Baby
BEEB13
I'm A Loser
BEEB13, CLASS2
The Night Before
BEEB13
Honey Don't
AUCTION, BEEB, BEEB13, WITHL
Dizzy Miss Lizzie
BACK, BBC, BEEB, BEEB13, BUG, CAVERN, 8ARMS, HEARD, HOWDO, POWER,
RECO, THOSE, WITHL
She's A Woman
BEEB13
Ticket To Ride (long)
BEEB, BEEB13, WITHL

24 Jun 65, *TODAY*
interview with John

3 Jul 65, *THE WORLD OF BOOKS*
John is interviewed and reads a poem

30 Aug 65, *THE BEATLES ABROAD*
interviews by Brian Matthew; recorded mid-Jun 65 in the USA

Nov 65, *POP PROFILE*
George is interviewed by Briant Matthew

Dec 65? *POP PROFILE*
John is interviewed by Brian Matthew

25 Dec 65, *SATURDAY CLUB*
chat

[25 Dec 65
a Christmas message on Radio Caroline]

[26 Dec 65, *POP'S HAPPENING*
prerecorded interview with Paul on Radio Caroline]

May 66, *POP PROFILE*
Paul is interviewed by Brian Matthew

May 66, *POP PROFILE*
Ringo is interviewed by Brian Matthew

6 Aug 66, *DAVID FROST AT THE PHONOGRAPH*
interview with Paul

29 Aug 66, *THE LENNON AND McCARTNEY SONGBOOK*
John & Paul are interviewed

20 Mar 67, *TOP OF THE POPS*
John and Paul are interviewed by Brian Matthew

20 May 67, *WHERE IT'S AT*
John, on tape, introduces cuts from **SGT. PEPPER**

[5 Aug 67
Ringo's farewell message to (and on) Radio London]

30 Sep 67, *SCENE AND HEARD*
George is interviewed by Miranda Ward, part 1

7 Oct 67, *SCENE AND HEARD*
George is interviewed by Miranda Ward, part 2

24 Nov 67, *WHERE IT'S AT*
John is interviewed

9 Jun 68, *THE KENNY EVERETT SHOW*
The Beatles are interviewed

BBC SONG INDEX
(VERSION 2.0)

Note that this index includes **THE BEATLES AT THE BEEB, VOL.S 12 & 13**, although they have not been examined in this book.

All I Want For Christmas Is A Beatle
    21 Dec 63   BEEB8
All My Loving
    21 Dec 63
    26 Dec 63   BEEB8
    15 Feb 64   BEEB9
    30 Mar 64   BEEB, BEEB9, BUG, WITHER, WITHL
And I Love Her
    16 Jul 64   BBC, BEEB, BEEB11, KNIGHT, WITHL
Anna (Go To Him)
    25 Jun 63   BEEB3, PLEASE
    27 Aug 63   LBEEB, STUDIO, STUD2
Ask Me Why
    15 Jun 62   LBEEB, MEET, W/PETE
    25 Jan 63
    29 Jan 63
    24 Sep 63   BEEB6, PLEASE
Baby It's You
    22 Apr 63
    11 Jun 63   BEEB2, BEEBCD, MONKEY, PLEASE
Beautiful Dreamer
    26 Jan 63   BEAUT, MEET, REINTRO, WOND, W/PETE
Besame Mucho
    15 Jun 62   LBEEB, MEET, W/PETE
Boys
    13 May 63   BEEB2, MONKEY
    25 May 63   BEEB1, BEEBCD, MONKEY
    24 Jun 63   BEEB1, BEEBCD, MONKEY, PLEASE
    25 Jun 63   BEEB3
    17 Sep 63   BEEB6, SOME, STUDIO, STUD2
    26 Dec 63   BEEB8
    3 Aug 64   BEEB11, PARL
Can't Buy Me Love
    30 Mar 64   BEEB, BEEB9, KNIGHT, 1964, SILVER, WITHL
    4 Apr 64   BEEB10
    18 May 64   BEEB10

Carol
    16 Jul 63   BBC, BEEB, BEEB3, BEEBCD, BROAD, DEMO, LINING, REINTRO,
                           SPLHCB

Chains
    25 Jan 63
    13 May 63   BEEB2, REINTRO
    25 Jun 63   BEEB3
    17 Sep 63   BEEB6, PLEASE, STUDIO, STUD2

Clarabella
    16 Jul 63   BBC, BEEB, BEEB3, BEEBCD, BROAD, REINTRO

"Crimble" medley
    21 Dec 63   BEEB8

Crying, Waiting, Hoping
    6 Aug 63   BEEB, BEEB4, DEMO, DON'T, PETE, REINTRO, SILVER, SUPER1,
                           THEIR, 21, WITHL, YEARS, YELL, YOUNG

(There's A) Devil In Her Heart
    20 Aug 63   BEEB5, STUDIO, STUD2
    24 Sep 63   BEEB6, WITHER, YOUNG

Dizzy Miss Lizzie
    7 Jun 65   BACK, BBC, BEEB, BEEB13, BUG, CAVERN, 8ARMS, HEARD,
                           HOWDO, POWER, RECO, THOSEWITHL

Do You Want To Know A Secret
    12 Mar 63
    28 Mar 63
    22 Apr 63
    25 May 63   BEEB1, BEEBCD, MONKEY
    4 Jun 63   BEEB2, COMPL, MONKEY, STONE, STUDIO, STUD1
    30 Jul 63   BEEB, BEEB4, BROAD, PLEASE

Don't Ever Change
    27 Aug 63   BBC, BEEB, BEEB5, DEMO, DON'T, REINTRO, THEIR, WITHL,
                           YELL

Dream Baby
    8 Mar 62   BEEB, LBEEB, MEET, 1234, REINTRO, WOND, W/PETE

Everybody's Trying To Be My Baby
    4 Jun 63   BEEB2, MONKEY
    4 Apr 64   BEEB10
    26 Nov 64   BEEB12
    26 Dec 64   AUCTION, BEEB, BEEB12, BROAD, DEC63, LINING, WHEN
    7 Jun 65   BEEB13

From Me To You
    7 Apr 63   MEET, W/PETE
    18 Apr 63   BEEB1, MONKEY
    22 Apr 63
    13 May 63
    25 May 63   BEEB1, BEEBCD, MONKEY
    3 Jun 63
    4 Jun 63
    18 Jun 63
    23 Jun 63   BEEB1, BEEBCD, MONKEY
    24 Jun 63   BEEB1, BEEBCD, MONKEY
    29 Jun 63   BEEB2, MONKEY, STUDIO, STUD1
    4 Jul 63
    3 Sep 63
    17 Sep 63   BEEB6, KNIGHT
    20 Oct 63   BEEB7

From Us To You
    various   BEEB, BEEB8, BEEB9, BEEB10, BEEB11, BUG, PARL, RARE,
                           REINTRO, ROUGH, SOME, WITHL

Glad All Over
    20 Aug 63   BEAUT, BEEB5, DEMO, DON'T, REINTRO, YELL
    24 Aug 63
Happy Birthday To You
    18 Jun 63   BEEB3, BEEBCD
    5 Oct 63   BEAT, BEEB, BEEB7, 1234, REINTRO, WOND
    18 May 64   BEEB10
A Hard Day's Night
    16 Jul 64   BEEB, BEEB11, BUG, KNIGHT, LAST, LOOKING, LONG, NASSAU,
                   MARY, POPS, ROAD, TOP, WITHL, YEARS
    3 Aug 64   BEEB11, PARL
The Hippy Hippy Shake
    16 Mar 63   MEET, W/PETE
    4 Jun 63   DEMO, LBEEB, STUD1, THEIR, 21
    30 Jul 63   BEEB, BEEB4, BROAD
    10 Sep 63   BEEB6, YOUNG
    15 Feb 64   BEEB9
Honey Don't
    3 Sep 63   BACK, BEEB5, BOTH, CASTS, LINING, POWER, SHOTS, SNAPS,
                   STUDIO, STUD2
    18 May 64   BEEB10
    26 Nov 64   BEEB12
    7 Jun 65   AUCTION, BEEB, BEEB13, WITHL
The Honeymoon Song
    6 Aug 63   BEAUT, BEEB, BEEB4, DEMO, DON'T, KNIGHT, THEIR, YELL
I Call Your Name
    4 Apr 64   BEEB10
I Feel Fine
    26 Nov 64   BEEB, BEEB12, BROAD
    26 Dec 64   BEEB12
I Forgot To Remember To Forget
    18 May 64   BEEB10, DEMO, HEARD, MAIL, 1234, RECO, YOUNG
I Got A Woman
    13 Aug 63   BEEB5, DEMO, DON'T, YELL
    4 Apr 64   BEEB, BEEB10, BROAD, DEMO, HOWDO, SOLDIER, SNAPS
I Got To Find My Baby
    11 Jun 63   BEEB2, BEEBCD, MONKEY, 1234, PLEASE, WOND
    29 Jun 63   BEAUT, BEEB, BEEB2, MONKEY
I Just Don't Understand
    20 Aug 63   BEEB, BEEB5, DEMO, DON'T, PLEASE, THEIR, YELL
I Saw Her Standing There
    16 Mar 63   MEET, W/PETE
    22 Apr 63
    25 May 63   BEEB1, BEEBCD, MONKEY
    3 Jun 63   BEEB1, MONKEY
    25 Jun 63   BEEB3
    21 Jul 63   MEET, W/PETE
    24 Sep 63   BEEB6, PLEASE, STUDIO, STUD2
    5 Oct 63   BEEB7
    20 Oct 63   BEEB7
    26 Dec 63   BEEB8
    18 May 64   BEEB10
I Should Have Known Better
    16 Jul 64   BEEB11?
    3 Aug 64   BEEB11, PARL, RARE

I Wanna Be Your Man
 15 Feb 64 BEEB9
 30 Mar 64 BBC, BEEB, BEEB9, BUG, RECO, WITHER, WITHL
I Want To Hold Your Hand
 21 Dec 63 BEEB8
 26 Dec 63 BEEB8
 15 Feb 64 BEEB9
I'll Be On My Way
 24 Jun 63 BEEB, BEEB1, BEEBCD, DIGIT, LINING, MONKEY, ROUGH,
 SOLDIER, 2MUCH, WALK, WITHER, WITHL, YEARS
I'll Follow The Sun
 26 Nov 64 AUCTION, BBC, BEEB, BEEB12, BROAD, DEC63
I'll Get You
 13 Aug 63 BEAUT, BEEB5
 24 Aug 63
 3 Sep 63
 10 Sep 63 BEEB6, KNIGHT
 5 Oct 63
I'm A Loser
 26 Nov 64 AUCTION, BEEB, BEEB12, BROAD
 26 Dec 64 BEEB12
 7 Jun 65 BEEB13, CLASS2
I'm Gonna Sit Right Down And Cry (Over You)
 6 Aug 63 BEAUT, BEEB4, DEMO, DON'T, PLEASE, THEIR, 21, YELL
I'm Happy Just To Dance With You
 3 Aug 64 BEEB11, KNIGHT, PARL
I'm Talking About You
 16 Mar 63 BEAUT, MEET, PLEASE, W/PETE
If I Fell
 16 Jul 64 BEEB11
 3 Aug 64 BEEB11, KNIGHT, PARL
Johnny B. Goode
 15 Feb 64 BEAT, BEAUT, BEEB, BEEB9
Kansas City/Hey-Hey-Hey-Hey!
 6 Aug 63 BEEB4, STUDIO, STUD1, YOUNG
 18 May 64 BEEB10
 3 Aug 64 (not broadcast?) BEEB11, PARL, RARE
 26 Dec 64 AUCTION, BEEB, BEEB12, DEC63, 1964, PETE, SILVER, WITHL
Keep Your Hands Off My Baby
 26 Jan 63 BEAUT, CASTS, MEET, PLEASE, SHOTS, WOND, W/PETE
Lend Me Your Comb
 16 Jul 63 BBC, BEEB, BEEB3, BEEBCD, BROAD, DEMO, LINING, PLEASE
Lonesome Tears In My Eyes
 23 Jul 63 BBC, BEEB, BEEB4, DEMO, DON'T, SILVER, WITHL, YELL
Long Tall Sally
 13 May 63 AUCTION, BEEB2, MONKEY
 25 May 63 BEEB1, BEEBCD, MONKEY
 13 Aug 63 BEEB5, STUDIO, STUD1
 24 Aug 63
 4 Apr 64 BEEB10, BROAD
 16 Jul 64 BEEB, BEEB11, LAST, LONG, LOOKING, MARY, NASSAU, POPS,
 ROAD, TOP
 3 Aug 64 BEEB11, PARL
Love Me Do
 26 Oct 62
 4 Dec 62
 26 Jan 63

                20 Feb 63
                11 Jun 63   BEEB2, MONKEY
                24 Jun 63
                23 Jul 63   8ARMS, LBEEB, RAREST, RECO, STUDIO, STUD1
                10 Sep 63   BEEB6, PLEASE
                20 Oct 63   BEEB7
Lucille
                17 Sep 63   BEEB6, DEMO, KNIGHT, SOME, STUD2, THEIR
                5 Oct 63   BEEB7, HAVE, RECO
Matchbox
                30 Jul 63   BEEB, BEEB4, BROAD
                18 May 64   BEEB10
Memphis
                8 Mar 62   LBEEB, MEET, WOND, W/PETE
                18 Jun 63   BEEB3, BEEBCD
                29 Jun 63   BEEB2, MONKEY, WITHER
                30 Jul 63   BEEB, BEEB4, BROAD
                5 Oct 63   BEAT, BEEB7, WHEN, WOND, YOUNG
Misery
                12 Mar 63
                16 Mar 63   MEET, W/PETE
                28 Mar 63
                7 Apr 63
                22 Apr 63
                4 Jun 63   COMPL, LBEEB, RECO, STONE, STUDIO, STUD1
                17 Sep 63   BEEB6, PLEASE
Money (That's What I Want)
                25 May 63   BEEB1, BEEBCD, MONKEY
                18 Jun 63   BEEB3, WITHER
                29 Jun 63   LBEEB, STUD1
                3 Sep 63   LBEEB, STUDIO, STUD2
                26 Dec 63   BEEB8
                15 Feb 64   BEEB9
The Night Before
                7 Jun 65   BEEB13
Nothin' Shakin' (But The Leaves On The Trees)
                23 Jul 63   BBC, BEEB, BEEB4, DEMO, DON'T, PETE, SILVER, WITHER,
                                WITHL, YELL
Ooh! My Soul
                27 Aug 63   BEAUT, BEEB5, 1234, WITHER, WOND, W/PETE
A Picture Of You
                15 Jun 62   LBEEB, MEET, 1234, WOND, W/PETE
Please Mr. Postman
                8 Mar 62   LBEEB, MEET, W/PETE
                30 Jul 63   BEEB, BEEB4, PETE, SILVER, WITHL, YEARS
                30 Mar 64   BEEB9, ROUGH, WITHER
Please Please Me
                25 Jan 63
                26 Jan 63
                29 Jan 63
                20 Feb 63
                12 Mar 63
                16 Mar 63   MEET, W/PETE
                28 Mar 63
                7 Apr 63
                22 Apr 3
                3 Jun 63   BEEB1, MONKEY

13 Aug 63   BEEB5, COMPL, 8ARMS, PLEASE, RAREST,STONE, STUDIO, STUD1
20 Oct 63   BEEB7
Pop Go The Beatles
various   BEEB, BEEB2, BEEB3, BEEB4, BEEB5, BEEB6, BEEBCD, BROAD, REINTRO
P.S. I Love You
26 Oct 62
4 Dec 62
25 Jun 63   BEEB3, PLEASE
Rock And Roll Music
26 Dec 64   BEEB, BEEB12, DEC63, PETE, SILVER, WITHL
Roll Over Beethoven
3 Jun 63
29 Jun 63   BEEB2, MONKEY, STUDIO, STUD1
3 Sep 63   BEEB5
21 Dec 63   BEEB8
26 Dec 63   BEEB8
15 Feb 64   BEEB9
30 Mar 64   BEEB, BEEB9, BUG, WITHER, WITHL
Rudolph The Red-Nosed Reindeer
21 Dec 63   BEEB8
She Loves You
13 Aug 63   BEEB5, KNIGHT
20 Aug 63   BEEB5, STUDIO, STUD2
24 Aug 63
27 Aug 63
10 Sep 63   BEEB6
24 Sep 63   BEEB6
5 Oct 63
20 Oct 63   BEEB7
3 Nov 63
21 Dec 63   BEEB8
26 Dec 63   BEEB8
She's A Woman
26 Nov 64   BEEB, BEEB12, BROAD
26 Dec 64   BEEB12
7 Jun 65   BEEB13
A Shot Of Rhythm And Blues
18 Jun 63   BEEB3, BEEBCD, WITHER, YOUNG
21 Jul 63   DEMO, DON'T, MEET, 21, WITHL, WOND, W/PETE
27 Aug 63   BBC, BEEB, LBEEB, DEMO, WOND, YELL
Side By Side
various   BEEB1, BEEB2, BEEBCD, MONKEY, REINTRO, YEARS
Slow Down
20 Aug 63   AUCTION, BEEB5, DON'T, HOWDO, YELL
So How Come (No One Loves Me)
23 Jul 63   BBC, BEEB, BEEB4, DEMO, DON'T, PETE, SILVER, WITHER, YELL
Soldier Of Love
16 Jul 63   BBC, BEEB, BEEB3, BEEBCD, BROAD, SOLDIER, THEIR, WITHER, YEARS
Some Other Guy
26 Jan 63   BEAUT, BEEB, CASTS, MEET, SHOTS, W/PETE
29 Jan 63
23 Jun 63   BEEB1, BEEBCD, MONKEY, WITHER, YEARS
Sure To Fall (In Love With You)
18 Jun 63   BEEB3, BEEBCD, YOUNG

24 Sep 63	BACK, BEEB6, DEMO, DON'T, POWER, REINTRO, STUD2, 21, YELL
4 Apr 64	BBC, BEEB, BEEB10, BROAD
18 May 64	BEEB10

Sweet Little Sixteen
23 Jul 63	BEAUT, BEEB, BEEB4, KNIGHT, 1234, YOUNG

A Taste Of Honey
26 Oct 62	
13 May 63	BEEB2, MONKEY
18 Jun 63	BEEB3, PLEASE
23 Jun 63	BEEB1, BEEBCD, MONKEY
4 Jul 63	
23 Jul 63	
10 Sep 63	BEEB6

Thank You Girl
13 May 63	BEEB2, MONKEY, WITHER
3 Jun 63	
23 Jun 63	BEEB1, BEEBCD, MONKEY

That's All Right, Mama
16 Jul 63	BEAUT, BEEB, BEEB3, BEEBCD, DIGIT, KNIGHT, 1234

There's A Place
16 Jul 63	BEAUT, BEEB3, BEEBCD, PLEASE
21 Jul 63	MEET, W/PETE
3 Sep 63	BEEB5, STUDIO, STUD2

Things We Said Today
16 Jul 64	BEEB, BEEB11, BOTH, BUG, KNIGHT, LAST, LOOKING, MARY, NASSAU, POPS, ROAD, TOP, 20X4, WITHL
3 Aug 64	BEEB11, PARL, RARE

This Boy
21 Dec 63	BEEB, BEEB8, KNIGHT, WITHL
30 Mar 64	BEEB9, 1964, PETE, ROUGH, SILVER, YEARS

Ticket To Ride (long version)
7 Jun 65	BEEB, BEEB13, WITHL

Ticket To Ride (short version)
7 Jun 65	BEEB13, PETE, SILVER

Tie Me Kangaroo Down, Sport
26 Dec 63	BEEB8

Till There Was You
11 Jun 63	BEEB2, MONKEY
29 Jun 63	LBEEB, STUDIO, STUD1
30 Jul 63	BEEB4, BROAD
10 Sep 63	
21 Dec 63	BEEB8
26 Dec 63	BEEB8
30 Mar 64	BEEB, BEEB9, WITHER

To Know Her Is To Love Her
6 Aug 63	BEAUT, BEEB, BEEB4, DEMO, DON'T, KNIGHT, 21, YELL

Too Much Monkey Business
16 Mar 63	MEET, W/PETE
11 Jun 63	BEAUT, BEEB2, MONKEY, 1234, WOND
24 Jun 63	BEEB1, BEEBCD, KNIGHT, MONKEY
10 Sep 63	BBC, BEEB, BEEB6, LINING, YOUNG

Twist And Shout
4 Dec 62	
18 Apr 63	BEEB1, MONKEY
25 Jun 63	BEEB3
4 Jul 63	
21 Jul 63	W/PETE

6 Aug 63	BEEB4
24 Aug 63	
27 Aug 63	BEEB5
24 Sep 63	BEEB6, PLEASE

Words Of Love

20 Aug 63	AUCTION, BEAUT, BEEB5, RECO, STUDIO, STUD2

You Can't Do That

30 Mar 64	BEEB9
4 Apr 64	BEEB10
18 May 64	BEEB10
16 Jul 64	BEEB11

You Really Got A Hold On Me

4 Jun 63	BEEB2, MONKEY, STUDIO, STUD1
13 Aug 63	BEEB5
24 Aug 63	
17 Sep 63	BEEB6, WITHER

Young Blood

11 Jun 63	BEAUT, BEEB2, BEEBCD, KNIGHT, MONKEY, 1234, WOND, YOUNG

A NEW GET BACK LISTING

The following songs are known to have been performed or spoken in part or in whole during the **GET BACK** sessions. Previous estimates have generally ranged from 100 to 125, but recent releases and careful examination have brought this up to (at least) 221, excluding unknown instrumentals and indecipherable songs; if we had access to the complete tapes, which may no longer exist, the number would surely exceed 300. Many of these are no more than brief snatches, and some are unquestionably improvisations.

Ach Du Lieber (Balls For Mr. Benglestein)
Across The Universe
Act Naturally
All Along The Watchtower
All I Want Is You (not **Dig A Pony**—improvisation?)
All Shook Up
All Things Must Pass
Almost Grown
Another Day
Around And Around
Baa Baa Black Sheep
(You're So Square) Baby I Don't Care
Back Seat Of My Car
Bad Boy
The Ball Of Inverary
Be-Bop-A-Lula
Besame Mucho
Blowin' In The Wind
Blue Suede Shoes
Bo Diddley
Bring It On Home To Me
Bring It To Jerome
Brown-eyed Handsome Man
Bye Bye Love
A Case Of The Blues
Cathy's Clown
Child Of Nature
Chopsticks
Commonwealth (improvisation)
Crackin' Up
Crying, Waiting, Hoping
Da-Doo-Run-Run
Danny Boy
(There's A) Devil In Her Heart

Dig A Pony
Dig It (different tune)
Dig It
Diggin' My Potatoes
Domino
Don't Be Cruel
Don't Let Me Down
Don't Let The Sun Catch You Crying
Early In The Morning
Early In The Morning (improvisation?)
Enoch Powell (improvisation)
Every Little Thing
Every Night
Feedback guitar
Flowing More Freely Than Wine (a real song, or a line from **I Me Mine**?)
Fools Like Me
For You Blue
Frere Jacques
Get Back
Gimme Some Lovin' (brief riff)
Gimme Some Truth
Go Johnny Go (probably a real song)
Gone, Gone, Gone
Good Rockin' Tonight
Great Balls Of Fire
A Hard Rain's Gonna Fall
Happiness Is A Warm Gun
Hare Krishna Mantra
Harry Lime (Third Man Theme)
Hava Nagila
Hear Me Lord
Hello Dolly
Hello Goodbye
Hello Mudduh, Hello Fadduh
Help!
Her Majesty
Hey Little Girl (In The High School Sweater)
Hi Heel Sneakers
The Hippy Hippy Shake
Hitchhike
Honey Hush
Hot As Sun
House Of The Rising Sun
I Me Mine
I Shall Be Released
I Threw It All Away
I Want You (She's So Heavy)
I'm Ready
I'm So Tired
I'm Talking About You
I've Got A Feeling
I've Got My Blue Fingers (improvisation?)
If Tomorrow Ever Comes (early Lennon-McCartney?)
In The Middle Of An Island
The Inner Light
Isadora Duncan (improvisation)
It Ain't Me Babe
Jambalaya
Jazz Piano Theme
Jenny Jenny

Johnny B. Goode
Just Fun
Kansas City
Lady Jane
Lady Madonna
Lawdy Miss Clawdy
Let It Be
Let It Down
Little Queenie
Little Yellow Pills
London Bridge Is Falling Down
The Long And Winding Road
Look Out! (probably a real song)
Long Tall Sally (John recites one line of lyric)
Love Is A Swingin' Thing
Love Is Like A Macaroni (improvisation)
Low Down Blues Machine (improvisation?)
Lucille
Madman (various)
Maggie Mae
Mailman, Bring Me No More Blues
Mama You Been On My Mind
Maxwell's Silver Hammer (various)
Maybe Baby
Maybe I'm Amazed
Mean Mister Mustard (various)
Midnight Special
Milk Cow Blues
Miss Ann
Money (That's What I Want) (instrumental)
Move It
Movin' Along The River Rhine (improvisation?)
Negro In Reserve (possibly based on a real song)
New Orleans
Norwegian Wood (instrumental)
Not Fade Away
Ob-La-Di, Ob-La-Da
Octopus's Garden
Oh! Darling
Once Upon A Time (improvisation?)
The One After 909
Papa's Got A Brand New Bag
Paul's Piano Theme
Penina
(Take Another) Piece Of My Heart
Please Mrs. Henry
Please Please Me
Polythene Pam (various)
Queen Of The Hop
A Quick One While He's Away
Rainy Day Woman #12 & 35
Ramblin' Woman (Dylan?)
Reach Out, I'll Be There
Rip It Up
Rock And Roll Music
Rock Island Line
Rocker (Link Track & Instrumental #42)
Roll Over Beethoven
Sabre Dance
(I Can't Get No) Satisfaction

Save The Last Dance For Me
School Days
Sexy Sadie
Shake, Rattle And Roll
Shakin' In The Sixties (improvisation)
She Came In Through the Bathroom Window
She Said She Said
Short Fat Fannie
A Shot Of Rhythm And Blues
Shout!
Singing The Blues
Slippin' And Slidin'
Soldier Of Love
Stand By Me
Strawberry Fields Forever
Suicide
Sun King (instrumental, as part of **Don't Let Me Down**)
Suzy Parker
Sweet Little Sixteen
Take This Hammer
Takin' A Trip To Carolina (A Ringo song in progress)
Tea For Two
Teddy Boy
Tennessee
That Would Be Something
That'll Be The Day
There Once Was A Beautiful Girl (probably a real song)
There You Go, Eddie
Thinking That You Love Me (early Lennon-McCartney?)
Thirty Days
This Song Of Love (probably a real song — not **It's For You**)
Three Cool Cats
Till There Was You
Time Is Tight (bass riff)
Too Bad About Sorrows
Tutti Frutti (John recites one line of lyric)
Two Of Us
Under The Boardwalk (brief riff)
Vacation Time
Wake Up In The Morning (early Lennon-McCartney)
The Walk
Watch Your Step
Watching Rainbows (Lennon)
Well All Right
What Do You Wanna Make Those Eyes At Me For?
What'd I Say
What's The Use Of Getting Sober?
When I'm Sixty-four
When Irish Eyes Are Smiling
When You're Drunk You Think Of Me (a real song)
Where Have You Been All My Life?
White Power (Get Off!) (improvisation)
Whole Lotta Shakin' Goin' On
Why Don't We Do It In The Road (Why Don't You Put It On The Toast)
The William Smith Boogie (probably based on a real song)
Woman
Won't You Please Say Goodbye (early Lennon-McCartney?)
Yer Blues
You Can't Do That
You Got Me Going (probably a real song)

You Got The Message (improvisation?)
You Gotta Get Back (improvisation)
You Really Got A Hold On Me
You Win Again
You're Going To Lose That Girl (You're Going To Shag That Girl)
You've Got Me Thinking
Your True Love

The following songs are reported to have surfaced:

Foxy Lady (Hendrix)
    According to *The Beatles Get Back*, George plays this riff while Yoko wails. It's pretty certain that the text refers to the piece I call "Feedback Guitar" (on **WATCHING RAINBOWS**) but, while the riffs are similar, I don't think they are close enough for a positive identification.
Good Golly, Miss Molly (Blackwell-Marascalco)
    on **THE BEATLES VS. LITTLE RICHARD AND LARRY WILLIAMS** and **CINELOGUE** (judging from where it appears on the albums, probably just **Miss Ann/Lawdy Miss Clawdy**; a reader confirmed that this was so).
Hey Jude (Lennon-McCartney)
    on **STUDIO OUTTAKES** (although I have not heard it myself, I have been informed by several readers that it is indeed the *Experiment In Television* version).
Hully Gully (Smith-Goldsmith)
    Appearance unknown; probably a misidentification.
It's For You (Lennon-McCartney)
    This is apparently just "This Song Of Love," which prominently features the line "It's just for you."
Some Other Guy (Leiber-Stoller-Barrett)
    on **BEATLEMANIA 1963-69** and **LET THEM BEATLES BE**. Apparently just the 22 Aug 62 Cavern film version tacked on).
Tutti Frutti (Penniman-La Bostrie-Lubin)
    on **BYE, BYE, BYE: SUPERTRACKS VOL. 2**. One reader suggested that this originates from Paul's recitation of some nonsense lyrics before the *Experiment In Television* performance of **Hey Jude**. John does recite one line of lyric on FILE1.
Yakety Yak (Leiber-Stoller)
    on **THE BLACK ALBUM** and various other places. This is actually **Honey Hush** (Turner), sometimes called **Hi Ho Silver** (Waller-Kirkeby). **Yakety Yak** was performed by the Coasters, who also did **Young Blood** and **Three Cool Cats**, so it's not impossible that the Beatles would have done a version.

In addition, the following titles have been reported to have been performed but have not yet surfaced:

Back In The U.S.S.R. (Lennon-McCartney)
Carol (Berry)
Carry That Weight (Lennon-McCartney)
Dizzy Miss Lizzie (Williams)
Get A Job (Silhouettes)
God Save The Queen (trad.) (30 Jan 69, Apple rooftop)
Going Up The Country (Wilson) (22 Jan 69, Apple)
I Left My Heart In San Francisco (Cory-Cross)
Isn't Is A Pity (Harrison) (26 Jan 69, Apple)
I'll Build A Stairway To Paradise (Gershwin-Desylva-Francis)
It's Only Make Believe (Twitty-Nance)
It's So Easy (Holly-Petty)
Lend Me Your Comb (Twomey-Wise-Weisman)
Love Me Do (Lennon-McCartney) (28 Jan 69, Apple)
Maybelline (Berry)
Memphis (Berry)
Michael, Row The Boat Ashore (trad.)

Nowhere Man (Lennon-McCartney)
Ooh! My Soul (Penniman)
The Right String But The Wrong Yo-Yo (Berryman)
Rocky Raccoon (Lennon-McCartney)
Send Me Some Lovin' (Marascalco-Price)
Somethin' Else (Cochran-Sheeley)
Sure To Fall (In Love With You) (Perkins-Claunch-Cantrell)
Think It Over (Holly-Allison-Petty)
The Tracks Of My Tears (Robinson-Moore-Tarplin) (26 Jan 69, Apple)
True Love Ways (Holly-Petty)
Turn Around (Bennett-Tepper)
Twenty Flight Rock (Cochran-Fairchild)
Whole Lotta Lovin' (Domino-Bartholomew)
You Are My Sunshine (Davis-Mitchell)

note: the original source for the report of many of the above songs would appear to be an _NME_ article, 23 Mar 74.

Here is an updated **GET BACK** chronology by the "slate numbers:"

slate(s)	disc	side
41	GET BACK JOURNALS	I
41, 42	SWEET APPLE TRAX, VOL. 3	C
43	GET BACK JOURNALS	J
45	SWEET APPLE TRAX, VOL. 3	D
120	"WORDS OF WISDOM"	(tape only)
127	CODENAME RUSSIA	B
137, 139, 140	THE BLACK ALBUM	E
140	ALMOST GROWN	A
142	BYE BYE LOVE	A
167	GET BACK JOURNALS	S
176	SOUNDCHECK	A
176, 177	THE BLACK ALBUM	B
181	THE BLACK ALBUM	D
181, 182	THE BLACK ALBUM	C
189	THE BLACK ALBUM	A
205	CODENAME RUSSIA	B
235	GET BACK JOURNALS	K
247	GET BACK JOURNALS	L
261	GET BACK JOURNALS	P
263	GET BACK JOURNALS	N
263, 265	GET BACK JOURNALS	P
289	GET BACK JOURNALS	O
298	GET BACK JOURNALS	O
311, 312, 314	GET BACK JOURNALS	Q
318, 319, 320	GET BACK JOURNALS	T
320	SINGING THE BLUES	B
322	WONDERFUL PICTURE OF YOU	B
323	SINGING THE BLUES	B
326	FILE UNDER: BEATLES	B
326, 327	GET BACK JOURNALS	K
354, 355	BYE BYE LOVE	B
423	IN A PLAY ANYWAY (appears in the _Get Back_ film)	C
431	CLASSIFIED DOCUMENT, VOL. 3	A

MAKING SENSE OF
THE LOST BEATLES SONGS

In *Do You Want To Know A Secret*, I guessed that of the estimated one hundred or so pre-success Beatles songs, we knew of perhaps fifteen percent. But, as I prepared this book, I began to wonder just how close my guess had been.

KNOWN SONGS

These are among the earliest known Beatles compositions, although the writing date of some of the 64 "giveaways" is unclear.

Bad To Me (Lennon-McCartney)
Released by Billy J. Kramer, John's 63 acetate demo is on **FILE UNDER: BEAT-LES, VOLUME ONE** and **NOT FOR SALE**.

Catswalk (McCartney)
We have a Spring 62 rehearsal tape of this instrumental. The commercial release was in 67 by the Chris Barber Band, as **Cat Call**.

Cry For A Shadow (Lennon-Harrison)
The commercial release is included with the Tony Sheridan material.

From A Window (Lennon-McCartney)
The commercial version was released in 64 by Billy J. Kramer and The Dakotas; no Beatles version is known to exist but there is probably a demo.

Hello Little Girl (Lennon-McCartney)
A Beatles version is available on the Decca tapes (1 Jan 62). The commercial release was in 63 by the Fourmost. There may be an EMI demo as well.

Hold Me Tight (Lennon-McCartney)
Although this was song being performed as early as 61, its first release was in 63 on **WITH THE BEATLES**.

Hot As Sun (McCartney)
Written and performed in the late '50s, it finally appeared on **McCARTNEY**. A **GET BACK** sessions version appears on **WONDERFUL PICTURE OF YOU**.

I Don't Want To See You Again (Lennon-McCartney)
The commercial version was released in 64 by Peter and Gordon; no Beatles version is known to exist but there is probably a demo.

I Fancy Me Chances (Lennon-McCartney)
Reported as being performed live in 62; no recorded version is known to exist.

I Lost My Little Girl (McCartney)
Paul does a bit of this song, his first, in the Melvin Bragg interview (Oct 77). A nearly-complete version is on **HOME REHEARSALS**.

I'll Be On My Way (Lennon-McCartney)
A Beatles version exists on the BBC tapes (24 Jun 63); the commercial version was released in 63 by Billy J. Kramer and The Dakotas, and there is probably a demo.

I'll Keep You Satisfied (Lennon-McCartney)
The commercial version was released in 63 by Billy J. Kramer and The Dakotas; no Beatles version is known to exist but there is probably a demo.

I'll Follow The Sun (Lennon-McCartney)
> The earliest known version is Spring 60, on the Quarry Men rehearsal tapes; the commercial version was released on **BEATLES FOR SALE** in 64.

I'm In Love (Lennon-McCartney)
> The commercial version was released in 63 by the Fourmost; no Beatles version is known to exist but there is probably a demo.

In Spite Of All The Danger (McCartney-Harrison)
> The only known copy is owned by Paul McCartney on the Quarry Men shellac.

It's For You (Lennon-McCartney)
> The commercial version was released in 64 by Cilla Black (and later by Three Dog Night); no Beatles version is known to exist but there is probably a demo.

Just Fun (Lennon-McCartney)
> Paul does a bit of this song in *Let It Be*, available on **IN A PLAY ANYWAY** and various **GET BACK** sessions recordings.

Keep Looking That Way (Lennon-McCartney)
> Reported as being performed in the late '50s, but no recorded version is known, although a Spring 62 rehearsal recording has been said to exist.

Like Dreamers Do (Lennon-McCartney)
> A Beatles version appears on the Decca tapes (1 Jan 62); the commercial version was released in 64 by the Applejacks.

Long Black Train (Lennon?)
> Reported as being performed in the late '50s, but no recorded version is known to exist. A song of this name was written and recorded by Conway Twitty in the late '50s—could they be the same?

Looking Glass (Lennon-McCartney)
> An instrumental, reported as being performed during the late '50s. Paul mentions this song during the **GET BACK** sessions but, if it was played, it has yet to surface. It has been said that there is an EMI 6 Jun 62 recording, but this would appear to be incorrect.

Love Of The Loved (Lennon-McCartney)
> A Beatles version is on the Decca tapes (1 Jan 62); the commercial version was released in 63 by Cilla Black.

Nobody I Know (Lennon-McCartney)
> The commercial version was released in 64 by the Peter and Gordon; no Beatles version is known to exist but there is probably a demo.

One After 909 (Lennon-McCartney)
> The earliest known (available) versions are from Spring 60, on the Quarry Men rehearsal tapes. There is a rehearsal version (probably from 62) and an EMI outtake from Mar 63. First official release was on **LET IT BE**.

One And One Is Two (Lennon-McCartney)
> The commercial release was in 64 by The Strangers with Mike Shannon; no Beatles version seems to exist but there is a Dick James demo, which appears on **ULTRA RARE TRAX VOL.S 3 & 4**.

Pinwheel Twist (Lennon-McCartney)
> Reported as being performed live in 62; no recorded version is known to exist.

Suicide (McCartney)
> Paul has recorded a number of versions of this song, originally written "for Frank Sinatra" in the late '50s. They are available on **SOUNDCHECK** (and **THE REAL CASE HAS JUST BEGUN**), **ONE HAND CLAPPING** and **HOME REHEARSALS**. A brief piece appeared on **McCARTNEY**.

That's My Woman (Lennon-McCartney)
> Reported as being performed in the late '50s, but no recorded version is known to exist.

Thinking Of Linking (Lennon-McCartney)
> Reported as being performed in the late '50s, but no recorded version is known to exist, although it has been said that there is a Spring 62 rehearsal recording. Paul talks about the song in *The Beatles: Recording Sessions*.

Tip Of My Tongue (Lennon-McCartney)
> The commercial version was released in 63 by Tommy Quickly; the Beatles recorded several takes at EMI on 26 Nov 62, which may remain in the EMI vaults; an acetate demo possibly exists.

Too Bad About Sorrows (Lennon-McCartney)
> Brief bits of this appear among the **GB** sessions; Paul also performs a brief rendition during the Oct 77 Melvin Bragg interview on **SUNSHINE SUPERMEN!!!**

What Goes On (Lennon-McCartney)
> It's unclear exactly when this was written, but Lewisohn says that it was "quite an old song" when the Beatles first attempted to record it on 5 Mar 63; the released version was recorded 3 Nov 65.

When I'm Sixty-Four (Lennon-McCartney)
> Written the the late '50s, reported as being performed live in 62, eventually recorded for **SERGEANT PEPPER**.

Winston's Walk (Lennon-McCartney)
> An instrumental, reported as being performed in the late '50s, but no recorded version is known to exist. The track given this title on **THE QUARRY MEN REHEARSE** is probably not the song. It has been said that there is a Spring 62 rehearsal recording.

World Without Love (Lennon-McCartney)
> The commercial version was released in 64 by Peter and Gordon; no Beatles version is known to exist but there is probably a demo (possibly Paul solo). In fact, a tape is currently making the rounds which is alleged to be such a demo, but it is not very convincing.

The Years Roll Along (Lennon-McCartney)
> Reported as being performed in the late '50s; no recorded version is known to exist but it has been said that there is a Spring 62 rehearsal recording.

FRAGMENTS WE MAY HAVE

PROBABLES:
> Our best evidence for these songs comes from a few precious moments on the **GET BACK** tapes. The accompanying dialogue is difficult to make out, but the following songs all seem to be early Lennon-McCartney originals:

If Tomorrow Ever Comes
> Performed briefly during the **GET BACK** sessions:
>> *I'll wait till tomorrow, till you come my way.*
>> *That's why I sit here alone and I pray.*
>> *But I'll wait till tomorrow, through a thousand setting suns.*
>> *I'll wait till tomorrow, if tomorrow ever comes.*
>> *I've got a love, I don't know where she's gone to.*
>> *I may be wrong, but I'm sure she didn't want to.*
>> *But I'll wait till tomorrow, through a thousand setting suns.*
>> *I'll wait till tomorrow, if tomorrow ever comes.*

Thinking That You Love Me (could this possibly be **Thinking Of Linking**?)
> Performed briefly during the **GET BACK** sessions:
>> *Well I've been thinking that you love me*
>> *Tell me that—*

Wake Up In The Morning
> Performed briefly during the **GET BACK** sessions:
>> *Wake up in the morning, I don't feel blue*
>> *'Cause I know I've got you.*
>> *Get a funny feeling all day and night.*
>> *Get the funny feeling you don't treat me right.*
>> *Should have read your letter and then I'd know.*
>> *I would have felt much better*
>> *Because I'd know you love me so.*

Won't You Please Say Good-bye
>Performed briefly during the **GET BACK** sessions:
>>*Won't you please say good-bye?*
>>*Love has long since grown cold.*
>>*Won't you please say good-bye?*
>>*How many times must you be told?*

There are also a number of yet-unidentified songs from the **GET BACK** sessions which may be early Lennon-McCartney tunes.

POSSIBLES

This material is all from the Spring 1960 Quarry Men rehearsal tapes. Any of these songs might actually be covers, but I have not been able to track them down so far.

Come On, People
>Performed on the Quarry Men rehearsal tapes.

Hey Darling
>Performed on the Quarry Men rehearsal tapes.

I Don't Know
>Performed on the Quarry Men rehearsal tapes.

Some Days
>Performed on the Quarry Men rehearsal tapes.

You Must Write Every Day (previously listed as "You Must Lie Every Day")
>Performed on the Quarry Men rehearsal tapes.

Unless (or until) more **GET BACK** or Quarry Men (said to exist, but to consist primarily of more instrumental jams) tapes surface, we will have to content ourselves with working on these.

All told, this may give us as many as forty-five out of an estimated hundred early Beatles songs. That is not nearly as bad as I had feared, although many of the others—even their titles—may be lost forever. Paul's notebook of early songs was reportedly thrown out by Jane Asher while tidying up. I know nothing of how trash is dealt with in and around London, but consider that the notebook may be buried somewhere right now, just waiting to be found...

MAKING SENSE OF
THE EARLY TELEVISION APPEARANCES
(Oct 1962-Dec 1963)

This list is compiled from a number of sources, none of which are complete or definitive, and much work remains to be done in this area. When two sources conflict, I have opted for the one which I suspect is more reliable.

Most of this material is not available through the usual audio or video trading circles, and much of it may be lost.

The prevailing opinion seems to be that most (if not all) *Thank Your Lucky Stars* appearances were lip-synched.

17 Oct 62, *People And Places*
   Their television debut; live, Manchester
   reportedly **Love Me Do, Ooh! My Soul**
2 Nov 62, *People And Places*
   Love Me Do
   This entry may be incorrect, as the Beatles were playing in Hamburg on this date; if the show was pre-recorded, no information has yet surfaced. It may also have been confused with the 17 Oct 62 show.
11 Nov 62, *Know The North* (scheduled—may not have been shown)
   filmed at the Cavern, probably 22 Aug 62
   Some Other Guy
3 Dec 62, *Discs-A-Gogo*
   TWW Studios, Bristol; material unknown
4 Dec 62, *Tuesday Rendezvous*
   Kingsway Studios, London
   Love Me Do (possibly the video which has them in dark, collarless suits in front of curtains)
17 Dec 62, *People And Places*
   live; reportedly **A Taste Of Honey**
8 Jan 63, *Round-Up*
   Glasgow
   Please Please Me
19 Jan 63, *Thank Your Lucky Stars*
   recorded 13 Jan 63, Birmingham
   Please Please Me; reportedly also **Ask Me Why**
23 Feb 63, *Thank Your Lucky Stars*
   recorded 17 Feb 63
   Please Please Me
9 Apr 63, *Tuesday Rendezvous*
   live from Kingsway Studios, London; material unknown

16 Apr 63, *The 6.25 Show*
    recorded 13 Apr 63, Lime Grove Studios, London
    From Me To You, Thank You Girl, Please Please Me
20 Apr 63, *Thank Your Lucky Stars*
    recorded 14 Apr 63, Teddington Studios
    From Me To You
16 May 63, *Pops And Lenny*
    live, BBC Television Theatre, Shepherd's Bush Green
    From Me To You, Please Please Me, After You've Gone (theme, with cast
    and other guests)
18 May 63, *Thank Your Lucky Stars*
    recorded 12 May 63
    From Me To You
29 Jun 63, *Juke Box Jury*
    recorded 22 Jun 63; John (solo; no performance)
29 Jun 63, *Thank Your Lucky Stars (Summer Spin)*
    recorded 23 Jun 63; material uncertain
    possibly **Twist And Shout** (the video with the band in dark turtlenecks, no jackets,
    and shadows in the background)
19 Aug 63, *Scene At 6.30* (formerly *People And Places*)
    recorded 14 Aug 63, Manchester; material unknown
    Pete Best was reportedly interviewed as well
24 Aug 63, *Thank Your Lucky Stars (Summer Spin)*
    recorded 18 Aug 63
    She Loves You, I'll Get You
7 Sep 63, *Big Night Out*
    recorded 1 Sep 63; material unknown
4 Oct 63, *Ready Steady Go!*
    performances were lip-synched; Kingsway Studios, London
    Twist And Shout, She Loves You, I'll Get You; the group wore their grey
    collarless suits and performed on the *RSG!* set, surrounded by fans; the first two
    songs are commercially available on *Ready Steady Go! Volume 2*
9 Oct 63, *The Mersey Sound*
    music recorded 27 Aug 63 at the Little Theatre, Southport
    interviews recorded 28 Aug 63 in Manchester
    **Twist And Shout, Love Me Do, I Saw Her Standing There, She Loves
    You** (the videos show the four on a small stage, performing in grey collarless suits;
    audience shots have been edited in)
    [note: this **She Loves You** was shown on *The Jack Parr Show*, 3 Jan 64]
13 Oct 63, *Sunday Night At The London Palladium*
    live on stage; London Palladium
    **I Want To Hold Your Hand, This Boy, All My Loving, Money, Twist And
    Shout** (this may instead be the lineup for the 12 Jan 64 show—see p. 235)
18 Oct 63, *Scene At 6.30*
    live; material unknown
26 Oct 63, *Thank Your Lucky Stars*
    recorded 20 Oct 63; material unknown
3 Nov 63, *Drop In*
    live in the studio; recorded 30 Oct 63, Sweden
    **She Loves You, Twist And Shout, I Saw Her Standing There, Long Tall
    Sally**, theme; they wore dark suits with velvet lapels and performed in front of a small
    audience
8 Nov 63, *Six O'clock*
    recorded that afternoon at the Ritz Cinema, Belfast
    one song plus interview
8 Nov 63, *Ready Steady Go!*
    repeats show of 4 Oct
10 Nov 63, *The Royal Variety Show*
    live on stage; filmed 4 Nov 63, Prince Of Wales Theatre, London
    She Loves You, Till There Was You, From Me To You, Twist And Shout

21 Nov 63, *CBS Evening News*
> concert footage (silent) filmed 16 Nov 63, Winter Gardens Theatre, Bournemouth; this marks the first U.S. television mention of the Beatles

27 Nov 63, *Scene At 6.30*
> music and chat (with Ken Dodd)
> possibly **I Want To Hold Your Hand**; the video has the giant "Daily Echo" in the background

3 Dec 63, *Day By Day*
> live?

7 Dec 63, *Juke Box Jury*
> filmed that afternoon at the Empire Theatre, Liverpool; no performance

7 Dec 63, *It's The Beatles*
> live on stage; taped the same day at the Empire Theatre, Liverpool
> **From Me To You, I Saw Her Standing There, All My Loving, Roll Over Beethoven, Boys, Till There Was You, She Loves You, This Boy, I Want To Hold Your Hand, Money (That's What I Want), Twist And Shout**

20 Dec 63, *Scene At 6.30*
> **This Boy**; the video may have the giant "Daily Echo" in the background

21 Dec 63, *Thank Your Lucky Stars*
> recorded 15 Dec 63
> **All My Loving, Twist And Shout, She Loves You, I Want To Hold Your Hand**

31 Dec 63, *Ready Steady Go!*
> repeats the show of 4 Oct

[note also:
22-29 Dec 63, *The Beatles Come To Town* (cinema newsreel)
> filmed 20 Nov 63, ABC Cinema, Ardwick, Manchester
> **From Me To You, She Loves You, Twist And Shout**]

MAKING SENSE OF
SESSIONS

If putting out an album is a battle, **SESSIONS** is the Bataan death march.

According to Brian Southall, the first time anyone at EMI officially went looking for unreleased Beatles material was in 76, when the Beatles' contract with them expired (on 6 Feb; Paul re-upped, George and Ringo left, and John went into retirement); company executives "sat down and listened to all the material that had not been released. In the main it existed in the form of rough mixes only and few were considered suitable for commercial release." Exactly what they had in mind is not clear but (EMI seems to start thinking about this when contract negotiations draw near), the result may have been **ROCK 'N' ROLL MUSIC**—and, perhaps, **THE BEATLES AT THE HOLLYWOOD BOWL**. It was apparently during this period that **How Do You Do It, Leave My Kitten Alone, That Means A Lot** and **If You've Got Trouble** were found.

After a couple years of picture discs, colored vinyl and boxed sets, a **SESSIONS**-like EP was considered for a Summer 80 release; it was to contain **Leave My Kitten Alone** and "several other alternate takes and demos" (*Beatlefan* Dec 81/Jan 82). The idea was delayed, then abandoned after the assassination of John Lennon.

But by early the next year an LP was being put together, as a follow-up to **RARITIES** (79 in the UK, 80 in the US). *Beatlefan* (Jun/Jul 81) carried a nearly correct, nearly complete title listing (**Come And Get It, That Means A Lot, If You've Got Trouble, Christmas Time (Is Here Again), One After 909, Mailman, Bring Me No More Blues** and—of course—**Leave My Kitten Alone**), including a song called **London Ball**, about which no more has ever been heard. This project never materialized.

In 82, as the Beatles' 20th anniversary approached, engineer John Barrett was assigned to listen to "every tape the Beatles had recorded for EMI and log any reference to material that was previously unknown." He reportedly found no new songs, but did locate several alternate (or working) versions of already-released cuts. **Leave My Kitten Alone** was again seriously considered for release, for Christmas 82, and again withdrawn.

During the Summer of 83, EMI presented *The Beatles At Abbey Road*, using much of the audio material uncovered by John Barrett. Afterward, with interest up, EMI executives sat down and listened to the old unreleased tracks, as well as the newly-discovered alternate versions. It was decided that most of the stereo tracks would have to be remixed, and that all of the material would need to be transferred to digital. The job was given to Geoff Emerick, who had engineered most of the Beatles' later work under George Martin.

[An interesting rumor has it that during a playback for EMI executives of unreleased Beatles material, someone present made a secret copy on a portable recorder. This tape, which probably dates from late 83 or early 84, is said to be the source of the various unreleased tracks on **FILE UNDER: BEATLES**, which are recorded off speakers and have extraneous voices and noises on them. Judging from sound quality, the following tracks derive from that "**SESSIONS** audition tape:" **Come And Get It, Shake, Rattle And Roll, Leave My Kitten Alone, Not Fade Away/Bo Diddley, Christmas Time (Is Here Again), Blue Suede Shoes, If You've Got Troubles, That Means A Lot, One After 909** and **Dig A Pony**. Whether this comes from EMI or Capitol, executives or engineers, the theory seems sound and is supported by what few facts we have.]

Writer Alan Kozinn related his brief association with the **SESSIONS** project in *Beatlefan* Apr/May 85. Kozinn, who had done reviews for, among others, the *New York*

Times, as well as some jacket notes for Angel (an EMI label), was hired in Aug 84 to write the liner notes for **SESSIONS**; he heard a tape (late Aug-early Sep) with the following lineup:

Side A

Christmas Time (Is Here Again)/Come And Get It
Leave My Kitten Alone (no false start; mono?)
Not Guilty
That Means A Lot (mono)
I'm Looking Through You
What's The New Mary Jane (stereo)

Side B

How Do You Do It (mono)
Besame Mucho (mono)
One After 909 (mono?)
If You've Got Trouble
(Not on the tape he heard, but he was told it was to come next; its absence may indicate it was a late choice and was still being worked on. If so, this dates the remixing as probably Aug-Sep 84.)
While My Guitar Gently Weeps
Mailman, Bring Me No More Blues
(called **Mailman Blues**)
Ob-La-Di, Ob-La-Da/Christmas Time (Is Here Again)

[This is essentially the same as the final lineup, except:
1) **Christmas Time** (Side A) was dropped to go on the single
2) **That Means A Lot** was bumped to Side B
3) **Ob-La-Di** was dropped to become the single.]

Kozinn had a number of interesting observations to make. He stated, for example, that the reason Capitol/EMI began and ended the LP with **Christmas Time** was because it was being released during that season (a short-sighted idea); he also suggested that the reason the LP is in such a chronological mess is because the label's marketing people felt that the earliest track, *Besame Mucho*, was also the weakest track on the LP (Did they truly feel that a browser will look only at the first cut? Apparently.). Once it was out of order, it seems, anything went.

At this point, according to Kozinn, the album was to be called **ONE-TWO-THREE-FOUR** (an earlier title proposal had been **BOOTS**, which may be why the Beatle boots appear on the back cover; this pun was rejected for obvious reasons, but it does show, I think, just how aware—one might even say knowledgeable—some industry people can be about bootlegs). Left hanging for several months, Kozinn finally heard in Dec 84 that his liner notes would not be used; Brian Southall's (then General Manager of Public Relations for EMI) would. EMI had scheduled **SESSIONS** for a Dec 84 (Christmas market) release, but this was dropped back a bit so as not to conflict with **GIVE MY REGARDS TO BROAD STREET** (and tick Paul off).

Production artwork (copied on the current **SESSIONS** disc and CD bootlegs—the black block in the corner contained the PARLOPHONE logo) was completed; the LP had a title (although not a very imaginative one), a catalogue number (EJ 2402701), and a release date (25 Feb 85); it was ready to go. The proposed single from the album was to be **Leave My Kitten Alone** b/w **Ob-La-Di, Ob-La-Da/Christmas Time (Is Here Again)**, catalogue number R6088 with a targeted release date of 28 Jan 85 (there are currently on the market apparent copies of the US picture sleeve, selling for about $300; it is black and white and not very attractive, but consistent with the proposed LP jacket). It, too, was ready to go.

An oddly defensive series of the questions and answers had been prepared, apparently to deal with an anticipated flood of inquiries regarding the new releases:

Q: Is this record being released because EMI needs the money?
A: The simple answer is no. EMI Music is a profitable company as shown by the Thorn EMI report and accounts.

But the Beatles, concerned over unpaid back royalties (and current royalties for that matter—see George's interview in the Dec 87 issue of *Creem* where, in apparent contradiction to many published sources, he states that in 1987, the Beatles' royalties are still just one penny per album), put a stop to it.

> *Q: What do the Beatles earn from this record?*
> *A: ...The royalty payments to the group will be in line with the contract in operation at the time of the original recording.*

And the whole project was dropped. Again.

Apple Corps Ltd. was at that time suing EMI for unpaid royalties (their claim was £2.3 million, plus interest; they were also suing Capitol for $42.5 million), and on 13 Dec 84, a judge ruled that "many matters need investigating," which began a complete audit that was not scheduled to be finished until 1986 (but is still dragging on). Negotiations continued through the early part of 85 to free up the project, but no agreement was ever reached and the release was cancelled. The inescapable conclusion is that what is truly keeping new Beatles material off the market is that Paul, George, Ringo and Yoko simply won't allow it until the money matters are settled (or don't want it out at all—an alarming prospect). This is sad, but understandable.

The ill-will between EMI and the Beatles (especially Paul) may not have gone deeper than financial considerations, but some very strange things were said. Kozinn says that he was told by John Carter, a producer for Capitol, that EMI "didn't want McCartney to know that the project was in the works until it was ready to be released ... they suspect McCartney would kill it if he had the chance."

> *Q: Did you ask the Beatles permission to release this record?*
> *A: ...Each of the Beatles are (sic) aware of this release and we haven't received any reaction at all.*

Some at EMI also seemed to be afraid that McCartney would demand the master tapes to all unreleased Beatles material as part of his upcoming contract negotiations and destroy them! (In fact, during 85 Paul did re-sign with Capitol/EMI for the U.S.—he had been with CBS—and he was promptly sued by George, Ringo & Yoko for accepting a preferred royalty rate.)

In the midst of this mess, someone apparently decided to take the matter into his own hands, and by late that year (or early the next), the first **SESSIONS** bootleg had appeared in Europe.

> *Q: Do you think you are guilty of exploiting/ripping off the Beatles by releasing tracks that they themselves never intended for release?*
> *A: Bootleggers and counterfeiters are guilty of ripping off the Beatles, not EMI who are the legal owners of this material.*

It was soon copied in the US with a colorful (but bogus) "Parlophone" jacket, and got a lot of publicity (in late 87, the very first Beatles bootleg CD was based on this release). Then in 88, there were two more US releases, one with **Ob-La-Di, Ob-La-Da** (framed by two **Christmas Time**s), using the correct cover art; this version was also available on CD.

> *Q: Technically, what did Emerick do to the tracks?*
> *A: Basically he remixed them and enhanced the overall sound quality by transferring the tapes to digital equipment.*

Well, he went a little farther than that. Working at AIR Studios in Montserrat, Emerick also did a certain amount of cutting and pasting, and here is a very good rationale for the existence of bootlegs, because without them we would have no way to judge the state of the material. At any rate, here is what Emerick ended up with, and what almost released:

Side A
Come And Get It
The initial appearance on **FILE UNDER: BEATLES** was shorter (and thus incomplete); it appears to be basically unchanged.
Leave My Kitten Alone
The initial appearance on **FILE UNDER: BEATLES** had a false start which has been left off. The cut on **ULTRA RARE TRAX VOL. 2** is the same as the **SESSIONS** version. [The version on **NOT FOR SALE** has the false start from the **SESSIONS** audition tape version edited onto the front of the **SESSIONS** version.]
Not Guilty
The initial appearance on **NOT GUILTY**, probably from an acetate, contains an extra brief guitar solo and one extra line: "Not guilty, for being on your street, getting underneath your feet;" the **SESSIONS** version also fades early. The EMI version Emerick worked with was probably identical to the acetate version.
I'm Looking Through You
The initial appearance from *The Beatles Live At Abbey Road* on **THE BEATLES LIVE AT ABBEY ROAD STUDIOS** was merely an excerpt of the track, but they appear to be identical. The cut on **ULTRA RARE TRAX VOL. 1** is the same, but with studio chat, riffs and a countdown at the beginning, and it proceeds to the end of the take instead of fading.
What's The New Mary Jane
The initial (best) appearance was on **WHAT A SHAME, MARY JANE HAD A PAIN AT THE PARTY**. The **SESSIONS** version would appear to be a drastic remix of version #1 (there may be no version #0, or it may be the version on **ULTRA RARE TRAX, VOL.S 5&6**), with the extraneous noises nearly eliminated, and echo and phasing added to the vocals.

Side B
How Do You Do It
The initial appearance was probably on **HOW DO YOU DO IT**; the **SESSIONS** version's ending has been edited so that the first (of three) "Wish I knew how you do it to me, I'd do it to you" lines has been replaced by "Wish I knew how you do it to me, but I haven't a clue," copied from the second verse. The version on **ULTRA RARE TRAX VOL. 1** has the original ending.
Besame Mucho
No prior appearance; however, it is probable that the ending was edited to repeat during the fade. The cut on **ULTRA RARE TRAX VOL. 1** is identical to the **SESSIONS** version.
One After 909
The initial appearance was on **FILE UNDER: BEATLES**. The **SESSIONS** version has a piece from an entirely different guitar solo edited in. The version on **ULTRA RARE TRAX VOL. 1** is a completely different take, with a still different guitar solo.
If You've Got Trouble
The initial appearance on **FILE UNDER: BEATLES** starts late and fades early; the next appearance on **NOT FOR SALE** is complete; on the **SESSIONS** version, Ringo has an extra "Rock on!" after his "Ah, rock on, anybody!" The cut on **ULTRA RARE TRAX VOL. 1** is the **SESSIONS** version.
That Means A Lot
The initial appearance on **FILE UNDER: BEATLES** starts late and fades early; otherwise they seem to be the same.
While My Guitar Gently Weeps
The initial appearance on **"IN ABBEY ROAD"** (and subsequent copies) from EMI's *The Beatles At Abbey Road* presentation ends with George strumming a final chord and then requesting playback: "Let's hear that back." The **SESSIONS** version is edited to repeat the last guitar phrase and fade.

Also, the faint electric organ has been brought forward a bit more in the **SESSIONS** version.

Mailman, Bring Me No More Blues

The initial appearance on **THE REAL CASE HAS JUST BEGUN** shows that this version has been severely edited. The original consists (roughly) of two verses separated by a brief instrumental break; the **SESSIONS** version fades in on the instrumental break, which then repeats; this is followed by the last half of the first verse, the instrumental break, then the first half of the first verse, then it fades on the last half of the last verse. The editing is excellent.

Christmas Time (Is Here Again)

The initial appearance on **FILE UNDER: BEATLES** is over six minutes long; the **SESSIONS** version consists of about the first minute of that.

Will a legitimate **SESSIONS** ever be released? The real question may be: will **SESSIONS** be released while anybody still cares?

TOMORROW NEVER KNOWS
(VERSION 2.0)

Here is an updated list of significant Beatles (collective & solo) recordings (excluding BBC, **GET BACK**, and most EMI sessions) which are known, or have been said, to exist but have not yet appeared on bootlegs. Some of these are working titles for songs which were later released. Some apparently do not exist at all and are included here for debunking purposes. Alternate takes are not included (there are hundreds, after all), unless they seem to be especially important.

After You've Gone (Creamer-Layton)
    16 May 63, UK tv; the Beatles sang the closing theme to *Pops And Lenny* along with the other guests; source: *Beatles Book Monthly* (Jun 80).
All Right (?)
    Apr-May 76, Ringo.
All Rocked Out (McCartney)
    mentioned by Paul's piano tuner (!) in the 9-22 Jun 86 issue of *Music Connection.*
ALL THINGS MUST PASS (outtakes)
    In his Oct 86 *Playboy* interview, Phil Collins tells that he played conga drums on a session which didn't make the final LP. In all likelihood, there are hours of unused material from these sessions.
All Those Years Ago (Harrison)
    The original version, recorded prior to John's assassination but never used.
Always And Only (McCartney)
    21 Sep 64 - 8 Oct 64 for **BEATLES FOR SALE**; supposedly written by Paul in May 64 while on vacation in the Virgin Islands; earliest reference traced to date: *NME*, 23 Mar 74; apparently does not exist.
Annie (McCartney)
    May-Jun 67, reportedly performed by Paul under the pseudonym "Busker Sam Sellers;" earliest reference traced to date: *NME*, 23 Mar 74. An alleged copy of this cut is making the tape trading rounds, but I have heard it and it sounds nothing like the Beatles or Busker Sam. The word is that it is actually the group Blonde (not Blondie), but I have been unable to confirm this; apparently does not exist.
Anything (Lennon-McCartney-Harrison-Starkey)
    also called "Drum Track (1);" an experimental percussion piece recorded 22 Feb 67 at EMI.
Ask Me Why (Lennon-McCartney)
    EMI 6 Jun 62; tape apparently destroyed.
Autumn Leaves (Mercer-Prevert-Kosma)
    Feb 70, Ringo; source: *Working Class Heroes.*
Baby Jane (?)
    (or "Baby Jane, I'm Sorry:" *Beatles A To Z*) Oct 65, for **RUBBER SOUL**; earliest reference traced to: *Beatles Discography* (Guzek, 76); according to Peter Doggett (*Beatles Book Monthly*, May 89) it was announced as a forthcoming bootleg single in a 1971 issue of *Disc And Music Echo*; but a correction was printed a couple of weeks later to the effect that it was not a Beatles song after all; apparently does not exist; it

has also been suggested that this may be a garbled reference to **What's The New Mary Jane**.

Bad Penny Blues (Lyttleton)
supposedly Summer 69 but, Ray Schweighardt (editor of *How Do You Do It?*) writes that it resulted from a misunderstanding of a 68 NME article (exact date unknown) which stated that the next Beatles single would be "the same old bad penny blues." The single in question was **Lady Madonna**, and the recording of **Bad Penny Blues** apparently does not exist. According to Lewisohn, **Lady Madonna** is "not totally unlike **Bad Penny Blues**, a minor chart hit for the Humphrey Lyttleton Band in 1956."

"The Beatles' chauffeur's" tapes
Some really interesting items came up for auction at Sotheby's in Aug 89: five reel-to-reel tapes, at least some of which are rumored to to have come from the Beatles' chauffeur, containing much material no one had ever heard before. Some of the items included: two alternate, unreleased takes of **It Won't Be Long** (EMI, 30 Jul 63?); the Fourmost's session for **Hello Little Girl** (EMI 24 Jul 63), with George and Ringo present; an informal tape of John and Paul singing **Tell Me True** and **Over The Rainbow**, some McCartney instrumentals, a **Michelle** instrumental (possibly by Paul), **Three Coins In The Fountain**, nursery rhymes with a child, and John and Paul singing "Rockin' And Rollin'" (**Reelin' And Rockin'**?); several attempts by John at a demo for **If I Fell**, in a non-studio location; George composing **Don't Bother Me** in a Bournemouth hotel room in Aug 63; and, finally, George, Paul and Gerry Marsden, joined by John, reading from *The Bible*, **The Lord Is My Shepherd**, sung by John and **There Is A Green Hill** sung by all (at Weston-super-Mare during the week of 22-27 Jul 63). Because the asking prices were so high, some of these tapes remain unsold.

Buy Me A Beer, Mr. Shane
10 Oct 69, Ringo; the latest and most likely theory is that this is simply *Bei Mir Bist Du Schon* (Shein/Cahn-Calvin), which is certainly weird enough to be true.

Carl Perkins jam
1 Jun 64? Perkins was at EMI to see the Beatles record **Matchbox**, although he did not play on the song; nevertheless, the book for **CARL PERKINS: THE SUN YEARS** (Charly Records, Sun Box 101) claims that "an unissued session remains of Carl jamming with the Beatles." Lewisohn says that there is no tape of this in the EMI archives.

Cavern Club tape
Jul 62. At the Sotheby's auction of 29 Aug 85, Paul bought a 1&3/4 ips tape of a Cavern Club performance. Recorded by a fan, it went for £2100 and contained the following songs: **Hey! Baby** (Channel-Cobb), **If You Gotta Make A Fool Of Somebody** (Clark), **The Hippy Hippy Shake** (Romero), **Please Mr. Postman** (Holland-Bateman-Gordy), **Roll Over Beethoven** (Berry), **Ask Me Why** (Lennon-McCartney), **Sharing You** (Goffin-King), **Your Feet's Too Big** (Benson-Fisher), **Words Of Love** (Holly), **Till There Was You** (Willson), **Dizzy Miss Lizzie** (Williams), **I Forgot To Remember To Forget** (Kesler-Feathers), **Matchbox** (Perkins), **Shimmy Shake** (South-Land), **Young Blood** (Leiber-Stoller-Pomus) and **Dream Baby** (Walker). No other Beatles version of some of these songs is known to exist. Lewisohn has said that the sound quality is extremely poor.

Circles (Harrison)
A Harrison Kinfauns demo which supposedly surfaced among the *Lost Lennon* material; possibly a "WHITE ALBUM" demo, the song eventually appeared on **GONE TROPPO**.

Colliding Circles (Lennon?)
mid-66; earliest reference traced to date: *NME*, 23 Mar 74; apparently does not exist; may refer to **Circles**.

Cottonfields (Ledbetter)
done by Paul & Wings during some performances of their Summer 72 tour; available on the tape of Wings live in Antwerp, 22 Aug 72.

Crawl Of The Wild (?)
Jun-Jul 78, **BACK TO THE EGG** sessions? Paul with Dave Mason? Oddly, a song called "The Crowd Of The Wild" is listed in *Beatles Discography* (Guzek, 1976) as a

overdubbed later) or the 78 date is incorrect (since it could have not appeared in a 76 listing).

Do You Like Me Just A Little Bit (?)

Ringo and Cilla Black, reportedly from Cilla Black's tv show of 6 Feb 68, the traditional date of their **Act Naturally** duet. Ringo was apparently also a guest on her show of 25 Apr 71, and the song may be from that show.

Do You Want To Know A Secret (Lennon-McCartney)

63 Dick James acetate, John and Paul; sold at auction.

ECHOES OF THE MERSEYSIDE

[3 Oct-8 Oct 64?] According to new information from Wiener (*Goldmine*, 3 Jun 88), this is not a song but a compilation album issued in 1971 by *The Liverpool Echo* (LPDE 101) which contained "interview clips of many sports and entertainment stars, including a five-second Lennon clip."

1882 (McCartney)

studio, recorded prior to Jul 72; source: 72 European tour program. This song was performed extensively on the Summer 72 tour, and many live versions are available.

Every Time Somebody Comes To Town (Harrison-Dylan?)

Summer 69?; a version of George and Bob Dylan (Nov 68?) doing this song is on **20X4**; earliest reference traced to date (where it is called "When I Come To Town"): *NME*, 23 Mar 74; Lewisohn does not report it as appearing in the EMI session logs.

Four Nights In Moscow (Lennon?)

Summer 69; earliest reference traced to date: *NME*, 23 Mar 74; this may in fact be a 71 **RINGO** outtake.

From A Window (Lennon-McCartney)

64; probably exists as an acetate.

Give My Regards To Broad Street jams

During rehearsal and filming, Dave Edmunds said (*Beatlefan* Jun/Jul 83), "We did all the old Everly Brothers, Jerry Lee and Elvis songs." At least two long jams were taped (but not filmed) at the warehouse location "for posterity." *Posterity?!* Lovely. Our grandchildren will have something to look forward to.

The Great Cock And Seagull Race (McCartney?)

According to an excerpt of *Strange Days: The Music Of John, Paul, George And Ringo Twenty Years On* in *Beatlefan* (Feb/Mar 87) this was a cut considered for an early version of **HOT HITS AND COLD CUTS** (circa 74). Recording date unknown.

"The Heart That You Broke"

recorded by Wings in Nashville, Summer 74. Source: *The Beatles A To Z*. This is just **Send Me The Heart** (McCartney-Laine); the confusion apparently resulted from its appearance (under the incorrect title) on a *Strawberry Fields Forever* Christmas flexi.

Heather (McCartney)

recorded in the (late) '60s; source: *McCartney Songwriter*; this is probably the version from the **POST CARD** sessions, which has appeared.

Hello Little Girl (Lennon-McCartney)

John's original tape demo for the Fourmost, possibly done while he was sitting on the toilet following a performance in Blackpool; source: *Let's Go Down The Cavern* and liner notes (by Tony Barrow) for **TRIBUTE TO THE CAVERN** (LP). Brian O'Hara still had the tape in the early '80s. Hullo, Brian? The assumed 62 and 64 recordings probably do not exist, but there may be a demo acetate.

Help Me (Williamson-Bass)

According to an excerpt of *Strange Days: The Music Of John, Paul, George And Ringo Twenty Years On* in *Beatlefan* (Feb/Mar 87) this was a cut considered for an early version of **HOT HITS AND COLD CUTS** (circa 74). There may be a studio version (recording date unknown), but a live version is available on **FIRST LIVE SHOW**. It should be emphasized that this is *not* a McCartney song, but a cover of an old blues number by Sonny Boy Williamson (compare with Van Morrison's rendition on his LP **"...IT'S TOO LATE TO STOP NOW..."**).

Helter Skelter (Lennon-McCartney)

18 Jul 68, the 24-minute version. Source: *The Long And Winding Road*. According to a letter in *The Beatles Book* (Feb 83), Brian Southall of EMI claimed that their vault contains "parts of" this track but not the complete long version. I have been told that

contains "parts of" this track but not the complete long version. I have been told that there is a bogus version of this, edited together from the album track, making the rounds among tape collectors. I have also heard rumors of a former EMI employee who claims to have a 10-minute version on acetate. According to Lewisohn, Paul made a copy for himself.

Hey Jude (Lennon-McCartney)
> A 10-minute version. According to a letter in *The Beatles Book* (Feb 83), Brian Southall of EMI claimed that their vaults contains "parts of" this track but not the complete long version.

Home (Van Steedson-Clarkson-Clarkson)
> 64; earliest reference traced to: *Beatles Discography* (Guzek, 76).

House Of The Rising Sun (trad.)
> 3 Oct 64, at London's Granville Theatre. The rest of the performance was recorded for broadcast on *Shindig*. (Lewisohn does not mention this, and it may be apocryphal, or performed as a warm-up as Wiener suggests.)

I Do Like To Be Beside The Seaside (Glover Kind)
> (traditionally) 17 Jul 65, ABC Theatre, Blackpool, England and broadcast 1 Aug 65 on *Blackpool Night Out* television show, perhaps as part of a skit. However, John and Paul do sing 5 seconds' worth of the song at the end of the *A Midsummer Night's Dream* Pyramus And Thisbee sketch on *Around The Beatles* (filmed 28 Apr 64, first broadcast in the UK on 6 May 64), so perhaps (even probably) that is the origin of this reference. As Pyramus (Paul) and Thisbee (John) die, they say:
>> "Adieu, adieu... I do like to be beside the seaside.
>> I do like to be beside the sea..."
>
> and then the audience cheers and the scene fades. The sketch is not on the official video of *Around The Beatles* (from Dave Clark's Picture Music International), but is on *Fun With The Fab Four* (Goodtimes 9015). This short bit has never been bootlegged, and is probably not worth doing. John sings a piece of the song in the medley on *THE LOST LENNON TAPES*, VOL. 2 as well.

I Don't Want To See You Again (Lennon-McCartney)
> 64; probably exists as an acetate.

I Lost My Little Girl (Lennon-McCartney)
> Spring 62 rehearsal? earliest traced reference: *Beatles Discography* (Guzek, 1976).

I Saw Her Standing There (Lennon-McCartney)
> Dec 62, Hamburg; an un-booted performance, possibly played on German tv or radio.

I Should Like To Live Up A Tree (Starkey)
> Mar 69; it has been claimed that this is an early working title for *Octopus's Garden*, which is possible; as apparently reported in a 69 *NME.*

Incantation (Lennon-Cicala)
> Written 74; source: *The Beatles A To Z.*

India (Harrison)
> A working title for one of the tracks (Lewisohn does not say which one) on George's **WONDERWALL** soundtrack, recorded at EMI 22/23 Nov 67.

"I'll Be Looking At The Moon"
> Feb 70, Ringo; this is no doubt:

I'll Be Seeing You (Fain-Kahal)
> Feb 70, Ringo; earliest traced reference: *Beatles Discography* (Guzek, 1976).

I'll Keep You Satisfied (Lennon-McCartney)
> Apparently no EMI recording, although it may exist as a Dick James acetate.

I'm In Love (Lennon-McCartney)
> Apparently no EMI recording, although it may exist as a Dick James acetate.

In Spite Of All The Danger (McCartney-Harrison)
> 1958, recorded by the Quarry Men. The only known copy is owned by Paul McCartney. Source: *The Beatles Live!*

It's All Too Much (Harrison)
> mid-Jun 67, excellent stereo; the version in the *Yellow Submarine* film has an extra verse. The video soundtrack for this song is mono.

It's For You (Lennon-McCartney)
> Apparently no EMI recording, although it may exist as a Dick James acetate.

It's Hard To Be Lovers (?)
> Apr-May 76, Ringo.

Jubilee (McCartney)
> Mar 69, an early version of **Junk**; also, EMI 31 Jul 69 (*Beatles Discography*, Guzek, 1976); does not appear in the session notes and may not exist. Earliest traced reference: a 70 (?) radio mention by Kenny Everett (?) as a song recorded "last year."

Just Dancing Around (?)
> Summer 69; earliest traced reference: *Beatles Discography* (Guzek, 1976).

Karate Chaos (McCartney)
> ©Jun 75; "abstract percussion piece" for *Empty Hand* documentary, released in 1977. Source: U.S copyright registry.

Keep Looking That Way (Lennon-McCartney)
> Spring 62 rehearsal recording? earliest traced reference: *Beatles Discography* (Guzek, 1976).

Keep Your Hands Off My Baby (Goffin-King)
> 11 Feb 63, as reported 22 Feb 63 in the *NME*, but the complete studio documentation does not mention this song, and the report may be an error. May-Jun 65, another version; also apparently does not exist.

Life Begins At Forty (Lennon)
> Recorded in the Summer of 80 for, but never used on, Ringo's **CAN'T FIGHT LIGHTNING** LP.

Like Dreamers Do (Lennon-McCartney)
> Apparently no EMI recording, although it may exist as a Dick James acetate.

Little Child (Lennon-McCartney)
> 63 Dick James acetate, with John and Paul; sold at auction.

Little Eddy (McCartney)
> see **GB** sessions, **There You Go, Eddie**.

London Ball (?)
> *Beatlefan* (Jun/Jul 81) mentions this as being on the "upcoming" [**SESSIONS**] LP.

Looking Glass (Lennon-McCartney)
> Spring 62 rehearsal? earliest traced reference: *Beatles Discography* (Guzek, 1976).

Maisy Jones (Lennon-McCartney?)
> Oct 65, for **RUBBER SOUL**; earliest reference traced to: *Beatles Discography* (Guzek, 76); apparently does not exist.

Midnight Special (trad.)
> late May 74, **PUSSYCATS** sessions. John and Paul (and many others) jamming in the studio.

Mind Train (Ono)
> Aug 72, One-To-One rehearsals; available on tape.

Mr. Shane
> see Buy Me A Beer, Mr. Shane.

Moonglow (Hudson-De Lange-Mills-Duning-Allen)
> 64? earliest traced reference: *Beatles Discography* (Guzek, 1976); apparently does not exist.

My Kind Of Girl (Briscuss?)
> Summer 69; earliest reference traced to: *Beatles Discography* (Guzek, 76); apparently does not exist.

Nobody I Know (Lennon-McCartney)
> 64; probably exists as a Dick James acetate.

Not Unknown (Harrison)
> The correct working title of **Only A Northern Song** (Feb 67) was "Not Known;" earliest reference traced to date: *NME*, 23 Mar 74; a tape of this "lost song" is making the rounds which sounds nothing like the Beatles (the word is that it is actually the group Blonde, but I have been unable to confirm this).

Ob-La-Di, Ob-La-Da (Lennon-McCartney)
> In the Jan 86 *Beatles Book*, a reader reports an acetate which has vocals only; from his description, this might be a bogus acetate of an OOPSed version.

Olympic Studios, 31 Oct 69
> George records with Eric Clapton, Rick Grech and Denny Laine.

On Moonlight Bay (Madden-Wenrich)
> Performed 18 Apr 64 on *Morcambe and Wise*.

Paul at AIR, Montserrat, 81
> **Boppin' The Blues** (Perkins), **Cut Across Shorty** (Walker-Wilkin), **Honey Don't** (Perkins), **Lend Me Your Comb** (Twomey-Wise-Weisman), **Red Sails In The Sunset** (Kennedy-Williams), **When The Saints Go Marching In** (trad.); some of these possibly with Carl Perkins.

Party (Starkey-Nilsson)
> date unknown; reported in *Book Of Beatles Lists* (Reinhart).

Peace Of Mind (?)
> excellent stereo version; apparently not the Beatles.

Penina (McCartney)
> 70, demo for Jotta Herre? Earliest reference traced to date: *NME*, 23 Mar 74; Lewisohn does not report it as appearing in the EMI session logs; a Dick James acetate may exist.

Pink Litmus Paper Shirt (Harrison?)
> working title, mid-66; earliest reference traced to date: *NME*, 23 Mar 74; Lewisohn does not report it as appearing, under this title, in the EMI session logs.

Please Please Me (Lennon-McCartney)
> EMI 11 Sep 62; original, slow version; Lewisohn reports the tape was destroyed. The original version was described as being like a Roy Orbison song, slow and very dramatic. When Orbison and Paul met some time ago, Orbison reportedly proposed that they re-record the song as it was originally written, with Paul doing the vocals and Orbison producing. Paul said he'd think about it. Too late now, Paul.

Portrait Of My Love (Ornadel-West)
> Summer 69; earliest reference traced to: *Beatles Discography* (Guzek, 76); in 88 he reports that he has been unable to confirm it; probably does not exist.

Proud As You Are (?)
> Summer 69; earliest reference traced to: *Beatles Discography* (Guzek, 76); in 88 he reports that he has been unable to confirm it; probably does not exist.

P.S. I Love You (Lennon-McCartney)
> EMI 6 Jun 62, with Pete Best; Lewisohn reports the tape was destroyed.

Raunchy (Justis-Manker)
> 64? earliest traced reference: *Beatles Discography* (Guzek, 1976); apparently does not exist.

Red Hot (Emerson)
> the complete song, excerpted on **WHEN IT SAYS BEATLES...** May be a Hamburg performance, or a Cavern Club tape. *Beatles Discography* (Guzek, 76) mentioned this as a Hamburg song two years before the tapes were commercially released.

Revolution 1 (Lennon-McCartney)
> (10:17) version. According to a letter in *The Beatles Book* (Feb 83), Brian Southall of EMI claimed that their vaults contain "parts of" this track but not the complete long version. Lewisohn explains that the last six minutes (consisting mostly of vocal weirdness) were "hived off to form the basis for **Revolution 9**."

Revolution 9 (Lennon-McCartney)
> 16 minute version making the rounds on tape is probably bogus and may be from the same source as the **FORETASTE** tape; at the 7 Apr 88 Sotheby's auction, an acetate of an "early, working version" sold for £800; another copy (or another version) was sold at auction in late 88.

Rock Peace (Lennon?)
> Summer 69; instrumental, by the Plastic Ono Band, reportedly withdrawn just before its intended release in Aug 69; this cut has allegedly surfaced among the *Lost Lennon* material, but there is a very slight possibility that it may be the tune making the rounds which was mis-identified as **12-Bar Original**.

Rode All Night (McCartney?)
> According to an excerpt of *Strange Days: The Music Of John, Paul, George And Ringo Twenty Years On* in *Beatlefan* (Feb/Mar 87) this was a cut considered for an early version of **HOT HITS AND COLD CUTS** (circa 74). Recording date unknown.

During Neil Innes' late 79 UK tour, Nasty and Barry performed three unreleased Rutles tunes. Anybody have these on tape? More unreleased material may also be included on the CD from Rhino—if it ever comes out.

Sea Dance (McCartney)
Wings, Jan-Apr 75, during the **VENUS AND MARS** sessions; ©Jun 75; source: U.S. copyright registry.

Soundstage Of Mind (Harrison)
74-5, George, studio version? may not exist.

Star-Club tapes
Dec 62, Hamburg; as many as five sets were reportedly recorded in Hamburg; one has appeared on **MACH SHAU**; pieces of that one and (at least) one other are on the official Star-Club release. Where are the others?

Studio outtakes, late 62
Dizzy Miss Lizzie (Williams), **I Forgot To Remember To Forget** (Kesler-Feathers), and **Lucille** (Collins-Penniman); earliest traced source: *A Day In The Life*. Here is apparently what happened: these three BBC cuts appeared on the 72 BBC radio special, *The Beatles Story* (where **I Forgot** was said to be Paul and **Lucille** was said to be John!) and were (first) copied onto **HAVE YOU HEARD THE WORD** with no liner notes. U.S collectors, knowing little about the Beatles' extensive BBC career, and possibly misled by some advertising (probably in catalogues) for the bootleg, came to understand that these were studio outtakes. The mistake was then repeated in text. In fact, the cuts referred to are BBC 7 Jun 65, 18 May 64, and 5 Oct 63.

Suicide (McCartney)
Summer 69; earliest reference traced to: *Beatles Discography* (Guzek, 76).

Summertime (Gershwin)
15 Oct 60, Hamburg; the only known copy is in Australia. Source: *The Beatles Live!*

Swinging Days (?)
Summer 69; earliest reference traced to: *Beatles Discography* (Guzek, 76); in 88 he reported that he has been unable to confirm it; probably does not exist.

Take It Away filming
23 Jun 82, Elstree Studios; Paul performed for British fan club members while filming *Take It Away*. Also performed for the fans were **Bo Diddley** (McDaniel), **Peggy Sue** (Holly-Allison-Petty), **Twenty Flight Rock** (Cochran-Fairchild), **Lucille** (Penniman-Collins), **Send Me Some Lovin'** (Marascalco-Price), **Cut Across Shorty** (Walker-Wilkin), **Searchin'** (Leiber-Stoller), **Reelin' And Rockin'** (Berry), **The Theme From Hill Street Blues** (as "Elstree Blues") and a number of untitled jams. For a complete description of the session, see *Beatles Book* Aug 82. No tapes of this performance have yet surfaced, darn it.

That'll Be The Day (Holly)
58, the Quarry Men; the only known copy is owned by Paul McCartney. Source: *The Beatles Live!* Paul has said that he has given tape copies to a few close friends.

Thinking Of Linking (Lennon-McCartney)
rehearsal recorded Spring 62? also Summer 69 (earliest reference traced to: *Beatles Discography* (Guzek, 76).

This Is Some Friendly (Starkey)
working title for **Don't Pass Me By**.

The Tip Of My Tongue (Lennon-McCartney)
26 Nov 62, EMI; this was under consideration as one side of the Beatles' second single, but they never got a take they liked; several takes may be stored in the EMI vaults; possibly exists as an acetate.

El Toro Passing (?)
May 77, Paul, instrumental.

We're All Water (Ono)
Aug 72, One-To-One rehearsals; available on tape.

What'd I Say (Charles)
On a French Gene Vincent bootleg which appeared in 88, this cut was claimed to have been recorded at the Cavern with the Beatles backing GV. The sound is decent mono, and the band could be the Beatles (they appeared on the same bill on 1 Jul 62), but there are no vocals to confirm it. Where is the rest of the set?

What'd I Say (Charles)
> On a French Gene Vincent bootleg which appeared in 88, this cut was claimed to have been recorded at the Cavern with the Beatles backing GV. The sound is decent mono, and the band could be the Beatles (they appeared on the same bill on 1 Jul 62), but there are no vocals to confirm it. Where is the rest of the set?

When I Was In Paris (McCartney?)
> According to an excerpt of *Strange Days: The Music Of John, Paul, George And Ringo Twenty Years On* in *Beatlefan* (Feb/Mar 87) this was a cut considered for an early version of **HOT HITS AND COLD CUTS** (circa 74). Recording date unknown.

Where Are You Going (?)
> Apr-May 76, Ringo.

Winston's Walk (Lennon-McCartney)
> Spring 62 rehearsal? earliest traced reference: *Beatles Discography* (Guzek, 1976).

Woman (McCartney as Webb)
> Apparently no EMI recording, although it may exist as a 64 Dick James demo acetate.

World Without Love (Lennon-McCartney)
> 64 Dick James acoustic demo? making the tape rounds, I am not convinced of its authenticity.

The Years Roll Along (Lennon-McCartney)
> Spring 62 rehearsal? also Summer 69; earliest reference traced to: *Beatles Discography* (Guzek, 76).

Yesterday (Lennon-McCartney)
> 65 Dick James demo acetate, Paul solo; sold at auction.

Yesterday (Lennon-McCartney)
> For the 65 tv special, *The Music Of Lennon And McCartney*, Paul reportedly shared vocals with Marianne Faithful (*Beatlefan*, Feb/Mar 87).

You Are My Sunshine (Davis-Mitchell)
> 64? earliest traced reference: *Beatles Discography* (Guzek, 1976); it has been suggested that this may refer to the cut by "The Beat Brothers" on the 64 MGM LP **THE BEATLES WITH TONY SHERIDAN AND THEIR GUESTS**.

You Are My Sunshine (Davis-Mitchell)
> 23 Oct 84, Paul on *The Tonight Show*; very brief.

You Know My Name (Lennon-McCartney)
> 67-69, the long version; according to the notes of **PAST MASTERS VOLUME TWO**, there were three remixes of the original mono master, which was more than six minutes long; reportedly, there has never been a stereo mix.

You'll Know What To Do (Harrison?)
> 21 Sep - 8 Oct 64 for **BEATLES FOR SALE**; earliest reference traced to date: *NME*, 23 Mar 74; apparently does not exist.

Your Feet's Too Big (Benson-Fisher)
> Spring 62 rehearsal recording?

Zero Is Just Another Even Number (Harrison?)
> Summer 69; earliest reference traced to: *Beatles Discography* (Guzek, 76); apparently does not exist.

It should be noted that a number of EMI/Apple outtakes (**How Do You Do It**, **If You've Got Trouble**, **Not Guilty**, **What's The New Mary Jane**, **Jazz Piano Song**, and **Suzy Parker**) reported in the 23 Mar 74 *NME* article (written with the help of Tony King of Apple Records and John Ingham of EMI) *have* surfaced.

BIBLIOGRAPHY

Here is a list of sources without which it would have been impossible to do an adequate job on such an undertaking as this. Some are signifcantly better than others (and many have almost nothing to do with the Beatles, yet are nonetheless interesting), but all were useful.

Belmer, Scott & L.R.E. King (ed's.)
Belmo's Beatleg News

Brown, Peter & Steven Gaines
The Love You Make
Macmillan, 1983

Carr, Roy & Tony Tyler
The Beatles: An Illustrated Record
Harmony Books, 1981

Castleman, Harry & Walter Podrazik
All Together Now
Pierian Press, 1976

Castleman, Harry & Walter Podrazik
The Beatles Again
Pierian Press, 1977

Castleman, Harry & Walter Podrazik
The End Of The Beatles?
Pierian Press, 1985

Cott, Jonathan & David Dalton
The Beatles Get Back
Apple Publishing, 1969

Davies, Hunter
The Beatles
McGraw-Hill, 1985

Dean, Johnny (ed.)
The Beatles Book
Beat Publications

Dean, Johnny (ed.)
The Record Collector
Diamond Publishing Group

Elson, Howard
McCartney Songwriter
W.H. Allen, 1986

Friede, Goldie & R. Titone & S. Weiner
The Beatles A To Z
Metheun, 1980

Gaiman, Neil
Don't Panic
Pocket, 1988

Glemser, Kurt
Hot Wacks - Book XII
Blue Flake Productions, 1987

Guzek, Arno
Beatles Discography
privately printed, 1976

Harrison, George
I Me Mine
Simon & Schuster, 1980

Harry, Bill
Beatlemania:
A History Of The Beatles On Film
Virgin Books, 1984

Howlett, Anthony
The Beatles At The Beeb 1962-65
BBC, 1982

King, Leslie T. (ed.)
Beatlefan
The Goody Press

King, L.R.E.
Do You Want To Know A Secret?
Storyteller Productions, 1988

King, L.R.E.
Help!
Storyteller Productions, 1988

Leigh, Spenser
Let's Go Down The Cavern
Vermillion, 1984

Lewisohn, Mark
The Beatles Live!
Pavillion Books, Ltd., 1986

Lewisohn, Mark
The Beatles: Recording Sessions
Harmony Books, 1988

Lewisohn, Mark
The Beatles: 25 Years In The Life
Sidgwick & Jackson, Ltd., 1987

Martin, George
All You Need Is Ears
St. Martin's Press, 1979

McCartney, Mike
The Macs
Delilah Books, 1981

McCoy, William & Mitchell McGeary
Every Little Thing
Ticket To Ryde, Ltd., 1979

Norman, Philip
Shout!
Simon & Schuster, 1981

Pang, May
Loving John
Warner Books, 1983

Perry, George
The Life Of Python
Little, Brown 1983

Pope, Joe (ed.)
Strawberry Fields Forever

Reinhart, Charles
You Can't Do That!
Pierian Press, 1981

Rees, Tony
Rare Rock — A Collector's Guide
Blandford Press (UK), 1985

Rehwagen, Thomas
The Beatles From Session To Session
Privately printed, 1987

Rosenay, Charles (ed.)
Good Day Sunshine

Russell, Jeff. P.
The Beatles On Record
Scribners, 1982

Sandahl, Linda
Enciclopedia Of Rock Music
Blandford Press (UK), 1987

Schaffner, Nicholas
The Beatles Forever
Cameron House, 1977

Schultheiss, Tom
A Day In The Life
Pierian Press, 1980

Schweighardt, Ray (ed.)
How Do You Do It?

Shepherd, Billy
The True Story Of The Beatles
Bantam, 1964

Stannard, Neville
The Long & Winding Road
Avon Books, 1982

Stannard, Neville & John Tobler
Working Class Heroes
Avon Books, 1983

Sulpy, Doug (ed.)
Illegal Beatles

Wiener, Allen J.
The Beatles: A Recording History
McFarland, 1986

THE DISCOGRAPHY

ABBEY ROAD WEST-MINSTER 1
THE BEATLES
Black Disc, 2441
Full color jacket (featuring an alternate **ABBEY ROAD** cover shot), with song listing on the back; label info matches.

Side A

Come Together (Lennon-McCartney) (4:07)
    30 Aug 72, MSG, evening; from tv broadcast
Something (Harrison) (3:09)
    2 May, EMI & 5 May, Olympic & 11 Jul 69, EMI; take 37
    This is a tape reduction of take 36, the basic take of the commercial version; it
        was intended (but never used) for overdubs.
I Need You (?) (1:37)
    source unknown; no apparent Beatles involvement
    from acetate, possibly Apple
Maxwell's Silver Hammer (Lennon-McCartney) (3:36)
    9/10/11 Jul 69, EMI; take 21; no synthesizer or guitar overdubs
Oh! Darling (Lennon-McCartney) (3:25)
    20/26 Apr 69, EMI; take 26; alternate lead vocals
    This may be the basic take 26 with a guide vocal, or one one of Paul's later
        (mid-Jul) overdub attempts. Since a second vocal is faintly audible, I'm
        assuming this is the first vocal take on top of the guide vocal.
Ringo tells all (0:06)
    17 Apr 78, *The Mike Douglas Show*; excellent mono
Octopus's Garden (Starkey) (2:47)
    26/29 Apr & 17 Jul 69, EMI; take 32
    piano, backing vocals and sound effects were dubbed in on this day; this track
        has the piano but no backing vocals or effects
I Want You (She's So Heavy) (Lennon-McCartney) (4:27)
    22 Feb 69, Trident; Paul vocals

Side B

Here Comes The Sun (Harrison) (3:26)
    18 Nov 76, *Saturday Night Live*; George & Paul Simon
26 Nov 64, BBC (0:06)
    chat: "A little bit of soul in the studio."
Instrumental (Lennon-Starkey?) (0:47)
    Sep 67; tape loops, with dialogue; from the *MMT* soundtrack
You Never Give Me Your Money (Lennon-McCartney) (3:50)
    6 May, Olympic & 1/11 Jul 69, EMI; take 30
    The basic tracks had been recorded 6 May at Olympic Studios; the vocals were
        added on 1 Jul and the bass on this date.

Sun King (Lennon-McCartney) (1:19)
>> Jan 69, **GET BACK** sessions
>> originally part of **Don't Let Me Down**

Polythene Pam (Lennon-McCartney) (0:53)
>> Jan 69, **GET BACK** sessions

Mean Mister Mustard (Lennon-McCartney) (3:02)
>> Jan 69, **GET BACK** sessions

She Came In Through The Bathroom Window (Lennon-McCartney) (2:03)
>> Jan 69, **GET BACK** sessions

Golden Slumbers/Carry That Weight (Lennon-McCartney) (3:02)
>> 2 Jul 69, EMI; take 13
>> 15 basic takes were recorded this day; takes 13 and 15 were edited together to form the basic take (still called take 13) of the commercial version, before overdubs, which is what this appears to be.

The End (Lennon-McCartney) (2:01)
>> 23 Jul & 5/7/8/15/18 Aug 69, EMI; take 7
>> the commercial version

Her Majesty (Lennon-McCartney) (0:23)
>> 2 Jul 69, EMI; take 3, with the final chord

SOURCE:
>> Varies; see individual entries.

SOUND QUALITY:
>> Very good to excellent mono (although most of the EMI outtake material was mixed in stereo only).

COMMENTS:
>> Another attempt to gather together alternate versions of the **ABBEY ROAD** tracks, with some extraneous material thrown in for bad effect. Black Disc bootlegs are reportedly Japanese.

ABC MANCHESTER
THE BEATLES
Wizardo, WRMB 361
Insert cover.

Side A
>> *The Beatles Come To Town* (6:38)
>>> This is from the soundtrack of the Pathé News cinema newsreel, show in UK theaters during the week of 22 Dec 63; very good mono; includes:
>> narration
>>> **From Me To You** (McCartney-Lennon) (commercial cut)
>> 20 Nov 63, ABC Cinema, Manchester
>>> **She Loves You** (Lennon-McCartney)
>>> **Twist And Shout** (Medley-Russell)
>> MBE announcement interview (3:37)
>>> mid-Jun 65, from newsreel; very good mono
>>> This particular version is copied from an unknown American source (probably also a newsreel: "Yes, it's those Beatles again!")
>> 5 Jun 66, *The Ed Sullivan Show*
>>> good to very good mono; includes:
>>> greetings & introduction (0:15)
>>> **Paperback Writer** (Lennon-McCartney) (2:23)
>>> 13/14 Apr 66, EMI; filmed 19/20 May 66
>>> mono mix #1?; a couple of seconds longer than the commercial release

> **Rain** (Lennon-McCartney) (3:00)
> 14/16 Apr 66, EMI; filmed 19/20 May 66
> identical to commercial release

Side B
> 13 Oct 63, the London Palladium (?) (14:23)
> > Val Parnell's *Sunday Night At The London Palladium* (?)
> > transmitted live on ATV
> > > **I Want To Hold Your Hand** (Lennon-McCartney)
> > > **This Boy** (Lennon-McCartney)
> > > chat
> > > **All My Loving** (Lennon-McCartney)
> > > screaming
> > > **Money (That's What I Want)** (Bradford-Gordy)
> > > **Twist And Shout** (Medley-Russell)
> > > bows

SOURCE:
> Varies; see individual entries.

SOUND QUALITY:
> Good to very good mono.

COMMENTS:
> All of this material is taken from film/video sources.

ARCHIVES, VOLUME ONE
JOHN LENNON
Paper Plane Music, 8RCH111
Duotone jacket with song titles and recording information on the back; labels say "Hawk Records, Test Pressing."

Side A
> **Strawberry Fields Forever** (Lennon-McCartney) (4:04)
> > 2 parts; includes:
> > Nov 66? John's acoustic demo
> > > (3-hour special, 24 Jan 88)
> > Nov 66, EMI; electric "arranging" demo
> > > (program 4, 15 Feb 88)
> **Peggy Sue** (Holly-Allison-Petty) (0:50)
> > Summer 71, St. Regis, NYC; from *Clock*; acoustic
> > the song is interrupted by a phone call, and is not the same as the acoustic "medley" version on **TEDDY BOY**
> > (3-hour special, 24 Jan 88)
> **Watching The Wheels** (Lennon) (3:02)
> > 2 parts; includes:
> > 80, Dakota; acoustic; excellent stereo
> > Aug 80, **DF** sessions; studio chat & riffs
> > > both from (3-hour special, 24 Jan 88)
> **Be-Bop-A-Lula** (Vincent-Davis) (1:00)
> > Aug 80, **DF** sessions
> > this previously appeared on **WINSTON O'BOOGIE**
> **God** (Lennon) (1:25)
> > Fall 70? an acoustic, almost folky version
> > (program 1, 25 Jan 88)
> **I'm Losing You** (Lennon) (1:20)
> > 2 parts; includes
> > 80, Dakota? acoustic with rhythm box
> > Aug 80, **DF** sessions, with slide guitar
> > > both (3-hour special, 24 Jan 88)

Beautiful Boy (Darling Boy) (Lennon) (3:01)
>2 parts; includes:
>take 1; acoustic (excerpt) with spoken intro
>>source unknown; possibly Jul 80, Bermuda, but this is a solo take and not the usual one from the Bermuda tape.
>>(3-hour special, 24 Jan 88)
>Jul 80, Bermuda; excellent stereo
>>with message to Sean (**DF** sessions); this is a better quality—but edited, and shorter—version of the track which appeared on **CONFIDENTIAL DOCUMENT**.
>(program 3, 8 Feb 88)

Life Begins At Forty (Lennon) (1:59)
>Fall 80, Dakota; with beatbox and spoken intro; excellent mono?
>(program 2, 1 Feb 88)

Power To The People (Lennon) (2:42)
>Feb 71; rough mix of the released take; excellent stereo?
>(program 2, 1 Feb 88)

Cleanup Time (Lennon) (2:58)
>80, Dakota; piano demo; excellent mono?
>(program 2, 1 Feb 88)

Side B

Mucho Mungo (Lennon) (7:10)
>Mar-May 74, **PUSSYCATS** sessions
>>this is a composite of the two pieces on **YING YANG** and does not include the take from *The Lost Lennon Tapes*. The "Jesse" mentioned is presumably Jesse Ed Davis.

Real Love (Lennon) (2:20)
>80; acoustic demo, excellent stereo
>(program 3, 8 Feb 88)
>This song (often mis-called "Girls And Boys," includes a gentler version of the middle eight of **Isolation** as its middle eight.

Woman (Lennon) (3:04)
>Jul 80, Bermuda? acoustic demo
>(program 3, 8 Feb 88)

The Rishikesh Song (Lennon) (1:49)
>unknown; acoustic demo
>(program 4, 15 Feb 88)

Rock Island Line (trad.) (2:32)
>70s, Dakota; acoustic, excellent stereo?
>(program 5, 22 Feb 88)

John Henry (trad.) (1:37)
>70s, Dakota; piano
>(program 5, 22 Feb 88)

Tennessee (Lennon) (1:52)
>Dakota, early 75? demo takes 1 & 4
>(program 5, 22 Feb 88)

Surprise, Surprise (Sweet Bird Of Paradox) (Lennon) (1:16)
>Summer 74? Dakota; acoustic
>(program 5, 22 Feb 88)

Child Of Nature (Lennon) (2:33)
>late May 68, Kinfauns; acoustic demo
>>The original version of **Jealous Guy**; apparently John solo and double-tracked. The group were working on this song (rather half-heartedly) as late as the Jan 69, **GET BACK** sessions.
>(program 6, 29 Feb 88)

SOURCE:
>Primarily various broadcasts of *The Lost Lennon Tapes*.

SOUND QUALITY:
Very good to excellent mono unless otherwise noted.

COMMENTS:
Most of this material has been edited, and the songs run together with no separation. This might be okay for casual listening, but I have to object (for all the good it does) to *any* tampering with the raw material, no matter who does it or what their intentions may be.

The jacket also implies that there is more here than there is. For example, it says that **Strawberry Fields Forever** has four parts (there are only two) and **Cleanup Time** has two parts (there is only one). The advance word on this series was that these versions would be from the raw tapes, with many versions being a few seconds longer, but this appears to have been hype. The only thing here which has not appeared elsewhere is the studio piece of **I'm Losing You**, which came from the three-hour special. There seems to be no advantage to this series over *THE LOST LENNON TAPES* series (despite the cute little dig at Bag Records).

ARCHIVES, VOLUME TWO
JOHN LENNON
Paper Plane Music, 8RCH222
Duotone jacket with song titles and recording information on the back; labels say "Maclen Records, Test Pressing."

Side A
The Luck Of The Irish (Lennon-Ono) (3:10)
    12 Nov 71; demo takes 1 & 2
    (program 7, 7 Mar 88)
Every Man Has A Woman Who Loves Him (Ono) (3:08)
    Aug 80, DF sessions; excellent stereo
    John sings lead, Yoko sings backing
    (program 7, 7 Mar 88)
He Said He Said (Lennon) (0:13)
    65-66, Kenwood? John solo acoustic
    just an idea at this point; very early, very different
    (program 7, 7 Mar 88)
She Said She Said (Lennon-McCartney) (0:50)
    66, Kenwood? John solo, acoustic
    Not yet fully worked out, the song heads toward a slightly different "middle 8"
        before it's cut short.
    (program 7, 7 Mar 88)
Grow Old With Me (Lennon) (2:46)
    Aug 80, Dakota? excellent stereo
    John with piano and rhythm box; Yoko has (later) voice-over at the end
    (program 7, 7 Mar 88)
Daddy's Little Sunshine Boy (?) (0:28)
    67? source unknown; vocals: Ringo
    (program 8, 14 Mar 88)
I'm The Greatest (Lennon) (1:20)
    late 70, Tittenhurst? John on piano
    home demo, very early and crude run-through
    (program 8, 14 Mar 88)
I'm The Greatest (Lennon) (2:33)
    71? studio demo; excellent stereo
    the "middle 8" is still quite different at this point
    (program 8, 14 Mar 88)
Make Love Not War (Lennon) (3:13)
    70; John on piano; excellent stereo?
    the early version of **Mind Games**
    (program 8, 14 Mar 88)

I Promise (Lennon) (1:55)
>   late 70; John on piano; excellent stereo?
>   A love song to Yoko which was apparently never completed; it utilizes part of **Make Love Not War/Mind Games**, and sounds a bit like **Oh! Darling**.
>   (program 8, 14 Mar 88)

   Goodnight Vienna (Lennon) (1:36)
>   Jun 74, W&B sessions; demo for Ringo; excellent stereo
>   Previously available on **GOODNIGHT VIENNA** and **JOHNNY MOONDOG**. This appearance is taken from the broadcast and is a good minute shorter than the version on *THE LOST LENNON TAPES, VOL. 1*, although the sound quality is superior.
>   (program 8, 14 Mar 88)

Side B

   Help! (Lennon-McCartney) (0:36)
>   late 70; John at the piano; excellent stereo
>   (program 9, 21 Mar 88)

   You Know My Name (Look Up The Number) (Lennon-McCartney) (0:58)
>   67? John composing on piano
>   (program 9, 21 Mar 88)

   How Do You Sleep? (Lennon) (8:04)
>   Jul 71, POB sessions; an alternate take; excellent stereo
>   (program 9, 21 Mar 88)

   John on **How Do You Sleep?** (0:07)
>   16 Apr 73, Hollywood
>   (program 9, 21 Mar 88)

   (Just Like) Starting Over (Lennon) (4:49)
>   Aug 80, Dakota; "take 3;" excellent stereo
>   John with acoustic and rhythm box; some different lyrics
>   (program 10, 28 Mar 88)

music hall medley ("Sea ditties") (2:33)
>   When I Was Young And In My Prime (?)
>   **My Old Man's A Dustman** (trad. arr. Donegan)
>   **I Do Like To Be Beside The Seaside** (Glover Kind)
>   **Leaning On A Lamp Post** (Gay)
>   **Chinese Laundry Blues** (Cottrell-Formby)
>   unknown; John and piano; his true musical roots!
>   (program 10, 28 Mar 88)

   Borrowed Time (Lennon) (2:29)
>   Jul 80, Bermuda; acoustic demo; excellent stereo?
>   not from the radio series; previously available on **CONFIDENTIAL DOCUMENT**

   I Don't Wanna Face It (Lennon) (2:44)
>   Aug 80, DF sessions; alternate mix; excellent stereo
>   not from the radio series; previously available on **CONFIDENTIAL DOCUMENT**

SOURCE:
>   Primarily from various broadcasts of *The Lost Lennon Tapes*.

SOUND QUALITY:
>   Very good to excellent mono unless otherwise noted.

COMMENTS:
>   No comment.
>   Well, okay, just one.
>   This is something which I cannot recall having happened before: CUT-THROAT BOOTLEG WAR!!, a competition between two ongoing series of bootlegs. As far as I can tell, the *LOST LENNON TAPES* people have won, although the **ARCHIVES** series went at least as far as eight volumes before cashing in. The bootleg market is not, after all, infinite (I

would guess 7000-10,000 *world*-wide), nor are its resources (do you tithe to your bootleggers?).

ARCHIVES, VOLUME THREE
JOHN LENNON
Paper Plane Music, 8RCH333
Duotone jacket with song titles and recording information on the back; labels say "Maclen Records, Test Pressing."

Side A
> **Whatever Gets You Through The Night** (Lennon) (5:21)
>> Summer 74, NYC?
>> John composes on the guitar, and and fills a blank spot with the lyrics of **Jealous Guy**.
>> (program 12, 11 Apr 88)
>
> **Dear John/September Song** (Lennon/Anderson-Weill) (4:15)
>> late Nov 80, Dakota; acoustic, with rhythm box; excellent stereo
>> possibly the last song he ever wrote
>> (program 12, 11 Apr 88)
>
> **Across The Universe** (Lennon-McCartney) (3:45)
>> 4/8 Feb 68, EMI; take 8 (unreleased mix)
>> This version features backward guitar and humming effects on the word "Om." Although there were eight takes of the song at EMI, although we have heard only the one (in all its versions).
>> According to Lewisohn (*Beatles Book Monthly*, Aug 88) this was an interim mix, and there is no copy of it in EMI's vaults, although the effects tape of the humming (recorded late on the 4th and called "Hums Wild") is there.
>> (program 13, 18 Apr 88)
>
> **What's The New Mary Jane** (Lennon) (2:34)
>> late May 68, Kinfauns
>> acoustic demo (w/ the Beatles, and somebody actually says the title!)
>> (program 13, 18 Apr 88)
>
> **Cookin' (In The Kitchen Of Love)** (Lennon) (2:28)
>> Spring 76, Dakota; John on piano; excellent stereo?
>> (program 13, 18 Apr 88)
>> commercial release: Sep 76, **RINGO'S ROTOGRAVURE**
>
> **Lord, Take This Makeup Off Me** (Lennon) (2:18)
>> date unknown, Dakota; acoustic, excellent stereo
>> A Dylan parody, probably ad-libbed, this time with vocal imitation and lots of Dylan lyrics.
>> (program 14, 25 Apr 88)
>
> **The News Of The Day (From Reuters)** (Lennon) (4:23)
>> late Nov 78, Dakota? acoustic, excellent stereo
>> Another Dylan parody, this one marginally cruel; John ad-libs current events in his best Dylan voice to some familiar chords.
>> If the news he was reading was current, this segment is dated from late Nov 78 (Nixon was in Paris on 28 Nov 78).
>> (program 14, 25 Apr 88)

Side B
> "Put the incense on…" (0:07)
>> spoken; source unknown
>> (program 6, 29 Feb 68)
>
> **Revolution** (Lennon-McCartney) (3:44)
>> late May 68, Kinfauns; acoustic demo
>> The rest of the Beatles clap along and provide some great Beach Boys harmony in spots
>> (program 6, 29 Feb 88)

Serve Yourself (Lennon) (5:24)
> date unknown, Dakota; excellent stereo
> A different version (reportedly there are at least twelve) from that on **YIN YANG** and **JOHNNY MOONDOG**. John accompanies himself on the piano, still playing **Mean Mr. Mustard**.
> (program 14, 25 Apr 88)

Good Morning Good Morning (Lennon-McCartney) (1:00)
> Feb 67? demo
> (program 15, 2 May 88)

Everybody Had A Hard Year (Lennon) (1:44)
> Fall 68, Kenwood; acoustic
> This is not the same version as appears on **JOHNNY MOONDOG** as **Theme From** *Rape*.
> (program 15, 2 May 88)

Everybody's Got Something To Hide Except Me And My Monkey (Lennon-McCartney) (2:59)
> late May 68, Kinfauns; acoustic demo
> The Beatles are probably on this, but the vocals are John, double-tracked. This version is weird and very interesting.
> (program 15, 2 May 88)

Mannish Boy (London-McDaniel-Morganfeld) (1:50)
> date unknown, Dakota?
> This song, originally done by Muddy Waters, is very similar to **I'm A Man** (McDaniel). Both were released in 55, but, from the vocals, it's obvious that John is doing Muddy Waters and not Bo Diddley, so I've gone with the corresponding title.
> (program 15, 2 May 88)

Brown-Eyed Handsome Man/Get Back (Berry/Lennon-McCartney) (2:13)
> date unknown, Dakota? excellent stereo
> two acoustic versions, one slow, one fast
> (program 15, 2 May 88)

"'Twas A Night Like Ethel Merman" (1:01)
> date unknown, Dakota; poem/recitation
> (program 15, 2 May 88)

Beyond The Sea/Blue Moon (Trenet-Lawrence/Rodgers-Hart) (3:32)
> date unknown, Dakota; excellent stereo
> lots of fractured French
> (program 15, 2 May 88)

Young Love (Cartey-Joyner) (0:35)
> date unknown, Dakota; excellent stereo (excerpt)
> a continuation of the previous segment
> (program 15, 2 May 88)

SOURCE:
> Various broadcasts of *The Lost Lennon Tapes*.

SOUND QUALITY:
> Very good to excellent mono unless otherwise noted.

COMMENTS:
> What the jacket claims is a demo for **Getting Better** is actually **Good Morning, Good Morning**. Too bad, and a sad case of either ignorance or false advertising.

ARCHIVES, VOLUME FOUR
JOHN LENNON
PAPER PLANE MUSIC, 8RCH444
2-color jacket with song titles and recording information on the back; labels are blank.

Side A
>**Power To The People** (Lennon) (2:45)
>>Feb 71; alternate take; excellent mono?
>>(program 16, 9 May 88)
>10 Dec 71, Chrylser Arena, Ann Arbor, Michigan (10:16)
>>**Attica State** (Lennon)
>>**The Luck Of The Irish** (Lennon-Ono)
>>**John Sinclair** (Lennon-Ono)
>>from unreleased film of the John Sinclair benefit, *Ten For Two*
>>(program 16, 9 May 88)
>**Rock And Roll People** (Lennon) (2:08)
>>electric composing demo; excellent stereo
>>(program 17, 16 May 88)
>**Rock And Roll People** (Lennon) (5:56)
>>4 Aug 73, take 5; alternate take; excellent stereo
>>(program 17, 16 May 88)

Side B
>**Real Life** (Lennon) (4:46)
>>Dakota, piano demo; excellent stereo?
>>an early version of **Steppin' Out**
>>(program 17, 16 May 88)
>**Steppin' Out** (Lennon) (4:33)
>>Jul 80, Bermuda; acoustic & rhythm box; excellent stereo?
>>(program 17, 16 May 88)
>**Tight A$** (Lennon) (3:20)
>>73? electric composing demo; excellent stereo
>>(program 17, 16 May 88)
>**Rock Island Line** (trad.) (2:45)
>>mid-70s, Dakota; electric version with rhythm box
>>crude but infectious, probably how the Quarry Men sounded (and where is
>>>that 74 version with John and Paul?)
>>(program 18, 23 May 88)
>**Love** (Lennon) (3:06)
>>82 remix for UK 45, not an alternate take; excellent stereo
>>not from the radio series

SOURCE:
>Primarily various broadcasts of *The Lost Lennon Tapes*.

SOUND QUALITY:
>Very good to excellent mono unless otherwise noted.

COMMENTS:
>More of the same.

ARRIVANO I «CAPELLONI»
THE BEATLES
Clean Sound Records, CS 1008
Black-on-grey printed jacket with song listing; labels are blank.

Side A
>27 Jun 65, *Teatro Adriano*, Rome? (17:03)
>>**Twist And Shout** (Medley-Russell)
>>**She's A Woman** (Lennon-McCartney)
>>**I'm A Loser** (Lennon-McCartney)
>>**Can't Buy Me Love** (Lennon-McCartney)
>>**Baby's In Black** (Lennon-McCartney)
>>**I Wanna Be Your Man** (Lennon-McCartney)
>>**A Hard Day's Night** (Lennon-McCartney)

Side B

27 Jun 65, *Teatro Adriano*, Rome? (continued) (12:14)
Everybody's Trying To Be My Baby (Perkins)
Rock And Roll Music (Berry)
I Feel Fine (Lennon-McCartney)
Ticket To Ride (Lennon-McCartney)
Long Tall Sally (Johnson-Penniman-Blackwell) (excerpt)
Interview (1:55)
late Jun 65, Italy; fair mono
The questions are in Italian, the answers in English (translations edited out); extremely brief and uninformative. This is the same interview which appears in a slightly shorter version on Side B of **LIVE IN ITALY** (EP). Wiener lists two tv interviews from the Italian tour: 24 Jun 65, from *Velodromo Vigorelli*, Milan, conducted by Carmela Anna Fortunata, and 27 Jun 65, from Rome. If the source of his information is from these bootlegs, however, they are the same interview; probably a tv broadcast, exact location and date unknown.
There was a "legit" issue of this interview on **THE BEATLES TALK DOWNUNDER, VOL. 2** (Raven, RVLP-1013).

SOURCE:
The Beatles played two shows per day here, 27-28 Jun 65.

SOUND QUALITY:
Poor to good mono audience tape, most of it quite listenable.

COMMENTS:
This may be a repackaging of (or may actually be) **THE BEATLES AT TEATRO ADRIANO ROME JUNE 27TH 1965**. The title I am using comes from the front of the jacket, which reproduces an Italian newspaper clipping (the complete headline is "*ARRIVANO I «CAPELLONI»: TEEN-AGERS GIA IN CODA.*").
According to Wiener, one of the Rome concerts was professionally recorded by EMI. This longstanding rumor, which has yet to be proven, is based on a limited-issue Parlophone (Italian) LP from 65, an offhand remark by John in a later interview, and (as usual) a lot of wishful thinking.
The gist of the tale is that Parlophone (Italy) was supposed to have issued a live album from the 65 tour, **THE BEATLES ITALY**. When the LP was finally unearthed by collectors, it was found to be common studio material in a special sleeve. Then the rumor mill said that the show had been recorded, but that it had been withdrawn at the last minute (and commercial tracks substituted) because the group didn't want the show released. The latest twist has it that the first hundred copies or so *were* live—then withdrawn and replaced by studio tracks. Rumors are extremely difficult to eliminate, and aside from John's (most probably wrong) remark, there is no evidence that I am aware of to support it.
THE BEATLES IN ITALY has apparently been legitimately reissued at least once—I have a copy on EMI (Holland—1A 062-04632) from, I think, the early '80s. Its track listing

Side A	Side B
Long Tall Sally	This Boy
She's A Woman	Slow Down
Matchbox	I Call Your Name
From Me To You	Thank You Girl
I Want To Hold Your Hand	Yes It Is
Ticket To Ride	I Feel Fine

only vaguely matches the songs performed on the tour.

BACK UPON US ALL—THE FOURTH AMMENDMENT
THE BEATLES
ZAP, 7864
Insert cover with track listing; labels are "World Records."

Side A

Day Tripper (Lennon-McCartney) (3:35)
    30 Jun 66, Nippon Budokan Hall, Tokyo
    excellent mono
Two Of Us (Lennon-McCartney) (3:36)
    24 Jan 69, Apple; excellent stereo
Maggie Mae (trad. arr. Lennon-McCartney-Harrison-Starkey) (0:39)
    24 Jan 69, Apple; excellent stereo
23 Aug 64, Hollywood Bowl (6:06)
    Twist And Shout (Medley-Russell)
    You Can't Do That (Lennon-McCartney)
    All My Loving (Lennon-McCartney)
        excellent mono
Dig It (Lennon-McCartney) (3:57)
    26 Jan 69, Apple; excellent stereo
Suzy Parker (Lennon-McCartney-Harrison-Starkey) (1:53)
    Jan 69, **GET BACK** sessions, excellent mono

Side B

Let It Be (Lennon-McCartney) (7:45)
    Jan 69, **GET BACK** sessions; excellent mono
    first rehearsal, with chord changes
Dizzy Miss Lizzie (Williams) (2:45)
    7 Jun 65, BBC; excellent mono
Sie Liebt Dich (Lennon-McCartney) (2:14)
    29 Jan 64, Paris; excellent mono
Honey Don't (Perkins) (2:06)
    3 Sep 63, BBC; very good mono
Sure To Fall (In Love With You) (Perkins-Claunch-Cantrell) (1:17)
    24 Sep 63, BBC; very good mono (excerpt)
I Need You (Harrison) (2:49)
    15/16 Feb 65, EMI; from *Help!* with dialogue; excellent mono
For You Blue (Harrison) (2:52)
    Jan 69, **GET BACK** sessions; excellent stereo

SOURCE:
    Varies; see individual entries.

SOUND QUALITY:
    Varies; see individual entries.

COMMENTS:
    A real hodge-podge, with nothing of note for present-day collectors.

THE BEATLES AT THE BEEB, VOLUME SEVEN
THE BEATLES
Beeb Transcription Records, 2178/S
Color jacket with song titles and notes on the back; labels say "Beating The Beeb."

Side A

5 Oct 63, *Saturday Club*
    I Saw Her Standing There (McCartney-Lennon) (2:30)
        The Beatles
    Memphis (Berry) (2:12)
        The Beatles
    Happy Birthday To You (Hill-Hill) (0:29)
        The Beatles
    Fools Rush In (Mercer-Bloom)
        Rick Nelson, no Beatles involvement (record)

Sally Ann (Klein)
>Joe Brown And His Bruvvers, no Beatles involvement

Autumn Leaves (Kosman-Prevert-Mercer)
>Joe Brown And His Bruvvers, no Beatles involvement

telegram from Bobby Vee

Take Good Care Of My Baby (Goffin-King)
>Bobby Vee, no Beatles involvement (record)

Walk Right Back (Curtis)
>The Everly Brothers, no Beatles involvement

All I Have To Do Is Dream (Bryant)
>The Everly Brothers, no Beatles involvement

greetings from Brenda Lee

A Picture Of You (Beveridge-Oakman)
>Joe Brown And His Bruvvers, no Beatles involvement

Bye Bye Love (Bryant-Bryant)
>The Everly Brothers, no Beatles involvement

Lucille (Collins-Penniman) (1:45)
>The Beatles

Side B

20 Oct 63, *Easy Beat*

I Saw Her Standing There (Lennon-McCartney) (2:27)
Love Me Do (McCartney-Lennon) (2:21)
Please Please Me (McCartney-Lennon) (1:52)
chat with Paul
From Me To You (McCartney-Lennon) (1:46)
She Loves You (Lennon-McCartney) (2:13)

10 Nov 63, ITV, *The Royal Variety Show* (11:38)
tv narration and introduction
>Dickie Henderson

From Me To You (McCartney-Lennon) (excerpt)
greetings
She Loves You (Lennon-McCartney)
"Sophie Tucker" remark
Till There Was You (Willson)
"...rattle your jewelry" remark
Twist And Shout (Medley-Russell)

Summer 63, unknown (tv broadcast?) (excerpt) (3:29)
chat
Twist And Shout (Medley-Russell)

SOURCE:
>Varies; see individual entries. Recording information as follows (Beatles only):
5 Oct 63, *Saturday Club*: 7 Sep 63, The Playhouse Theatre, London
20 Oct 63, *Easy Beat*: 16 Oct 63, The Playhouse Theatre, London
10 Nov 63, *Royal Variety Show*: 4 Nov 63, Prince Of Wales Theatre, London

SOUND QUALITY:
>Side A is excellent mono; Side B is very good mono.

COMMENTS:
>Also broadcast, but not on this disc were:
>5 Oct 63, *Saturday Club*
>>**She Loves You** (Lennon-McCartney)
>>**I'll Get You** (Lennon-McCartney)
>>These two songs recently surfaced as part of *The Beeb's Lost Beatles Tapes*.

As interesting as the non-Beatles cuts are on the 5th birthday *Saturday Club*, it's hard to believe that Rick Nelson or Bobby Vee (or even—gasp—Joe Brown and His Bruvvers) are more worthy of the vinyl than the Beatles.

The jacket notes claim that the **Twist And Shout** on Side B is from an *Easy Beat*, but the only show on which they performed that song was that of 21 Jul 63 (which is on **THE BEATLES AT THE BEEB WITH PETE BEST**) and they are not the same. In the introduction, Paul names **Twist And Shout** as "the title of our last EP." The EP was released 12 Jul 63; the follow-up was released 6 Sep 63, so the performance must fall somewhere between the two dates. Judging from the sound and the visual nature of John's performance, it may have been a tv broadcast.

THE BEATLES AT THE BEEB, VOLUME EIGHT
THE BEATLES
Beeb Transcription Records, 2179/S
Color jacket with song titles and notes on the back; labels say "Beating The Beeb."

Side A
  21 Dec 63, *Saturday Club*
    chat and requests
    This Boy (Lennon-McCartney) (2:13)
    All I Want For Christmas Is A Beatle (Benton) (0:07)
      sung as "All I Want For Christmas Is A Bottle"
    requests
    I Want To Hold Your Hand (Lennon-McCartney) (2:14)
    Till There Was You (Willson) (2:09)
    Roll Over Beethoven (Berry) (2:08)
    Christmas messages
    She Loves You (Lennon-McCartney) (2:07)
    "Crimble" medley (0:28)
      The riff played underneath the recitation of titles is from **Shazam!**
        (Eddy-Hazelwood), recorded by Duane Eddy (identification by
        Doug Sulpy).
      Love Me Do (McCartney-Lennon)
      Please Please Me (McCartney-Lennon)
      From Me To You (McCartney-Lennon)
      She Loves You (Lennon-McCartney)
      I Want To Hold Your Hand (Lennon-McCartney)
      Rudolph The Red-Nosed Reindeer (Marks)
  26 Dec 63, *From Us To You* #1
    From Us To You (McCartney-Lennon) (0:51)
    Roll call
    She Loves You (Lennon-McCartney) (2:13)
    All My Loving (Lennon-McCartney) (1:59)
    Roll Over Beethoven (Berry) (2:12)
    Till There Was You (Willson) (2:08)
    Boys (Dixon-Farrell) (1:43) (excerpt)
Side B
  26 Dec 63, *From Us To You* #1 (continued)
    Money (That's What I Want) (Bradford-Gordy) (2:38)
    I Saw Her Standing There (McCartney-Lennon) (2:28)
    Tie Me Kangaroo Down Sport (Harris) (2:41)
      guest host Rolf Harris and the Beatles
      with new Beatles-related lyrics
    I Want To Hold Your Hand (Lennon-McCartney) (2:18)
    From Us To You (McCartney-Lennon) (0:40)
      This version differs from all others available (to date) by having vocals
        all the way through, instead of having an instrumental break
        for the announcer's voice-over.
  8 Feb 64, *Saturday Club*
    Malcolm Davis reports from New York (8:40)
      interview with Murray The K
      WINS Radio, New York: Beatles sweatshirt plug

Kennedy airport: interviews with teenagers
Kennedy airport: arrival of the Beatles' plane
Fans in front of the Plaza Hotel, New York
Beatle chat (phone call)
> This chat is an edited version of a phone call between the Bea-
> tles and Brian Matthew; the complete (?) call appears
> on **WITHERED BEATLES**.

SOURCE:
Various BBC broadcasts. Recording information as follows:
21 Dec 63, *Saturday Club*: 17 Dec 63, The Playhouse Theatre, London
26 Dec 63, *From Us To You* #1: 18 Dec 63, BBC Paris Studio, London
8 Feb 64, *Saturday Club*: 7-8 Feb 64, New York City

SOUND QUALITY:
Excellent mono, except for Davis's report, which is very good mono.

COMMENTS:
Also broadcast, but not on this disc were:
> 21 Dec 63,*Saturday Club*
> > **All My Loving** (Lennon-McCartney)
> 8 Feb 64, *Saturday Club*
> > live phone call with Brian Matthew
> > (available on **WITHERED BEATLES**)

THE BEATLES AT THE BEEB, VOLUME NINE
THE BEATLES
Beeb Transcription Records, 2180/S
2-color jacket with song titles and notes on the back; labels say "Beating The Beeb."

Side A
15 Feb 64, *Saturday Club*
> **All My Loving** (Lennon-McCartney) (1:54)
> **Money (That's What I Want)** (Bradford-Gordy) (2:36)
> requests
> **The Hippy Hippy Shake** (Romero) (1:46)
> chat & requests
> **I Want To Hold Your Hand** (Lennon-McCartney) (2:15)
> **Roll Over Beethoven** (Berry) (2:14)
> **Johnny B. Goode** (Berry) (2:46)
> **I Wanna Be Your Man** (Lennon-McCartney) (2:06)
22 Feb 64, *Saturday Club*
> telephone conversation with Brian Matthew (4:04)
> > from London Airport, after returning to England
Side B
30 Mar 64, *From Us To You* #2
> **From Us To You** (McCartney-Lennon) (0:55)
> **You Can't Do That** (Lennon-McCartney) (2:28)
> chat
> **Roll Over Beethoven** (Berry) (2:15)
> chat
> **Till There Was You** (Willson) (2:12)
> chat
> **I Wanna Be Your Man** (Lennon-McCartney) (2:14)
> chat & dedications
> **Please Mr. Postman** (Holland-Bateman-Gordy) (2:17)
> **All My Loving** (Lennon-McCartney) (2:02)
> chat
> **This Boy** (Lennon-McCartney) (2:13)

chat
Can't Buy Me Love (Lennon-McCartney) (2:06)
From Us To You (McCartney-Lennon) (0:56)

SOURCE:
Various BBC broadcasts.
Recording information:
15 Feb 64, *Saturday Club*: 7 Jan 64, The Playhouse Theatre, London
30 Mar 64, *From Us To You* #2: 28 Feb 64, Picadilly Theatre, London

SOUND QUALITY:
Excellent mono.

COMMENTS:
Both shows are musically complete as they appear here.

THE BEATLES AT THE BEEB, VOLUME TEN
THE BEATLES
Beeb Transcription Records, BB 2181/S
3-color jacket with song listing and liner notes; labels say "Beating the Beeb."

Side A
4 Apr 64, *Saturday Club*
Everybody's Trying To Be My Baby (Perkins) (2:17)
I Call Your Name (Lennon-McCartney) (2:02)
I Got A Woman (Charles-Richards) (2:26)
chat & requests
You Can't Do That (Lennon-McCartney) (2:27)
requests
Can't Buy Me Love (Lennon-McCartney) (1:59)
chat
Sure To Fall (In Love With You) (Perkins-Claunch-Cantrell) (2:07)
Long Tall Sally (Johnson-Penniman-Blackwell) (1:57)
Side B
18 May 64, *From Us To You* #3
From Us To You (McCartney-Lennon) (0:52)
chat
Happy Birthday To You (Hill-Hill) (0:20)
as "Whit Monday To You"
I Saw Her Standing There (McCartney-Lennon) (2:32)
Kansas City/Hey-Hey-Hey-Hey! (Leiber-Stoller/Penniman) (2:11)
chat
I Forgot To Remember To Forget (Kesler-Feathers) (2:05)
chat & requests
You Can't Do That (Lennon-McCartney) (2:30)
Sure To Fall (In Love With You) (Perkins-Claunch-Cantrell) (2:09)
chat & requests
Can't Buy Me Love (Lennon-McCartney) (2:03)
chat
Matchbox (trad. arr. Perkins) (1:51)
Honey Don't (Perkins) (2:18)
vocals: John
From Us To You (McCartney-Lennon) (0:10)

SOURCE:
Various BBC broadcasts.
Recording information:
Saturday Club: 31 Mar 64, Playhouse Theatre, Manchester
From Us To You: 1 May 64, BBC Paris Studio, London.

SOUND QUALITY:
Very good to excellent mono; these tapes are recorded off the air and contain faint signals from other stations; the sound is also slightly distorted.

COMMENTS:
Although entries 1-9 in this series were produced in Europe, volumes 10 & 11 were apparently produced in the US. This may be the reason why their sound quality is not as good as on previous volumes.

Both shows are complete. Note that despite the listing in *The Beatles At The Beeb* by Howlett, John sings lead on the **Honey Don't** from 18 May 64, making this the second Beeb broadcast on which he did so (also 3 Sep 63).

THE BEATLES AT THE BEEB, VOLUME ELEVEN
THE BEATLES
Beeb Transcription Records, BB 2182/S
Full color jacket with song listing and liner notes; labels say "Beating the Beeb."

Side A
    16 Jul 64, *Top Gear*
        Long Tall Sally (Johnson-Penniman-Blackwell) (1:55)
        Things We Said Today (Lennon-McCartney) (2:19)
        chat
        A Hard Day's Night (Lennon-McCartney) (2:28)
        chat
        And I Love Her (Lennon-McCartney) (2:17)
        I Should Have Known Better (Lennon-McCartney) (2:38)
            This is the commercial cut.
        If I Fell (Lennon-McCartney) (2:06)
        You Can't Do That (Lennon-McCartney) (2:27)
Side B
    3 Aug 64, *From Us To You* #4
        From Us To You (McCartney-Lennon) (0:55)
        chat & requests
        Long Tall Sally (Johnson-Penniman-Blackwell) (2:00)
        If I Fell (Lennon-McCartney) (2:12)
        I'm Happy Just To Dance With You (Lennon-McCartney) (1:54)
        requests
        Things We Said Today (Lennon-McCartney) (2:30)
        I Should Have Known Better (Lennon-McCartney) (2:36)
        requests
        Boys (Dixon-Farrell) (2:02)
        Kansas City/Hey-Hey-Hey-Hey! (Leiber-Stoller/Penniman) (2:34)
        requests
        A Hard Day's Night (Lennon-McCartney) (2:30)
        From Us To You (McCartney-Lennon) (0:53)

SOURCE:
Various BBC broadcasts.
Recording information:
Top Gear: 14 Jul 64, Broadcasting House, London
From Us To You #4: 17 Jul 64, BBC Paris Studio, London

SOUND QUALITY:
Very good to excellent mono; these tapes are recorded off the air and contain faint signals from other stations; the sound is also slightly distorted.

COMMENTS:

Both shows are complete, perhaps. The 16 Jul 64 *Top Gear* includes an **I Should Have Known Better** which is a copy of the commercial version, and may or may not have been as broadcast.

This *Top Gear* is where Paul and Ringo talk about writing **Don't Pass Me By**; it is also the show which was cannibalized to produce the fake *Top Of The Pops* tape on some older boots.

From Us To You #4 is the show for which the recording session appears on **FROM US TO YOU, A PARLOPHONE REHEARSAL SESSION**. Oddly, although both Lewisohn and Howlett fail to mention that **Kansas City/Hey-Hey-Hey-Hey!** was broadcast (Lewisohn does not mention it as even having been recorded—nor does it appear here on the album jacket or label), here it is, and with a very specific vocal tag. The alternatives seem to be that either it was broadcast but that the written records are faulty (more likely) or that these tapes come from a pre-broadcast recording (more intriguing).

THE BEATLES AT THE BEEB W/PETE BEST

THE BEATLES
Drexel Records, BEEB 6263
2-color jacket with track listing and recording info on the back; label info matches.

Side A

8 Mar 62, *Teenager's Turn*
    Dream Baby (Walker) (1:49)
    Memphis (Berry) (2:14)
    Please Mr. Postman (Holland-Bateman-Gordy) (1:59)
15 Jun 62, *Here We Go*
    Ask Me Why (McCartney-Lennon) (2:14)
    Besame Mucho (Velazquez-Skylar) (2:24)
    A Picture Of You (Beveridge-Oakman) (2:13)
26 Jan 63, *Saturday Club*
    Some Other Guy (Leiber-Stoller) (2:06)
    Keep Your Hands Off My Baby (Goffin-King) (2:35)
    Beautiful Dreamer (Foster) (1:51)
7 Apr 63, *Easy Beat*
    From Me To You (McCartney-Lennon) (1:55)
        introduced by Gerry Marsden

Side B

16 Mar 63, *Saturday Club*
    I Saw Her Standing There (McCartney-Lennon) (2:35)
    Misery (McCartney-Lennon) (1:47)
    Too Much Monkey Business (Berry) (1:47)
    I'm Talking About You (Berry) (1:54)
    Please Please Me (McCartney-Lennon) (1:52)
    The Hippy Hippy Shake (Romero) (1:41)
21 Jul 63, *Easy Beat*
    I Saw Her Standing There (McCartney-Lennon) (2:36)
    A Shot Of Rhythm And Blues (Thompson) (2:12)
    There's A Place (McCartney-Lennon) (1:48)
    Twist And Shout (Isley-Isley-Isley) (2:24)
27 Aug 63, *Pop Go The Beatles*
    Ooh! My Soul (Penniman) (1:36)

SOURCE:

Various BBC broadcasts.

SOUND QUALITY:

Good to very good mono.

COMMENTS:

This is a cheapo American almost-reissue of **MEET THE BEEB**. The slicks on my copy were full of wrinkles and looked as if they'd been pasted on by hand (bootleg records—a new cottage industry?). The disc is copied from a noisy original, and adds new noise of its own. Perhaps each copy was hand-carved?

The manufacturers have dropped the *Pop Chat* and **Abilene** from **MEET THE BEEB**, and added the **Twist And Shout** (its first and, so far, only appearance on vinyl) and **Ooh! My Soul**, which has appeared before (excerpted on BEEB5 and complete on **BEAUTIFUL DREAMER**).

BEATLES FOR AUCTION
THE BEATLES
"Apple Records," SAPCOR 32
Full color jacket, with track listing on the back; labels say "Rubber Soul" and have track listing.

Side A

I'm A Loser (Lennon-McCartney) (2:35)
26 Nov 64, BBC
Baby's In Black (Lennon-McCartney) (2:14)
19 Aug 65, Sam Houston Coliseum, Houston, afternoon
the last few seconds of the commercial release have been edited onto the end
Rock And Roll Music (Berry) (2:06)
26 Dec 64, BBC
I'll Follow The Sun (Lennon-McCartney) (1:52)
26 Nov 64, BBC
Kansas City/Hey-Hey-Hey-Hey! (Leiber-Stoller/Penniman) (2:47)
26 Dec 64, BBC
Honey Don't (Perkins) (2:27)
7 Jun 65, BBC

Side B

Everybody's Trying To Be My Baby (Perkins) (2:25)
26 Dec 64, BBC
Words Of Love (Holly) (1:52)
20 Aug 63, BBC
Long Tall Sally (Johnson-Penniman-Blackwell) (1:53)
13 Aug 63, BBC
Slow Down (Williams) (2:36)
20 Aug 63, BBC
Matchbox (trad. arr. Perkins) (1:58)
30 Jul 63, BBC
The Beatles' Third Christmas Record (6:22)
8 Nov 65, EMI

SOURCE:

Varies; see individual entries.

SOUND QUALITY:

Very good to excellent mono unless otherwise stated.

COMMENTS:

Pfui! What is so clever about rearranging common, previously available material to produce alternate versions of the albums?

The SAPCOR series, reportedly domestic product sold as imports to command higher prices, consists of:

SAPCOR 28	**RE-INTRODUCING THE BEATLES**
SAPCOR 29	**PLEASE RELEASE ME**
SAPCOR 30	**WITHERED BEATLES**
SAPCOR 31	**A KNIGHT'S HARD DAY**

SAPCOR 32	**BEATLES FOR AUCTION**
SAPCOR 33	**FUCK!**
SAPCOR 34	**RABBI SAUL**
SAPCOR 35	**REVOLTING**
SAPCOR 36/37	**TRAGICAL HISTORY TOUR/DR. PEPPER**
SAPCOR 38	**LITTLE RED ALBUM**
SAPCOR 39	**MELLOW YELLOW**
SAPCOR 40	**BROAD ROAD**
SAPCOR 41	**HEY JULIAN**
SAPCOR 42	**LET IT END**
SAPCOR 43	**LIFTING MATERIAL FROM THE WORLD**
SAPCOR NZ1964	**GRAVE POSTS**

BEATLES 4 EVER
THE BEATLES
Beat Riff Records
Full color jacket with song listing on the back; labels are generic "See For Miles."

Side A
>24 Jun 66, *Circus-Krone-Bau*, Munich (13:08)
>>**Rock And Roll Music** (Berry)
>>**She's A Woman** (Lennon-McCartney) (intro only)
>>**Baby's In Black** (Lennon-McCartney)
>>**I Feel Fine** (Lennon-McCartney)
>>**Yesterday** (Lennon-McCartney)
>>**Nowhere Man** (Lennon-McCartney)
>>**I'm Down** (Lennon-McCartney)
>>>good to very good mono line recording (tv)
>interview: London Hilton (3:37)
>>date unknown; questions and answers mostly in German
>>very good mono, heavy surface noise
>>Copied from a small giveaway cardboard record, from German *OK* magazine, Nov 65
>George's acceptance speech for the 1966 *Bravo* Award (0:45)
>>23 Jun 66, Munich; excellent mono; in German
>>This was copied from a 7-inch flexi giveaway from *Bravo* magazine, **Die Goldenen OTTO—Sieger 1966**, which also contained messages from Marie Versini, Robert Fuller, Manuela, Drafi Deutscher and Pierre Brice. Date of issue unknown.

Side B
>24 Jun 65 *Velodromo Vigorelli*, Milan? (5:11)
>>**Twist And Shout** (Medley-Russell)
>>**She's A Woman** (Lennon-McCartney)
>>**I'm A Loser** (Lennon-McCartney) (excerpt)
>>>good to very good mono line recording (probably tv)
>>>see **LIVE IN ITALY** (EP) for discussion
>4 Nov 63, live at the *Royal Variety Show*, Prince Of Wales Theatre (10:25)
>>broadcast on ITV, 10 Nov 63.
>>**From Me To You** (McCartney-Lennon) (excerpt)
>>greetings
>>**She Loves You** (Lennon-McCartney)
>>"Sophie Tucker" remark
>>**Till There Was You** (Willson)
>>"...rattle your jewelry" remark
>>**Twist And Shout** (Medley-Russell)
>>>good to very good mono line recording (tv); this appearance has a pause between the second and third songs (thus this is copied from the **BY ROYAL COMMAND** EP)

SOURCE:
    Varies; see individual entries.

SOUND QUALITY:
    Varies; see individual entries.

COMMENTS:
    Apparently, this is the inspiration for **THE LIVE BEATLES: RECORDED LIVE IN MUNICH, WEST GERMANY, JUNE 24TH, 1966** (Document Records, DR 005 LP) and its copy, **LIVE AT THE CIRCUS CRONE** (Fabulous Four Records, L 30157).
    Oddly, *Hot Wacks* claims that the London Hilton interview is not on the disc, presumably because both of the talk pieces are in German.

BEATLES INTERVIEW (EP)
THE BEATLES & THE DAVE CLARK FIVE
No manufacturer listed, 610 X 11
7-inch EP in black & white picture sleeve; labels match.

Side A
    21 Aug 64, Seattle (6:53)
        press conference with The Beatles
        good to very good mono
Side B
    24 Nov 64, Seattle (6:02)
        press conference with The Dave Clark Five
        good to very good mono

SOURCE:
    Varied; see individual entries.

SOUND QUALITY:
    Very good mono

COMMENTS:
    At the Seattle press conference, the Beatles were very low key.
    The Dave Clark (since he does most of the speaking) interview presents an interesting contrast with the Beatles interview. At first, he fields all the usual dumb questions about hair and success but, lacking the Beatles' wit and ability to see the humorous absurdity of the situation (while sharing their honesty), his contempt is all too obvious. At last, someone asks him if they get tired of being compared to the Beatles:
        "Well, the point is, this doesn't arise in England at all. Over here it does, which we accept for the simple reason that the Beatles were first into this country. If *we* were first, people would compare the Beatles with us... But when people get a bit stupid about it we get annoyed, 'cause if you play any of our records and any of the Beatles' records, they're completely different."
    It's not often we get a chance to hear how other groups, with totally different personalities, coped with the pressures and inanities of those '60s press conferences.

BEATLES 1964
THE BEATLES
Beat Riff Records, MNS (3) 54009
Full color jacket, with song titles and recording information on the back; labels are blank.

Side A

Kansas City/Hey-Hey-Hey-Hey! (Leiber-Stoller/Penniman) (2:41)
26 Dec 64, BBC
This Boy (Lennon-McCartney) (2:05)
30 Mar 64, BBC
Can't Buy Me Love (Lennon-McCartney) (1:58)
30 Mar 64, BBC
Medley: (McCartney-Lennon) (3:52)
19 Apr 64, IBC; for *Around The Beatles*
Love Me Do
Please Please Me
From Me To You
She Loves You
I Want To Hold Your Hand
Misery (McCartney-Lennon) (1:36)
11/20 Feb 63, EMI; take 16
The jacket claims that this is an alternate take but, aside from being too fast, this is identical to the commercial version.
A Taste Of Honey (Marlow-Scott) (1:50)
11 Feb 63, EMI; take 7
The jacket claims that this is an alternate take but, aside from being too fast, this is identical to the commercial version.

Side B

12 Jun 64, Centennial Hall, Adelaide, Australia (14:55)
excellent mono line recording
I Saw Her Standing There (McCartney-Lennon)
greetings and thanks
All My Loving (Lennon-McCartney)
She Loves You (Lennon-McCartney)
Till There Was You (Willson)
Roll Over Beethoven (Berry)
chat
Can't Buy Me Love (Lennon-McCartney)

SOURCE:
Varies; see individual entries.

SOUND QUALITY:
Excellent mono; most of these cuts are too fast and Side B noticeably changes speed several times.

COMMENTS:
I suppose it was naive of me to think that, with the Beeb series getting wide distribution, people would stop trying to pass BBC material off as EMI outtakes (the first three cuts on Side A are lifted from **JOHNNY AND THE MOONDOGS: SILVER DAYS**, right down to the incorrect recording date for **Kansas City/Hey-Hey-Hey-Hey!**), but this is the first time I've encountered commercial tracks being passed off as outtakes of themselves! Aside from a nice cover, this piece is essentially worthless.

BEFORE THEIR TIME
THE BEATLES
Shalom, 4749 DJG
Front and back covers are pasted-on photocopies, with song titles (incorrect) on the back; labels are generic Shalom.

Side A (14:25)
I Saw Her Standing There (McCartney-Lennon)
Roll Over Beethoven (Berry)
The Hippy Hippy Shake (Romero)

Sweet Little Sixteen (Berry)
Lend Me Your Comb (Twomey-Wise-Weisman)
Your Feet's Too Big (Benson-Fisher)
Side B (14:33)
Twist And Shout (Medley-Russell)
Mr. Moonlight (Johnson)
A Taste Of Honey (Marlow-Scott)
Besame Mucho (Velazquez-Skylar)
Reminiscing (Curtis)
Kansas City/Hey-Hey-Hey-Hey! (Leiber-Stoller/Penniman)

SOURCE:
This is Disc One of **STARS OF '63**, which is a pirate (an unauthorized copy which does not try to pass itself off as an original) of the Bellaphon commercially-released set from 77. The original recordings are, of course, from late (allegedly 31) Dec 62, The *Star-Club*, Hamburg.

SOUND QUALITY:
Very good to excellent mono (rechannelled as stereo); comparable to the original.

COMMENTS:
The back cover lists the songs from DISC TWO. See **STARS OF '63**.

BELGIUM 1972
PAUL McCARTNEY & WINGS
No manufacturer listed, PM-1016
Insert cover with song titles; labels are generic, unknown (*Hot Wacks* says Contra Band).

Side A (20:50)
Lucille (Collins-Penniman)
excerpt
Give Ireland Back To The Irish (McCartney)
Turkey In The Straw (trad.)
acapella
Blue Moon Of Kentucky (Monroe)
introducing the band
Help Me (Williamson-Bass)
Some People Never Know (P. McCartney-L. McCartney)
Side B (19:15)
The Mess (McCartney)
Bip Bop (P. McCartney-L. McCartney)
Say Darling (McCartney)
Smile Away (McCartney)
My Love (McCartney)
excerpt

SOURCE:
Despite the title, 11 Feb 72, Hull University.

SOUND QUALITY:
Poor to good mono, audience recording; the tape has been edited.

COMMENTS:
While this is undoubtedly taken from the same original tape as a Wizardo release, **FIRST LIVE SHOW SPRING 72**, it is not copied from that set. **FIRST LIVE**, for example, is missing the intro to **Say Darling**.

THE BEST OF TOBE MILO PRODUCTIONS
THE BEATLES
Tobe Milo, 10Q&1/2
Black-on-red jacket ©1978 with track listings and recording information; labels match.

Side A
excerpt from unknown television broadcast (1:35)
> The jacket claims this is from a weekly radio series based on *The Guiness Book Of World Records*, but since the narrator mentions that they are showing the Cavern Club film, it would more likely be a tv show. Also present is a brief and highly uninformative excerpt of an interview with Paul, date unknown.
>
> Since the narration appears to be by Flip Wilson, it may be part of the introduction for Paul & Wings' appearance on 12 Oct 72 (the video for **Mary Had A Little Lamb** was shown).
>
> During 73-75, ABC ran a series of five *Guiness Book Of World Records* specials, as part of their late-night *Wide World Of Entertainment* show, hosted by David Frost: 24 Oct 73 (rerun 24 Jul 74), 10 Apr 74 (rerun 28 Aug 74), 7 Nov 74 (rerun 19 Mar 75), 7 May 75, and 21 Dec 75. The *TV Guide* notes for these shows makes no mention of either the Beatles, or of Flip Wilson, although Frost apparently did have co-hosts.
>
> It could originate from the 21 May 75 late-night David Frost special about the Beatles; *TV Guide* reports that the Cavern film was to be shown. On the other hand, it also gives the impression that the show would consist mostly of Frost interviews (with George Martin and Mal Evans, among others) and no mention is made of Flip Wilson.
>
> In Oct 79, the *Guiness Book Of Records* honored Paul as the most successful composer and recording artist ever, but this cut does not seem to be a result of that award, and almost certainly predates it (as it talks about Lennon-McCartney as successful songwriters).
>
> This entry may originate from any of these shows; it may also be from something else completely. Sorry.

My Carnival (McCartney) (2:58)
> 12 Feb 75, New Orleans; for tv news

Now Hear This Song Of Mine (McCartney) (0:30)
> Spring 71, from Apple SPRO-6210, **BRUNG TO EWE BY HAL SMITH**

Una Sensazionale Intervista (6:30)
> 5-6 Jun 68, EMI; from (Italian) Apple DPR-108
>
> The Kenny Everett interview, with lots of fooling around and vocal improvisations; includes **Cottonfields**, Goodbye Jingle, Tiny Tim For President, and so on.
>
> Regarding the dating of this interview, John mentions that they were working on Ringo's first song, the second for their new LP. The first song recorded was **Revolution 1** (30/31 May & 4 Jun), after which they began **Don't Pass Me By** (5-6 Jun).

Kenny Everett (0:48)
> Summer 68, EMI
>
> Kenny Everett describes the Beatles at work in the studio, as they fool around in the background; this may or may not be part of *Intervista* (but probably not).

Now Hear This Song Of Mine (McCartney) (0:30)
> Spring 71, from Apple SPRO-6210, **BRUNG TO EWE BY HAL SMITH**

Bel Air mansion interview (4:10)
> 23-25 Aug 64, Los Angeles (?)
>
> John and Paul at the piano; they talk about songwriting, how they met, and their future. Source unknown, but this has the sound of an open-end interview.

Side B

Hey Jude (Lennon-McCartney) (2:46)
  30 Jul 68, EMI; mostly take 9; from *Experiment In Television*
"And the roof almost came down when…" (5:14)
  source unknown
    This appears to be a piece of a television show, possibly a tribute to Ed Sulli-
      van. It contains brief statements by Sullivan, George Harrison (of the
      Liverpool Echo), Brian Epstein and Dick Cavett, as well as excerpts
      from various *Ed Sullivan Shows* and Shea Stadium.
    With Brian Matthew doing the narration, this really ought to be an excerpt
      from *The Beatles Story* radio special (72, see below). But it isn't.
    In any case, this is not nearly as interesting as it sounds. It is possible that the
      Cavett/Sullivan piece does come from a Dick Cavett show, possibly a
      Sullivan tribute.
Day Tripper (Lennon-McCartney) (3:15)
  30 Jun 66, Nippon Budokan Hall, Tokyo
Now Hear This Song Of Mine (McCartney) (0:53)
  Spring 71, from Apple SPRO-6210, **BRUNG TO EWE BY HAL SMITH**
The Beatles Story (3:32)
  72, BBC (excerpt)
    This was a 13-hour (it was booted as an extremely rare 13 picture disc set—
      and even rarer blue vinyl pressing—as well as on black vinyl in the late
      '70s) BBC radio special, broadcast in 72. Hosted by Brian Matthew, it
      documented the entire career of the Beatles and, as well as music
      (mostly studio versions), featured interviews with the group and many
      who interacted with them during their career.
    It also provided the material for a number of early bootlegs, much of it misat-
      tributed, and this bad information is still causing problems today (see
      the section **Tomorrow Never Knows** for examples).
    This brief excerpt features a brief intro by Murray The K, and bits of the 7 Feb
      64 JFK airport (?) press conference, with Brian Matthew dubbing in
      the questions.
  promo for a forthcoming Houston bootleg (2:11)

SOURCE:
  Varies; see individual entries.

SOUND QUALITY:
  Very good to excellent mono.

COMMENTS:
  A very rare record, high on collectibility but low on content.

BROAD ROAD
THE BEATLES
"Apple Records," SAPCOR 40
Full color jacket with song listing on the back; labels say "Rubber Soul" and have song titles.

Side A

Come Together (Lennon-McCartney) (3:52)
  18 Aug 72, Butterfly Studios; *One To One* rehearsals
Something (Harrison) (3:04)
  2 May, EMI & 5 May, Olympic & 11 Jul 69, EMI; take 37
    This is a tape reduction of take 36, the basic take of the commercial version; it
      was intended (but never used) for overdubs.
Maxwell's Silver Hammer (Lennon-McCartney) (3:44)
  9/10/11 Jul 69, EMI; take 21; no synthesizer or guitar overdubs

Oh! Darling (Lennon-McCartney) (2:09)
　　　　mid-Jul 69, EMI; lead vocals only
　　　　on 17, 18, & 22 Jul, Paul recorded lead vocal takes which were not used (the
　　　　　　final version was done on 23 Jul)
Oh! Darling (Lennon-McCartney) (2:32)
　　　　27 Jan 69, Apple? with one spoken verse
Octopus's Garden (Starkey) (2:53)
　　　　26/29 Apr & 17 Jul 69, EMI; take 32
　　　　piano, backing vocals and sound effects were dubbed in on this day; this track
　　　　　　has the piano but no backing vocals or effects
Side B
Here Comes The Sun (Harrison) (3:05)
　　　　18 Nov 76, *Saturday Night Live*; George & Paul Simon
Because (Lennon-McCartney) (2:10)
　　　　1/4/5 Aug 69, EMI; take 16; very good stereo
　　　　the original source is *The Beatles Live At Abbey Road* show; this version fea-
　　　　　　tures harpsicord, vocals & synthesizer only and may be the unused
　　　　　　stereo mix from 12 Aug 69
You Never Give Me Your Money (Lennon-McCartney) (6:00)
　　　　6 May, Olympic & 1/11 Jul 69, EMI; take 30
　　　　The basic tracks had been recorded 6 May at Olympic Studios; the vocals were
　　　　　　added on 1 Jul and the bass on this date.
Sun King (Lennon-McCartney) (113)
　　　　Jan 69, **GET BACK** sessions
　　　　originally part of **Don't Let Me Down**
Mean Mister Mustard (Lennon-McCartney) (3:16)
　　　　Jan 69, **GET BACK** sessions
Polythene Pam (Lennon-McCartney) (1:39)
　　　　Jan 69, **GET BACK** sessions
She Came In Through The Bathroom Window (Lennon-McCartney) (1:56)
　　　　Jan 69, **GET BACK** sessions
Golden Slumbers/Carry That Weight (Lennon-McCartney) (3:16)
　　　　2 Jul 69, EMI; take 13
　　　　15 basic takes were recorded this day; takes 13 and 15 were edited together
　　　　　　to form the basic take (still called take 13) of the commercial version,
　　　　　　which is what this appears to be.
Her Majesty (Lennon-McCartney) (1:59)
　　　　Jan 69, **GET BACK** sessions

SOURCE:
　　　　Varies; see individual entries.

SOUND QUALITY:
　　　　Very good to excellent mono, unless otherwise noted.

COMMENTS:
　　　　Yet another alternate version of **ABBEY ROAD; I Want You (She's So
Heavy)** is listed on the jacket and label but is not on the record. This alternate cover shot is
the same one used on **RETURN TO ABBEY ROAD**.

BROADCASTS
JOHN LENNON & THE BEATLES
Boxtop Records, GN 70083
Disc is colored vinyl, in generic Boxtop jacket with photo affixed; label is generic "*Annuit Co-
eptis.*"

Side A
Some Other Guy (Leiber-Stoller-Barrett) (1:55)
　　　　26 Jan 63, BBC; very good mono

Keep Your Hands Off My Baby (Goffin-King) (2:24)
  26 Jan 63, BBC; very good mono
Honey Don't (Perkins) (2:09)
  3 Sep 63, BBC; very good mono
4 Nov 63, Royal Variety Show, Prince Of Wales Theatre (2:57)
  Broadcast on ITV, 10 Nov 63; very good mono
  "...rattle your jewelry" remark
   Twist And Shout (Medley-Russell)
Lady Marmalade (Crewe-Nolan) (0:43)
  Mar 75 interview ad-lib; very good mono
Be My Baby (Spector-Greenwich-Barry) (4:30)
  Oct-Dec 73, from **ROOTS: JOHN LENNON SINGS THE GREAT
   ROCK & ROLL HITS** (Adam VIII A8018); excellent stereo
Angel Baby (Ponci) (3:04)
  Oct-Dec 73, from **ROOTS: JOHN LENNON SINGS THE GREAT
   ROCK & ROLL HITS** (Adam VIII A8018); excellent stereo
John does commercials (2:49)
  Oct 74; KHJ-AM, Los Angeles; excellent mono
  Another John-as-dj spot, this time subbing for Charlie Van Dyke on the
  morning show during "Superstar Week!" He was absolutely crazed as
  he took phone calls (this is where he answered the question about
  Have You Heard The Word) and requests (for songs from his
  new album) from hysterical fans.

Side B

All I Want Is You (Lennon-McCartney?) (0:47)
  Jan 69, **GET BACK** sessions; excellent mono
Roll Over Beethoven (Berry) (1:31)
  Paul reads the news while the band improvises
  Jan 69, **GET BACK** sessions; excellent mono
Bad Boy (Williams) (3:11)
  Jan 69, **GET BACK** sessions; excellent mono
Almost Grown (Berry) (1:43)
  Jan 69, **GET BACK** sessions; excellent mono
Child Of Nature (Lennon) (1:45)
  Jan 69, **GET BACK** sessions; very good mono
Ob-La-Di, Ob-La-Da (Lennon-McCartney) (1:19)
  Jan 69, **GET BACK** sessions; very good mono
Help!/Please Please Me (Lennon-McCartney) (0:50)
  Jan 69, **GET BACK** sessions; very good mono
dialogue (0:18)
  Jan 69, **GET BACK** sessions; very good mono
Madman (Lennon) (7:09)
  Jan 69, **GET BACK** sessions, extended rehearsal; very good mono
dialogue (2:35)
  Jan 69, **GET BACK** sessions; very good mono

SOURCE:
  Varied; see individual entries.

SOUND QUALITY:
  Varied; see individual entries.

COMMENTS:
  This is a reissue of DISC ONE of **SNAP SHOTS**, with extra **GET BACK** dialogue
(copied from **GET BACK JOURNALS**) replacing a **Mean Mr. Mustard** rehearsal at the
end of Side B.

BUG CRUSHER "LIVE"
THE BEATLES
No manufacturer listed, TMOQ 71076
Insert cover and back, with song listing; labels are blank.

Side A
Have You Heard The Word (Kipner-Groves) (2:46)
74, the Fut; no Beatles involvement
Don't Let Me Down/Those Were The Days
(Lennon-McCartney/Raskin) (1:50)
traditionally Fall 68, John, press conference ad-lib; it has also been (more logi-
cally) suggested that it may be from a Spring 69 bed-in (possibly
Amsterdam, 21-28 Mar 69)
This appearance is about two seconds longer than the usual.
What's The New Mary Jane (Lennon) (3:16)
14 Aug 68, EMI; take 4, stereo remix 4 (excerpt)
possibly from the version from the unreleased Apple 45
Cottonfields (Ledbetter) (0:20)
5-6 Jun 68, EMI; excerpt from *Una Sensazionale Intervista*, (Italian)
Apple DPR-108
Twist And Shout (Medley-Russell) (2:44)
24 Oct 63, *Karlaplannstudion*, Stockholm
broadcast on *Pop '63*, Swedish radio
Dizzy Miss Lizzie (Williams) (2:43)
7 Jun 65, BBC
Side B
You Really Got A Hold On Me (Robinson) (2:58)
24 Oct 63, *Karlaplannstudion*, Stockholm
broadcast on *Pop '63*, Swedish radio
30 Mar 64, *From Us To You*
chat with George
Roll Over Beethoven (Berry) (2:16)
chat with John
All My Loving (Lennon-McCartney) (2:07)
chat with Ringo
I Wanna Be Your Man (Lennon-McCartney) (2:13)
16 Jul 64, *Top Gear*
chat about *A Hard Day's Night*
A Hard Day's Night (Lennon-McCartney) (1:35)
This appearance is almost a minute shorter than elsewhere, since the
middle of the song (including the add-on solo) has been ex-
pertly edited out. The suspicion that the other BBC version is
padded with excerpts from the commercial version would appear to be incorrect as there are slight lyric differences.
chat
Things We Said Today (Lennon-McCartney) (2:15)
As with the so-called *Top Of The Pops* versions, this has the original
intro by Brian Matthew, which differs from that on *The Beatles At The Beeb* radio special—more evidence of editing.
From Us To You (McCartney-Lennon) (0:27)
63-4, BBC

SOURCE:
Varies; see individual entries.

SOUND QUALITY:
Very good to excellent mono, unless otherwise stated.

COMMENTS:
       This is a reissue (or, more likely, a repackaging) of **SPICY BEATLES SONGS** (TMOQ 71076, and others) and the same as **MARY JANE** (CBM 3585). A typical early compilation, but the **A Hard Day's Night** on Side B is unique and (except for copies) has appeared nowhere else in this form that I know of. Perhaps it was broadcast like this, but more likely is editing on the part of the original bootlegger.

BUMBLE WORDS (SUPER STUDIO SERIES 3)
THE BEATLES
Instant Analysis, 3624A/3626A
Insert cover with song titles.

Side A
       L.S. Bumble Bee (Moore) (2:32)
              Peter Cook & Dudley Moore; no Beatles involvement
              from UK Decca 45 F12551 (Jan 67)
     from the film, *Let It Be*
              Don't Let Me Down (Lennon-McCartney) (0:49)
                    with wah-wah (excerpt)
              chat
              Maxwell's Silver Hammer (Lennon-McCartney) (2:05)
                    film edit (early/late)
              Two Of Us (Lennon-McCartney) (1:38)
                    "Oo-oo" version (excerpt)
              I've Got A Feeling (Lennon-McCartney) (0:57)
                    "Oh yeah?" version (excerpt)
               guitar lessons for George
              I've Got A Feeling (Lennon-McCartney) (1:17)
                    "Good morning!" version (excerpt)
               Oh! Darling (Lennon-McCartney) (0:12)
                    Paul with piano
              chat about early songwriting; includes acapella:
                    Just Fun (Lennon-McCartney) (0:09)
                    One After 909 (Lennon-McCartney) (0:09)
               One After 909 (Lennon-McCartney) (0:59)
                    (excerpts)
              Paul doesn't annoy George
               Across The Universe (Lennon-McCartney) (1:21)
                    (excerpt)
               Dig A Pony (Lennon-McCartney) (0:57)
                    "killed a hound dog" version (excerpt)
Side B
       Have You Heard The Word (Kipner-Groves) (3:21)
              74, The Fut; no Beatles involvement
     from the film, *Let It Be*
               You Really Got A Hold On Me (Robinson) (2:24)
                        26 Jan 69, Apple; vocals: John, George, Paul
              The Long And Winding Road (Lennon-McCartney) (0:37)
                    cha-cha version
              Maxwell's Silver Hammer (Lennon-McCartney) (1:31)
                    late version (with anvil)
              Jazz Piano Song (McCartney-Starkey) (0:53)
                    Paul & Ringo; vocals: Paul
              Besame Mucho (Velazquez-Skylar) (1:53)
                    29 Jan 69, Apple; vocals: Paul, John
              Octopus's Garden (Starkey) (1:25)
                    George helps Ringo and everybody joins in
              I Me Mine (Harrison) (2:21)
                    film edit: first performance/"I-I-Me-Me-Mine"

Don't Let Me Down (Lennon-McCartney) (3:08)
30 Jan 69, Apple rooftop (excerpt)

SOURCE:
Two non-Beatles songs; the rest are Jan 69, **GET BACK** sessions excerpted from *Let It Be*.

SOUND QUALITY:
Very good to excellent mono.

COMMENTS:
Side A is a reissue of Side A of **L. S. BUMBLEBEE** (Contra Band 3626); Side B is a reissue of Side B of **HAVE YOU HEARD THE WORD** (Contra Band 3624). Non-essential.

BYE BYE LOVE
THE BEATLES
Tiger Beat Records, TBR/LP 3
Full color jacket with track listing on the back; labels are blank.

Side A
[142] **All Things Must Pass** (Harrison) (9:55)
extended rehearsal, riffs & chat (excerpts)
feedback jam (improvisation) (2:17)
vocals: Yoko (excerpts)
instrumental jam (improvisation) (0:29)
(excerpt)
chat
Get Back (Lennon-McCartney) (0:24)
John, riffs only
question: "Are you going to release **Get Back**?"
John: "Well, we'll try and record it first."
chat
Get Back (Lennon-McCartney) (0:30)
riffs only; John demonstrates his man-tone
[355] **Let It Be** (Lennon-McCartney) (1:08)
rehearsal (excerpt)
Let It Be (Lennon-McCartney) (1:02)
playback, with chat and singalong (excerpts)
Let It Be (Lennon-McCartney) (2:16)
rehearsal
Side B
London Bridge Is Falling Down (trad.) (0:04)
vocals: John; as "Glynnis, will you take-" (excerpt)
chat & riffs
Let It Be (Lennon-McCartney) (0:10)
rehearsal (excerpt)
chat
Take This Hammer (Terry-McGhee) (0:05)
George, spoken
tape weirdness
For You Blue (Harrison) (0:08)
playback (excerpt)
Early In The Morning (Darin-Harris) (0:15)
vocals: Paul; brief; this is the actual song and not the improvisation from
SWEET APPLE TRAX (and the **BLACK ALBUM**)
[354] **Let It Be** (Lennon-McCartney) (0:53)
rehearsal (excerpts)
chat

Let It Be (Lennon-McCartney) (1:30)
    rehearsal (excerpt)
chat & riffs
Let It Be (Lennon-McCartney) (0:13)
    rehearsal (excerpt)
A Hard Rain's Gonna Fall (Dylan) (0:02)
    vocals: Paul; very brief
Two Of Us (Lennon-McCartney) (0:33)
    rehearsal (excerpt); "sock it to me" version
Bye Bye Love (Bryant-Bryant) (0:02)
    vocals: all; very brief excerpt
Two Of Us (Lennon-McCartney) (1:32)
    rehearsal (excerpts)
chat
[339] **Two Of Us** (Lennon-McCartney) (5:40)
    working on the harmonies (excerpts)
Let It Be (Lennon-McCartney) (0:26)
    "Let it B-C-D" versions; (excerpt)
You Really Got A Hold On Me (Robinson) (0:09)
    riffs only
instrumental jam (2:26)
    some Yoko vocals (excerpts)
harmonies & chat
instrumental jam (0:42)
    some Heather vocals
Dig It (Lennon-McCartney) (0:55)
    playback (excerpt)

SOURCE:
    Video outtake footage of the **GET BACK** sessions; slates 142, 339, 354, and 355.
Bye Bye Love at least) dates from 25 Jan; **You Really Got A Hold On Me** dates from
26 Jan.

SOUND QUALITY:
    Very good to excellent mono.

COMMENTS:
    The soundtrack from approximately an hour of *Let It Be* outtake footage has been
making the tape-trading rounds for a year or so. Someone has at last put it on vinyl (it con-
cludes on Side A of **CLASSIFIED DOCUMENT VOLUME THREE**).
    A mixture of color and b&w, Twickenham and Apple, sound and silent, most of the
footage focuses exclusively on Yoko and John; the theory is that this is footage culled for the
preparation of a program about Yoko (precisely which one is uncertain).
    Since the concentration is on the video image, most of the music consists of ex-
cerpts, some of them very brief. However, there are a number of songs (or pieces of songs)
here we have not encountered before.
    One interesting bit occurs during the **All Things Must Pass** rehearsal on Side A.
Paul is helping George with the song, finding the harmonies and such, and he asks him, "Do
You fancy doing it just on your own, acoustic? 'Cause it does work." George is noncommital,
implying that he wouldn't feel comfortable with that. Since this occurs early on, at Twickenham, it should offset somewhat the "Paul the bully" impression which resulted from the im-
mortal "I'll play what you want me to play" remark.

CAVERN DAYS (SUPER STUDIO SERIES 5)
THE BEATLES
Shalom, 3906A/3907A
Insert cover with song listing; labels are generic Shalom.

Side A
>6 May 64, *Around The Beatles*; good mono
>>Medley: (McCartney-Lennon) (4:30)
>>>**Love Me Do**
>>>**Please Please Me**
>>>**From Me To You**
>>>**She Loves You**
>>>**I Want To Hold Your Hand**
>>**Can't Buy Me Love** (Lennon-McCartney) (2:09)
>>**Long Tall Sally** (Johnson-Penniman-Blackwell) (1:48)
>**She Loves You** (Lennon-McCartney) (2:19)
>>9 Feb 64, *The Ed Sullivan Show*

Side B
>**You Really Got A Hold On Me** (Robinson) (2:59)
>>This cut begins with the intro and performance from the *Pop '63* Swedish radio show and ends with the commercial version. From *The Beatles Story* (BBC, 72).
>**Have You Heard The Word** (Kipner-Groves) (2:47)
>>74, the Fut; no Beatles involvement; very good mono
>**Don't Let Me Down/Those Were The Days**
>(Lennon-McCartney/Raskin) (1:48)
>>traditionally Fall 68, John, press conference ad-lib; it has also been (more logically) suggested that it may be from a Spring 69 bed-in (possibly Amsterdam, 21-28 Mar 69); very good mono
>**Mean Mister Mustard** (Lennon-McCartney) (0:18)
>>Jul 69? the "short, bouncy" version; good mono
>>from a Kenny Everett broadcast, probably Kenney Everett only with no Beatles involvement
>All Together On The Wireless Machine (McCartney?) (0:58)
>>unknown; possibly Fall 67, Paul with Kenny Everett
>>good mono
>**Step Inside Love** (Lennon-McCartney) (2:15)
>>Feb 68, Dick James? demo for Cilla Black? poor to fair mono
>>>from a British radio broadcast (source unknown, but again possibly Kenny Everett)
>Bye Bye Bye (?) (2:47)
>>unknown, possibly no Beatles involvement
>>good mono; see **THEIR GREATEST UNRELEASED**
>**Cottonfields** (Ledbetter) (0:19)
>>5-6 Jun 68, EMI; excerpt from *Una Sensazionale Intervista*, (Italian) Apple DPR-108; very good mono
>**Twist And Shout** (Medley-Russell) (2:46)
>>24 Oct 63, *Karlaplannstudion*, Stockholm
>>broadcast on *Pop '63*, Swedish radio; very good mono
>**Dizzy Miss Lizzie** (Williams) (2:44)
>>7 Jun 65, BBC; excellent mono

SOURCE:
>Varies; see individual entries.

SOUND QUALITY:
>Varies; see individual entries.

COMMENTS:
>Side A is a copy of Side A of **CAVERN CLUB** (Contra Band 3906); Side B is a copy of Side A of **THOSE WERE THE DAYS** (Contra Band 3907) and **ABBEY ROAD REVISITED** (also Contra Band 3907). Thus the title.

CHICAGO 11 30 74
GEORGE HARRISON
No manufacturer listed, GH-1044
Insert cover; labels are blank.

Side A (22:06)
      While My Guitar Gently Weeps (Harrison)
      Something (Harrison)
      Sue You Sue Me Blues (Harrison)
      For You Blue (Harrison)
      Give Me Love (Harrison)
Side B (23:18)
      In My Life (Lennon-McCartney)
      Dark Horse (Harrison)
      What Is Life (Harrison)
      My Sweet Lord (Harrison)

SOURCE:
      30 Nov 74, Chicago (excerpts)

SOUND QUALITY:
      An audience tape, good stereo.

COMMENTS:
      Hot Wacks claims that this is a Contra Band record.

CIRCUIT SONGS
THE BEATLES
Boxtop Records, TWK 2262
Generic Boxtop jacket with photo affixed; labels are Circuit Records, with song titles.

Side A
      set up at Twickenham
      Paul's Piano Theme (McCartney?) (1:23)
            I have played this track for a number of people extremely familiar with classical
            piano music, and no one has been able to identify it; most suggest
            that it is an original (excerpt)
      Don't Let Me Down (Lennon-McCartney) (0:49)
            with wah-wah (excerpt)
      chat
      Maxwell's Silver Hammer (Lennon-McCartney) (2:05)
            movie edit; one early & one late (with anvil)
      electric shocks
      Two Of Us (Lennon-McCartney) (1:38)
            "Oo-oo" version (excerpt)
      I've Got A Feeling (Lennon-McCartney) (0:57)
            "Oh yeah?" version (excerpt)
      guitar lessons for George
      I've Got A Feeling (Lennon-McCartney) (1:17)
            "Good morning!" version (excerpt)
      Oh! Darling (Lennon-McCartney) (0:12)
            Paul with piano
      chat about early songwriting; includes acapella:
            Just Fun (Lennon-McCartney) (0:09)
            One After 909 (Lennon-McCartney) (0:09)
      One After 909 (Lennon-McCartney) (0:59)
            (excerpts)

Jazz Piano Song (McCartney-Starkey) (0:56)
      Paul & Ringo; vocals: Paul
Two Of Us (Lennon-McCartney) (0:13)
      John is off-mic
Paul doesn't annoy George
Across The Universe (Lennon-McCartney) (1:21)
      (excerpt)
Dig A Pony (Lennon-McCartney) (0:57)
      "killed a hound dog" version (excerpt)
Suzy Parker (Lennon-McCartney-Harrison-Starkey) (0:50)
      the usual version
I Me Mine (Harrison) (2:25)
      movie edit; first performance/"I-I-Me-Me-Mine"
Side B
For You Blue (Harrison) (2:47)
      long intro, with slide guitar (edited)
Da-Doo-Run-Run (Spector-Greenwich-Barry) (0:04)
      John
chat about their visit with the Maharishi
Besame Mucho (Velazquez-Skylar) (1:56)
      29 Jan 69, Apple; vocals: Paul, John
Octopus's Garden (Starkey) (3:04)
      George helps Ringo and everybody joins in
chat
Isadora Duncan (improvisation?) (0:11)
      vocals: John
You Really Got A Hold On Me (Robinson) (2:28)
      26 Jan 69, Apple; vocals: John, George, Paul
The Long And Winding Road (Lennon-McCartney) (0:37)
      cha-cha version
The Long And Winding Road (Lennon-McCartney) (0:24)
      Paul vamps
Shake, Rattle And Roll (Calhoun) (2:06)
      26 Jan 69, Apple; vocals: Paul, John
Kansas City/Miss Ann/Lawdy Miss Clawdy
(Leiber-Stoller/Dolphy/Price) (2:33)
      26 Jan 69, Apple; vocals: John, Paul
Dig It (Lennon-McCartney) (3:26)
      26 Jan 69, Apple

SOURCE:
    Let It Be soundtrack. Side A is from Twickenham Film Studios rehearsals, Side B is from Apple.

SOUND QUALITY:
    Very good mono.

COMMENTS:
    This is merely a repackaging of DISC ONE of **IN A PLAY ANYWAY**.

CLASSIFIED DOCUMENT VOLUME TWO
THE BEATLES
Tiger Beat Records, TBLP-1
One-color jacket with track listing and some recording information on the back; labels are blank.

Side A

Goodbye (McCartney) (2:15)

Mary Hopkin; 1-2 Mar 69, excellent stereo?

This appears to be an earlier mix of the commercial version, only faster and murkier, with heavier bass and lacking some overdubs. Probably from an acetate.

Come And Get It (McCartney) (2:13)

Badfinger; Sep 69, excellent stereo?

This appears to be the basic take, only faster and murkier; the remixed commercial version is vastly superior. A brief bit of studio chat at the end tends to confirm this. Probably from an acetate.

5 Nov 75, Wings at Apollo Stadium, Adelaide, Australia (5:31)

audience tape, good to very good mono

Junior's Farm (McCartney)

A unique performance; the band starts, then stops to tune up before beginning again. The jacket to **A DOLL'S HOUSE** claims that the song was retired after this show.

Give Peace A Chance (Lennon-McCartney) (1:08)

Oct 69? John, Yoko & acoustic, with spoken intro in Japanese from John & Yoko

source unknown; very good mono

from a promo film for Warner Brothers staff (0:59)

George thanks WEA salespeople and sings

Go Your Own Way (Buckingham)

very good mono

I'm A Loser (Lennon-McCartney) (2:19)

7 Jun 65, BBC (excerpt)

John sings "...beneath this wig I am wearing a tie."

Pipes Of Peace (McCartney) (3:33)

82, AIR? very good stereo

This is apparently an early version of the commercial release, lacking some overdubs and having a long synthesizer ending.

Side B

8 Oct 82, *Parkinson In Australia* (tv) (5: 40)

Honey Don't (Perkins)

Honey Don't/Blue Suede Shoes (Perkins)

filmed 28 Sep 82, very good mono; vocals: mostly Glenn Shorrock (ex-Little River Band); Ringo drums and sings a little; after the first **Honey Don't**, somebody says, "I hope we passed the audition."

6 Sep 72, *Jerry Lewis Muscular Distrophy Telethon* (tv) (8:05)

Imagine (Lennon) (excerpt)

chat

Give Peace A Chance (Lennon-McCartney)

recorded off tv speakers; good to very good mono

Daytime Nighttime Suffering (McCartney) (3:07)

Jan 79, Replica Studios? good to very good stereo

This is not a demo or an alternate take; the rhythm guitar and backing vocals appear identical to the commercial version, as do the lead vocals, except for a few bars near the end. Almost certainly this represents Paul's original production, before Chris Thomas helped out to create the commercial version.

Singing The Blues (Endsley) (2:21)

12 Dec 81, *Parkinson* (UK tv), excellent mono (excerpt)

personnel included Ringo (drums, some vocals), Michael Parkinson (vocals), Harry Stoner (piano), Tim Rice and Jimmy Tarbuck

Let's Twist Again (Mann-Appel) (3:06)

a reggae version, supposedly Jan 74, David Bowie with John; neither is really evident, as the vocals are heavily compressed; possibly no Beatles involvement; very good stereo?

SOURCE:
  Varies; see individual entries.

SOUND QUALITY:
  Varies; see individual entries.

COMMENTS:
  The sound quality is a little disappointing, but the material is interesting (unless you already have it—which I didn't). Some of it is collected from other (obscure) bootlegs, and some appears here for the first time (from tapes which have been making the rounds).

CLASSIFIED DOCUMENT VOLUME THREE
THE BEATLES
Tiger Beat Records, TBR/LP 4
One-color jacket with track listing and some recording information on the back; labels are blank.

Side A
  Jan 69, **GET BACK** sessions
          very good mono
          Suzy Parker (Lennon-McCartney-Harrison-Starkey) (0:06)
                  playback (excerpt), riff only
          I Want You (She's So Heavy) (Lennon-McCartney) (0:40)
                  John and guitar with Billy Preston (excerpt)
          I've Got A Feeling (Lennon-McCartney) (0:51)
                  rehearsal, mostly riffs
          Dig It (Lennon-McCartney) (0:32)
                  24 Jan 69, Apple (excerpt); early ("Can You Dig It?") version
[431]   **All Things Must Pass** (Harrison) (1:16)
                  (excerpts)
          chat: Paul's driving problems
          chat & riffs & instrumentals
                  includes:
                  The Long And Winding Road (Lennon-McCartney) (0:07)
                          piano intro only
                  Gimme Some Lovin' (Davis) (0:07)
                          riff only, segues into
                  Under The Boardwalk (Resnick-Young) (0:27)
                          riff only (with hints of **Teddy Boy**)
                  organ jam (w/ Billy Preston) (0:31)
                          (excerpt)
          3 Dec 71, *The David Frost Show* (2:58)
                  sitar play and discussion with George; very good mono
          Help! (Lennon-McCartney) (2:25)
                  13 Apr 65, EMI; take 12; excellent stereo
                  commercial version with countdown; taken from *SPLHCB*
          The Beatles Open-End Interview (1:45)
                  Jun-Dec 83, ABC FM network; excellent mono
                  conducted by Ringo, from *Ringo's Yellow Submarine*
          The History Of Rock And Roll (1:53)
                  National Lampoon, no Beatles involvement; excellent stereo
          Only You (Ram-Rand) (3:21)
                  Summer 74, excellent stereo
                  John's studio demo for Ringo; this cut differs from the version broadcast on
                          The Lost Lennon Tapes, which did not have the spoken verse.
Side B
  Jan 69, **GET BACK** sessions
          chat & riffs

Don't Let Me Down (Lennon-McCartney) (1:10)
("take 2") "Dickie Murdock" version
with 2 false starts (excerpt)
Two Of Us (Lennon-McCartney) (0:33)
"Daddy...Mama" version
chat
Oh! Darling (Lennon-McCartney) (0:02)
Paul, acapella
chat & riffs
1 May 70, CBS Nashville?
Bob Dylan with George; excellent stereo
Corrine, Corrina (Williams-Chatman-Parrish) (0:32)
vocals: George (one line)
Yesterday (Lennon-McCartney) (3:09)
vocals: Dylan
I Lost My Little Girl (McCartney) (3:11)
Fall 80? from the home rehearsal tape; good mono
probably the most complete version we'll ever hear
18 Aug 72, Butterfly Studios; One To One Rehearsals
excellent stereo
Tequila jam (Rio) (3:11)
Bunny Hop jam (Anthony-Auletti) (2:26)
Junior's Farm (McCartney) (4:27)
One Hand Clapping sessions; very good stereo
the previously-unbooted performance

SOURCE:
Varies; see individual entries.

SOUND QUALITY:
Varies; see individual entries.

COMMENTS:
As with volume 2, some of this material is collected from other (obscure) bootlegs, and some appears here for the first time. The **GET BACK** material on Side A continues the video outtakes from **BYE BYE LOVE** (Slate 431 is the latest known available to date); those on Side B are taken from the **SONGS FROM THE PAST** import CD.

CODENAME: RUSSIA
THE BEATLES
Core 8869
Full color jacket, with song listing on the back; labels are generic "Rockwell & Goode."

Side A
taping footsteps
Another Day (McCartney) (1:25)
Paul & piano
George arrives, chat & bird imitations
One After 909 (Lennon-McCartney) (0:10)
Paul, acapella, very brief, in pieces
chat about "the show"
Hello Dolly (Herman) (1:20)
Paul & piano
riffs
Please Mrs. Henry (Dylan) (0:34)
vocals: Paul
chat about Dylan's tapes
Ramblin' Woman (Dylan?) (0:55)
vocals: George (another version)

unknown (?) (0:34)
    vocals: George
Takin' A Trip To Carolina (Starkey) (1:14)
    A song in progress.
riffs
Brown-eyed Handsome Man (Berry) (0:30)
    vocals: George?
Well All Right (Petty-Holly-Allison-Mauldin) (0:45)
    vocals: George
riffs & chat about oldies in "the show"
Every Little Thing (Lennon-McCartney) (0:21)
    vocals: Paul, George (trying to remember the song)
more chat
(Take Another) Piece Of My Heart (Berns-Ragovoy) (0:30)
    vocals: George
organizing their career & riffs
Sabre Dance (Katchiturian) (0:12)
    instrumental, John on organ
chat
***Frere Jacques*/It Ain't Me Babe** (trad./Dylan) (0:35)
    vocals: George, Paul
Two Of Us (Lennon-McCartney) (0:22)
    vocals: George
Hear Me Lord (Harrison) (1:35)
    vocals: George, John
chat
Lady Madonna (Lennon-McCartney) (0:03)
    vocals: George (one line)
Low-Down Blues Machine (improvisation?) (1:48)
    vocals: Paul
What'd I Say/Shout! (Charles/Isley-Isley-Isley) (1:48)
    vocals: George, Paul ("How Lulu did it.")
chat & riffs & the power of positive thinking
Side B
A Shot Of Rhythm And Blues (Thompson) (1:48)
    vocals: John, Paul
(You're So Square) Baby I Don't Care (Leiber-Stoller) (0:42)
    vocals: John, Paul, George
Across The Universe (Lennon-McCartney) (0:41)
    vocals: John
[127] **Rock And Roll Music** (Berry) (1:48)
    vocals: John, Paul
Don't Let Me Down (Lennon-McCartney) (4:10)
    vocals: Paul, John, George
    a rehearsal, getting the phrasing and harmonies
(There's A) Devil In Her Heart (Drapkin) (1:21)
    vocals: John, Paul
echo play
Hello Mudduh, Hello Fadduh (Sherman-Busch) (0:08)
    vocals: John
    probably the least likely of all **GET BACK** sessions songs!
riffs & chat: Ringo's codename: Russia; George is France; discussion about the diffi-
    culties of playing live, scheduling the sunrise, looking nice, good vibes, a boat
    full of Beatlemaniacs, and bedtime
Jenny Jenny/Slippin' And Slidin'
(Penniman-Johnson/Penniman-Bocage-Collins-Smith) (2:11)
    vocals: Paul, John
That'll Be The Day (Holly-Allison-Petty) (1:21)
    vocals: Paul (some talking over)
chat: it's Thursday

[205] **Hi Heel Sneakers** (Higginbottom) (2:33)
     vocals: John, Paul (excerpts)
  chat & riffs
  Till There Was You (Willson) (0:16)
     vocals: Paul
  Don't Be Cruel/In The Middle Of An Island
  (Blackwell-Presley/Varnic-Acquaviva) (1:29)
     vocals: John, Paul
      In The Middle Of An Island was a hit for Tony Bennett (!) in 57, but the
        original lyrics do not mention a bossa nova, so there may be a piece of
        a third song in here as well.
  rehearsal's over; it's a wrap

SOURCE:
  Jan 69, **GET BACK** sessions; from (at least) slates 127 and 205.

SOUND QUALITY:
  Very good to excellent mono

COMMENTS:
  A lot of new material here, musical and verbal. Despite their obvious disagreements
about how (or even if) to proceed with the film, concert and LP, the Beatles get along quite
well and manage to talk around their differences without anyone quitting during these 45 minutes. The end of Side B may represent the end of filming at Twickenham (although there is a
break between **Don't Be Cruel** and this chat, so it's impossible to be certain that 205 is the
last Twickenham slate).
  This is an American reissue of a European piece.

A COLLECTION OF "ROCK'N'ROLL" REHEARSALS
JOHN LENNON
No manufacturer listed, WI-86
Sepia-tone picture disc (possibly limited to 200 copies) with song listing on the back.

Side A
    Ain't That A Shame (Domino-Bartholomew) (1:01)
    Bring It On Home To Me/Send Me Some Lovin'
    (Cooke/Price-Marascalco) (3:33)
    Ya Ya (Robinson-Dorsey-Lewis) (2:33)
      with one false start
    That'll Be The Day (Holly-Allison-Petty) (2:25)
      with one false start
    Do You Want To Dance? (Freeman) (3:15)
    Stand By Me (King-Leiber-Stoller) (3:28)
    Ain't That A Shame (Domino-Bartholomew) (2:32)
Side B
    Do You Want To Dance? (Freeman) (3:33)
    Rip It Up/Ready Teddy (Blackwell-Marascalco) (1:26)
    Bring It On Home To Me/Send Me Some Lovin'
    (Cooke/Price-Marascalco) (3:26)
    Peggy Sue (Holly-Allison-Petty) (2:06)
    Be-Bop-A-Lula (Davis-Vincent) (1:48) (excerpt)
    Slippin' And Slidin' (Penniman-Bocage-Collins-Smith) (1:54)
       excerpt
  guitar jam (1:58)
      including **Rumble** (Wray-Cooper) (0:44) and
       Whole Lotta Love (Plant-Page-Jones-Bonham) (0:09)
    Thirty Days (Berry) (0:59) (excerpt)
    Slippin' And Slidin' (Penniman-Bocage-Collins-Smith) (2:07)

SOURCE:
> **ROCK 'N' ROLL** sessions, Oct-Dec 73.

SOUND QUALITY:
> Significantly sharper than **THE MAY PANG TAPES**, which it duplicates. Very good to excellent mono? (stereo ambiance but little separation—maybe this is what Spector thinks stereo should sound like?). There is a strong bleed over from previous tracks during the between-song silences which is annoying.

COMMENTS:
> This is a picture-disc version of **THE MAY PANG TAPES**, although the artwork is different. Because of the better sound quality, **THE MAY PANG TAPES** may in fact be copied from this disc.

COMMONWEALTH
THE BEATLES
Shogun, 13112
2-disc set on colored vinyl, in full color jacket, with song titles on the back; label info matches

DISC ONE
Side A [duplicates **GET BACK JOURNALS**, Side A]
> **Tennessee** (Perkins) (1:59)
>> vocals: John, Paul, George
> **Across The Universe** (Lennon-McCartney) (0:10)
>> the last version
> **House Of The Rising Sun** (trad.) (2:33)
>> vocals: John, Paul
> chat
> Commonwealth (improvisation) (3:56)
>> vocals: Paul, John
> Enoch Powell (improvisation) (0:20)
>> vocals: Paul
> White Power (Get Off!) (improvisation) (6:48)

[189]
>> vocals: Paul, John (excerpts); includes:
>>> **Why Don't We Do It In The Road** (Lennon-McCartney) (0:03)
>>>> as "Why Don't You Put It On The Toast"
> **Honey Hush** (Turner) (2:08)
>> vocals: John, George, Paul
> **For You Blue** (Harrison) (2:02)
>> all-electric version
> **Let It Be** (Lennon-McCartney) (2:33)
>> *Record Mirror* version

Side B [duplicates **GET BACK JOURNALS**, Side H]
> **Sun King/Don't Let Me Down** (Lennon-McCartney) (1:38)
>> (continued from **GET BACK JOURNALS**, Side G)
> **Don't Let Me Down** (Lennon-McCartney) (2:30)
>> rehearsal, with clapping (excerpts)
> Go Johnny Go (?) (0:39)
>> vocals: John, Paul, George
> chat about rehearsal
>> instrumentals while everyone talks:
>>> **Don't Let Me Down** (Lennon-McCartney) (0:13)
>>> **Sun King** (Lennon-McCartney) (0:17)
>>> **Don't Let Me Down** (Lennon-McCartney) (0:18)
> Paul at the piano
>> **Tea For Two** (Youmans-Caesar) (0:57)
>>> slow version
>> **Tea For Two** (Youmans-Caesar) (0:24)
>>> fast version

Chopsticks (trad.) (0:23)
(According to *McCartney Songwriter*, Paul's extensive musical hold-
ings include this song, but others insist it's public domain.)
Whole Lotta Shakin' Goin' On (Williams-David) (0:48)
vocals: Paul
Crackin' Up (McDaniel) (0:23)
vocals: George
All Shook Up/Your True Love (Blackwell-Presley/Perkins) (2:50)
vocals: Paul, George, John
Blue Suede Shoes (Perkins) (1:28)
vocals: George, Paul, John
Three Cool Cats (Leiber-Stoller) (2:06)
vocals: George, Paul, John
requests
Blowin' In The Wind (Dylan) (0:31)
vocals: George, Paul, John (excerpt)
Lucille (Collins-Penniman) (2:28)
vocals: Paul (excerpt)

DISC TWO
Side C [duplicates **GET BACK JOURNALS**, Side E]
[137]   chat: less harmful than alcohol; "My Guitar," by Henry Gibson
Early In The Morning/**Honey Hush** (improv./Turner) (2:19)
vocals: Paul, George (excerpt)
Stand By Me (King-Glick) (2:02)
vocals: Paul
Hare Krishna (improvisation) (2:13)
vocals: Paul
Two Of Us (Lennon-McCartney) (2:59)
mumbled version
[139]   You Got Me Going (improvisation?) (0:21)
vocals: Paul
Don't Let Me Down (Lennon-McCartney) (3:07)
"Rubbed me" version
I've Got A Feeling (Lennon-McCartney) (3:25)
"Good morning!" version
chat
[140]   **One After 909** (Lennon-McCartney) (3:08)
"Hit me, babe!" version, with break
Side D [duplicates **GET BACK JOURNALS**, Side N]
chat
John reads a newspaper report about George and the band jams.
includes: I've Got My Blue Fingers (improvisation?) (0:05)
vocals: John
Every Night (McCartney) (1:12)
early rehearsal
Dig A Pony/Watch Your Step (Lennon-McCartney/Parker-Belmonte) (2:59)
playback? "skylight" version (excerpt) with false start
New Orleans (Guida-Royster) (2:33)
vocals: John, Paul, George
Madman (Lennon) (1:55)
rehearsal, full band
Dig A Pony (Lennon-McCartney) (1:03)
"fine line" version (excerpt)
Hi Heel Sneakers (Higginbottom) (1:53)
vocals: John
Milk Cow Blues (Arnold) (0:41)
vocals: John (excerpt)
Bring It To Jerome (Green) (0:03)
vocals: John (excerpt)
chat and half a million quid

[263] **Little Queenie** (Berry) (0:55)
 vocals: John, with false start
tuning
When Irish Eyes Are Smiling (Olcott-Graff-Ball) (0:16)
 vocals: John
more tuning & chat
Queen Of The Hop (Harris) (0:37)
 vocals: Paul, John (excerpt)
chat and riffs

SOURCE:
 GET BACK sessions; jacket says 16 Jan-20 Jan 69.

SOUND QUALITY:
 Good to excellent mono.

COMMENTS:
 A reissue of another piece of the **GET BACK JOURNALS** box.

COMPLETE ITALY & PARIS (SUPER LIVE CONCERT SERIES 3)
THE BEATLES
No manufacturer listed, ITA/3688
Insert cover with song titles.

Side A
 20 Jun 65, *Palais des Sports*, Paris, evening show (13:21)
 Twist And Shout (Medley-Russell)
 She's A Woman (Lennon-McCartney)
 Ticket To Ride (Lennon-McCartney)
 Can't Buy Me Love (Lennon-McCartney)
 I'm A Loser (Lennon-McCartney)
Side B
 Boys (Dixon-Farrell) (1:57)
 23 Aug 64, Hollywood Bowl
 Do You Want To Know A Secret (McCartney-Lennon) (1:43)
 4 Jun 63, BBC (skips)
 All My Loving (Lennon-McCartney) (1:58)
 23 Aug 64, Hollywood Bowl
 Please Please Me (McCartney-Lennon) (1:53)
 13 Aug 63, BBC
 Misery (McCartney-Lennon) (1:42)
 4 Jun 63, BBC
 23 Aug 64, Hollywood Bowl (3:37)
 Twist And Shout (Medley-Russell)
 You Can't Do That (Lennon-McCartney)

SOURCE:
 Varies; see individual entries.

SOUND QUALITY:
 Side A is good mono; Side B is very good mono.

COMMENTS:
 Paris? Yes. Italy? Not even close. Complete? It is to laugh.
 Side A is a copy of either **PARIS AGAIN** (CBM, 3688) or **LIVE AT THE PARIS OLYMPIA** (Shalom, 3688), judging by the matrix number. The Paris evening show is available complete and with much better sound on **HOT WAX**.

Side B is a copy of Side A of **THE BEATLES AND THE ROLLING STONES** (Joker, SM 3591).
What a mess!

DEAD STICK
GEORGE HARRISON & ERIC CLAPTON
ZAP, 7879
Insert cover with song titles; labels are "World Records."

Side A
10 Nov 74, George, Long Beach Arena (10:09)
While My Guitar Gently Weeps (Harrison)
Something (Harrison)
[Eric Clapton, live 74
Badge (Harrison-Clapton)
Layla]
Side B
10 Nov 74, George, Long Beach Arena (9:48)
Give Me Love (Harrison)
In My Life (Lennon-McCartney)
[Eric Clapton, live 74
I Shot The Sheriff
Let It Grow]

SOURCE:
George's material from his 74 tour.

SOUND QUALITY:
An audience recording, very good mono.

COMMENTS:
The Clapton cuts are (obviously) not from the same source as the Harrison cuts, and may be from the 74 tour boot **LIVE IN LONDON**.

DOCTOR WINSTON O'BOOGIE ON THE *TOMORROW* SHOW
JOHN LENNON
No manufacturer listed, CX 297
Insert cover with no printed information; labels have title only.

Side A
Part One (22:35)
Side B
Part Two (20:12)

SOURCE:
28 Apr 75, on *Tomorrow*, hosted by Tom Snyder; complete except for commercials and one glitch.

SOUND QUALITY:
Very good to excellent mono.

COMMENTS:
Despite a certain awkwardness, an interesting interview with John and his lawyer; currently available on commercial video. The same pressing was also available as **ALL WE NEED IS JOHN**.

A DOLL'S HOUSE
THE BEATLES
Maidenhead Records, MHR JET 909-1
2-disc set in full color jacket, with track listing and some recording information on the back;
labels say "Jet I" and "Jet II."

DISC ONE
Side A

A message from John & Yoko (0:29)
Oct 69? in Japanese; excellent mono

Give Peace A Chance (Lennon-McCartney) (0:36)
John, Yoko & acoustic; excellent mono
source unknown, continued from previous track

Instant Karma! (Lennon) (1:58)
12 Feb 70, *Top Of The Pops*
very good mono (excerpt)

All Together On The Wireless Machine (McCartney?) (0:55)
unknown; possibly Fall (Dec?) 67, Paul with Kenny Everett
good mono

Step Inside Love (McCartney) (2:13)
Feb 68, Dick James? demo for Cilla Black? poor to fair mono
from a British radio broadcast (source unknown, but possibly Kenny
Everett)

Dark Horse (Harrison) (4:17)
Sep-Oct 74? acoustic demo, excellent mono (?)

A message from Yoko (part 1) (4:01)
Oct 69? in Japanese; excellent mono
Yoko talks while John plays acoustic guitar, including a brief version of **Sun
King**.
The content is similar to most of their peace messages from 69, but contains
several clues which allow us to make a good guess at a date. Yoko
talks about **Give Peace A Chance** (released Jul 69), their time in
Toronto (Sep 69), the fact that it would be snowing in Japan (fall or
winter), and that she will be well soon. In Oct 69, Yoko had another
miscarriage in King's College Hospital, and we know from **LIFE
WITH THE LIONS** that, during her previous hospital stay, she and
John occupied themselves with a portable (cassette?) recorder. This
message to fans back in Japan was probably made during that period.

A message from Yoko (part 2) (4:30)
Oct 69? in Japanese; excellent mono
Yoko talks while John plays acoustic guitar, including brief versions of **Sun
King** (continued) and **Dear Prudence**.
The manner in which the message is broken in half, with each half being about
4:30 strongly suggests that this material is taken from a 45 of some
kind.

Side B

Sound Stage Of Mind (Harrison) (4:04)
4 Nov 74, Seattle Center Coliseum, Seattle, Washington
a line recording, very good to excellent mono

Old Siam Sir (McCartney) (4:14)
Jul 78; very good stereo (weak separation)
This appears to be the basic take for the commercial cut; while the vocals and
lead guitar are identical (although the drumming was apparently overdubbed later) there is a longer break between the verses, and it ends,
followed by brief studio chat, instead of fading. Copied from the extremely rare **SCRAMBLED EGG** EP (MPL-001), this is not the
same version as is on **EGGS UP**. The balance of **SCRAMBLED
EGG** appears on **SUITABLE FOR FRAMING** (MPL, JPM-40IF).

Junior's Farm (McCartney) (4:14)
> 4 Nov 75; Wings at Apollo Stadium, Adelaide, Australia
> audience tape, very good mono

1882 (McCartney) (5:54)
> Summer 72, European tour; this is not the version of 16 Aug 72 (Hanover) or
> > that of 17 Aug 72 (Rotterdam)
> audience tape, very good stereo (best version to date)

Rock And Roller (Lawrie-Starkey) (3:08)
> Billy Lawrie; 73, from a UK 45; excellent stereo

One Hand Clapping (McCartney) (1:18)
> Fall 75, *One Hand Clapping* sessions
> the usual version; excellent stereo

Holding On To A Dream (?) (0:30)
> unknown; possibly some Wings involvement
> very good mono (excerpt); with a bit of *One Hand Clapping* sessions studio
> > chat tacked onto the front of it

DISC TWO
Side C

> 12 Jun 64, Centennial Hall, Adelaide, South Australia (24:00)
> excellent mono line recording (speed changes occasionally)
> apparently from a tv broadcast 13 Jun 64
> **I Saw Her Standing There** (McCartney-Lennon)
> **I Want To Hold Your Hand** (Lennon-McCartney)
> **All My Loving** (Lennon-McCartney)
> **She Loves You** (Lennon-McCartney)
> **Till There Was You** (Willson)
> **Roll Over Beethoven** (Berry)
> **Can't Buy Me Love** (Lennon-McCartney)
> **This Boy** (Lennon-McCartney)
> **Twist And Shout** (Russell-Medley)
> **Long Tall Sally** (Johnson-Penniman-Blackwell) (excerpt)

Side D

Now Hear This Song Of Mine (McCartney) (9:32)
> Spring 71, from Apple SPRO-6210, **BRUNG TO EWE BY HAL SMITH**
> 15 more-or-less different versions; excellent stereo

Goodbye (McCartney) (2:10)
> Mary Hopkin; 1-2 Mar 69, excellent stereo
> This appears to be an earlier mix of the commercial version, only faster and
> > murkier, with heavier bass and lacking some overdubs. Probably from
> > an acetate.

Come And Get It (McCartney) (2:08)
> Badfinger; Sep 69, excellent stereo
> This appears to be the basic take, only faster and murkier; the remixed com-
> > mercial version is vastly superior. A brief bit of studio chat at the end
> > tends to confirm this. Probably from an acetate.

> 5 Nov 75, Wings at Apollo Stadium, Adelaide, Australia
> audience tape, very good mono
> **Junior's Farm** (McCartney) (5:15)
> > A unique performance; the band starts, then stops to tune up before
> > beginning again. The jacket claims that the song was retired
> > after this show.
> **Little Woman Love/C Moon** (P. McCartney-L. McCartney) (4:32)

SOURCE:
> Varies; see individual entries.

SOUND QUALITY:
> Varies; see individual entries.

COMMENTS:
"A Doll's House" was a working title of **THE BEATLES** ("The White Album").
This set has several new interesting (if relatively minor) pieces.
The complete 12 Jun 64 Adelaide show is on **300,000 BEATLES FANS CAN'T BE WRONG** (notice that there's no **I Wanna Be Your Man**, as Ringo was still out sick).

DON'T PASS ME BY
THE BEATLES
Contra Band, CBM-2
2-disc set with insert cover; labels are generic CBM.

DISC ONE
Side A
        [Nothing Is Easy
           Jethro Tull, live]
        Dig It (Lennon-McCartney) (4:47)
           26 Jan 69, Apple
        The Beatles' Third Christmas Record (6:25)
           8 Nov 65, EMI
        Pantomime: Everywhere It's Christmas (6:40)
           aka **The Beatles' Fourth Christmas Record**
           25 Nov 66, Dick James
Side B
        Christmas Time (Is Here Again) (6:25)
           aka **The Beatles' Fifth Christmas Record**
           28 Nov 67, EMI
        The Beatles' Sixth Christmas Record (7:50)
           Nov 68
        The Beatles' Seventh Christmas Record (7:42)
           Nov 69?
DISC TWO
Side C
        When The Saints Go Marching In (trad. ar. Sheridan) (3:04)
           May 61, Hamburg, with Tony Sheridan
           the commercial version
        Glad All Over (Bennett-Tepper-Schroeder) (1:45)
           20 Aug 63, BBC
        I Just Don't Understand (Wilkin-Westberry) (2:39)
           20 Aug 63, BBC
        Slow Down (Williams) (2:26)
           20 Aug 63, BBC
        Don't Ever Change (Goffin-King) (1:58)
           27 Aug 63, BBC
        A Shot Of Rhythm And Blues (Thompson) (2:09)
           27 Aug 63, BBC
        Sure To Fall (In Love With You) (Perkins-Claunch-Cantrell) (2:13)
           24 Sep 63, BBC
Side D
        My Bonnie (Pratt) (1:57)
           May 61, Hamburg, with Tony Sheridan
           the commercial version, no intro
        I Got A Woman (Charles-Richards) (2:25)
           13 Aug 63, BBC (excerpt)
        Nothin' Shakin' (But The Leaves On The Trees)
        (Fontaine-Colacrai-Lampert-Gluck) (2:47)
           23 Jul 63, BBC
        Lonesome Tears In My Eyes (Burnette-Burnette-Burlison-Mortimer) (2:24)
           23 Jul 63, BBC

So How Come (No One Loves Me) (Bryant) (1:45)
  23 Jul 63, BBC
I'm Gonna Sit Right Down And Cry (Over You) (Thomas-Biggs) (1:53)
  6 Aug 63, BBC
Crying, Waiting, Hoping (Holly) (2:01)
  6 Aug 63, BBC
To Know Her Is To Love Her (Spector) (2:37)
  6 Aug 63, BBC
The Honeymoon Song (Theodorakis) (1:33)
  6 Aug 63, BBC

SOURCE:
  Varies; see individual entries.

SOUND QUALITY:
  Very good to excellent mono.

COMMENTS:
  DISC ONE is a repackaging of **COMPLETE CHRISTMAS COLLECTION** (CBM, 2) and **BEST OF THE BEATLES AND JETHRO TULL** (CBM). DISC TWO is a repackaging of the Shalom version of **YELLOW MATTER CUSTARD (AS SWEET AS YOU ARE**, with the two Hamburg tracks added).

ED'S REALLY BIG BEATLES BLASTS
THE BEATLES
Melvin Records, MM05
Black and white jacket, ©1978, with song listing on the back; label info matches.

Side A
  9 Feb 64, *The Ed Sullivan Show*
    First set (7:12)
      Introduction
      All My Loving (Lennon-McCartney)
      Till There Was You (Willson)
      She Loves You (Lennon-McCartney)
      Dedications
    Second set (6:04)
      Introduction
      I Saw Her Standing There (McCartney-Lennon)
      I Want To Hold Your Hand (Lennon-McCartney)
      Thanks
  16 Feb 64, *The Ed Sullivan Show*
    First set: (7:19)
      Introduction
      She Loves You (Lennon-McCartney)
      This Boy (Lennon-McCartney)
      Paul: "Good evening."
      All My Loving (Lennon-McCartney)
Side B
  16 Feb 64, *The Ed Sullivan Show* (continued)
    Second set: (7:50)
      Introduction (mention of Sonny Liston vs. Cassius Clay)
      I Saw Her Standing There (McCartney-Lennon)
      From Me To You (McCartney-Lennon)
      Paul: "Sophie Tucker" remark
      I Want To Hold Your Hand (Lennon-McCartney)
    The boys chat with Ed; congratulations from Richard Rodgers

23 Feb 64, *The Ed Sullivan Show*
>> First set (4:54)
>>>> Introduction
>>>> **Twist And Shout** (Medley-Russell)
>>>> **Please Please Me** (McCartney-Lennon)
>>>> Ed
>> Second set (3:00)
>>>> **I Want To Hold Your Hand** (Lennon-McCartney)

SOURCE:
>> The first three *Ed Sullivan Show* broadcasts.

SOUND QUALITY:
>> Good to very good mono.

COMMENTS:
>> Although the 9 Feb and 23 Feb performances are available on **THE BEATLES CONQUER AMERICA**, this is one of the few appearances of the 16 Feb broadcast (**BEATLES CONQUER** has the 15 Feb rehearsal). Introductions and chat are preserved, and the sound quality is acceptable.

EIGHT ARMS TO HOLD YOU
THE BEATLES
Kimber Records, BEAT 1
2-disc set in full color jacket, with song titles on the back; labels have wrong titles.

DISC ONE
Side A
>> 23 Aug 64, Hollywood Bowl 64 (13:21)
>>>> **Twist And Shout** (Medley-Russell)
>>>> **You Can't Do That** (Lennon-McCartney)
>>>> **All My Loving** (Lennon-McCartney)
>>>> **She Loves You** (Lennon-McCartney)
>>>> **Things We Said Today** (Lennon-McCartney)
>>>> **Roll Over Beethoven** (Berry)
>> **Love Me Do** (McCartney-Lennon) (2:20)
>>>> 23 Jul 63, BBC; very good mono
>> **Please Please Me** (McCartney-Lennon) (1:53)
>>>> 13 Aug 63, BBC; very good mono
Side B
>> 23 Aug 64, Hollywood Bowl 64 (15:48)
>>>> **Can't Buy Me Love** (Lennon-McCartney)
>>>> **If I Fell** (Lennon-McCartney)
>>>> **I Want To Hold Your Hand** (Lennon-McCartney)
>>>> **Boys** (Dixon-Farrell)
>>>> **A Hard Day's Night** (Lennon-McCartney)
>>>> **Long Tall Sally** (Johnson-Penniman-Blackwell)
>> 17 Jun 64, Festival Hall, Melbourne, Australia (5:21)
>>>> good to very good mono
>>>> **Till There Was You** (Willson)
>>>> **I Saw Her Standing There** (McCartney-Lennon)
DISC TWO
Side C
>> 30 Jun 66, Nippon Budokan Hall, Tokyo (22:10)
>>>> **Rock And Roll Music** (Berry)
>>>> **She's A Woman** (Lennon-McCartney)
>>>> **If I Needed Someone** (Harrison)
>>>> **Day Tripper** (Lennon-McCartney)
>>>> **Baby's In Black** (Lennon-McCartney)
>>>> **I Feel Fine** (Lennon-McCartney)

Yesterday (Lennon-McCartney)
I Wanna Be Your Man (Lennon-McCartney)
Ain't She Sweet (Ager-Yellen) (2:10)
May 61, Hamburg; the commercial version

Side D
P.S. I Love You (McCartney-Lennon) (2:00)
11 Sep 62, EMI; take 10 (the commercial version)
There's A Place (McCartney-Lennon) (1:47)
11/20 Feb 63, EMI; take 13 (the commercial version)
Misery (McCartney-Lennon) (1:46)
11 Feb 63, EMI; take 16 (the commercial version)
Dizzy Miss Lizzie (Williams) (2:39)
7 Jun 65, BBC
16 Feb 64, *The Ed Sullivan Show*
This Boy (Lennon-McCartney) (2:26)
From Me To You (McCartney-Lennon) (1:54)
30 Jun 66, Nippon Budokan Hall, Tokyo (7:38)
Nowhere Man (Lennon-McCartney)
Paperback Writer (Lennon-McCartney)
I'm Down (Lennon-McCartney)

SOURCE:
Varied; see individual entries.

SOUND QUALITY:
Excellent mono unless otherwise stated.

COMMENTS:
This is a reissue of an older title, **SECOND TO NONE**, which itself is apparently a reissue of **THE VERY BEST OF THE BEATLES RAREST, VOLUMES 2** and **3**. Another bootleg with this same jacket front and title, but with different material, has also been issued.

ELVIS MEETS ... THE BEATLES
ELVIS PRESLEY/THE BEATLES
Backstage Records, BSR ES-LP-50
Insert cover with song listing; label info matches.

Side A
[Elvis Presley]
Side B
The Long And Winding Road (Lennon-McCartney) (3:30)
31 Jan 69, Apple & 1 Apr 70, EMI
take 18 (the commercial version)
My Bonnie (Pratt) (2:34)
May 61, Hamburg (the commercial version)
Tony Sheridan, with English intro
Money (That's What I Want) (Bradford-Gordy) (2:19)
1 Jan 62, Decca audition
Sweet Georgia Brown (Bernie-Pinkard-Casey) (2:02)
Tony Sheridan; Apr 62, Hamburg (music)/early 64 (vocals)
commercial version with Beatles reference
You're Going To Lose That Girl (Lennon-McCartney) (2:13)
19 Feb 65, EMI; take 3 (the commercial version)
Girl (Lennon-McCartney) (2:22)
11 Nov 65, EMI; take 2 (the commercial version)

SOURCE:
Varies; see individual entries.

SOUND QUALITY:
>Very good to excellent mono; some of the cuts appear to be just one channel of a stereo version.

COMMENTS:
>Utterly without interest, except perhaps to completists. This is not the LP listed in *Hot Wacks* as **ELVIS VS. THE BEATLES** (Superstar Records).

EMI OUTTAKES
THE BEATLES
No manufacturer listed, 1374
Insert cover with track listing; labels have side numbers only.

Side A
>John's apology (0:39)
>>12 Aug 66, Chicago; very good mono
>**What's The New Mary Jane** (Lennon) (2:58)
>>14 Aug 68, EMI; take 4, stereo remix 4; (excerpt)
>>possibly the unreleased Apple 45; excellent stereo
>interview (0:35)
>>Paul on how he and John write together
>>probably 66, very good mono
>**Penny Lane** (Lennon-McCartney) (2:53)
>>29/30 Dec 66 & 4/5/6/9/10/12/17 Jan 67, EMI; very good mono
>>take 9 (mono remix #11), with trumpet ending
>interview (0:57)
>>George on how they try to improve with each album
>>probably 66, very good mono
>**Blue Jay Way** (Harrison) (3:37)
>>6/7 Sep & 6 Oct 67, EMI; take 3 (mono remix #27)
>>with different backing vocals; excellent mono
>interview (0:27)
>>with a fan; very good mono; source unknown US tv program
>**All My Loving** (Lennon-McCartney) (2:01)
>>30 Jul 63, EMI; take 14; very good "true" stereo
>interview (0:51)
>>Ed Sullivan and Happy Rockefeller (!?), very good mono
>>source unknown, probably circa 64
>*Sie Liebt Dich* (Lennon-McCartney) (2:03)
>>29 Jan 64, Paris; take 14 (commercial version); excellent mono

Side B
>interview (0:39)
>>with a fan after a concert
>>source unknown, very good mono
>6 May 64, *Around The Beatles* (14:41)
>>good to very good mono
>>**Twist And Shout** (Medley-Russell)
>>**Roll Over Beethoven** (Berry)
>>**I Wanna Be Your Man** (Lennon-McCartney)
>>**Long Tall Sally** (Johnson-Penniman-Blackwell)
>>Medley (McCartney-Lennon)
>>>**Love Me Do**
>>>**Please Please Me**
>>>**From Me To You**
>>>**She Loves You**
>>>**I Want To Hold Your Hand**
>>**Can't Buy Me Love** (Lennon-McCartney)

SOURCE:
    Varies; see individual entries.

SOUND QUALITY:
    Varies; see individual entries.

COMMENTS:
    The interviews are by far more unusual than the musical cuts on this collection (Happy Rockefeller was the wife of Nelson Rockefeller, a former Governor of New York and Vice President of the United States under Gerald Ford.)

EXTENDED SESSIONS
THE BEATLES
Rock Solid Records, RSR 7007-2
2-disc set in full color jacket, with song listing on the back; labels are blank. Jacket says "limited to 1000 copies."

DISC ONE
Side A
    Oh! Darling (Lennon-McCartney) (2:01)
        mid-Jul 69, EMI; lead vocals only
        on 17, 18, & 22 Jul, Paul recorded lead vocal takes which were not used (the final version was done on 23 Jul)
    Oh! Darling (Lennon-McCartney) (3:17)
        26 Apr 69, EMI; take 26; alternate lead vocals
        This may be the basic take 26 with a guide vocal, or one one of Paul's later overdub attempts. Since a second vocal is faintly audible, I'm assuming this is the first vocal take on top of the guide vocal.
    Golden Slumbers/Carry That Weight (Lennon-McCartney) (2:56)
        2 Jul 69, EMI; take 13
        15 basic takes were recorded this day; takes 13 and 15 were edited together to form the basic take (still called take 13) of the commercial version, which is what this appears to be.
    Her Majesty (Lennon-McCartney) (0:23)
        2 Jul 69, EMI; take 3, with the final chord
    You Never Give Me Your Money (Lennon-McCartney) (5:33)
        6 May, Olympic & 1/11 Jul 69, EMI; take 30
        The basic tracks had been recorded 6 May at Olympic Studios; the vocals were added on 1 Jul and the bass on this date.
    Octopus's Garden (Starkey) (2:37)
        26/29 Apr & 17 Jul 69, EMI; take 32
        piano, backing vocals and sound effects were dubbed in on this day; this track has the piano but no backing vocals or effects
    Maxwell's Silver Hammer (Lennon-McCartney) (3:27)
        9/10/11 Jul 69, EMI; take 21; no synthesizer or guitar overdubs
Side B
    Across The Universe (Lennon-McCartney) (3:33)
        4/8 Feb 68 & 2 Oct 69 EMI; take 8 (WWF version)
        excellent stereo
    Lady Madonna (Lennon-McCartney) (1:58)
        3/6 Feb 68, EMI; take 4; very good stereo
        the basic track (take 3) was recorded on 3 Feb; the backing vocals, handclaps and a second lead vocal were added on 6 Feb, as were the brass overdubs; this take would appear to be from this 6 Feb overdubbing session, prior to the addition of the brass.
        off speakers, from *The Beatles Live At Abbey Road*
    Ob-La-Di, Ob-La-Da (Lennon-McCartney) (2:37)
        3/4/5 Jul 68, EMI; take 5; very good stereo
        from the cancelled **SESSIONS** 45

Christmas Time (Is Here Again) (Lennon-McCartney-Harrison-Starkey) (0:52)
    28 Nov 67, EMI; very good stereo
    from the cancelled **SESSIONS** 45
Let It Be (Lennon-McCartney) (3:42)
    31 Jan 69, Apple; a finished take; excellent mono
Something (Harrison) (4:43)
    11 Jul 69, EMI; take 37
    This is a tape reduction of take 36, the basic take of the commercial version; it
        was intended (but never used) for overdubs.
Christmas Time (Is Here Again) (Lennon-McCartney-Harrison-Starkey) (5:21)
    28 Nov 67, EMI; very good mono, off speakers
    from the "EMI board room" tape

DISC TWO
Side C
Come And Get It (McCartney) (2:20)
    24 Jul 69, EMI; take 1; Paul's demo; very good stereo
Your Mother Should Know (Lennon-McCartney) (2:12)
    22 Aug 67, Chappell; take 8? the basic tracks
    no bass or organ, different backing vocals; very good mono
Goodbye (McCartney) (2:15)
    late 68? Dick James; Paul's demo; excellent mono
I'm So Tired (Lennon-McCartney) (2:10)
    Jan 69, **GET BACK** sessions
    vocals: Paul; excellent mono
Birthday (Lennon-McCartney) (2:35)
    18 Sep 68, EMI; take 22
    commercial version, OOPSed; excellent mono
Dig It (Lennon-McCartney) (7:59)
    26 Jan 69, Apple; excellent mono
I Me Mine (Harrison) (1:30)
    3 Jan 70, EMI; take 16; excellent stereo
    Although this appears to have an announcement of "take 8" at the beginning,
        it must be take 16 as it is an early version of the commercial release
        (pre-Spector). There is a chance that this is Glyn John's 5 Jan 70
        remix for the second version of **GET BACK**, although it does not
        contain the spoken preamble Lewisohn describes.
Side D
We Can Work It Out (Lennon-McCartney) (2:05)
    20/29 Oct 65, EMI; take 2; excellent stereo
    with countdown, otherwise identical to commercial release
    from **SPLHCB: A HISTORY OF THE BEATLE YEARS**
Not Guilty (Harrison) (3:09)
    8/9/12 Aug 68, EMI; take 102
    84 **SESSIONS** remix; excellent stereo
While My Guitar Gently Weeps (Harrison) (3:12)
    25 Jul 68, EMI; take 1; acoustic; excellent mono
Across The Universe (Lennon-McCartney) (3:14)
    4/8 Feb 68, EMI; take 8 (acetate version); very good stereo
    This would appear to be Glyn John's 5 Jan 70 remix for the second version of
        GET BACK, as it contains John's spoken preamble, "Are you all
        right, Richie?"
Penny Lane (Lennon-McCartney) (2:47)
    29/30 Dec 66 & 4/5/6/9/10/12/17 Jan 67, EMI; very good mono
    take 9 (mono remix #11), with trumpet ending
A Day In The Life (Lennon-McCartney) (4:28)
    19/20 Jan & 3/10/22 Feb 67, EMI; edit of takes 6 & 7
    commercial version, with clean intro
What's The New Mary Jane (Lennon) (5:55)
    14 Aug 68, EMI; take 4, 84 **SESSIONS** remix; very good stereo

SOURCE:
Varies; see individual entries.

SOUND QUALITY:
Varies; see individual entries. Most of these cuts are too fast and have a very flat sound to them.

COMMENTS:
Another RSReissue of bits and pieces from here and there. Yawn.

FALCONER
DELANEY & BONNIE (WITH ERIC CLAPTON & GEORGE HARRISON)
Contra Band, 54450
Insert cover; labels are generic CBM.

Side A (18:36)
Poor Elijah/Tribute To Johnson (Bramlett-Ford/Bramlett-Russell)
Don't Know Why (Bramlett-Clapton)
Eric Clapton
Where There's A Will, There's A Way (Bramlett-Whitlock)
My Baby Specializes (?)
Side B (23:09)
You're My Girl (?)
That's What My Man Is For (Griffin)
Comin' Home (Bramlett-Clapton)
Little Richard medley:
Tutti Frutti (LaBostrie-Penniman)
The Girl Can't Help It (Troup)
Long Tall Sally (Johnson-Penniman-Blackwell)
Jenny, Jenny (Johnson-Penniman)

SOURCE:
12 Dec 69, *Falkonercenter*, Copenhagen, Denmark; George and Eric Clapton with Delaney & Bonnie on a tour of Scandinavia. The source of this tape may be an FM radio broadcast.

SOUND QUALITY:
A line recording, very good mono (too much bass!).

COMMENTS:
If George is here, you can't prove it by listening. Clapton's guitar work is clearly evident—maybe George wasn't plugged in? Delaney introduces the band at the end of **Comin' Home**: Billy Preston (electric piano), Bobby Whitlock, Jim Gordon (drums), Carl Radle (bass) Eric Clapton and George Harry (?) (guitars). Most of these people would help in recording **ALL THINGS MUST PASS** the next year.
George is also supposed to be on the legitimate commercial album, **DELANEY AND BONNIE ON TOUR**, recorded a week earlier (7 Dec 69) at Fairfield Hall, Croyden (US Atco 33-326, released 7 Apr 70).

FOREST HILLS TENNIS STADIUM
THE BEATLES
King Kong Records, FH1058
Insert cover; labels are Instant Analysis and have song listing.

Side A
    15 Aug 65, Shea Stadium, NYC (5:25)
        introduction (Ed Sullivan, "a truly great American!")
        I Feel Fine (Lennon-McCartney)
        Dizzy Miss Lizzie (Williams)
    Lucille (Collins-Penniman) (2:27)
        17 Sep 63, BBC
        with overdubbed screaming to make it seem part of the show
    15 Aug 65, Shea Stadium, NYC (continued) (7:19)
        Help! (Lennon-McCartney)
        I'm Down (Lennon-McCartney)
        Baby's In Black (Lennon-McCartney)
Side B
    24 Oct 63, *Karlaplannstudion*, Stockholm, Sweden (8:08)
        broadcast on *Pop '63* Swedish radio
        I Saw Her Standing There (McCartney-Lennon)
        From Me To You (McCartney-Lennon)
        Money (That's What I Want) (Bradford-Gordy)
    2 Dec 65, *Top Of The Pops* (4:55)
        Day Tripper (Lennon-McCartney)
            16 Oct 65, EMI; take 3 (the commercial version)
        We Can Work It Out (Lennon-McCartney)
            20/29 Oct 65, EMI; take 2 (the commercial version)
        the group lip-synched; this film was also shown in the US on *Hullabaloo*, 3
        Jan 66

SOURCE:
    Varies; see individual entries.

SOUND QUALITY:
    Side A is fair mono; Side B is good mono.

COMMENTS:
    Side A was allegedly broadcast live on radio station WBOX in Sep 65, an attribution which overlooked the fact that the Beatles played Forest Hills (two shows) on 28-29 Aug 64; since the lineup is clearly from 65, neither the date (the 65 tour was in Aug) nor the location could be correct. The tape is a mess; only just listenable (recorded from a tv broadcast—background noises can be heard occasionally), it has been edited and rearranged. Yecch.
    Side B seems to be lifted from **ON STAGE**.
    This title was also available on Wizardo, Shalom and Contra Band.

FT. WORTH/SEATTLE
PAUL McCARTNEY & WINGS
King Kong, 4599
Insert cover; labels are generic.

Side A
    3 May 76, Tarrant County Convention Hall, Forth Worth, Texas (18:05)
        Silly Love Songs (McCartney)
        Beware My Love (McCartney)
        introducing the band
        Letting Go (McCartney)
Side B
    3 May 76, Tarrant County Convention Hall, Forth Worth, Texas (11:55)
        Band On The Run (McCartney)
        applause
        Hi, Hi, Hi (McCartney)

interview (3:42)
>   probably 3 May 76, Fort Worth; possibly tv news
>   includes **Silly Love Songs** (McCartney)
>>   commercial version, possibly from video (excerpt)
>   28 Jun 76, *Goodnight America* (tv) (7:30)
>   Paul, Linda and Wings are interviewed by Geraldo Rivera
>   includes:
>>   10 Jun 76, The Kingdome, Seattle
>>   **Band On The Run** (McCartney) (excerpt)
>>   **Yesterday** (Lennon-McCartney)

SOURCE:
>   Varies; see individual entries.

SOUND QUALITY:
>   Concert is a very good to excellent mono audience tape (there is a break between **Silly Love Songs** and **Beware My Love**); interview material is good to very good mono.

COMMENTS:
>   Fort Worth was Paul's first U.S. show on the 76 tour, and is apparently continued here from **FIRST AMERICAN CONCERT** (Shalom, 4598). Although the Seattle footage was first shown just 18 days after it was shot, *Rockshow* (which uses primarily Seattle footage) would not premiere until Nov 80, four and one-half years later.

FROM A WHISPER TO A SHOUT!

THE BEATLES
No manufacturer listed, DISCO ONE
Full color jacket, with song listing and some recording information on the back; labels are blank.

Side A
>   **Savoy Truffle** (Harrison) (2:29)
>>   3/5 Oct 68, Trident & 11/14 Oct 69, EMI (the commercial version)
>>   outfake of somebody singing along with the record
>   **Honey Pie** (Lennon-McCartney) (2:01)
>>   1/2/4 Oct 68, Trident (the commercial version)
>>   outfake of somebody singing along with the record (again)
>   "White album jam" (0:02)
>>   somebody says the words (honest!)
>   **What's The New Mary Jane** (Lennon) (6:17)
>>   14 Aug 68, EMI; take 4 (stereo remix #4)
>>   excellent stereo, recorded off disc
>   **I Saw Her Standing There** (McCartney-Lennon) (2:58)
>>   good mono; source unknown
>>   John's "Okay George, take it" at the beginning is unrelated to the rest of the tape, and comes from "Feedback Guitar" (Jan 69, **GB** sessions). *You Can't Do That!* suggests that this may be the Who (presumably based on the guitar work).
>   Instrumental (improvisation) (2:47)
>>   Jan 69, **GET BACK** sessions
>>   This is from the jam which usually follows "Watching Rainbows."
> [139]   You Got Me Going (?) (0:26)
>>   Jan 69, **GET BACK** sessions
>   **Don't Let Me Down** (Lennon-McCartney) (3:08)
>>   Jan 69, **GET BACK** sessions
>>   Dirty Mac, with Rocky and the Rubbers
>   **Maxwell's Silver Hammer** (Lennon-McCartney) (2:48)
>>   Jan 69, **GB** sessions
>>   somebody sings along with various versions (excerpts)

Side B

      My Love (McCartney) (4:03)
      Little Woman Love (P. McCartney-L. McCartney) (0:09)
      chat
      Little Woman Love/C Moon (P. McCartney-L. McCartney) (4:16)
      tuning
      Maybe I'm Amazed (McCartney) (4:29)
          with "novel opening"
      chat
      Bluebird (McCartney) (3:09)
      chat
      Blackbird (Lennon-McCartney) (2:23)
          74, from Paul's unreleased *Backyard* film
          3 takes, "dedicated to Edie"
      Jet (McCartney) (3:39)

SOURCE:
      Side A: varied; see individual listings. Side B: *One Hand Clapping* sessions (except for **Blackbird**); for a discussion of the dating of these sessions (album jacket says these are Elstree, May 75), see the entry for **ONE HAND CLAPPING** in *Do You Want To Know A Secret?*

SOUND QUALITY:
      Side A: good to very good mono unless otherwise stated. Side B: very good stereo (but too fast).

COMMENTS:
      This is a recent reissue of an older piece.
      Except for the killer **I Saw Her Standing There**, Side A is worthless—especially when someone is trying to create "new" versions by having someone do a lousy Paul imitation along to a record.
      All of this *One Hand Clapping* material (and much more) is now available on **ONE HAND CLAPPING** (except for **Blackbird**, which is on **WATCHING RAINBOWS**), although this may have been its first appearance.

FROM SESSION TO SESSION...

THE BEATLES
Alternative Record Company, Ltd., ARC 0072
Full color jacket ©1983 with song listing on the back; labels have artist and titles only.

Side A

      Angel Baby (Ponci) (3:08)
          Oct-Dec 73, **ROCK'N'ROLL** sessions
          excellent stereo; from **ROOTS: JOHN LENNON SINGS THE GREAT
               ROCK AND ROLL HITS** (Adam VIII A 8018)
      Be My Baby (Spector-Greenwich-Barry) (4:39)
          Oct-Dec 73, **ROCK'N'ROLL** sessions
          excellent stereo; from **ROOTS: JOHN LENNON SINGS THE GREAT
               ROCK AND ROLL HITS** (Adam VIII A 8018)
      How Do You Do It (Murray-Edmond) (1:58)
          4 Sep 62, EMI; take 2; excellent mono
      Come And Get It (McCartney) (2:24)
          Badfinger, Sep 69; the commercial version; excellent stereo
      Let It Be (Lennon-McCartney) (8:18)
          Jan 69, **GET BACK** sessions; excellent mono
          first rehearsal with chord changes

Side B

> **Yesterday** (Lennon-McCartney) (2:30)
>> 30 Jun 66, Nippon Budokan Hall, Tokyo
>
> **Get Back** (Lennon-McCartney) (3:58)
>> Jan 69, **GET BACK** sessions; excellent mono
>> "No Pakistanis" version
>
> **Get Back** (Lennon-McCartney) (2:06)
>> Jan 69, **GET BACK** sessions; excellent mono
>> fast version, John shares lead vocals
>
> **Don't Let Me Down** (Lennon-McCartney) (3:26)
>> Jan 69, **GET BACK** sessions; excellent mono
>
> **House Of The Rising Sun** (trad.) (2:35)
>> Jan 69, **GET BACK** sessions
>
> **Across The Universe** (Lennon-McCartney)
>> Jan 69, **GET BACK** sessions; excellent mono
>> the last version
>
> **Let It Be** (Lennon-McCartney) (2:36)
>> Jan 69, **GET BACK** sessions; excellent mono
>> *Record Mirror* version

SOURCE:
> Varies; see individual entries.

SOUND QUALITY:
> Varies; see individual entries.

COMMENTS:
> Nothing remarkable; probably made to capitalize on the interest in **SESSIONS**.

FUCK!
THE BEATLES
"Apple Records," SAPCOR 33
2-disc set in full color jacket, with track listing and recording information on the back, says "Made In New Zealand;" labels say "Rubber Soul" and have song titles.

DISC ONE
Side A

> **Help!** (Lennon-McCartney) (2:18)
>> 12 Sep 65, *The Ed Sullivan Show*
>
> **Ticket To Ride** (Lennon-McCartney) (3:03)
>> 7 Jun 65, BBC
>
> **Act Naturally** (Russell-Morrison) (2:28)
>> 12 Sep 65, *The Ed Sullivan Show*
>
> **Yesterday** (Lennon-McCartney) (1:42)
>> 16 Apr 73, *James Paul McCartney*
>
> **Dizzy Miss Lizzie** (Williams) (2:47)
>> 7 Jun 65, BBC
>
> **That Means A Lot** (Lennon-McCartney) (2:31)
>> 20 Feb 65, EMI; take 2

Side B

> **I Feel Fine** (Lennon-McCartney) (2:08)
>> 26 Nov 64, BBC
>
> **She's A Woman** (Lennon-McCartney) (3:16)
>> 26 Nov 64, BBC (ending has been edited)
>
> **I'm Down** (Lennon-McCartney) (2:07)
>> 12 Sep 65, *The Ed Sullivan Show*
>
> **Yes It Is** (Lennon-McCartney) (2:47)
>> 16 Feb 65, EMI; take 14; excellent stereo
>> studio chat lifted from **I'm A Loser** on *SPLHCB*

Medley: (McCartney-Lennon) (4:08)
> **Love Me Do**
> **Please Please Me**
> **From Me To You**
> **She Loves You**
> **I Want To Hold Your Hand**
>> 19 Apr 64, IBC; for *Around The Beatles*
>> Reverts to live at the end of the last song.

This Boy (Lennon-McCartney) (2:14)
> 17 Oct 63, EMI; edit of takes 15 & 17
> commercial version, in excellent stereo

DISC TWO
Side C

I Got A Woman (Charles-Richards) (2:47)
> 13 Aug 63, BBC

Johnny B. Goode (Berry) (2:20)
> 15 Feb 64, BBC

Honey Don't (Perkins) (2:11)
> 3 Sep 63, BBC

Shout! (Isley-Isley-Isley) (2:00)
> 19 Apr 64, IBC; for *Around The Beatles*

The Hippy Hippy Shake (Romero) (1:51)
> 30 Jul 63, BBC

I Forgot To Remember To Forget (Kesler-Feathers) (2:04)
> 18 May 64, BBC; good to very good mono
> two different tapes edited together

Side D

Beatleviews (23:22)
> Bob Rogers interviews the Beatles during their Australasian tour. In general, much of this material appears on **THE BEATLES TALK DOWN UNDER**, although these seem to be the raw tapes (some things were edited out for the legitimate LP). There is also material on the legitimate LP which does not appear here.

SOURCE:
> Varies; see individual listings.

SOUND QUALITY:
> Varies; see individual listings.

COMMENTS:
> I could have lived a full and productive life without this jacket, but some people seem to find it hilarious. As a point of interest, the semaphore positions here do correctly spell the title; on **HELP!**, the positions spell **R** (or **N**) **V U J**.

GET BACK SESSION
THE BEATLES
No manufacturer listed, DISCO 2
Full color jacket, says "Manufactured by Beatles Fans Club—Amsterdam—Printed in Holland," with song titles on the back; labels are blank.

Side A

Tennessee (Perkins) (1:59)
> vocals: John, Paul, George

Across The Universe (Lennon-McCartney) (0:10)
> the last version

House Of The Rising Sun (trad.) (2:33)
> vocals: John, Paul

Commonwealth (improvisation) (3:56)
    vocals: Paul, John
Enoch Powell (improvisation) (0:20)
    vocals: Paul
White Power (Get Off!) (improvisation) (6:48)
[189]   vocals: Paul, John (excerpts); includes:
    Why Don't We Do It In The Road (Lennon-McCartney) (0:03)
        as "Why Don't You Put It On The Toast"
Honey Hush (Turner) (2:08)
    vocals: John, George, Paul
For You Blue (Harrison) (2:02)
    all-electric version
Let It Be (Lennon-McCartney) (2:33)
    Record Mirror version

Side B
Get Back (Lennon-McCartney) (2:00)
    fast version, John shares lead vocals
Don't Let Me Down (Lennon-McCartney) (3:07)
    with Leslied guitar
[176] **Two Of Us** (Lennon-McCartney) (2:01)
    excerpt
chat and tea
Baa Baa Black Sheep (trad.) (0:17)
    vocals: John
[177] **Don't Let Me Down** (Lennon-McCartney) (3:10)
    screaming version
Suzy Parker (Lennon-McCartney-Harrison-Starkey) (1:52)
    the usual version
I've Got A Feeling (Lennon-McCartney) (3:48)
    "facelift" version
Get Back (Lennon-McCartney) (3:40)
    "No Pakistanis" version

SOURCE:
    Jan 69, **GET BACK** sessions.

SOUND QUALITY:
    Excellent mono.

COMMENTS:
    This is a copy of **SWEET APPLE TRAX VOLUME ONE** (literally—you can hear the ends of the sides) and is a recent reissue of an older piece.

THE GOLDEN BEATLES (CD)
THE BEATLES
Overseas Records, 30CP-56
CD, made in Japan; comes with transcript booklet in Japanese.

introduction (0:49)
    Summer 69, EMI
    Someone (probably Kenny Everett) describing the scene while the Beatles bang and crash around on various instruments.
Oi Gevalt (Lennon-McCartney-Yeadles?) (3:10)
    A parody of **Ob-La-Di, Ob-La-Da** by "The Yeadles;" commercial release unknown. Not very interesting.
The Kenny Everett interview (12:52)
    5-6 Jun 68, EMI. Regarding the dating of this interview, John mentions that they were working on Ringo's first song, the second for their new LP. The first song recorded was **Revolution 1** (30/31 May & 4 Jun), after which they

began **Don't Pass Me By** (5-6 Jun); the accompanying notes date this interview as 18 Jul 68. This is unlikely as the interview was broadcast on 9 Jun 68.

This is a much longer version of Kenny Everett's interview and contains over six minutes of material which does not appear on *Una Sensazionale Intervista* (Italian Apple DPR-108). Tony Rees, writing in *Rare Rock*, claims that there is a 13-minute EMI-Disc acetate in existence. If so, that acetate is probably the source of this recording (or, perhaps, *vice-versa*).

Beatle Rap (Qworymen) (3:39)

An interesting and often humorous Beatles parody. This cut has been commercially released by Rhino Records as a rather ugly black-and-white 8-inch picture disc (Erika Records ER-107) and on the LP **BEATLESONGS** (RNLP 803).

KFWBeatles (1:42)

a copy of Capitol Custom RB-2637, released on 5 Jun 64 in Los Angeles by KFWB and includes:

KFWB music spot #1

to the tune of **She Loves You**; very good mono
no Beatles involvement

greetings

to Wink Martindale & Jolly Joe Yoakum; very good mono
the poor editing may be present on the original

KFWB music spot #2

to the tune of **It Won't Be Long**; very good mono
no Beatles involvement

Help! (open-ended?) interview (9:59)

Spring 65; exact dates and places of original recordings uncertain; questions apparently read by Wink Martindale (whose name also appears frequently, interestingly enough, on **KFWBeatles**); original release of promo: Aug 65

The booklet dates this as 6 Jun 65, Nassau, during the filming of *Help!* but the internal evidence suggests a compilation of more than one interview, none of them on the 6th. The Beatles were on separate vacations between 27 May and about 7 Jun (Paul was definitely gone until the 11th), so that date is clearly wrong.

The trip to the Bahamas lasted from 22 Feb to 10 Mar. Since Ringo talks about being married "a month," (he and Pattie were married on 11 Feb), parts of the interview could have taken place during the first week in Mar in the Bahamas.

Also, they mention the trip to Austria (13-22 Mar; "Quiet," Paul says), which came after the Bahamas. And John specifically mentions the title song **Help!** (written 4 Apr, recorded EMI 13 Apr), so other parts of the interview must post-date that.

The Beatles had an advance screening *Help!* on the morning of 12 Jun (it premiered 29 Jul in London, went into general UK release on 1 Aug, and opened in New York on 14 Aug); since they give the impression they have seen at least a rough cut of the film, the non-Bahamas material may postdate 12 Jun. From the background noises on parts of the tape, Twickenham seems a likely location; they were there on 16 Jun to do some work on the soundtrack (this material is obviously pretty late, since they refer to publicity material—"Will John live to sleep in his pit again?"—and so on) and may have been interviewed at that time.

SOURCE:

Varies; see individual entries.

SOUND QUALITY:

Very good to excellent mono.

COMMENTS:

This is (apparently—Japan has the same 20-year, non-renewable copyright as Italy) not a bootleg, but is included because of the complete Kenny Everett interview. This package is also available as an import LP, which may be a copy or a foreign release of the LP **THE GOLDEN BEATLES** (Silhouette, S.M. 10015), released in the U.S. Jul 85.

GOLDMINE
THE BEATLES
Suma Records, 8086591
2-disc set, on colored vinyl, in full color jacket, with song titles on the back; label info matches.

DISC ONE
Side A [duplicates **GET BACK JOURNALS**, Side K]
      tuning & riffs
[326] **Get Back** (Lennon-McCartney) (2:36)
          listless version, with Billy Preston
    Get Back (Lennon-McCartney) (0:37)
          instrumental
    riffs & chat
    Bad Boy (Williams) (3:15)
          vocals: John, two takes
    riffs & chat
[327] **Sweet Little Sixteen/Around And Around** (Berry) (2:48)
          vocals: John
    Almost Grown (Berry) (1:45)
          vocals: John
    chat & riffs
    School Days (Berry) (0:30)
          vocals: John (excerpt)
    riffs & chat
    Yer Blues (Lennon-McCartney) (0:02)
          vocals: Paul
    chat & riffs & Yoko
    Get Back (Lennon-McCartney) (0:40)
          excerpts
[235] **Get Back** (Lennon-McCartney) (1:11)
          rehearsal, working on the lyrics (excerpts)
Side B [duplicates **GET BACK JOURNALS**, Side I]
    I'm So Tired (Lennon-McCartney) (2:16)
          vocals: Paul
    Ob-La-Di, Ob-La-Da (Lennon-McCartney) (1:21)
          vocals: Paul, John, George
    Harry Lime (*Third Man* Theme) (Karas) (1:39)
          instrumental
    Negro In Reserve (?) (0:41)
          vocals: Paul, John
    Don't Let Me Down (Lennon-McCartney) (2:41)
          another rehearsal (excerpts)
    One After 909 (Lennon-McCartney) (3:05)
          first runthrough?
    chat & riffs
    Wake Up In The Morning (Lennon-McCartney?) (2:29)
          vocals: Paul, John
    One After 909 (Lennon-McCartney) (0:30)
          rehearsal (excerpt)
    chat & riffs
[41] If Tomorrow Ever Comes (Lennon-McCartney?) (0:57)
          vocals: Paul, John
    Love Is Like A Macaroni (improv.) (0:03)
          vocals: John
    Thinking That You Love Me (Lennon-McCartney?) (0:17)
          vocals: Paul, John
    Won't You Please Say Goodbye (Lennon-McCartney?) (0:45)
          vocals: Paul, John

DISC TWO
Side C [duplicates **GET BACK JOURNALS**, Side Q]
    I've Got A Feeling (Lennon-McCartney) (0:15)
        (excerpts)
    Help!/Please Please Me (Lennon-McCartney) (0:50)
        vocals: John, Paul
[311]   John chats about bagism, Billy Preston joining the Beatles and plays
        riffs from:
    Get Back (Lennon-McCartney) (0:34)
    (I Can't Get No) Satisfaction (Jagger-Richards) (0:28)
        and others
[312]   more chat and more playing
    For You Blue/Ob-La-Di, Ob-La-Da (Harrison/Lennon-McCartney) (0:47)
        instrumental/vocals: Paul
    Get Back (Lennon-McCartney) (1:37)
        "get back to where your mama is" version (excerpts)
    chat about the **GET BACK** book
    Soldier Of Love (Cason-Moon) (0:31)
        vocals: John, Paul
    Soldier Of Love/Cathy's Clown (Cason-Moon/Everly-Everly) (0:40)
        vocals: John, Paul, George
[314]   **Where Have You Been All My Life?** (Weil-Mann) (0:27)
        vocals: John, Paul, George
    Soldier of Love (Cason-Moon) (0:07)
        vocals: Paul
    Love Is A Swingin' Thing (Dixon-Owens-Denson) (0:46)
        vocals: George, John, Paul
    Child Of Nature (Lennon) (1:42)
    Two Of Us (Lennon-McCartney) (2:53)
        rehearsing "being loose"
Side D [duplicates **GET BACK JOURNALS**, Side B]
    Get Back (Lennon-McCartney) (2:00)
        fast version, John shares lead vocals
    Don't Let Me Down (Lennon-McCartney) (3:07)
        with Leslied guitar
[176]   **Two Of Us** (Lennon-McCartney) (2:01)
        excerpt
    chat and tea
    Baa Baa Black Sheep (trad.) (0:17)
        vocals: John
    chat and riffs
[177]   **Don't Let Me Down** (Lennon-McCartney) (3:10)
        screaming version
    Suzy Parker (Lennon-McCartney-Harrison-Starkey) (1:52)
        the usual version
    I've Got A Feeling (Lennon-McCartney) (3:48)
        "facelift" version
    Get Back (Lennon-McCartney) (3:40)
        "No Pakistanis" version

SOURCE:
    GET BACK sessions, Jan 69.

SOUND QUALITY:
    Very good to excellent mono.

COMMENTS:
    More reissues of the **GET BACK JOURNALS** box.

GRAVE POSTS
THE BEATLES
"Apple Records," SAPCOR NZ 1964
2-disc set in full color jacket, with song listing on the back, says "Made In New Zealand;" labels say "Rubber Soul" and have song titles.

DISC ONE
Side A [duplicates **GET BACK JOURNALS**, Side M]
    Take This Hammer (trad.) (2:50)
        vocals: John
  riffs
    Johnny B. Goode (Berry) (1:42)
        vocals: John (excerpt)
  Paul discusses promoting Mary Hopkin's album with Derek Taylor
  Drum solo (Paul) (0:26)
    I Shall Be Released (Dylan) (1:20)
        faint vocals (excerpts)
  jam (1:11)
    I've Got A Feeling (Lennon-McCartney) (13:04)
        extended rehearsal, lots of riffs and chat, including:
        country guitar
        "soft drink" version
        "I had a dream" version
        chat about Martin Luther King, Jr.
        "Our last single"
Side B [duplicates **GET BACK JOURNALS**, Side N]
  chat
  John reads a newspaper report about George and the band jams.
        includes: I've Got My Blue Fingers (improvisation?) (0:05)
            vocals: John
    Every Night (McCartney) (1:12)
        early rehearsal
    Dig A Pony/Watch Your Step (Lennon-McCartney/Parker-Belmonte) (2:59)
        playback? "skylight" version (excerpt) with false start
    New Orleans (Guida-Royster) (2:33)
        vocals: John, Paul, George
  Madman (Lennon) (1:55)
        rehearsal, full band
    Dig A Pony (Lennon-McCartney) (1:03)
        "fine line" version (excerpt)
    Hi Heel Sneakers (Higginbottom) (1:53)
        vocals: John
    Milk Cow Blues (Arnold) (0:41)
        vocals: John (excerpt)
    Bring It To Jerome (Green) (0:03)
        vocals: John (excerpt)
  chat and half a million quid
[263] **Little Queenie** (Berry) (0:55)
        vocals: John, with false start
  tuning
    When Irish Eyes Are Smiling (Olcott-Graff-Ball) (0:16)
        vocals: John
  more tuning & chat
    Queen Of The Hop (Harris) (0:37)
        vocals: Paul, John (excerpt)
  chat and riffs
DISC TWO
Side C [duplicates **GET BACK JOURNALS**, Side S]
  George chats about John's 1969 diary (for *Aspen* magazine), watching tv, and the inspiration for his new song.

I Me Mine (Harrison) (1:00)
    (excerpts)
George and Ringo talk about watching tv and Hamburg. George plays his new song for Paul.
I Me Mine (Harrison) (1:34)
George worries about grammar.
Let It Be (Lennon-McCartney) (0:47)
    playback
Maybe I'm Amazed/That Would Be Something (McCartney) (2:16)
    Paul working through some riffs on guitar
Discussion about the difficulties of playing live in Arabia, scheduling
[167]   the sunrise, looking nice, good vibes, a boat full of Beatlemaniacs, and bedtime.
Don't Let Me Down (Lennon-McCartney) (0:10)
Get Back (Lennon-McCartney) (0:45)
    jam
Side D [duplicates **GET BACK JOURNALS**, Side T]
[319] **Teddy Boy** (McCartney) (15:13)
[318]   24 Jan 69, Apple; extended rehearsal, with chord changes
        includes the usual usual version and
        The Ball Of Inverary (trad.) (0:05)
        Ach Du Lieber (trad.) (0:04)
           as "Balls For Mr. Benglestein"
chat
Two Of Us (Lennon-McCartney) (0:08) (excerpt)
chat
Two Of Us (Lennon-McCartney) (0:40) (Paul solo)
lunch & riffs
Polythene Pam (Lennon-McCartney) (1:32)
    rehearsal; vocals: John, Paul
[320] jam (0:55)
Two Of Us (Lennon-McCartney) (0:22)
    (excerpts)
Maggie Mae (trad.) (0:34)
    24 Jan 69, Apple; the usual version
Teddy Boy (McCartney) (1:31)
    playback of earlier rehearsal (excerpts)

SOURCE:
    GET BACK sessions, Jan 69. Some cuts on Side T are from 24 Jan 69, Apple, but given the nature of **GET BACK** tapes, it is probably too much to say that all of Side T is from the same day (although it may be).

SOUND QUALITY:
    Very good to excellent mono.

COMMENTS:
    Merely a copy of two discs of the **GET BACK JOURNALS**.

GREAT TO HAVE YOU WITH US
THE BEATLES
No manufacturer listed [Maidenhead Records], MHR-JET-909-3
2-disc set in 2-color jacket, says "Made In France," with track listing and recording information on the back; labels say "Jet IV" and "Jet V."

DISC ONE
Side A

    No Values (McCartney) (4:59)

        from the soundtrack of the film, *Give My Regards To Broad Street*

        excellent mono

The following cuts are from a 14 Oct 84 *South Bank* tv show documenting *The Making Of Give My Regards To Broad Street*. It was shown in the US as part of the *Film On Film* series on PBS (date unknown). Very good mono

        Broad Street music (McCartney) (2:07)

            Paul and George Martin try out some chords and effects

        For No One (Lennon-McCartney) (1:58)

        acoustic run-through

        Corridor Music (McCartney) (0:57)

    from the **GIVE MY REGARDS TO BROAD STREET** C D

        excellent stereo

        So Bad (McCartney) (3:16)

        Goodnight Lonely Princess (McCartney) (3:50)

    Thingumybob (Lennon-McCartney) (1:42)

        John Foster & Son Ltd. Black Dyke Mills Band

        30 Jun 68, from (US 45) Apple 1800; excellent mono

Side B

    Bel Air mansion interview (2:02)

        23-25 Aug 64, Los Angeles (?)

        John and Paul at the piano; they talk about songwriting, how they met, and their future. Source unknown, but this has the sound of an open-end interview.

        excellent mono, recorded off disc

    Fab Four On Film (6:00)

        from 82 Capitol promo P-B-5100 (interview recorded Apr 64?)

        excellent mono, recorded off disc

    The Beatles Open-End Interview (2:50)

        from Capitol promo PRO 2459 (Feb 64)

64, from Capitol promo PRO 2720; excellent mono

        John's intro for Cilla Black (0:33)

        Paul's intro for Peter and Gordon (0:27)

    KFWBeatles (1:35)

        a copy of Capitol Custom RB-2637, released on 5 Jun 64 in Los Angeles by KFWB and includes:

        KFWB music spot #1

            to the tune of **She Loves You**; very good mono

            no Beatles involvement

        greetings

            to Wink Martindale & Jolly Joe Yoakum; very good mono

            the poor editing may be present on the original

        KFWB music spot #2

            to the tune of **It Won't Be Long**; very good mono

            no Beatles involvement

    The Beatles Decade (0:58)

        74 radio spot, long version; excellent stereo

    The Beatles Decade (0:31)

        74 radio spot, short version; excellent stereo

    Interview (2:34)

        16 Jul 64, *Top Gear*; excellent mono

        excerpts from the **TOP OF THE POPS** (EP)

Dialogue from the film *Let It Be* (4:11)
 from an Apple promo 45? excellent mono
 Jan 69, **GET BACK** sessions includes
  chat about early songwriting, with
   Just Fun (Lennon-McCartney)\ (0:09)
   One After 909 (Lennon-McCartney) (0:09)
  Paul talks to John about films, audiences and nerves
   Da-Doo-Run-Run (Spector-Greenwich-Barry) (0:04)
  Maharishi memories

DISC TWO
Side C

I Lost My Little Girl (McCartney) (0:25)
 filmed Oct 77, EMI; broadcast 14 Jan 78, *South Bank Show*
 Paul talks about his first song and plays a short version
 from the Melvin Bragg interview; very good mono
I Lost My Little Girl (McCartney) (0:06)
 possibly 9 Jun 84, *Aspel And Company*
 excellent mono; source unknown
excerpts from the Melvin Bragg interview (2:40)
 very good mono
 filmed Oct 77, EMI; broadcast 14 Jan 78, *South Bank Show*
  Lucille (Collins-Penniman) unknown Wings rehearsal
  Too Bad About Sorrows (Lennon-McCartney)
  Melvin Bragg (improvisation)
  Mull Of Kintyre (McCartney-Laine)
That'll Be The Day (Allison-Holly-Petty) (1:51)
 9 Jun 84, *Aspel And Company* (UK tv);Paul, with Tracey Ullman
 This is more complete than the version on **BOTH SIDES**
30 Jan 82, excerpts from *Desert Island Discs* (3:02)
 very good mono; Paul talks about and sings along with
  Searchin' (Leiber-Stoller) The Coasters
  Beautiful Boy (Darling Boy) (Lennon) John Lennon
tv spot for **McCARTNEY II** (0:25)
 source unknown; very good mono
tv spot for **WINGS' GREATEST** (0:18)
 source unknown; some original material; good to very good mono
from a promo film for Warner Brothers staff (0:57)
 George thanks WEA salespeople and sings
  Go Your Own Way (Buckingham)
  very good mono
Dark Horse (Harrison) (1:47)
 from video clip; source of performance unknown (74)
radio spot for *Concert For Bangla Desh* (film) (0:53)
 good to very good mono
radio spot for **BAND ON THE RUN** (0:59)
 Dec 73; good to very good mono
17 Jun 64, Festival Hall, Melbourne, Australia (7:30)
 jacket says Sydney, Australia; this tape has been edited to eliminate the Melbourne reference
 a line recording, good to very good mono
  I Saw Her Standing There (McCartney-Lennon)
  greetings
  All My Loving (Lennon-McCartney)
  Can't Buy Me Love (Lennon-McCartney)

Side D
Too Many Cooks (Holland-Dozier-Holland?) (3:27)
    Mar 74? L.A., Record Plant West
    Recording produced by John, with Mick Jagger doing the vocals. Musicians
        included Jack Bruce on bass, Harry Nilsson on backing vocals, Jim
        Keltner on drums, and some of the Hollywood Horns. John played
        this on the radio in Sep 74 in an interview with Tom Donohue on
        KSAN, and that broadcast may be the source of the tape; excellent
        mono
God Bless California (Fradkin) (3:29)
    Thornton, Fradkin, & Unger and The Big Band, with Paul on bass and backing
        vocals; excellent stereo
    Jan 71, from Esp-Disc ESP 45-63019 (released Jun 74)
Dance The Do (McCartney-McGear) (2:51)
    Mike McGear; from UK 45 Warner BrothersS K 16573
    Jan-May 74? excellent stereo
Ten Years After On Strawberry Jam (P. McCartney-L. McCartney) (2:47)
    Scaffold; from UK 45 Warner Brothers K 16400
    Jan-May 74? excellent stereo
What Do We Really Know? (McCartney) (1:10)
    Mike McGear, from UK LP Warner Brothers K 56051
    Jan-May 74; excellent stereo (excerpt)
Givin' Grease A Ride (McCartney-McGear) (1:41)
    Mike McGear, from UK LP Warner Brothers K 56051
    Jan-May 74; excellent stereo (excerpt)
The Holdup (Harrison-Bromberg) (2:52)
    David Bromberg; from US LP Columbia C31104
    72; excellent stereo
Let's Love (McCartney) (2:45)
    Peggy Lee, from US LP Atlantic SD 18108
    mid-Jun 74; excellent mono
guitar solos (1:48)
    a collection of George's guitar solos for other artists
    excellent stereo, but did we really need this?

SOURCE:
    Varied; see individual entries.

SOUND QUALITY:
    Varied; see individual entries.

COMMENTS:
    This set collects a lot of older 45s (boot and legitimate) together in one place, but to
very little effect.

HEADLINES
THE BEATLES
Rock Solid Records, RSR-1001
2-disc set in full color jacket, with song titles on the back; label info matches; limited to 1000
copies?

DISC ONE
Side A
The Walk (McCracklin-Gorlic) (0:54)
    27 Jan 69, Apple; the usual version; very good stereo
Teddy Boy (McCartney) (5:45)
    24 Jan 69, Apple; excellent stereo
    the usual version

Two Of Us (Lennon-McCartney) (3:40)
    24 Jan 69, Apple; excellent stereo
    "good-bye" version, with two false starts
I've Got A Feeling (Lennon-McCartney) (2:44)
    24 Jan 69, Apple; "on your what?" version; excellent stereo
The Long And Winding Road (Lennon-McCartney) (3:36)
    31 Jan 69, Apple; take 19; very good stereo
For You Blue (Harrison) (2:30)
    25 Jan 69, Apple; with false start and laughing; excellent stereo
Dig A Pony (Lennon-McCartney) (3:36)
    24 Jan 69, Apple; laughing version; excellent stereo

Side B

Across The Universe (Lennon-McCartney) (3:40)
    4/8 Feb 68 & 2 Oct 69 EMI; take 8 (WWF version)
    excellent stereo, from the LP
The Inner Light (Harrison) (2:30)
    12 Jan 68, Bombay & 6/8 Feb 68, EMI; take 6
    excellent mono, from the 45
Let It Be (Lennon-McCartney) (3:46)
    31 Jan 69, Apple & 30 Apr 69/4 Jan 70, EMI; take 30
    excellent stereo, from the 45
Don't Let Me Down (Lennon-McCartney) (3:30)
    28 Jan 69, Apple; excellent stereo, from the 45
Get Back (Lennon-McCartney) (3:07)
    28 Jan 69, Apple; excellent stereo, from the 45
I'm Down (Lennon-McCartney) (2:30)
    14 Jun 65, EMI; take 7; excellent mono, from the 45
Instant Karma! (Lennon) (3:13)
    27 Jan 70, Apple? excellent stereo, from the 45

DISC TWO
Side C

Honey Pie (Lennon-McCartney) (2:32)
    1/2/4 Oct 68, Trident (the commercial version); good mono
    outfake of somebody singing along with the record
Jan 69, **GET BACK** sessions; very good to excellent mono
    Get Back (Lennon-McCartney) (1:54)
        fast version, John shares lead vocals
    Tennessee (Perkins) (1:55)
    Across The Universe (Lennon-McCartney) (0:10)
        the last version
chat
    House Of The Rising Sun (trad.) (2:27)
chat & riffs
    Commonwealth (improvisation) (3:20)
    Enoch Powell (improvisation) (0:20)
    White Power (Get Off!) (improvisation) (6:04)
        includes:
        Why Don't We Do It In The Road (Lennon-McCartney) (0:03)
            as "Why Don't You Put It On The Toast"
    Honey Hush (Turner) (2:03)

Side D

A Day In The Life (Lennon-McCartney) (4:10)
    19/20 Jan 67, EMI; take 6; very good stereo?
    from acetate; no orchestra & alternate vocals for Paul
Strawberry Fields Forever (Lennon-McCartney) (2:27)
    24 Nov 66, EMI; take 1; excellent stereo
Strawberry Fields Forever (Lennon-McCartney) (2:58)
    28 Nov 66, EMI; takes 3 (false start) & 4; excellent stereo

Strawberry Fields Forever (Lennon-McCartney) (3:15)
  15 Dec 66, EMI; overdub onto take 25; excellent stereo
  George Martin conducts his score
Strawberry Fields Forever (Lennon-McCartney) (3:11)
  8/9/15/21 Dec 66, EMI; take 26; excellent stereo
A Day In The Life (Lennon-McCartney) (4:56)
  19/20 Jan & 3/10/22 Feb 67, EMI; edit of takes 6 & 7
  commercial version with clean intro; excellent stereo

SOURCE:
  Varies; see individual entries.

SOUND QUALITY:
  Varies; see individual entries.

COMMENTS:
  DISC ONE is a reissue of **RENAISSANCE MINSTRELS VOL. II**. Side C is lifted mostly from **THE BLACK ALBUM**. Very boring stuff, this—just another chance for the RSR people to stick their hands in your pockets.

HEY JULIAN
THE BEATLES
"Apple Records," SAPCOR 41
2-disc set in full color jacket with track listing on the back; labels say "Rubber Soul" and have song titles.

DISC ONE
Side A
  4 Sep 68, Twickenham (8:01)
    filmed for *Frost On Sunday* (broadcast 8 Sep 68).
    good to very good mono
    The David Frost Theme (Martin) (0:20)
      Often referred to as "A Perfect Rendition"
    It's Now Or Never (DiCapua-Gold-Schroeder) (0:06)
    Hey Jude (Lennon-McCartney) (7:13)
      The video performance consists of new vocals (4 Sep 68, Twickenham) performed to pre-recorded backing tracks (for the commercial version: 31 Jul & 1 Aug 68, Trident; take 1).
    Revolution (Lennon-McCartney) (3:26)
      The video performance consists of new vocals (4 Sep 68, Twickenham) performed to pre-recorded backing tracks (10/11/12 Jul 68, EMI; take 16). This was done because of strict Musician's Union rules about miming.
      broadcast 19 Sep 68, *Top Of The Pops*; good to very good mono
    Paperback Writer (Lennon-McCartney) (2:23)
      13/14 Apr 66, EMI; take 2; excellent stereo; no echo mix
      with added countdown from **We Can Work It Out** (from *SPLHCB: A History Of The Beatle Years*)
    Come And Get It (McCartney) (2:32)
      24 Jul 69, EMI; take 1; Paul's demo; excellent stereo
    Don't Let Me Down (Lennon-McCartney) (3:06)
      Jan 69, **GET BACK** sessions
    Suicide (McCartney) (1:29)
      Fall 75? *One Hand Clapping* sessions
Side B
    The Beatles' Seventh Christmas Record (7:39)
      Nov 69?

All Together On The Wireless Machine (McCartney?) (0:59)
>> unknown; possibly Fall (Dec?) 67, Paul with Kenny Everett
>> good mono

Step Inside Love (McCartney) (2:21)
>> Feb 68, Dick James? demo for Cilla Black? poor to fair mono
>> > from a British radio broadcast (source unknown, but possibly Kenny Everett)

Thank You Guru Dev/**Happy Birthday To You** (McCartney-?/Hill-Hill) (2:41)
>> 15 Mar 68, Rishikesh, India, with the Beach Boys
>> With Wolfman Jack's voice-over

Lady Madonna (Lennon-McCartney) (2:11)
>> 3/6 Feb 68, EMI; take 4; very good stereo
>> the basic track (take 3) was recorded on 3 Feb; the backing vocals, handclaps and a second lead vocal were added on 6 Feb, as were the brass overdubs; this take would appear to be from this 6 Feb overdubbing session, prior to the addition of the brass.
>> off speakers, from *The Beatles Live At Abbey Road*

Peace Of Mind (?) (3:15)
>> unknown; allegedly Jun 67; probably no Beatles involvement

DISC TWO
Side C
>> *Ringo's Yellow Submarine* (21:33)
>> Jun-Dec 83, ABC FM network; excerpts (part 5)
>> very good to excellent stereo (some hiss, static and fading)

Side D
>> *Ringo's Yellow Submarine* (22:21)
>> Jun-Dec 83, ABC FM network; excerpts (part 6)
>> very good to excellent stereo (some hiss, static and fading)

SOURCE:
>> Varies; see individual entries.

SOUND QUALITY:
>> Very good to excellent mono, unless otherwise noted.

COMMENTS:
>> By far the most valuable pieces here are the excerpts from *Ringo's Yellow Submarine*. On Side C he has some advice about signing contracts, and on Side D he demonstrates the problems of a left-handed drummer. Interesting stuff. Parts 1-4 are on **MELLOW YELLOW** (SAPCOR 39).

HI HO SILVER! (SUPER STUDIO SERIES 1)
THE BEATLES
King Kong Records, 4438, GT-8410
Insert cover with song titles.

Side A
>> **Get Back** (Lennon-McCartney) (1:57)
>> > fast version, John shares vocals
>> **Tennessee** (Perkins) (1:43)
>> > vocals: John, Paul, George
>> **House Of The Rising Sun** (trad.) (2:28)
>> > vocals: John, Paul
>> Commonwealth (improvisation) (3:27)
>> > vocals: Paul, John
>> Enoch Powell (improvisation) (0:22)
>> > vocals: Paul
>> White Power (Get Off!) (improvisation) (2:21)
>> > vocals: Paul, John (excerpt)

I Threw It All Away/Mama You Been On My Mind (Dylan) (2:52)
George, solo acoustic
Across The Universe (Lennon-McCartney) (3:30)

Side B
Honey Hush (Turner) (2:04)
vocals: John, Paul, George
Suzy Parker (Lennon-McCartney-Harrison-Starkey) (1:52)
the usual version
Get Back (Lennon-McCartney) (3:42)
"No Pakistanis" version

[177] **Don't Let Me Down** (Lennon-McCartney) (3:07)
I've Got A Feeling (Lennon-McCartney) (3:45)
For You Blue (Harrison) (1:48)
all-electric version
Move It/Good Rocking' Tonight (Samwell/Brown) (1:33)
vocals: John
Two Of Us (Lennon-McCartney) (1:50)
Let It Be (Lennon-McCartney) (2:40)
Record Mirror version

SOURCE:
Jan 69, **GET BACK** sessions.

SOUND QUALITY:
Very good to excellent mono.

COMMENTS:
These are basically excerpts from the first disc of **THE BLACK ALBUM**.

HOMOGENIZED BEATLES
THE BEATLES
Avocado Records, 2812
Plain white jacket; sticker has song titles; labels are generic TMOQ.

Side A
The Walk (McCracklin-Gorlic) (0:53)
27 Jan 69, Apple; the usual version
Teddy Boy (McCartney) (5:35)
24 Jan 69, Apple; the usual version
Two Of Us (Lennon-McCartney) (3:38)
24 Jan 69, Apple; "good-bye" version with two false starts
I've Got A Feeling (Lennon-McCartney) (2:46)
24 Jan 69, Apple; "on your what?" version
The Long And Winding Road (Lennon-McCartney) (3:33)
31 Jan 69, Apple; & 30 Apr 69, EMI; take 19; very good stereo
this is the basic version of that which would later appear on **LET IT BE**
For You Blue (Harrison) (2:26)
25 Jan 69, Apple; with two false starts and laugh (edited)
chat
Dig A Pony (Lennon-McCartney) (3:32)
24 Jan 69, Apple; laughing version, with one false start

Side B
Across The Universe (Lennon-McCartney) (3:38)
4/8 Feb 68 & 2 Oct 69 EMI; take 8 (WWF version)
from the LP
The Inner Light (Harrison) (2:29)
12 Jan 68, Bombay & 6/8 Feb 68, EMI; take 6
excellent mono, from the 45

Let It Be (Lennon-McCartney) (3:44)
    31 Jan 69, Apple & 30 Apr 69/4 Jan 70, EMI; take 30
    from the 45
Don't Let Me Down (Lennon-McCartney) (3:28)
    28 Jan 69, Apple; from the 45
Get Back (Lennon-McCartney) (3:06)
    28 Jan 69, Apple; from the 45
I'm Down (Lennon-McCartney) (2:28)
    14 Jun 65, EMI; take 7; excellent mono, from the 45
Instant Karma! (Lennon) (3:10)
    27 Jan 70, Apple? from the 45

SOURCE:
    Side A Jan 69, **GET BACK** sessions (excerpted from early **GET BACK** bootlegs).
Side B varies; see individual entries.

SOUND QUALITY:
    Excellent stereo, except as noted.

COMMENTS:
    This material was more commonly available as (and is identical to) **RENAISSANCE MINSTRELS VOL. II**. Most of the cuts on Side A are from the **GET BACK** acetate (or tape) which produced **GET BACK TO TORONTO**, **KUM BACK** and others, and prove to be the same versions as on the cancelled **GET BACK** LP, but with clean intro's. Side B is essentially (pre-**PAST MASTERS**) uncollected songs.

HOUND DOG/LONG TALL SALLY
JOHN LENNON /PAUL McCARTNEY & WINGS
Heavy Records, HVY-101
7-inch 45 in black & white picture sleeve, with song titles; labels match and have recording dates.

Side A
    Hound Dog (Leiber-Stoller) (2:55)
        John Lennon & Elephants Memory Band
        30 Aug 72, Madison Square Garden, evening show
        a line recording, very good mono
Side B
    Long Tall Sally (Johnson-Penniman-Blackwell) (2:18)
        Paul McCartney & Wings, from *James Paul McCartney*
        filmed 18 Mar 73, at Borehamwood Studio; broadcast 16 Apr 63
        a line recording, good to very good mono

SOURCE:
    Varied; see individual entries.

SOUND QUALITY:
    Varied; see individual entries.

COMMENTS:
    A cute concept, but the material is of little interest today.

IT'S ALL TOO MUCH
THE BEATLES
No manufacturer listed, B-6
Full color jacket says ©1985 and "made in Belgium" (sorry, neither), with song titles and recording information on the back; label info matches.

Side A
>Hospital announcement of John's death (0:24)
>"I Sat Belonely" (0:43)
>>Apr 64? John reads his poem
>>from **As It Happened**, Murray The K's fan club disc
>**Love Of The Loved** (Lennon-McCartney) (1:44)
>>1 Jan 62, Decca audition; distorted
>**Some Other Guy** (Leiber-Stoller-Barrett) (1:51)
>>22 Aug 62, Cavern Club (film); fair to good mono
>**How Do You Do It** (Murray-Edmond) (1:54)
>>4 Sep 62, EMI; take 2; distorted
>**I'll Be On My Way** (Lennon-McCartney) (2:00)
>>24 Jun 63, BBC
>**One After 909** (Lennon-McCartney) (2:43)
>>5 Mar 63, EMI; unknown take; distorted
>**Bad To Me** (Lennon-McCartney) (1:23)
>>Feb 63? Dick James; demo acetate, distorted
>**Leave My Kitten Alone** (Turner-McDougall) (2:41)
>>14 Aug 64, EMI; take 5; distorted
>**That Means A Lot** (Lennon-McCartney) (2:01)
>>20 Feb 65, EMI; take 2; distorted
>**If You've Got Trouble** (Lennon-McCartney) (1:43)
>>18 Feb 65, EMI; take 1; distorted
>**It's All Too Much** (Harrison) (2:33)
>>25/26 May & 2 Jun 67, De Lane Lea; take 32 (mono remix #1)
>>with extra verse, from the *Yellow Submarine* soundtrack
>>fair to good mono
>"The Fat Budgie" (0:17)
>>3 Jul 65, BBC; *The World Of Books*; John reads his poem
>>Spliced onto the end of this poem is a brief segment of an interview from *Top Gear* (BBC 26 Nov 64) which does not belong there; in addition, **In My Life** runs underneath it. This indicates that the source of this tape is the 72 BBC special, *The Beatles Story*.
>Paul talks to John about films, audiences and nerves (1:46)
>>Jan 69, **GET BACK** sessions; dialogue from *Let It Be*

Side B
>**Revolution** (Lennon-McCartney) (3:24)
>>The video performance consists of new vocals (4 Sep 68, Twickenham) performed to pre-recorded backing tracks (10/11/12 Jul 68, EMI; take 16). This was done because of strict Musician's Union rules about miming.
>>broadcast *Top Of The Pops*, 19 Sep 68; distorted
>**What's The New Mary Jane** (Lennon) (6:33)
>>14 Aug 68/26 Nov 69, EMI; take 4 (stereo remix #5)
>>very good stereo
>22 Jan 69, Apple, from the original **GET BACK** LP (1:46)
>>**Rocker** (McCartney)
>>>aka "Link Track" and "Instrumental 42"
>>**Save The Last Dance For Me/Don't Let Me Down**
>>(Pomus-Schuman/Lennon-McCartney)
>>excellent stereo
>**Don't Let Me Down** (Lennon-McCartney) (3:02)
>>Jan 69, **GET BACK** sessions; version with Leslied guitar
>**Something** (Harrison) (5:22)
>>11 Jul 69, EMI; take 37, extended
>>This is a tape reduction of take 36, the basic take of the commercial version; it was intended (but never used) for overdubs.
>**Goodbye** (Lennon-McCartney) (2:01)
>>late 68, Dick James; demo acetate

Her Majesty (Lennon-McCartney) (0:22)
>> 2 Jul 69, EMI; take 3, with the final chord

"The National Health Cow" (0:38)
>> 65, BBC (original date unknown); John reads his poem
>> this poem also apparently from *The Beatles Story*

Ringo says, "What's happening, baby?" (0:05)
>> source unknown (**As It Happened** w/ Murray The K?)

Paul doesn't annoy George (1:42)
>> dialogue, Jan 69, **GET BACK** sessions; from *Let It Be*

SOURCE:
>> Varied; see individual entries.

SOUND QUALITY:
>> Very good to excellent mono, unless stated otherwise. A number of cuts are badly distorted.

COMMENTS:
>> Nothing important and new here, except the announcement of John's death, and only a moron would want to hear that more than once. A waste of vinyl.

JOSHUA TREE TAPES
JOHN LENNON
Kornyfone/TAKRL, TKRWM 1803
Insert cover with song listing; labels are "World," with incorrect titles.

Side A
Imagine (Lennon) (3:20)
>> 14-18 Feb 72, *The Mike Douglas Show*

30 Aug 72, MSG, evening concert (17:21)
>> **Mother** (Lennon)
>> **Come Together** (Lennon-McCartney)
>> **Give Peace A Chance** (Lennon-McCartney)

outro (0:03)
>> 14-18 Feb 72, *The Mike Douglas Show*

Side B
Yer Blues (Lennon-McCartney) (8:18)
>> 11 Dec 68, *Rock And Roll Circus*

13 Jan 72, live on *The David Frost Show*
>> **John Sinclair** (Lennon) (2:23)
>> **It's So Hard** (Lennon) (1:59)
>> **The Luck Of The Irish** (Lennon-Ono) (2:49)
>>> This cut is notable because the "God"s have been blipped out of the "God damn"s

11 May 72, live on *The Dick Cavett Show*
>> **Woman Is The Nigger Of The World** (Lennon-Ono) (5:08)

16 Feb 72, live on *The Mike Douglas Show*
>> **Johnny B. Goode** (Berry) (2:57)

SOURCE:
>> Varies; see individual entries.

SOUND QUALITY:
>> Excellent mono.

COMMENTS:
>> Except for the edited **The Luck Of The Irish**, there is nothing here of interest.

JUDY
THE BEATLES
Kustom Rekord, ASC-003
Printed jacket, black on yellow, with paraphrased song listing; labels match.

Side A
Hey Jude (Lennon-McCartney) (7:02)
31 Jul/1 Aug 68, Trident; take 1
Lady Madonna (Lennon-McCartney) (2:13)
3/6 Feb 68, EMI; take 5
The Ballad Of John And Yoko (Lennon-McCartney) (2:54)
14 Apr 69, EMI; take 10
Rain (Lennon-McCartney) (2:55)
14/16 Apr 66, EMI; take 7
Old Brown Shoe (Harrison) (3:15)
16/18 Apr 69, EMI; take 4
This Boy (Lennon-McCartney) (2:10)
17 Oct 63, EMI; take 15
Side B
All You Need Is Love (Lennon-McCartney) (3:41)
14 Jun 67, Olympic, & 19/23/24/25 Jun 67, EMI; take 58
The Inner Light (Harrison) (2:29)
12 Jan, Bombay & 6/8 Feb 68, EMI; take 6
Baby You're A Rich Man (Lennon-McCartney) (2:59)
11 May 67, Olympic; take 2
I'm Down (Lennon-McCartney) (2:31)
14 Jun 65, EMI; take 7
Penny Lane (Lennon-McCartney) (2:56)
29/30 Dec 66 & 4/5/6/9/10/12/17 Jan 67; take 9
Strawberry Fields Forever (Lennon-McCartney) (4:05)
24/28/29 Nov & 8/9/15/21 Dec 66; edit of takes 7 & 26

SOURCE:
Commercial cuts, copied from 45s.

SOUND QUALITY:
Very good to excellent mono (jacket says "stereo").

COMMENTS:
Technically, this is a pirate an not a bootleg. I have included it because it's rare and the paraphrased song titles might mislead.

A KNIGHT'S HARD DAY
THE BEATLES
"Apple Records," SAPCOR 31
2-disc set in 3-color jacket, with track listing on the back; labels say "Rubber Soul" and have titles.

DISC ONE
Side A
A Hard Day's Night (Lennon-McCartney) (2:28)
16 Jul 64, BBC
The guitar solo, which was the commercial version dubbed into the radio take, has been replaced here by the version from the 17 Jul 64 BBC session for 3 Aug 64. The result is absolutely terrible.
I Should Have Known Better (Lennon-McCartney) (3:06)
17 Jul 64; session for BBC 3 Aug 64 (with false start)
good to very good mono

If I Fell (Lennon-McCartney) (2:13)
    17 Jul 64; session for BBC 3 Aug 64
    good to very good mono
I'm Happy Just To Dance With You (Lennon-McCartney) (2:03)
    17 Jul 64; session for BBC 3 Aug 64
    good to very good mono
And I Love Her (Lennon-McCartney) (2:24)
    16 Jul 64, BBC
Things We Said Today (Lennon-McCartney) (2:20)
    16 Jul 64, BBC
Can't Buy Me Love (Lennon-McCartney) (2:10)
    30 Mar 64, BBC

Side B

From Me To You (McCartney-Lennon) (1:49)
    17 Sep 63, BBC
She Loves You (Lennon-McCartney) (2:10)
    10 Sep 63, BBC
I'll Get You (Lennon-McCartney) (2:01)
    10 Sep 63, BBC
I Want To Hold Your Hand (Lennon-McCartney) (2:19)
    19 Jan 64, Paris Olympia
This Boy (Lennon-McCartney) (2:12)
    21 Dec 63, BBC
Bad To Me (Lennon-McCartney) (1:30)
    Feb 63? Dick James; demo acetate
You Can't Do That (Lennon-McCartney) (2:24)
    23 Aug 64, Hollywood Bowl

DISC TWO

Side C

Sweet Little Sixteen (Berry) (2:23)
    23 Jul 63, BBC
That's All Right Mama (Crudup) (2:56)
    16 Jul 63, BBC
To Know Her Is To Love Her (Spector) (2:49)
    6 Aug 63, BBC
Too Much Monkey Business (Berry) (2:06)
    24 Jun 63, BBC
Young Blood (Leiber-Stoller-Pomus) (1:54)
    11 Jun 63, BBC
The Honeymoon Song (Theodorakis) (1:42)
    6 Aug 63, BBC
Lucille (Collins-Penniman) (2:26)
    17 Sep 63, BBC

Side D

Another Beatles Christmas Record (3:52)
    26 Oct 64, EMI
Beatleviews (22:19)
    interviews with Bob Rogers
    from the 64 New Zealand/Australia tour

SOURCE:
    Varies; see individual entries.

SOUND QUALITY:
    Very good to excellent mono, except as noted.

COMMENTS:
    As with most of the records in this series, there is nothing here of importance.

LASER BEAMS
PAUL McCARTNEY & WINGS
Wizardo, WRMB 382
Insert cover with song titles; labels are generic Wizardo reissue.

Side A (22:16)
> **Live And Let Die** (McCartney)
> **Picasso's Last Words** (McCartney)
> **Richard Corey** (Simon)
> **Bluebird** (McCartney)
> **I've Just Seen A Face** (Lennon-McCartney)
> **Blackbird** (Lennon-McCartney)
> **The Star-Spangled Banner** (trad. arr. Key)
> > brief, joke intro to:
> **Yesterday** (Lennon-McCartney)

Side B (23:24)
> **Magneto And Titanium Man** (McCartney)
> **Go Now** (Banks-Bennett)
> **Band On The Run** (McCartney)
> **Hi, Hi, Hi** (McCartney)
> **Soily** (McCartney)

SOURCE:
> 23 Jun 76, L.A. Forum.

SOUND QUALITY:
> Audience tape, very good to excellent mono; the tape has been carefully edited.

COMMENTS:
> A good show; the audience is rowdy (in his between-song chat before the acoustic set, Paul asks if anyone in the audience knows what a rhythm box is. "Your wife!" someone shouts) and the band was tight.

THE LAST ALBUM
THE BEATLES
No manufacturer listed, 01971
Insert cover with track listing; labels are blank.

Side A
> **People Say** (Szigeti-Lichterman) (2:38)
> > "John & Paul," 65, from US 45 Tip 1021
> > good mono; no Beatles involvement
> **I'm Walkin'** (Szigeti-Lichterman) (2:08)
> > "John & Paul," 65, from US 45 Tip 1021
> > good mono; no Beatles involvement
> **Hey Jude** (Lennon-McCartney) (7:03)
> > The video performance consists of new vocals (4 Sep 68, Twickenham) performed to pre-recorded backing tracks (for the commercial version: 31 Jul & 1 Aug 68, Trident; take 1). This was done because of strict Musician's Union rules about miming.
> > broadcast 8 Sep 68, *Frost On Sunday*
> **Revolution** (Lennon-McCartney) (3:26)
> > The video performance consists of new vocals (4 Sep 68, Twickenham) performed to pre-recorded backing tracks (10/11/12 Jul 68, EMI; take 16).
> > broadcast 19 Sep 68, *Top Of The Pops*
> **The Beatles' Seventh Christmas Record** (1:13)
> > Nov 69? various (excerpt)

16 Jul 64, *Top Gear* (4:28)
>[*Top Of The Pops* intro]
>**Long Tall Sally** (Johnson-Penniman-Blackwell)

Side B

16 Jul 64, *Top Gear* (continued) (5:42)
>interview
>**A Hard Day's Night** (Lennon-McCartney)
>**Things We Said Today** (Lennon-McCartney)
>[*Top Of The Pops* closing]
>>excellent mono

Shout! (Isley-Isley-Isley) (0:41)
>6 May 64, *Around The Beatles* (excerpt)
>from **As It Happened**, with "Murray The K's" voice-over

Pantomime: Everywhere It's Christmas (2:56)
>aka **The Beatles' Fourth Christmas Record**
>25 Nov 66, Dick James (excerpt)

Christmas Time (Is Here Again) (1:49)
>aka **The Beatles' Fifth Christmas Record**
>28 Nov 67, EMI (excerpt)

Sie Liebt Dich (Lennon-McCartney) (2:14)
>29 Jan 64, Paris; take 14

SOURCE:
>Varies; see individual entries.

SOUND QUALITY:
>Very good mono, unless otherwise stated.

COMMENTS:
>This is very similar to **TOP OF THE POPS** (LP) and exactly the same as **LIVE AT NASSAU COLISSEUM** ("Zapple Records" 999, Contra Band Z999) and **LIVE FROM GERMANY**—peculiar titles for a collection of (mostly) studio material!

LEEDS, ENGLAND
PAUL McCARTNEY & WINGS
King Kong Records, 1050
3-color insert cover with song listing; labels are generic King Kong.

Side A (21:07)
>**Soily** (McCartney)
>**Big Barn Bed** (McCartney)
>**When The Night** (McCartney)
>**Wild Life** (P. McCartney-L. McCartney)
>**Seaside Woman** (L. McCartney)

Side B (24:17)
>**Little Woman Love/C Moon** (P. McCartney-L. McCartney)
>**Live And Let Die** (McCartney)
>**Maybe I'm Amazed** (McCartney)
>**My Love** (McCartney)
>**Go Now** (Banks-Bennett)
>**The Mess** (McCartney)

SOURCE:
>19 May 73, Leeds University

SOUND QUALITY:
>Good to very good audience recording; there are a number of edits in the tape. This is a noisy pressing, with noticeable tape drag (or battery drain) on **The Mess**.

COMMENTS:
        According to Wiener, **Long Tall Sally** and **Say You Don't Mind** (Laine) were also performed. **Say You Don't Mind** can be heard on **LIVE IN HANOVER GERMANY, 1972**, and **PAUL McCARTNEY IN SCOTLAND**. **Hi, Hi, Hi**, listed on the jacket but not present on the record, may also have been performed as it was commonly done during the 73 shows. **Live And Let Die**, reportedly recorded Oct 72, would not be released for another two weeks (1 Jun 73) in the UK, while **Seaside Woman**, possibly written in 70 and recorded in 72, would not see its first release for another four years (US, 31 May 77).

LET IT BE AND 10 OTHER SONGS
THE BEATLES
"Apple Records," 1-33-30
Full color jacket, possibly reproducing an original, unused design, with song titles on the back; labels are blank.

Side A
        Rocker (McCartney) (0:29)
                22 Jan 69, Apple; aka "Link Track" and "Instrumental 42"
        Save The Last Dance For Me/Don't Let Me Down
        (Pomus-Shuman/Lennon-McCartney) (0:49)
                22 Jan 69, Apple
        Don't Let Me Down (Lennon-McCartney) (3:29)
                22 Jan 69, Apple
        Dig A Pony (Lennon-McCartney (3:44)
                24 Jan 69, Apple; laughing version
        I've Got A Feeling (Lennon-McCartney) (2:40)
                24 Jan 69, Apple; cocked-up version
        Get Back (Lennon-McCartney) (3:10)
                28 Jan 69; the 45 version
        One After 909 (Lennon-McCartney) (2:42)
                30 Jan 69, Apple rooftop; with **Danny Boy** (Weatherly) (0:02)
Side B
        For You Blue (Harrison) (2:40)
                25 Jan 69, Apple; with false start and laughing
        Teddy Boy (McCartney) (3:40)
                24 Jan 69, Apple; the usual version
        Two Of Us (Lennon-McCartney) (3:40)
                24 Jan 69, Apple; "good-bye" version
        Maggie Mae (trad.) (0:37)
                24 Jan 69, Apple; same as commercial release
        Dig It (Lennon-McCartney) (4:01)
                26 Jan 69, Apple; longer version of commercial take
        Let It Be (Lennon-McCartney) (3:50)
                31 Jan 69, Apple; take 27
                the basic take for both released versions
        The Long And Winding Road (Lennon-McCartney) (3:48)
                31 Jan 69, Apple; take 19
                the basic take for the commercial release
        Get Back (reprise) (Lennon-McCartney) (0:37)
                28 Jan 69, Apple; laughing version (excerpt)

SOURCE:
        This is a copy of an earlier bootleg (possibly **THE VERY BEST OF THE BEATLES RAREST, VOLUME 6**).

SOUND QUALITY:
        Very good stereo; however, the source tape is extremely variable.

COMMENTS:

This would not appear to represent a legitimate lineup of the **GET BACK** material, and the reason for this arrangement of the material is unclear.

The main difference between this and **GET BACK** is the placement of **One After 909** at the end of Side A (it fades quickly, eliminating the "passed the audition" remark). Except for discrepancies which could be the result of indifferent amateur mastering (tempo changes, early fades—**Rocker** begins about 5 seconds later on this version), careful comparison reveals only one difference in the music. The **Get Back (reprise)** fades about one second later than any other version I have been able to compare it to.

This is a reissue; the earlier pressing may have come with a copy of a letter by Peter Brown which accompanied the legendary (and possibly non-existent) early promo-only (acetate?) issue of the album in 69. The LP was allegedly played once or twice on various radio stations before being recalled. It may have been taped off the air or copied by radio station personnel.

According to Doug Sulpy, a **GET BACK** acetate was aired on WBCN, Boston, sometime during Sep 69. It was identified as having been played previously by a station in Buffalo (!?) New York, and consisted of the material which contributed to the earliest **GET BACK** bootlegs (**GET BACK TO TORONTO**, etc.). Sulpy lists the lineup as:

Side A

Get Back
I've Got A Feeling (excerpt)
One After 909 (possibly, excerpt)
Teddy Boy
Two Of Us
I've Got A Feeling
The Long And Winding Road

Side B

Let It Be
Don't Let Me Down
For You Blue
Get Back
The Walk

According to Ray Schweighardt, there are two other possible sources for the bootleg copies of the **GET BACK** album. A copy of the master tape was supposedly stolen from an engineer's luggage at a NYC airport, presumably when the tape was being transferred to Capitol. This is an interesting story, but I have never seen anything to document it.

Also, John may have lent a (his?) copy of the master tape to a NYC radio station with permission to play it. An early **GET BACK** bootleg (extremely rare, on Lemon Records) apparently carried the following note:

I'd like to thank all of the people who made this project possible. And an especial thanks to the Baily Brothers for their support—John

and may be the source of this rumor.

LET IT END

THE BEATLES
"Apple Records," SAPCOR 42
2-disc set in full color jacket, with track listing and recording information on the back, says "Made In New Zealand;" labels say "Rubber Soul" and have song titles.

DISC ONE
Side A

Two Of Us (Lennon-McCartney) (2:16)
in a variety of accents
Two Of Us (Lennon-McCartney) (2:49)
"Oo-oo" version

Dig A Pony (Lennon-McCartney) (1:14)
  "skylight" version (excerpt)
Dig A Pony (Lennon-McCartney) (0:58)
  "girl" version (excerpt)
Dig A Pony (Lennon-McCartney) (0:15)
  "girl" version (the ending is repeated)
Across The Universe (Lennon-McCartney) (3:32)
I Me Mine (Harrison) (1:38)
  "I-I-Me-Me-Mine" version
Dig It (Lennon-McCartney) (0:53)
  different tune
Let It Be (Lennon-McCartney) (2:40)
  Record Mirror version
The Walk (McCracklin-Gorlic) (0:53)
  27 Jan 69, Apple; very good stereo

Side B

I've Got A Feeling (Lennon-McCartney) (3:54)
  "facelift version"
One After 909 (Lennon-McCartney) (3:10)
  2 versions edited together
Teddy Boy (McCartney) (2:02)
  24 Jan 69, Apple; an excerpt of the long rehearsal
The Long And Winding Road (Lennon-McCartney) (0:39)
  cha-cha version
The Long And Winding Road (Lennon-McCartney) (3:39)
  31 Jan 69, Apple; finished version from *Let It Be*
For You Blue (Harrison) (1:53)
  all-electric version
Get Back (Lennon-McCartney) (2:02)
  fast version, John shares lead vocals

DISC TWO
Side C

Take This Hammer (trad.) (2:49)
  vocals: John
New Orleans (Guida-Royster) (3:05)
  vocals: John, Paul, George
Madman (Lennon) (0:39)
  John
Little Queenie (Berry) (0:40)
  vocals: John
Be-Bop-A-Lula (Vincent-Davis) (0:31)
  vocals: Paul
There You Go, Eddie (McCartney) (3:58)
  Paul
Singing The Blues (Endsley) (2:47)
  vocals: Paul
Back Seat Of My Car (McCartney) (2:25)
  Paul and piano
This Song Of Love (Adams?) (1:54)
  Paul and piano
Woman (Lennon-McCartney) (0:35)
  Paul and piano
Bad Boy (Williams) (3:14)
  vocals: John

Side D

Shake, Rattle And Roll (Calhoun) (2:08)
  26 Jan 69, Apple; vocals: John, Paul
Kansas City/Miss Ann/Lawdy Miss Clawdy
(Leiber-Stoller/Dolphy/Price) (3:52)
  26 Jan 69, Apple; vocals: John, Paul

Blue Suede Shoes (Perkins) (2:10)
    vocals: Paul, John
Gone, Gone, Gone (Perkins) (1:56)
    vocals: John
Ramblin' Woman (Dylan?) (1:53)
    George, solo acoustic
I Threw It All Away (Dylan) (2:08)
    George, solo acoustic
Mama, You Been On My Mind (Dylan) (2:00)
    George, solo acoustic
Domino (Kaye-Ferrari) (0:55)
    vocals: Paul
Tea For Two (Youmans-Caesar) (1:34)
    Paul and piano
Chopsticks (trad.) (0:25)
    Paul and piano
Feedback guitar (improvisation) (1:14)
    vocals: Yoko

SOURCE:
    Jan 69, **GET BACK** sessions.

SOUND QUALITY:
    Very good to excellent mono, unless otherwise noted.

COMMENTS:
    The slice-and-dice job which attempts to pass for editing on DISC ONE is just terrible.

LIFE WITH THE LENNON'S
JOHN & YOKO
Tobe Milo, TMLP 4Q 13/14
7-inch EP in black & white jacket, with track listing and lyrics (!) on the back; label info matches; limited to 1000 copies?

Side A
    Song For John
        Let's Go On Flying (Ono) (1:07)
        Snow Is Falling All The Time (Ono) (1:24)
        Don't Worry Kyoko (Ono) (2:12)
    No Bed For Beatle John (Lennon-Ono) (4:45)
Side B
    Radio Play (Lennon) (7:56)

SOURCE:
    21-22 Nov 68? "outtakes" from **UNFINISHED MUSIC NO. 2: LIFE WITH THE LIONS**, made with a portable recorder during Yoko's stay at Queen Charlotte's Hospital, London. This is a reprint of the *Aspen* Flexi Disc (Issue 7, Section 11), Spring /Summer 69.

SOUND QUALITY:
    Very good to excellent mono.

COMMENTS:
    The first two cuts on Side A consist of Yoko ad-libbing acapella; the third has some guitar accompaniment by John; the last cut has both of them ad-libbing acapella to different newspaper reports. Side B is John playing with the radio dial.

LIFTING MATERIAL FROM THE WORLD
THE BEATLES (SOLO)
"Apple Records," SAPCOR 43
2-disc set in full color jacket, ©1988, with track listing and recording information on the back, says "Made In New Zealand;" labels say "Rubber Soul" and have song titles.

DISC ONE
Side A
> **Shanghai Surprise** (Harrison) (5:11)
> > 86, from the soundtrack of *Shanghai Surprise*
> > duet with Vicki Brown; from a promo-only release
> **Someplace Else** (Harrison) (3:33)
> > 86, from the soundtrack of *Shanghai Surprise*
> > the commercial version appears on **CLOUD NINE**
> **Breath Away From Heaven** (Harrison) (2:56)
> > 86, from the soundtrack of *Shanghai Surprise*
> > the commercial version appears on **CLOUD NINE**
> **I Don't Want To Do It** (Dylan) (2:19)
> > 84 demo?
> **Abandoned Love** (Dylan) (4:10)
> > 84? source unknown
> **Sue Me Sue You Blues** (Harrison) (2:55)
> > 72 demo? George and slide guitar
> **Every Time Somebody Comes To Town** (Harrison-Dylan?) (1:29)
> > late Nov 68? good to very good mono
> > George and Bob Dylan, supposedly at Dylan's Woodstock home
> **I'd Have You Anytime** (Harrison-Dylan) (2:06)
> > late Nov 69? good to very good mono
> > George and Bob Dylan, supposedly at Dylan's home
> George interviewed in Adelaide for the *Grand Prix* (1:57)
> > 198-? Australian tv? excellent mono
> George talks about the *Grand Prix* (1:14)
> > 198-? Australian tv? excellent mono

Side B
> 77, excerpts from the LP **SCOUSE THE MOUSE**
> > **Living In A Pet Shop** (Brown) (2:36)
> > **Scouse's Dream** (Brown) (1:54)
> > **Running Free** (Brown) (2:29)
> > **Boat Ride** (Brown) (1:59)
> > **Scouse The Mouse** (Brown) (2:44)
> > **I Know A Place** (Brown-O'Lochlainn-Pleasence) (1:33)
> > **S.O.S.** (Brown) (1:58)
> > **A Mouse Like Me** (O'Lochlainn) (4:23)

DISC TWO
Side C
> 16 Apr 73, *James Paul McCartney*
> > very good to excellent mono
> > **Big Barn Bed** (McCartney) (3:22)
> > > in concert, Borehamwood, 18 Mar 73
> > **Little Woman Love/C Moon** (P. McCartney-L.McCartney) (2:37)
> > **Gotta Sing, Gotta Dance** (McCartney) (2:24)
> > > edited to eliminate some of the dancing
> > acoustic medley: (3:54)
> > > **Blackbird** (Lennon-McCartney)
> > > **Bluebird** (McCartney)
> > > **Michelle** (Lennon-McCartney)
> > > **Heart Of The Country** (McCartney)
> > **Mary Had A Little Lamb** (McCartney) (3:44)
> > **The Mess** (McCartney) (4:00)
> > > in concert, Borehamwood, 18 Mar 73

commercial for **Hi, Hi, Hi**/**C Moon** (2:35)
>> Nov 72; excellent mono

73, acoustic medley (outtakes from *JPMc*?) (3:49)
>> good mono
>> **Bluebird** (McCartney)
>> **Momma's Little Girl** (McCartney)
>> **Michelle** (Lennon-McCartney)
>> **Heart Of The Country** (McCartney)

Side D

Imagine (Lennon) (3:17)
>> 17 Dec 71, Apollo Theatre

10 Dec 71, Ann Arbor, Michigan; John Sinclair benefit (12:49)
>> introduction & sound problems
>> **Attica State** (Lennon-Ono)
>> **The Luck of The Irish** (Lennon-Ono)
>> **John Sinclair** (Lennon)
>> good to very good mono
>> [**Sisters, O Sisters** (Ono) was also performed]

Give Peace A Chance (Lennon-McCartney) (2:26)
>> 1 Jun 69, Montreal; rehearsal? very good mono

Comment to a bleary-eyed Bob Dylan (0:16)
>> 27 May 66, *Eat The Document* outtake; excellent mono
>> for discussion, see the entry for **TEDDY BOY** in *Do You Want To Know A Secret?*

John interviewed by Howard Cosell (1:27)
>> 9 Dec 74, ABC-TV, *Monday Night Football*; excellent mono

John talks about meeting Chuck Berry (0:23)
>> 28 Sep 74, WNEW

John sings and talks about Paul's **RAM** lyrics (0:15)
>> source unknown (probably late 71) excellent mono

28 Sep 74, WNEW-FM; excellent mono (2:45)
>> Listen To This Radio Spot (0:39)
>>> Ringo does a **WALLS AND BRIDGES** commercial
>> John does a **GOODNIGHT VIENNA** commercial (0:34)
>> WNEW excerpts (1:27)

acoustic "medley" (2:01)
>> **Well (Baby, Please Don't Go)** (Ward)
>> **Rock Island Line** (trad. arr. Donegan)
>> **Maybe Baby** (Holly-Petty)
>> **Peggy Sue** (Holly-Allison-Petty)
>>> Summer 72, San Francisco; fair to good mono
>>> from an unknown *Eyewitness News* tv broadcast

SOURCE:
>> Varies; see individual entries.

SOUND QUALITY:
>> Excellent stereo, unless otherwise noted.

COMMENTS:
>> This is the final album in the SAPCOR series.

LIGHT AS A FEATHER
PAUL McCARTNEY & WINGS
ZAP, 7875
Insert cover with song titles; labels have side numbers only.

Side A (20:04)
>> **Venus And Mars** (McCartney)
>> **Rock Show** (McCartney)

Jet (McCartney)
Let Me Roll It (McCartney)
Spirits Of Ancient Egypt (McCartney)
Side B (24:41)
Medicine Jar (McCulloch-Allen)
Maybe I'm Amazed (McCartney)
Call Me Back Again (McCartney)
Lady Madonna (Lennon-McCartney)
The Long And Winding Road (Lennon-McCartney)

SOURCE:
15 May 76, Capitol Center, Largo, Maryland

SOUND QUALITY:
An audience recording, very good mono.

COMMENTS:
Part two of this show appears on **WINGS OVER AMERICA—LANDING GEAR DOWN** (ZAP, 7876), and part three appears on Side B of **9 MM. AUTOMATIC** (ZAP, 7878).

THE LITTLE RED ALBUM
THE BEATLES
"Apple Records," SAPCOR 38
2-disc set in full color jacket, with song listing on the back, says "Made In New Zealand;" labels say "Rubber Soul" and have song titles.

DISC ONE
Side A
Back In the USSR (Lennon-McCartney) (3:04)
4 Jul 85, Washington DC; the Beach Boys with Ringo
line recording, excellent stereo
This cut was included on a limited (but legitimate) album released by the [Mike] Love Foundation For American Music, **FOURTH OF JULY: A ROCKIN' CELEBRATION OF AMERICA**.
Ob-La-Di, Ob-La-Da (Lennon-McCartney) (2:45)
3/4/5 Jul 68, EMI; take 5; very good stereo
from the cancelled **SESSIONS** 45; this has the ending from the album version tacked on to replace the usual segue into **Christmas Time (Is Here Again)**.
While My Guitar Gently Weeps (Harrison) (3:27)
25 Jul 68, EMI; take 1 (acoustic) excellent stereo?
I'm So Tired (Lennon-McCartney) (2:18)
Jan 69, **GET BACK** sessions; excellent mono
vocals: Paul
Blackbird (Lennon-McCartney) (1:32)
74, from Paul's unreleased *Backyard* film
Hey Jude (Lennon-McCartney) (5:16)
30 Jul 68, EMI; mostly take 9
from *Experiment In Television*; very good mono
At one point during the rehearsal, Paul sings and plays a few bars of I Hate To See The Evening Sun Go Down (?). A much more complete piece of this song appears on **ULTRA RARE TRAX VOLS. 5 & 6**. It may be an improvisation, or it may be based on **In The Evening (When The Sun Goes Down)** (Carr), which was recorded by Ray Charles.
Side B
Birthday (Lennon-McCartney) (2:43)
18 Sep 68, EMI; take 22 (the commercial take)
OOPSed, excellent mono

Yer Blues (Lennon-McCartney) (4:05)
>   11 Dec 68, from *Rock And Roll Circus*
>   excellent mono; includes the countdown from the LP version

Goodbye (Lennon-McCartney) (2:22)
>   late 68, Dick James; acetate demo; excellent mono?

Not Guilty (Harrison) (3:22)
>   8/9/12 Aug 68, EMI; take 102
>   **SESSIONS** remix, excellent stereo

Heather (McCartney) (2:01)
>   Nov 68-Jan 69, EMI? during **POST CARD** sessions
>   excellent mono

What's The New Mary Jane (Lennon) (7:02)
>   14 Aug 68/26 Nov 69, EMI; take 4 (stereo remix #5); excellent stereo

Good Night (Lennon-McCartney) (0:26)
>   late Mar—early Apr 69, from the **WEDDING ALBUM**; excellent mono

DISC TWO
Side C

The Beatles' Sixth Christmas Record (7:37)
>   Nov 68; excellent mono

15 May 68; John & Paul on *Newsfront* (PBS) (19:30)
>   good to very good mono
>   A very tough interview. They seem to have a hard time opening up (example: "What do you think about young people?" John: "I think they're young."), although they do have a few interesting things to say.

15 May 68; John and Paul on *The Tonight Show* (0:32)
>   fair to good mono
>   Commenting on their *Newsfront* appearance.

Side D

15 May 68; John & Paul on *Newsfront* (continued) (9:19)
>   it gets a little better

Beatleviews:
>   Brief interview snippets, hopelessly jumbled.

SOURCE:
>   Varied; see individual entries.

SOUND QUALITY:
>   Varied; see individual entries.

COMMENTS:
>   The back cover has a photo of what the liner notes claim is the original artwork concept for **THE BEATLES** (The White Album). The interviews are by far the most interesting material here.

LIVE AT NASSAU COLISEUM

THE BEATLES
"Zapple," 999
Insert cover with track listing; label information matches.

Side A

People Say (Szigeti-Lichterman) (2:38)
>   "John & Paul," 65, from (UK) 45 Tip 1021
>   good mono; no Beatles involvement

I'm Walkin' (Szigeti-Lichterman) (2:08)
>   "John & Paul," 65, from (UK) 45 Tip 1021
>   good mono; no Beatles involvement

Hey Jude (Lennon-McCartney) (7:03)
>> The video performance consists of new vocals (4 Sep 68, Twickenham) performed to pre-recorded backing tracks (for the commercial version: 31 Jul & 1 Aug 68, Trident; take 1). This was done because of strict Musician's Union rules about miming.
> broadcast 8 Sep 68, *Frost On Sunday*

Revolution (Lennon-McCartney) (3:26)
>> The video performance consists of new vocals (4 Sep 68, Twickenham) performed to pre-recorded backing tracks (10/11/12 Jul 68, EMI; take 16).
> broadcast 19 Sep 68, *Top Of The Pops*

The Beatles' Seventh Christmas Record (1:13)
> Nov 69? various (excerpt)

16 Jul 64, *Top Gear* (4:28)
> [*Top Of The Pops* intro]
>> **Long Tall Sally** (Johnson-Penniman-Blackwell)

Side B

16 Jul 64, *Top Gear* (continued) (5:42)
> interview
>> **A Hard Day's Night** (Lennon-McCartney)
>> **Things We Said Today** (Lennon-McCartney)
> [*Top Of The Pops* closing]
>> excellent mono

Shout! (Isley-Isley-Isley) (0:41)
> 6 May 64, *Around The Beatles* (excerpt)
> from **As It Happened**, with Murray The K's voice-over

Pantomime: Everywhere It's Christmas (2:56)
> aka **The Beatles' Fourth Christmas Record**
> 25 Nov 66, Dick James (excerpt)

Christmas Time (Is Here Again) (1:49)
> aka **The Beatles' Fifth Christmas Record**
> 28 Nov 67, EMI (excerpt)

Sie Liebt Dich (Lennon-McCartney) (2:14)
> 29 Jan 64, Paris; take 14

SOURCE:
> Varies; see individual entries.

SOUND QUALITY:
> Very good mono, unless otherwise stated.

COMMENTS:
> Also available as Contra Band Z999 and as **LIVE FROM GERMANY**; this is very similar to **TOP OF THE POPS** (LP).

LIVE AT THE CIRCUS CRONE
THE BEATLES
Fabulous Four Records, L 30157
Full color jacket, with tracks listed on the back (date is incorrectly listed as 25 Jun 66 instead of 24 Jun 66); labels say "Live In Germany" and have matching info.

Side A (13:55)
> 24 Jun 66, *Circus-Krone-Bau*, Munich
>> **Rock And Roll Music** (Berry) (excerpt)
>> **She's A Woman** (Lennon-McCartney) (intro only)
>> **Baby's In Black** (Lennon-McCartney)
>> **I Feel Fine** (Lennon-McCartney)
>> **Yesterday** (Lennon-McCartney)
>> **Nowhere Man** (Lennon-McCartney)

Side B

I'm Down (Lennon-McCartney)

24 Jun 66, *Circus-Krone-Bau*, Munich (13:35)
Rock And Roll Music (Berry)
She's A Woman (Lennon-McCartney) (intro only)
I Feel Fine (Lennon-McCartney)
Yesterday (Lennon-McCartney)
Nowhere Man (Lennon-McCartney)
I'm Down (Lennon-McCartney)

interview: London Hilton (?) (3:43)
date unknown; questions and answers mostly in German
very good mono, heavy surface noise
Copied from a small giveaway cardboard record, from German *OK* magazine, Nov 65

George's acceptance speech for the 1966 *Bravo* Award (0:46)
23 Jun 66, Munich; excellent mono; in German
Copied from a 7-inch flexi giveaway from *Bravo* magazine, **Die Goldenen OTTO—Sieger 1966**, which also contained messages from Marie Versini, Robert Fuller, Manuela, Drafi Deutscher and Pierre Brice. Date of issue unknown.

SOURCE:
Varies; see individual entries.

SOUND QUALITY:
The concert excerpts are a line recording, good to very good mono (with lots of hiss), probably taped off a speaker; the tape has been severely edited (**She's A Woman** disappears after seven seconds of the intro—there is the slight possibility it was performed this way—and **I'm Down** is missing a substantial part of the song); otherwise as noted.

COMMENTS:
This is apparently a quickie domestic reissue of **THE LIVE BEATLES: RECORDED LIVE IN MUNICH, WEST GERMANY, JUNE 24TH, 1966**. Like the parent disc, this is of marginal interest. The concert and *Bravo* award speech were previously available on Side A of **BEATLES 4 EVER** (Beat Riff Records). Some copies were pressed on red vinyl.

THE LIVE BEATLES: RECORDED LIVE IN MUNICH, WEST GERMANY, JUNE 24TH, 1966

THE BEATLES
Document Records, DR 005 LP
3-color jacket, same design front and back; labels have title and track listing. This is probably an Italian piece.

Side A (13:55)
24 Jun 66, *Circus-Krone-Bau*, Munich
Rock And Roll Music (Berry) (excerpt)
She's A Woman (Lennon-McCartney) (intro only)
Baby's In Black (Lennon-McCartney)
I Feel Fine (Lennon-McCartney)
Yesterday (Lennon-McCartney)
Nowhere Man (Lennon-McCartney)
I'm Down (Lennon-McCartney)

Side B
24 Jun 66, *Circus-Krone-Bau*, Munich (13:35)
Rock And Roll Music (Berry)
She's A Woman (Lennon-McCartney) (intro only)
I Feel Fine (Lennon-McCartney)

Yesterday (Lennon-McCartney)
Nowhere Man (Lennon-McCartney)
I'm Down (Lennon-McCartney)
interview: London Hilton (?) (3:43)
      date unknown; questions and answers mostly in German
      very good mono, heavy surface noise
      Copied from a small giveaway cardboard record, from German *OK* magazine,
         Nov 65
George's acceptance speech for the 1966 *Bravo* Award (0:46)
      23 Jun 66, Munich; excellent mono; in German
      This was copied from a 7-inch flexi giveaway from *Bravo* magazine, **Die
         Goldenen OTTO—Sieger 1966**, which also contained messages
         from Marie Versini, Robert Fuller, Manuela, Drafi Deutscher and Pierre
         Brice. Date of issue unknown.

SOURCE:
      Varies; see individual entries.

SOUND QUALITY:
      The concert excerpts are a line recording, good to very good mono (with lots of
hiss), probably taped off a speaker; the tape has been severely edited (**She's A Woman**
disappears after seven seconds of the intro—there is the slight possibility it was performed
this way—and **I'm Down** is missing a substantial part of the song); otherwise as noted.

COMMENTS:
      Yes, these are the same performances on both sides. This material was previously
available on Side A of **BEATLES 4 EVER** (Beat Riff Records), and this entire disc has
been copied as **LIVE AT THE CIRCUS CRONE** (Fabulous Four Records, L 30157).
Some of this issue came with a sticker claiming the concert was from Essen.
      The 9:00 show was filmed by ZDF, the national tv station. The sound quality here is a
step up from its earlier appearance on **ON STAGE**, but it's not worth getting excited about,
and these tapes contain no songs which were not previously available (although they are now
in correct order).
      It's a shame that better quality tapes of these shows are not around, as the
performance is pretty good (especially compared to the Tokyo shows, just a few days later)—
although they completely lose it during **I'm Down**).
      This disc would be of interest only to completists.

THE LIVE BEATLES: TOKIO JULY 2, 1966
THE BEATLES
Bulldog Records, BDCD-002
Compact disc, ©1987, made in Italy.

30 Jun 66; Nippon Budokan Hall, Tokyo (29:46)
      tuning
      Rock And Roll Music (Berry)
      She's A Woman (Lennon-McCartney)
      If I Needed Someone (Harrison)
      Day Tripper (Lennon-McCartney)
      Baby's In Black (Lennon-McCartney)
      I Feel Fine (Lennon-McCartney)
      Yesterday (Lennon-McCartney)
      I Wanna Be Your Man (Lennon-McCartney)
      Nowhere Man (Lennon-McCartney)
      Paperback Writer (Lennon-McCartney)
      I'm Down (Lennon-McCartney)

SOURCE:
Although the jacket says that this is the Budokan performance which is traditionally dated as 2 Jul 66, it is in fact the show traditionally dated 30 Jun 66.

SOUND QUALITY:
Very good mono, recorded off a disc (surface noise).

COMMENTS:
One of two Italian CDs of Budokan material, allegedly issued due to the difference in Italian copyright laws (a 20 year limit—thus the subtitle, "It was more than 20 years ago."). Bulldog was rumored to have been closed down, but this is incorrect.

THE LIVE BEATLES SINGLES COLLECTION
THE BEATLES
Bulldog Records, BGS-14
13-disc set, on green vinyl, in black & white sleeves, with notes in Italian, in deluxe box; labels are ©1987 and have recording information; package includes two black & white postcards.

DISC ONE
Side A
> **Twist And Shout** (Medley-Russell) (1:11)
>> 27 Jun 65, *Teatro Adriano*, Rome
>> good to very good mono audience recording

Side B
> **I Saw Her Standing There** (McCartney-Lennon) (2:44)
>> 12 Jun 64, Centennial Hall, Adelaide

DISC TWO
Side C
> **Please Please Me** (McCartney-Lennon) (3:18)
>> 11 Feb 64, Washington Coliseum
>> fair to good mono line recording

Side D
> **I Wanna Be Your Man** (Lennon-McCartney) (3:26)
>> 11 Feb 64, Washington Coliseum
>> fair to good mono line recording

DISC THREE
Side E
> **From Me To You** (McCartney-Lennon) (1:17)
>> 7 Dec 63, Empire Theatre, Liverpool
>> label gives traditional date of 22 Dec 63; for discussion, see **YOUNG-BLOOD** in *Do You Want To Know A Secret?*

Side F
> **Rock And Roll Music** (Berry) (2:28)
>> 27 Jun 65, *Teatro Adriano*, Rome
>> good to very good mono audience recording

DISC FOUR
Side G
> **She Loves You** (Lennon-McCartney) (2:32)
>> 22 Aug 64, Empire Stadium, Vancouver

Side H
> **Roll Over Beethoven** (Berry) (2:20)
>> 2 Sep 64, Convention Hall, Philadelphia?
>> label says 18 Aug 65, Atlanta Stadium, Atlanta

DISC FIVE
Side I
> **I Want To Hold Your Hand** (Lennon-McCartney) (2:31)
>> 19 Jan 64, Olympia Theatre, Paris
>> label says 16 Jan 64; for discussion, see **HOT WAX** in *Do You Want To Know A Secret?*

Side J
>
> **This Boy** (Lennon-McCartney) (2:35)
>> 7 Dec 63, Empire Theatre, Liverpool
>> label gives traditional date of 22 Dec 63

DISC SIX
Side K
>
> **Can't Buy Me Love** (Lennon-McCartney) (2:40)
>> 20 Jun 65, evening show, *Palais des Sports*, Paris

Side L
>
> **You Can't Do That** (Lennon-McCartney) (2:44)
>> 16 Jun 64, Festival Hall, Melbourne

DISC SEVEN
Side M
>
> **A Hard Day's Night** (Lennon-McCartney) (3:00)
>> 27 Jun 65, *Teatro Adriano*, Rome
>> good to very good mono audience recording

Side N
>
> **Things We Said Today** (Lennon-McCartney) (2:25)
>> 22 Aug 64, Empire Stadium, Vancouver

DISC EIGHT
Side O
>
> **I Feel Fine** (Lennon-McCartney) (2:30)
>> 24 Jun 66, *Circus-Krone-Bau*, Munich; evening show
>> good to very good mono line recording

Side P
>
> **She's A Woman** (Lennon-McCartney) (3:02)
>> 24 Jun 65, *Velodromo Vigorelli*, Milan?
>> good to very good mono line recording

DISC NINE
Side Q
>
> **Ticket To Ride** (Lennon-McCartney) (2:58)
>> 19 Aug 65, evening show, Sam Houston Coliseum, Houston

Side R
>
> **Baby's In Black** (Lennon-McCartney) (2:39)
>> 20 Jun 65, evening show, *Palais des Sports*, Paris

DISC TEN
Side S
>
> **Help!** (Lennon-McCartney) (2:35)
>> 19 Aug 65, Sam Houston Coliseum, Houston; afternoon show

Side T
>
> **I'm Down** (Lennon-McCartney) (3:40)
>> 19 Aug 65, Sam Houston Coliseum, Houston; afternoon show

DISC ELEVEN
Side U
>
> **Day Tripper** (Lennon-McCartney) (3:25)
>> 29 Aug 66, Candlestick Park, San Francisco

Side V
>
> **If I Fell** (Lennon-McCartney) (2:01)
>> 23 Aug 64, Hollywood Bowl
>> label says 24 Jun 65, *Velodromo Vigorelli*, Milan

Side W
>
> **Paperback Writer** (Lennon-McCartney) (2:22)
>> 2 Jul 66, Nippon Budokan Hall, Tokyo

Side X
>
> **All My Loving** (Lennon-McCartney) (2:42)
>> 12 Jun 64, Centennial Hall, Adelaide

DISC THIRTEEN
Side Y
>
> **Yesterday** (Lennon-McCartney) (2:50)
>> 29 Aug 66, Candlestick Park, San Francisco

Side Z
   Nowhere Man (Lennon-McCartney) (2:44)
      24 Jun 66, *Circus-Krone-Bau*, Munich; evening show
      good to very good mono line recording

SOURCE:
   Varies; see individual listings. All of this material has been previously available (although the Milan performance is hard to find—see **LIVE IN ITALY**).

SOUND QUALITY:
   Very good to excellent mono line recordings, unless otherwise stated.

COMMENTS:
   Bulldog Records of Italy has semi-legitimately issued a number of old bootleg items under their "It Was More Than 20 Years Ago" banner, based on the idea that Italian copyright law (reportedly) covers only twenty years.

LIVE IN ITALY (EP)
THE BEATLES
No manufacturer listed, ITA 128
7-inch EP in black & white picture sleeve, with song titles and recording information on the back; labels have title only.

Side A
   Interview (1:38)
      late Jun 65, Italy; good mono
      The questions are in Italian, the answers in English (translations edited out); extremely brief and uninformative. This is the same interview which appears in a slightly longer version on Side B of **ROMA** (and its apparent source, *ARRIVANO I «CAPPELIONI»*). Wiener lists two tv interviews from the Italian tour: 24 Jun 65, from *Velodromo Vigorelli*, Milan, conducted by Carmela Anna Fortunata, and 27 Jun 65, from Rome. If the source of his information is from these bootlegs, however, they are the same interview; probably a tv broadcast, exact location and date unknown.
      There was a legitimate issue of this interview on **THE BEATLES TALK DOWN UNDER, VOL. 2** (Raven, RVLP-1013).
Side B
   24 Jun 65, *Velodromo Vigorelli*, Milan? (5:11)
      Twist And Shout (Medley-Russell)
      She's A Woman (Lennon-McCartney)
      I'm A Loser (Lennon-McCartney) (excerpt)
         In all the Beatles performed eight shows at three locations while in Italy (two In Milan on 24 Jun, two in Genoa on 25 Jun, and four in Rome on 27-28 Jun).
         This is a line recording, very good mono, sounds like a tv or radio broadcast, and may be from the same tape as Side A. Although we cannot be certain which show it is (my dating comes from the picture sleeve), Paul's attempt at introducing a song in Italian at least confirms the country. Contrary to the listing in *Hot Wax*, the Beatles never performed in Gilâu (which is a small village in Romania).

SOURCE:
   See individual entries.

SOUND QUALITY:
   See individual entries.

COMMENTS:
　　　The brief interview is a total waste of time, but the concert excerpts on Side B appear rarely. The mix is poor, with everything but John and Paul's vocals and John's guitar nearly inaudible; this speaks against its source being the supposed EMI recording.

LIVE IN JAPAN 1964 (CD)
THE BEATLES
Document Records, DR 002 CD
Compact disc, ©1987, made in Italy. Jacket has song listing and recording information.

30 Jun 66, Nippon Budokan Hall, Tokyo (30:16)
　　　introduction & tuning
　　　Rock And Roll Music (Berry)
　　　She's A Woman (Lennon-McCartney)
　　　If I Needed Someone (Harrison)
　　　Day Tripper (Lennon-McCartney)
　　　Baby's In Black (Lennon-McCartney)
　　　I Feel Fine (Lennon-McCartney)
　　　Yesterday (Lennon-McCartney)
　　　I Wanna Be Your Man (Lennon-McCartney)
　　　Nowhere Man (Lennon-McCartney)
　　　Paperback Writer (Lennon-McCartney)
　　　I'm Down (Lennon-McCartney)
　　　announcements
2 Jul 66, Nippon Budokan Hall, Tokyo; afternoon (30:16)
　　　introduction & tuning
　　　Rock And Roll Music (Berry)
　　　She's A Woman (Lennon-McCartney)
　　　If I Needed Someone (Harrison)
　　　Day Tripper (Lennon-McCartney)
　　　Baby's In Black (Lennon-McCartney)
　　　I Feel Fine (Lennon-McCartney)
　　　Yesterday (Lennon-McCartney)
　　　I Wanna Be Your Man (Lennon-McCartney)
　　　Nowhere Man (Lennon-McCartney)
　　　Paperback Writer (Lennon-McCartney)
　　　I'm Down (Lennon-McCartney)

SOURCE:
　　　The usual two Budokan concerts (complete), from 66—not 64, as the package says. The jacket dates the second show (traditionally 2 Jul 66) as 1 Jul 66.

SOUND QUALITY:
　　　Very good to excellent mono; some tape hiss.

COMMENTS:
　　　One of two Italian CDs of Budokan material, allegedly issued due to the difference in Italian copyright laws (a 20-year limit).

LIVE IN MELBOURNE, AUSTRALIA
THE BEATLES
Instant Analysis, MB 1034
Insert cover with song titles; labels are generic Instant Analysis.

Side A (10:58)
　　　I Saw Her Standing There (McCartney-Lennon)
　　　You Can't Do That (Lennon-McCartney)

All My Loving (Lennon-McCartney)
She Loves You (Lennon-McCartney)
Side B (13:11)
Till There Was You (Willson)
Roll Over Beethoven (Berry)
Can't Buy Me Love (Lennon-McCartney)
This Boy (Lennon-McCartney)
Long Tall Sally (Johnson-Penniman-Blackwell)

SOURCE:
17 Jun 64, Festival Hall, Melbourne, Australia; the last Melbourne show.

SOUND QUALITY:
A line recording, good to very good mono; the tape has been crudely edited in a number of places.

COMMENTS:
This piece, the last of six Melbourne shows—two each over three days—is far less common that the 16 Jun 64 *The Beatles Sing For Shell* performance.

LIVE IN VANCOUVER
GEORGE HARRISON
SODD, 005
2-disc set with insert cover with song titles; labels have side number only.

DISC ONE
Side A (13:30)
Dark Horse (Harrison)
Nothing From Nothing (Preston)
performed by Billy Preston and the band
What Is Life (Harrison)
Side B (17:08)
introducing the band
Tomcat (Scott)
performed by Tom Scott and the band
Maya Love (Harrison)
Outa-Space (Preston-Greene)
performed by Billy Preston and the band
DISC TWO
Side C (14:42)
Give Me Love (Harrison)
Sound Stage Of Mind (Harrison)
In My Life (Lennon-McCartney)
Side D (16:03)
While My Guitar Gently Weeps (Harrison)
My Sweet Lord (Harrison)

SOURCE:
2 Nov 74, Pacific Coliseum, Vancouver, British Columbia, Canada

SOUND QUALITY:
This is an audience tape, fair to good stereo.

COMMENTS:
The first show of George's 74 tour.

LIVE TRACKS—PREVIOUSLY ITALIAN E.P.
THE BEATLES
No manufacturer listed, EPB 1967
Full color jacket; labels are blank.

Side A (5:00)
      24 Jun 65,*Velodromo Vigorelli*, Milan?
          Twist And Shout (Medley-Russell)
          She's A Woman (Lennon-McCartney)
          chat & chant
          I'm A Loser (Lennon-McCartney) (excerpt)
Side B (4:15)
      23 Aug 64, The Hollywood Bowl
          If I Fell (Lennon-McCartney)
          I Want To Hold Your Hand (Lennon-McCartney)

SOURCE:
      Varies; see individual entires.

SOUND QUALITY:
      Good to very good line recordings; Side A is probably taken off a speaker (tv?).

COMMENTS:
      Still Italian E.P. See **LIVE IN ITALY** for discussion.
      Side B has a *"grazzi"* tacked onto the end of it, to give the impression that it is part of the Italian show.

LONG TALL SALLY/A HARD DAY'S NIGHT
THE BEATLES
Beat Records, 12-142
7-inch 45, on red vinyl, in 2-color picture sleeve, with song titles on the back; labels match.

Side A
      Long Tall Sally (Johnson-Penniman-Blackwell) (1:58)
Side B
      A Hard Day's Night (Lennon-McCartney) (2:26)

SOURCE:
      16 Jul 64, *Top Gear*; not studio outtakes.

SOUND QUALITY:
      Excellent mono.

COMMENTS:
      Nothing of interest.

LOOK BACK
THE BEATLES (INDIVIDUALLY) WITH MANY OTHERS
Boxtop Records, LB 72-7985
2-disc set in generic Boxtop jacket with stamped title and photo affixed; song titles are on sticker; labels are generic TMOQ.

DISC ONE
Side A (24:22)
      14 Sep 79, Hammersmith Odeon, London
          introducing Don Everly
          chat

Walk Right Back (Curtis)
    Don Everly
'Til I Kissed You (Everly)
    Don Everly & Albert Lee
Cathy's Clown (Everly-Everly)
    Don Everly & Albert Lee
All I Have To Do Is Dream (Bryant)
    Don Everly & Albert Lee
Bye Bye Love (Bryant-Bryant)
    Don Everly & Albert Lee
Raining In My Heart (Bryant-Bryant)
    Denny Laine with Don Everly
It's So Easy (Holly-Petty)
    Paul with Linda & Denny
Bo Diddley (McDaniel)
    this "grand finale" includes Paul, Linda, Denny, Steve, Laurence, The Crickets (Jerry Allison, Joe Mauldin, Sonny Curtis), Albert Lee, Bob Montgomery, Rick Gretch and Don Everly. Paul does most of the vocals.

Side B
    21 Nov 85, Limehouse Studios, London (17:58)
    opening titles
Boppin' The Blues (Perkins-Griffin)
    Carl Perkins
Put Your Cat Clothes On (Perkins)
    Carl
Honey Don't (Perkins)
    Ringo
Matchbox (trad. arr. Perkins)
    Carl, Ringo & Eric Clapton
Mean Woman Blues (Demetrius)
    Carl & Clapton

DISC TWO
Side C
    21 Nov 85, Limehouse Studios, London (continued) (18:09)
Turn Around (Bennett-Tepper)
    Carl
Jackson (Rogers-Wheeler)
    Carl & Roseanne Cash
What Kinda Girl (Forbert)
    Roseanne Cash
Everybody's Trying To Be My Baby (Perkins)
    George
Your True Love (Perkins)
    Carl, George & Dave Edmunds

Side D
    21 Nov 85, Limehouse Studios, London (continued) (19:53)
The World Is Waiting For The Sunrise (Bell-Lockhart-Seitz)
    Carl—guitar instrumental
Sun Records Medley
    That's All Right, Mama (Crudup)
    Blue Moon Of Kentucky (Monroe)
    Night Train To Memphis (Smith-Hughes-Bradley)
    Amen (trad.)
        Carl & All
Glad All Over (Bennett-Tepper-Schroeder)
    George & Carl
Whole Lotta Shakin' Goin' On (Williams-David)
    Carl

> **Gone, Gone, Gone** (Perkins)
> Carl
> **Blue Suede Shoes** (Perkins)
> Carl & All
> 16 Feb 72, *The Mike Douglas Show* (8:35)
> John and Chuck Berry
> introduction
> **Memphis** (Berry)
> chat
> **Johnny B. Goode** (Berry)

SOURCE:
Side A: This was filmed and recorded by MPL. Entitled *The Music Lives On*, it was shown only briefly on UK television (at 1:30 a.m. and again a few hours later on a different channel) on 8 Sep 84.
Sides B-D (except for the last two cuts): *Blue Suede Shoes*—the Carl Perkins Cinemax special (excerpt), broadcast 5 Jan 86, on Cinemax (cable).

SOUND QUALITY:
Side A, excellent stereo; all else excellent mono.

COMMENTS:
According to Wiener, *The Music Lives On* is only 14 minutes long (as on **RAVE ON**); if that is correct, then Side A comes from another source.

LOOKING BACK ON ABBEY ROAD
THE BEATLES
No manufacturer listed, CX 320
Insert cover with song titles; labels are blank except for title.

Side A
> John talks about **How Do You Do It** (0:43)
> Fall 74, RKO interview? very good mono
> **How Do You Do It** (Murray-Edmond) (1:57)
> 4 Sep 62, EMI; take 2; good mono;
> Someone has added a spoken intro, and there is whispering throughout the cut; according to Castleman & Podrazik (*The Beatles Again*, p.96), this tape would therefore come from the 76 RKO broadcast.
> **Long Tall Sally** (Johnson-Penniman-Blackwell) (1:59)
> 16 Jul 64, BBC
> **Things We Said Today** (Lennon-McCartney) (2:19)
> 16 Jul 64, BBC
> **A Hard Day's Night** (Lennon-McCartney) (2:26)
> 16 Jul 64, BBC
> **Octopus's Garden** (Starkey) (2:44)
> 26/29 Apr & 17 Jul 69, EMI; take 32
> piano, backing vocals and sound effects were dubbed in on this day; this track has the piano but no backing vocals or effects
> **Her Majesty** (Lennon-McCartney) (0:23)
> 2 Jul 69, EMI; take 3, with the final chord
Side B
> **Golden Slumbers/Carry That Weight** (Lennon-McCartney) (3:08)
> 2 Jul 69, EMI; take 13
> 15 basic takes were recorded this day; takes 13 and 15 were edited together to form the basic take (still called take 13) of the commercial version, which is what this appears to be.

You Never Give Me Your Money (Lennon-McCartney) (5:37)
>>6 May, Olympic & 1/11 Jul 69, EMI; take 30, extended
>>The basic tracks had been recorded 6 May at Olympic Studios; the vocals were added on 1 Jul and the bass on this date.

Oh! Darling (Lennon-McCartney) (3:21)
>>20/26 Apr 69, EMI; take 26; alternate lead vocals
>>This may be the basic take 26 with a guide vocal, or one one of Paul's later overdub attempts. Since a second vocal is faintly audible, I'm assuming this is the first vocal take on top of the guide vocal.

Maxwell's Silver Hammer (Lennon-McCartney) (3:29)
>>9/10/11 Jul 69, EMI; take 21; no synthesizer or guitar overdubs

Something (Harrison) (5:21)
>>2 May, EMI & 5 May, Olympic & 11 Jul 69, EMI; take 37, extended
>>This is a tape reduction of take 36, the basic take of the commercial version; it was intended (but never used) for overdubs.

SOURCE:
>>Varies; see individual entries.

SOUND QUALITY:
>>All cuts are excellent mono unless otherwise stated.

COMMENTS:
>>This is a repackaging of **ROCK 'N' ROAD**. Not much here of interest.

THE LOST BEEBS
THE BEATLES
Tiger Beat Records, TBR/LP 2
2-color jacket with track listing and recording information on the back; labels are blank.

Side A
>>8 Mar 62, *Teenager's Turn*
>>>**Dream Baby** (Walker) (1:50)
>>>**Memphis** (Berry) (2:15)
>>>**Please Mr. Postman** (Holland-Bateman-Gordy) (2:00)
>>15 Jun 62, *Here We Go*
>>>**Ask Me Why** (McCartney-Lennon) (2:13)
>>>**Besame Mucho** (Velazquez-Skylar) (2:24)
>>>**A Picture Of You** (Beveridge-Oakman) (2:11)
>>8 Feb 64, *Saturday Club* (4:34)
>>>telephone interview from NYC with Brian Matthew; too slow

Side B
>>4 Jun 63, *Pop Go The Beatles* #1
>>>**Misery** (McCartney-Lennon) (1:49)
>>>**The Hippy Hippy Shake** (Romero) (1:46)
>>29 Jun 63, *Saturday Club*
>>>**Money (That's What I Want)** (Bradford-Gordy) (2:32)
>>>**Till There Was You** (Willson) (2:13)
>>23 Jul 63, *Pop Go The Beatles* #6
>>>**Love Me Do** (McCartney-Lennon) (2:31)
>>27 Aug 63, *Pop Go The Beatles* #11
>>>**Anna (Go To Him)** (Alexander) (2:58)
>>>**A Shot Of Rhythm And Blues** (Thompson) (2:19)
>>3 Sep 63, *Pop Go The Beatles* #12
>>>**Money (That's What I Want)** (Bradford-Gordy) (2:48)

SOURCE:
>>Various BBC broadcasts.

SOUND QUALITY:
     Good to very good mono.

COMMENTS:
     Side A primarily reprints material which first appeared on **MEET THE BEEB**, but this is a much cleaner pressing; this version of the *Saturday Club* phone call is longer than that on BEEB8, and also appears on **WITHERED BEATLES**. Side B collects the tracks from **STUDIO SESSIONS VOL.s 1 & 2** which have not appeared on the BEEB albums. These cuts were recorded from a radio speaker and the sound quality suffers accordingly.

THE LOST LENNON TAPES, VOLUME ONE
JOHN LENNON
Bag Records, 5073
Full color jacket with track listing on the back; labels say "Musketeer Gripweed Presents The Lost Tapes" and have Lennon artwork.

Side A
     Strawberry Fields Forever (Lennon-McCartney) (2:55)
          Nov 66, EMI? electric "arranging" demo
          (program 4, 15 Feb 88)
     The Rishikesh Song (Lennon) (1:49)
          unknown; acoustic demo
          (program 4, 15 Feb 88)
     Rock Island Line (trad.) (2:28)
          70s, Dakota; acoustic, excellent stereo?
          (program 5, 22 Feb 88)
     John Henry (trad.) (1:34)
          70s, Dakota; piano
          (program 5, 22 Feb 88)
     Surprise, Surprise (Sweet Bird Of Paradox) (Lennon) (1:20)
          Summer 74? Dakota; acoustic
          (program 5, 22 Feb 88)
     Keep Right On To The End Of The Road (improvisation?) (0:38)
          Summer 71, from the *Oz* magazine flexi
     Goodnight Vienna (Lennon) (2:47)
          Jun 74, W&B sessions; demo for Ringo
          Previously available on **GOODNIGHT VIENNA** and **JOHNNY MOON-DOG**, this appearance is not from the radio show; it is longer but the sound quality is noticeably worse.
     Tennessee (Lennon) (1:52)
          Dakota, early 75? demo takes 1 & 4
          piano/piano & rhythm box
          (program 5, 22 Feb 88)
     God Save Us (Lennon-Ono) (3:01)
          Jun 71; demo
          The jacket lists the title as "God Save Oz" and, for this demo, those do indeed seem to be the lyrics. This song, apparently not from the series, is available in excellent stereo on **JOHNNY MOONDOG**.
     With A Little Help From My Friends (Lennon-McCartney) (0:35)
          Fall 79, Dakota
          Sean sings, and John tries to remember the title
          (program 3, 8 Feb 88)
Side B
     Power To The People (Lennon) (2:25)
          Feb 71; rough mix of the released take; excellent stereo?
          (program 2, 1 Feb 88)

Here We Go Again (Lennon-Spector) (1:17)
>   possibly 73-74; excellent mono
>   apparently not from the series; a clearer, slightly shorter version of this track
>   was previously available on **FILE UNDER: BEATLES, VOLUME
>   TWO**

Mucho Mungo (Lennon) (2:07)
>   late 75 - early 76, Dakota
>   (program 1, 25 Jan 88)
>   different from the versions previously available on **YIN YANG** (a baby Sean
>   cries in the background) and elsewhere

God (Lennon) (1:23)
>   Fall 70? an acoustic, almost folky version
>   (program 1, 25 Jan 88)

Life Begins At Forty (Lennon) (1:58)
>   Fall 80, Dakota; with beatbox and spoken intro; excellent mono?
>   (program 2, 1 Feb 88)

Woman (Lennon) (3:01)
>   Jul 80, Bermuda? acoustic demo
>   (program 3, 8 Feb 88)

Real Love (Lennon) (2:16)
>   80; acoustic demo, excellent stereo
>   (program 3, 8 Feb 88)
>   This song (often mis-called "Girls And Boys," includes a gentler version of the
>   middle eight of **Isolation** as its middle eight.

Cleanup Time (Lennon) (3:03)
>   80, Dakota; piano demo; excellent mono?
>   (program 2, 1 Feb 88)

Beautiful Boy (Darling Boy) (Lennon) (2:41)
>   Jul 80, Bermuda; excellent stereo
>   with message to Sean (**DF** sessions); this is a better quality—but edited, and
>   shorter—version of the track which appeared on **CONFIDENTIAL
>   DOCUMENT**.
>   (program 3, 8 Feb 88)

SOURCE:
>   Original source varies; most material from the first few episodes of *The Lost Lennon
Tapes.

SOUND QUALITY:
>   Very good to excellent mono, unless otherwise noted..

COMMENTS:
>   As these cuts are lifted directly from the radio series, most of them are excerpts; all
narration and voice-overs have been eliminated. Also included are a couple of cuts, previously
available, which do not seem to have been from the series.

THE LOST LENNON TAPES, VOLUME TWO

JOHN LENNON
Bag Records, 5074
Full color jacket (black & white front, full color back) ©1988 with track listing and recording
information; labels have artwork/photo.

Side A
>   "Put the incense on..." (0:07)
>   spoken; source unknown
>   (program 6, 29 Feb 88)

Revolution (Lennon-McCartney) (3:48)
 late May 68, Kinfauns; acoustic demo
 The rest of the Beatles clap along and provide some great Beach Boys
  harmony in spots
 (program 6, 29 Feb 88)
Child Of Nature (Lennon) (2:34)
 late May 68, Kinfauns; acoustic demo
 The original version of **Jealous Guy**; apparently John solo and double-
  tracked. The group were working on this song (rather half-heartedly)
  as late as the Jan 69, **GET BACK** sessions.
 (program 6, 29 Feb 88)
He Said He Said (Lennon) (0:13)
 65-66; John solo acoustic
 just an idea at this point; very early, very different
 (program 7, 7 Mar 88)
She Said She Said (Lennon-McCartney) (0:51)
 66? John solo, acoustic
 Not yet fully worked out, the song heads toward a slightly different "middle 8"
  before it's cut short.
 (program 7, 7 Mar 88)
I'm The Greatest (Lennon) (1:21)
 late 70, Tittenhurst; John on piano
 home demo, very early and crude run-through
 (program 8, 14 Mar 88)
Make Love Not War (Lennon) (3:15)
 70; John on piano; excellent stereo?
 the early version of **Mind Games**
 (program 8, 14 Mar 88)
How Do You Sleep? (Lennon) (8:14)
 Jul 71, **POB** sessions; an alternate take; excellent stereo
 (program 9, 21 Mar 88)
Daddy's Little Sunshine Boy (?) (0:28)
 67? source unknown; vocals: Ringo
 (program 8, 14 Mar 88)
Side B
Down In Eastern Australia I Met Her (?) (0:16)
 source unknown; John and electric organ
 (program 9, 21 Mar 88)
I'm The Greatest (Lennon) (2:35)
 71? studio demo; excellent stereo
 the "middle 8" is still quite different at this point
 (program 8, 14 Mar 88)
The Luck Of The Irish (Lennon-Ono) (3:14)
 12 Nov 71; takes 1 & 2; excellent stereo
 (program 7, 7 Mar 88)
Every Man Has A Woman Who Loves Him (Ono) (3:18)
 Aug 80, **DF** sessions; excellent stereo
 John sings lead, Yoko sings backing
 (program 7, 7 Mar 88)
(Just Like) Starting Over (Lennon) (4:56)
 Aug 80, Dakota; "take 3;" excellent stereo
 John with acoustic and rhythm box; some different lyrics
 (program 10, 28 Mar 88)
I Promise (Lennon) (1:57)
 late 70; John on piano; excellent stereo?
 A love song to Yoko which was apparently never completed; it utilizes part of
  Make Love Not War/Mind Games, and sounds a bit like **Oh!**
  Darling.
 (program 8, 14 Mar 88)

music hall medley ("Sea ditties") (2:36)
>When I Was Young And In My Prime (?)
>**My Old Man's A Dustman** (trad. arr. Donegan)
>**I Do Like To Be Beside The Seaside** (Glover Kind)
>**Leaning On A Lamp Post** (Gay)
>**Chinese Laundry Blues** (Cottrell-Formby)
>>unknown; John and piano; his true musical roots!
>(program 10, 28 Mar 88)

Grow Old With Me (Lennon) (3:21)
>Aug 80, Dakota? excellent stereo
>John with piano and rhythm box; Yoko has (later) voice-over at the end
>(program 7, 7 Mar 88)

SOURCE:
>Original material varies; most cuts taken from the radio series, *The Lost Lennon Tapes*.

SOUND QUALITY:
>Very good to excellent mono, unless otherwise noted.

COMMENTS:
>This marks the first appearance on disc of the late May 68, Kinfauns demos for **THE BEATLES**. They are certain to be copied for years to come.

THE LOST LENNON TAPES, VOLUME THREE

JOHN LENNON
Bag Records, 5075
Full color jacket ©1988 with track listing and recording information; labels say "Bag Records" and have track listing.

Side A
>We Come Along On Saturday Morning (?) (0:05)
>>source unknown
>>(3-hour special, 24 Jan 88)

Strawberry Fields Forever (Lennon-McCartney) (2:35)
>Nov 66, EMI? electric demo
>(program 11, 4 Apr 88)

What's The New Mary Jane (Lennon) (2:35)
>late May 68, Kinfauns
>acoustic demo (w/ the Beatles, and somebody actually says the title!)
>(program 13, 18 Apr 88)

Julia (Lennon-McCartney) (3:39)
>late May 68, Kinfauns; acoustic demo
>(program 11, 4 Apr 88)

Across The Universe (Lennon-McCartney) (3:45)
>4/8 Feb 68, EMI; take 8 (unreleased mix)
>This version features backward guitar and humming effects on the word "Om." Although there were eight takes of the song at EMI, although we have heard only the one (in all its versions).
>According to Lewisohn (*Beatles Book Monthly*, Aug 88) this was an interim mix, and there is no copy of it in EMI's vaults, although the effects tape of the humming (recorded late on the 4th and called "Hums Wild") is there.
>(program 13, 18 Apr 88)

You Know My Name (Look Up The Number) (Lennon-McCartney) (0:59)
>67? John composing on piano
>(program 9, 21 Mar 88)

Help! (Lennon-McCartney) (0:41)
>late 70; John at the piano; excellent stereo
>(program 9, 21 Mar 88)

Whatever Gets You Through The Night (Lennon) (5:27)
    Summer 74, NYC?
    John composes on the guitar, and and fills a blank spot with the lyrics of
        Jealous Guy.
    (program 12, 11 Apr 88)
18 Jun 65, BBC1, *Tonight* (1:04)
    (excerpts) includes:
    "We Must Not Forget The General Erection"
    "The Wumberlog (Or, The Magic Dog)"
    (program 9, 21 Mar 88)

Side B

Dear John/September Song (Lennon/Anderson-Weil) (4:14)
    late Nov 80, Dakota; acoustic, with rhythm box; excellent stereo
    possibly the last song he ever wrote
    (program 12, 11 Apr 88)
Whatever Happened To...? (Lennon) (4:56)
    80, Dakota; acoustic; excellent stereo
    from a planned musical, *The Ballad Of John And Yoko*, for which John and
        Yoko were going to contribute original music (reported in *People*, 20
        Feb 84, although the *LLT* was the first time I ever heard it mentioned).
        In an earlier episode, Yoko revealed that **Every Man Has A Wo-
        man Who Loves Him** was also written with that production in
        mind, for a scene where Yoko waits in London while John was in
        Rishikesh.
    (program 11, 4 Apr 88)
Cookin' (In The Kitchen Of Love) (Lennon) (2:28)
    Spring 76, Dakota; John on piano; excellent stereo?
    (program 13, 18 Apr 88)
    commercial release: Sep 76, **RINGO'S ROTOGRAVURE**
Peggy Sue (Holly-Allison-Petty) (0:54)
    Summer 71, St. Regis, NYC; from *Clock*; acoustic
    the song is interrupted by a phone call, and is not the same as the acoustic
        "medley" version on **TEDDY BOY**
    (3-hour special, 24 Jan 88)
Watching The Wheels (Lennon) (0:36)
    80, Dakota; on piano; excellent stereo
    (3-hour special, 24 Jan 88)
Watching The Wheels (Lennon) (1:44)
    80, Dakota; acoustic; excellent stereo
    (3-hour special, 24 Jan 88)
I'm Losing You (Lennon) (0:44)
    80, Dakota? acoustic with rhythm box
    (3-hour special, 24 Jan 88)
Beautiful Boy (Darling Boy) (Lennon) (0:52)
    take 1; acoustic (excerpt) with spoken intro
    source unknown; possibly Jul 80, Bermuda, but this is a solo take and not the
        usual one from the Bermuda tape.
    (3-hour special, 24 Jan 88)
Beautiful Boy (Darling Boy) (Lennon) (0:47)
    Aug 80, **DF** sessions
    mostly playback and studio chat
    (3-hour special, 24 Jan 88)
Cleanup Time (Lennon) (2:22)
    Aug 80, **DF** sessions; mostly studio chat
    (3-hour special, 24 Jan 88)
One To One radio spot outtakes (1:23)
    Aug 72; (excerpt); not from the series
    same material as on **WILLOWBROOK REHEARSALS**

SOURCE:
Original material varies; most cuts taken from the radio series, *The Lost Lennon Tapes.*

SOUND QUALITY:
Very good to excellent mono, unless otherwise noted. Stereo reverb has been added to a number of the home demos, making it difficult to tell mono from stereo.

COMMENTS:
A couple more Kinfauns demo are the highlights here, although **Dear John** showed extraordinary promise—another painful reminder of what we lost. Also included are things not from the radio series, and some minor items from a flashback to the initial 3-hour special.

THE LOST LENNON TAPES, VOLUME FOUR
JOHN LENNON
Bag Records, 5076
Full color jacket ©1988 with track listing and recording information; labels say "Bag Records" and have track listing.

Side A
    Revolution (Lennon-McCartney) (3:25)
        10 Jul 68, EMI; take 13; excellent mono
        the basic take for the 45 version, lacking the overdubs (most noticeably Nicky
            Hopkins' electric piano) of the 11th & 12th; to deal with voice-over
            problems from the radio show, this cut has the beginning of the com-
            mercial version edited (very well) onto it.
        (program 16, 9 May 88)
    Power To The People (Lennon) (2:47)
        Feb 71; alternate take; excellent mono?
        this is a weaker (and probably earlier) take than that on **VOLUME ONE**
        (program 16, 9 May 88)
10 Dec 71, Chrysler Arena, Ann Arbor, Michigan (10:27)
    Attica State (Lennon)
    The Luck Of The Irish (Lennon-Ono)
    John Sinclair (Lennon-Ono)
        from the unreleased film of the John Sinclair benefit, *Ten For Two*; excellent
            stereo
        (program 16, 9 May 88)
    Mannish Boy (London-McDaniel-Morganfeld) (1:52)
        Dakota, date unknown
        This song, originally done by Muddy Waters, is very similar to **I'm A Man**
            (McDaniel). Both were released in 55, but, from the vocals, it's
            obvious that John is doing Muddy Waters and not Bo Diddley, so I've
            gone with the corresponding title.
        (program 15, 2 May 88)
    "'Twas A Night Like Ethel Merman" (1:02)
        Dakota, date unknown; poem/recitation
        (program 15, 2 May 88)
    Beyond The Sea/Blue Moon (Trenet-Lawrence/Rodgers-Hart) (3:36)
        Dakota, date unknown; excellent stereo
        lots of fractured French
        (program 15, 2 May 88)
    Young Love (Cartey-Joyner) (0:35)
        Dakota, date unknown; excellent stereo (excerpt)
        a continuation of the previous segment
        (program 15, 2 May 88)

Side B

Cleanup Time (Lennon) (3:25)
Aug 80, **DF** sessions; excellent stereo
unreleased mix utilizing children's voices and other sound effects
(program 15, 2 May 88)
Good Morning Good Morning (Lennon-McCartney) (1:01)
Feb 67? demo
(program 15, 2 May 88)
Everybody's Got Something To Hide Except Me And My Monkey
(Lennon-McCartney) (2:55)
late May 68, Kinfauns; acoustic demo
The Beatles are probably on this, but the vocals are John, double-tracked. This
version is weird and very interesting.
(program 15, 2 May 88)
Everybody Had A Hard Year (Lennon) (1:34)
Fall 68, Kenwood; acoustic
this is not the same version as appears on **JOHNNY MOONDOG** as
Theme From *Rape*
(program 15, 2 May 88)
Brown-Eyed Handsome Man/Get Back (Berry/Lennon-McCartney) (2:15)
Dakota, date unknown; excellent stereo
two acoustic versions, one slow, one fast
(program 15, 2 May 88)
Serve Yourself (Lennon) (5:29)
Dakota, date unknown; excellent stereo
A different version (reportedly there are at least twelve) from that on **YIN
YANG** and **JOHNNY MOONDOG**. John accompanies himself on
the piano, still playing **Mean Mr. Mustard**.
(program 14, 25 Apr 88)
Lord, Take This Makeup Off Me (Lennon) (2:20)
Dakota, date unknown; acoustic, excellent stereo
A Dylan parody, probably ad-libbed
(program 14, 25 Apr 88)
The News Of The Day (From Reuters) (Lennon) (4:27)
Dakota, late Nov 78? acoustic, excellent stereo
Another Dylan parody, this one marginally cruel; John ad-libs current events in
his best Dylan voice to some familiar chords.
If the news he was reading was current, this segment is dated from late Nov
78 (Nixon was in Paris on 28 Nov 78).
(program 14, 25 Apr 88)

SOURCE:
Original material varies; all cuts taken from the radio series, *The Lost Lennon Tapes*.

SOUND QUALITY:
Very good to excellent mono, unless otherwise noted.

COMMENTS:
Lots of excellent material here. Of the three demos of Beatles material, probably the
most intriguing is the acoustic version of what would be one of their loudest, most raucous
electric songs.

THE LOST LENNON TAPES, VOLUME FIVE
JOHN LENNON
Bag Records, 5077
Full color cover with track listing and recording info on the back; labels info matches.

Side A
Dear Prudence (Lennon-McCartney) (4:41)
late May 68, Kinfauns; acoustic demo
Very close to the final version; John relates how they sang to Prudence (Mia
Farrow's sister) at Rishikesh.
(program 20, 6 Jun 88)
Jealous Guy (Lennon) (4:04)
Jul 71, **IMAGINE** sessions; an alternate take, excellent stereo
(program 20, 6 Jun 88)
God Save Us (Lennon) (1:55)
71; acoustic (with bongos) demo; excellent stereo
(program 19, 30 May 88)
Rock And Roll People (Lennon) (2:08)
73? electric composing demo; excellent stereo
(program 17, 16 May 88)
Rock Island Line (trad.) (2:46)
mid-70s, Dakota; electric version with rhythm box
crude but infectious, probably how the Quarry Men sounded (and where is
that 74 version with John and Paul?)
(program 18, 23 May 88)
Real Life (Lennon) (4:50)
Dakota, piano demo; excellent stereo?
an early version of **Steppin' Out**
(program 17, 16 May 88)
Side B
My Life (Lennon) (0:55)
take 1, piano demo
the earliest version of one of the melodies which became **(Just Like)
Starting Over**
(program 21, 13, Jun 88)
My Life (Lennon) (2:38)
take 3, acoustic demo
a more developed version of the song
(program 21, 13, Jun 88)
Don't Be Crazy (Lennon) (1:37)
piano demo, excellent stereo
an early version of the "middle 8" melody of **(Just Like) Starting Over**
(program 21, 13, Jun 88)
(Just Like) Starting Over (Lennon) (3:27)
Jul 80, Bermuda; demo take 3
acoustic, with rhythm box; excellent stereo
the two melodies have come together; the lyrics are different but some of the
rhymes are already in place
(program 21, 13, Jun 88)
studio chat (2:30)
Aug 80, **DF** sessions; excellent stereo
arranging the song in the studo
mostly John's mic, from the producer's tape
(program 21, 13, Jun 88)
(Just Like) Starting Over (Lennon) (4:21)
Aug 80, **DF** sessions; first vocal take; excellent stereo
mostly John's mic, from the producer's tape
(program 21, 13, Jun 88)
(Just Like) Starting Over (Lennon) (4:14)
Aug 80, **DF** sessions; first vocal take; excellent stereo
full playback of the previous take
(program 21, 13, Jun 88)

SOURCE:
Original material varies; all cuts taken from the radio series, *The Lost Lennon Tapes.*

SOUND QUALITY:
>Very good to excellent mono unless noted.

COMMENTS:
>I got two copies and both were warped. Nevertheless, there's a lot of good material here. Especially interesting is Side Two, which shows the development of **(Just Like) Starting Over**. This is an excellent use of the archive material.

THE LOST LENNON TAPES, VOLUME SIX
JOHN LENNON
Bag Records, 5078
Full color cover with track listing and recording info on the back; labels song titles.

Side A
>**Maggie Mae** (trad.) (0:23)
>>Aug 80, **DF** sessions; acoustic
>>(program 22, 20 Jun 88)
>
>**Honey Don't** (Perkins) (1:36)
>>Oct 70, **POB** sessions; excellent stereo
>>(program 22, 20 Jun 88)
>
>**Don't Be Cruel** (Blackwell-Presley) (1:26)
>>Oct 70, **POB** sessions; excellent stereo
>>(program 22, 20 Jun 88)
>
>**Matchbox** (Perkins) (1:46)
>>Oct 70, **POB** sessions; excellent stereo
>>(program 22, 20 Jun 88)
>
>**Dear Prudence** (Lennon-McCartney) (3:54)
>>28/29/30 Aug 68, Trident; take 1 (with overdubs)
>>As Lewisohn points out, while there was only one official take of this song, it was the result of numerous recordings and overdubs.
>>This version is almost identical in content to the commercial version, but with extended fade & chat, applause & fluglehorn at the end. The only other difference is that two of John's "Dear Prudence"s are missing from the last verse; they were dubbed in later.
>>(program 20, 6 Jun 88)
>
>**Cold Turkey** (Lennon) (3:35)
>>Sep 69, acoustic demo; excellent stereo?
>>(program 23, 27 Jun 88)
>
>**Here We Go Again** (Lennon-Spector) (3:00)
>>73? first complete acoustic demo
>>(program 23, 27 Jun 88)
>
>**Woman** (Lennon) (3:27)
>>Jul 80, Bermuda; acoustic w/rhythm box; excellent stereo
>>(program 22, 20 Jun 88)
>
>"The Neville Club" (0:35)
>>10 Dec 63; Gaumont Theatre, Doncaster? John reads his poem excerpted from an interview which appears on **THE BEATLES 'ROUND THE WORLD** (Cicadelic, CICLP-1965)
>>(program 18, 23 May 88)

Side B
>**Rock And Roll People** (Lennon) (5:59)
>>4 Aug 73, take 5; alternate take; excellent stereo
>>(program 17, 16 May 88)
>
>**Not Fade Away** (Hardin-Petty) (0:59)
>>Summer 71, St. Regis Hotel, NYC; excellent stereo
>>(program 22, 20 Jun 88)

Sweet Little Sixteen (Berry) (4:18)
>73 **R&R** sessions; excellent stereo
>(program 23, 27 Jun 88)

You Can't Catch Me (Berry) (3:28)
>73 **R&R** sessions; excellent stereo
>a performance which really demonstrates the similarity between this tune and
>>**Come Together**
>(program 23, 27 Jun 88)

Mirror, Mirror (Lennon) (2:34)
>Dakota; piano; take 1; not much of a song yet
>This was one of the tunes intended for **The Ballad Of John And Yoko**
>>play
>(program 20, 6 Jun 88)

Mirror, Mirror (Lennon) (2:37)
>Dakota; piano; take 5, still not much of a song
>(program 20, 6 Jun 88)

SOURCE:
>Original material varies; all cuts taken from the radio series, *The Lost Lennon Tapes*.

SOUND QUALITY:
>Very good to excellent mono unless noted.

COMMENTS:
>Some nice oldies here; the complete take of **Dear Prudence** and the acoustic demo of **Cold Turkey** are also memorable.

THE LOST LENNON TAPES, VOLUME SEVEN

JOHN LENNON
Bag Records, 5079
Full color cover with track listing and recording info on the back; labels have artwork and song titles.

Side A

Mind Games (Lennon) (4:03)
>Sep 73, NYC; alternate take; excellent stereo
>(program 24, 4 Jul 88)

Cold Turkey (Lennon) (4:56)
>30 Sep 69; alternate take, from an acetate; excellent stereo?
>(program 23, 27 Jun 88)

One Of The Boys (3:12)
>Dakota; acoustic "take 2;" excellent stereo?
>(program 24, 4 Jul 88)

request for **Tight A\$** (0:12)
>Oct 74, KHJ-AM, Los Angeles; from the call-in
>(program 17, 16 May 88)

Tight A\$ (Lennon) (3:20)
>73? electric composing demo; excellent stereo
>(program 17, 16 May 88)

studio chat (2:09)
>Aug 80, **DF** sessions
>mostly John's mic, from the producer's tape
>(program 22, 20 Jun 68)

Woman (Lennon) (2:45)
>Aug 80, **DF** sessions; alternate vocal take
>mostly John's mic, from the producer's tape
>(program 22, 20 Jun 88)

Side B
  Dear Yoko (Lennon) (3:43)
    Jul 80, Bermuda; acoustic; excellent stereo
    (program 21, 13 Jun 88)
  I Don't Wanna Face It (Lennon) (2:02)
    Jul 80, Bermuda? acoustic; excellent stereo
    (program 24, 4 Jul 88)
  Watching The Wheels (Lennon) (0:15)
    date unknown, Dakota; an abandoned piano take
    (program 21, 13 Jun 88)
  Watching The Wheels (Lennon) (3:36)
    date unknown, Dakota; piano run-through, some different lyrics
    (program 21, 13 Jun 88)
  I'm Stepping Out (Lennon) (4:32)
    Jul 80, Bermuda; acoustic & rhythm box; excellent stereo?
    (program 17, 16 May 88)
  Clean-up Time (Lennon) (2:58)
    date unknown, Dakota; piano run-through
    (program 23, 27 Jun 88)
  Woman (Lennon) (3:14)
    Aug 80, **DF** sessions; alternate take; excellent stereo
    (program 22, 20 Jun 88)

SOURCE:
  Original material varies; all cuts taken from the radio series, *The Lost Lennon Tapes.*

SOUND QUALITY:
  Very good to excellent mono unless noted.

COMMENTS:
  Plenty of **DOUBLE FANTASY**-oriented material here (for those who like it); my favorite cut is the alternate **Cold Turkey**.

MAGTRAX
THE BEATLES
Suma Records, 8084250
2-disc set, on colored vinyl, in full color jacket; label info matches.

DISC ONE
Side A [duplicates **GET BACK JOURNALS**, Side G]
  Two Of Us (Lennon-McCartney) (11:30)
    first? rehearsal with chord changes (excerpt)
    includes brief **Jambalaya** (Williams) (0:06)
  Child Of Nature (Lennon) (1:48)
    vocals: John, George (excerpt)
  I Shall Be Released (Dylan) (1:46)
    vocals: George, John
  Sun King/Don't Let Me Down (Lennon-McCartney) (4:10)
    interesting segue into early rehearsal (excerpts)
    At this point, the instrumental which would later appear as **Sun King** on
      ABBEY ROAD seems to have been part of **Don't Let Me Down**.
Side B [duplicates **GET BACK JOURNALS**, Side D]
  riffs & chat
  Norwegian Wood (Lennon-McCartney) (0:36)
    instrumental, while everyone talks
[181] **She Came In Through The Bathroom Window** (Lennon-McCartney) (2:10)
    "one more" version (excerpts)
  Penina (McCartney) (0:52)
    vocals: Paul

Shakin' In The Sixties (improvisation?) (0:37)
    vocals: John
Move It/Good Rockin' Tonight (Samwell/Brown) (1:37)
    vocals: John
Across The Universe (Lennon-McCartney) (3:29)
    vocals: John, Paul
Two Of Us (Lennon-McCartney) (1:53)
    fast version, with backing vocals
bass improvisation (0:46)
    Paul
Ramblin' Woman (Dylan?) (2:00)
    George, solo acoustic
I Threw It All Away/Mama You Been On My Mind (Dylan) (3:59)
    George, solo acoustic
chat
Flowing More Freely Than Wine (?) (0:03)
    vocals: John
    Is this a reference to **I Me Mine** or to another song?
I Me Mine (Harrison) (2:26)
    rehearsing the bridge
chat
Domino (Kaye-Ferrari) (1:24)
    vocals: Paul
DISC TWO
Side C [duplicates **GET BACK JOURNALS**, Side J]
    Bring It On Home To Me (Cooke) (1:50)
        vocals: George, Paul
    Hitchhike (Gaye-Paul-Stevenson) (2:00)
        vocals: George, Paul
    You Can't Do That (Lennon-McCartney) (2:12)
        vocals: George, Paul, John
[43]   **The Hippy Hippy Shake** (Romero) (2:27)
        vocals: George, Paul
    chat & riffs
    Two Of Us (Lennon-McCartney) (1:17)
        vocals: Paul; "keep going" version
    All Along The Watchtower (Dylan) (0:12)
        vocals: George, Paul (excerpt)
    Short Fat Fannie (Williams) (2:45)
        vocals: George, Paul
    Midnight Special (trad.) (2:00)
        vocals: John, Paul
When You're Drunk You Think Of Me (?) (0:09)
    vocals: George
What's The Use Of Getting Sober (When You're Gonna Get Drunk Again) (Meyers) (0:07)
    vocals: John
What Do You Wanna Make Those Eyes At Me For? (Monaco-McCarthy-Johnson) (1:00)
    vocals: Paul, George, John
chat & riffs
Money (That's What I Want) (Bradford-Gordy) (0:25)
    instrumental while everybody talks
chat
Gimme Some Truth (Lennon) (1:58)
    vocals: Paul, John; discussion and rehearsal

Side D [duplicates **GET BACK JOURNALS**, Side T]
[319]   **Teddy Boy** (McCartney) (15:13)
[318]   24 Jan 69, Apple; extended rehearsal, with chord changes
                includes the usual version and
                The Ball Of Inverary (trad.) (0:05)
                Ach Du Lieber (trad.) (0:04)
                    as "Balls For Mr. Benglestein"
        chat
        Two Of Us (Lennon-McCartney) (0:08) (excerpt)
        chat
        Two Of Us (Lennon-McCartney) (0:40) (Paul solo)
        lunch & riffs
        Polythene Pam (Lennon-McCartney) (1:32)
                rehearsal; vocals: John, Paul
[320]   jam (0:55)
        Two Of Us (Lennon-McCartney) (0:22)
                (excerpts)
        Maggie Mae (trad. arr. Lennon-McCartney-Harrison-Starkey) (0:34)
                24 Jan 69, Apple; the usual version
        Teddy Boy (McCartney) (1:31)
                playback of earlier rehearsal (excerpts)

SOURCE:
        Jan 69, **GET BACK** sessions.

SOUND QUALITY:
        Very good to excellent mono.

COMMENTS:
        Of interest only if the **GET BACK JOURNALS** are not available. Side D may be
entirely from 24 Jan 69, Apple.

MAILMAN BLUES
THE BEATLES
Apple Ghost Records [Maidenhead], JET3
Full color jacket with song listing and some recording information on the back; labels say JET
III.

Side A
        Not Guilty (Harrison) (3:16)
                8/9 Aug 68, EMI; take 102, from acetate; very good stereo
                from **NOT GUILTY**; faster and fades early
        Mailman, Bring Me No More Blues (Roberts-Katz-Clayton) (1:24)
                29 Jan 69, Apple; **SESSIONS** remix
                excellent stereo; starts late, fades early
        commercial for **Hi, Hi, Hi/C Moon** (2:23)
                Nov 72; excellent mono (too much high end)
        8 Oct 82, *Parkinson In Australia* (tv) (5:31)
                Honey Don't (Perkins)
                Honey Don't/Blue Suede Shoes (Perkins)
                filmed 28 Sep 82, excellent mono; vocals: mostly Glenn Shorrock (ex-Little
                        River Band); Ringo drums and sings a little; after the first **Honey
                        Don't**, somebody says, "I hope we passed the audition."
        Singing The Blues (Endsley) (2:19)
                12 Dec 81, *Parkinson* (UK tv), excellent mono (excerpt)
                personnel included Ringo (drums, some vocals), Michael Parkinson (vocals),
                        Harry Stoner (piano), Tim Rice and Jimmy Tarbuck
        I Forgot To Remember To Forget (Kesler-Feathers) (1:02)
                18 May 64, BBC (excerpt); very good mono (hiss)

Ringo interview (3:44)
>   Summer 74, Los Angeles; excellent mono
>   This is an interview with Ringo (by "Bob") for the employees of Apple
>   /EMI/Capitol. Ringo reveals that "It's all down to goodnight Vienna" is
>   a Liverpudlian expression meaning "I'm getting out of here," which
>   helps explain the jacket's spaceship theme.

Rock And Roll People (Lennon) (2:37)
>   Johnny Winter, Oct 74; from his album **JOHN DAWSON WINTER III**
>   (US) Blue Sky PZ 33292
>   very good stereo (distortion)

King Of Fuh (Friedland) (0:53)
>   This is from a rare Apple single (UK Apple 8) by Brute Force (Steven Fried-
>   land), produced in promotional copies only. The idea is that the "King
>   of Fuh" was the "Fuh King." Get it? Nudge nudge, wink wink, smirk
>   smirk, yawn yawn. Maybe that was clever in 69—or maybe not, since
>   EMI declined to press or distribute it. The song had an independent
>   release in the US in 71.
>   excellent mono (excerpt); mercifully fades after the first verse. If you must
>   hear the whole thing, it's on **A NIGHTMARE IS ALSO A
>   DREAM**.

Side B

(Just Like) Starting Over (Lennon) (4:12)
>   Aug 80; the long promo version (Geffen PRO-A-919)
>   excellent stereo
>   21 May 85, Julian live in Sydney, Australia (13:29)
>   **Stand By Me** (King-Leiber-Stoller)
>   **Day Tripper** (Lennon-McCartney)
>   **Slippin' And Slidin'** (Penniman-Bocage-Collins-Smith)
>   an audience recording, fair to good mono

Una Sensazionale Intervista (6:01)
>   5-6 Jun 68, EMI; from (Italian) Apple DPR-108 (excerpt)
>   The Kenny Everett interview, with lots of fooling around and vocal improvisa-
>   tions; includes **Cottonfields**, Goodbye Jingle, Tiny Tim For Presi-
>   dent, and so on; excellent mono
>   Regarding the dating of this interview, John mentions that they were working
>   on Ringo's first song, the second for their new LP. The first song
>   recorded was **Revolution 1** (30/31 May & 4 Jun), after which they
>   began **Don't Pass Me By** (5-6 Jun).

SOURCE:
>   Varies; see individual entries.

SOUND QUALITY:
>   Varies; see individual entries.

COMMENTS:
>   Several new (if minor) items here. Regarding the title, there is a song called **Mailman
Blues** (52, written and recorded by Lloyd Price, and originally titled **Korea Boogie**), but
this, of course, is not it. However, this incorrect song title was used during early production
of the **SESSIONS** LP.

MAPLE LEAF GARDENS
PAUL McCARTNEY & WINGS
ZAP, 7887
Insert cover with song titles.

Side A (27:18)
>   **Rock Show** (McCartney)
>   **Jet** (McCartney)

Let Me Roll It (McCartney)
Spirits Of Ancient Egypt (McCartney)
Medicine Jar (McCulloch-Allen)
Maybe I'm Amazed (McCartney)
Side B (24:03)
Call Me Back Again (McCartney)
Lady Madonna (Lennon-McCartney)
The Long And Winding Road (Lennon-McCartney)
Live And Let Die (McCartney)
Picasso's Last Words (McCartney)
Richard Corey (Simon)
Bluebird (McCartney)

SOURCE:
9 May 76, Maple Leaf Gardens, Toronto

SOUND QUALITY:
Audience tape, good mono.

COMMENTS:
Unremarkable, unless you were there, and then it's *your* concert.

"MARY JANE"
THE BEATLES
No manufacturer listed, 93
Insert cover with song titles; labels have side numbers only.

Side A
What's The New Mary Jane (Lennon) (2:35)
14 Aug 68, EMI; take 4 (stereo remix #4); very good mono (excerpt)
possibly from the unreleased Apple 45
Shout! (Isley-Isley-Isley) (2:21)
Around The Beatles, broadcast 6 May 64; very good mono
phone interview with George (1:12)
c.65; source unknown; good mono (excerpts)
People Say (Szigeti-Lichterman) (2:45)
"John & Paul," 65, from (UK) 45 Tip 1021
good to very good mono; no Beatles involvement
You Know My Name (Lennon-McCartney) (4:10)
17 May & 7/8Jun 67 (instrumentals)/30 Apr 69 (vocals), EMI
take 30; from the 45; excellent mono
Side B
16 Jul 64, *Top Gear* (10:53)
[*Top Of The Pops* intro]
Long Tall Sally (Johnson-Penniman-Blackwell)
interview
A Hard Day's Night (Lennon-McCartney)
Things We Said Today (Lennon-McCartney)
[*Top Of The Pops* closing]
very good mono, too slow
I'm Walkin' (Szigeti-Lichterman) (2:12)
"John & Paul," 65, from (UK) 45 Tip 1021
good to very good mono; no Beatles involvement
Sie Liebt Dich (Lennon-McCartney) (2:23)
29 Jan 64, Paris; take 14; from the 45

SOURCE:
Varies; see individual entries.

SOUND QUALITY:
>   Varies; see individual entries.

COMMENTS:
>   Another reworking of **LIVE AT NASSAU COLISEUM**; this is *not* the same **MARY JANE** (CBM 3585) which is a reissue of **SPICY BEATLES SONGS**. The *Top Gear* is obviously copied from another boot, since it has the break just before **A Hard Day's Night**.

MEET THE BEEB
THE BEATLES
Beeb Transcription Records, BB 2190/9
Black & white jacket with track listing and recording info on the back; labels are blank.

Side A
>   8 Mar 62, *Teenager's Turn*
>   **Dream Baby** (Walker) (1:49)
>   **Memphis** (Berry) (2:14)
>   **Please Mr. Postman** (Holland-Bateman-Gordy) (1:59)
>   15 Jun 62, *Here We Go*
>   **Ask Me Why** (McCartney-Lennon) (2:14)
>   **Besame Mucho** (Velazquez-Skylar) (2:24)
>   **A Picture Of You** (Beveridge-Oakman) (2:13)
>   26 Jan 63, *Saturday Club*
>   **Some Other Guy** (Leiber-Stoller) (2:06)
>   **Keep Your Hands Off My Baby** (Goffin-King) (2:35)
>   **Beautiful Dreamer** (Foster) (1:51)
>   7 Apr 63, *Easy Beat*
>   **From Me To You** (McCartney-Lennon) (1:55)
>   introduced by Gerry Marsden

Side B
>   16 Mar 63, *Saturday Club*
>   **I Saw Her Standing There** (McCartney-Lennon) (2:35)
>   **Misery** (McCartney-Lennon) (1:47)
>   **Too Much Monkey Business** (Berry) (1:47)
>   **I'm Talking About You** (Berry) (1:54)
>   **Please Please Me** (McCartney-Lennon) (1:52)
>   **The Hippy Hippy Shake** (Romero) (1:41)
>   21 Jul 63, *Easy Beat*
>   **I Saw Her Standing There** (McCartney-Lennon) (2:36)
>   **A Shot Of Rhythm And Blues** (Thompson) (2:12)
>   **There's A Place** (McCartney-Lennon) (1:48)
>   30 Aug 63, *Non Stop Pop* (2:09)
>   interview recorded 30 Jul 63, Manchester
>   The interview is followed by a piece of **I Got A Woman** from *Pop Go The Beatles* #9, 13 Aug 63.
>   **Abilene** (trad. arr. Loudermilk) (2:17)
>   63 BBC broadcast? fair mono; no Beatles involvement
>   This song (a hit for George Hamilton IV in 1963) is a small mystery. I think it very unlikely that the Beatles would cover a current hit in 63, and it is almost definitely not them (the sound quality is poor enough that it's impossible to be certain). If a British group released it as a 45, that may be the group here.

SOURCE:
>   Various BBC broadcasts.

SOUND QUALITY:
>   Good to very good mono, except as noted.

COMMENTS:
    A very noisy pressing, especially sad given the nature of the material on Side A. This is the first appearance on disc of the complete lineup the the Beatles' first two BBC shows, recorded with Pete Best on drums, and includes the first BBC performance of a Lennon-Mc-Cartney original. A much better pressing can be found on **THE LOST BEEBS.** The 26 Jan 63 *Saturday Club* material has been available before, and with better sound, on **BEAUTIFUL DREAMER.** Of the 16 Mar 63 *Saturday Club* material, only **I'm Talking About You** has appeared previously (also on **BEAUTIFUL DREAMER**).

MELLOW YELLOW
THE BEATLES
"Apple Records," SAPCOR 39
2-disc set in full-color jacket, with song listing on the back; says "Made In New Zealand;" labels say "Rubber Soul" and have song titles.

DISC ONE
Side A
    Yellow Submarine (Lennon-McCartney) (1:07)
        26 Apr 78, from *Ringo* tv special; very good mono
        This is an excerpt of a longer production number, and includes the six-second
        "drum bit," copied from **OGNIR RRATS GREATEST HITS.**
    It's All Too Much (Harrison) (2:31)
        25/26 May & 2 Jun 67, De Lane Lea; take 32 (mono remix #1)
        with extra verse, from the *Yellow Submarine* soundtrack
        very good mono
    All You Need Is Love (Lennon-McCartney) (5:08)
        14 Jun 67, Olympic & 19/23/24/25 Jun 67, EMI; take 58
        broadcast version, from the *Our World* tv special
        excellent mono; this includes all of the pre-performance chat and preparation
            in much better sound quality than usual
    Ringo's Yellow Submarine (11:00)
        Jun-Dec 83, ABC FM network; excerpts (part 1)
        very good to excellent stereo (some hiss, static and fading)
Side B
    Ringo's Yellow Submarine (22:40)
        Jun-Dec 83, ABC FM network; excerpts (part 2)
        very good to excellent stereo (some hiss, static and fading)
DISC TWO
Side C
    Ringo's Yellow Submarine (20:34)
        Jun-Dec 83, ABC FM network; excerpts (part 3)
        very good to excellent stereo (some hiss, static and fading)
        This side contains a wonderful sequence as Ringo conducts the **Beatles'
            Open-End Interview**.
Side D
    Ringo's Yellow Submarine (18:47)
        Jun-Dec 83, ABC FM network; excerpts (part 4)
        very good to excellent stereo (some hiss, static and fading)

SOURCE:
    Varies; see individual entries.

SOUND QUALITY:
    Varies; see individual entries.

COMMENTS:
    This may be the first time that significant material from *Ringo's Yellow Submarine* has appeared on bootleg, although the material has been edited so that all that remains is Ringo's

narration and reminiscences. Some of it's quite interesting, and is continued on **HEY JU-LIAN** (SAPCOR 41).

MIXED BLESSING
THE BEATLES
Boxtop Records, GN 70077
2-disc set, one on colored vinyl, in generic Boxtop jacket, with photo and song listing attached; one label is generic TMOQ, the other is blank.

DISC ONE
Side A
       One After 909 (Lennon-McCartney) (3:09)
           30 Jan 69, Apple rooftop; with **Danny Boy** (Weatherly) (0:05)
       Rocker (McCartney) (0:45)
           22 Jan 69, Apple; aka "Link Track" & "Instrumental 42"
       Save The Last Dance For Me/Don't Let Me Down
       (Pomus-Shuman/Lennon-McCartney) (0:51)
           22 Jan 69, Apple
       Don't Let Me Down (Lennon-McCartney) (3:38)
           22 Jan 69, Apple
       Dig A Pony (Lennon-McCartney (3:49)
           24 Jan 69, Apple; laughing version
       I've Got A Feeling (Lennon-McCartney) (2:43)
           24 Jan 69, Apple; cocked-up version
       Get Back (Lennon-McCartney) (3:12)
           28 Jan 69; the 45 version
Side B
       For You Blue (Harrison) (2:40)
           25 Jan 69, Apple; with false start and laughing
       Teddy Boy (McCartney) (3:40)
           24 Jan 69, Apple; the usual version
       Two Of Us (Lennon-McCartney) (3:40)
           24 Jan 69, Apple; "good-bye" version
       Maggie Mae (trad. arr. Lennon-McCartney-Harrison-Starkey) (0:37)
           24 Jan 69, Apple; same as commercial release
       Dig It (Lennon-McCartney) (3:57)
           26 Jan 69, Apple; longer version of commercial take
       Let It Be (Lennon-McCartney) (3:52)
           31 Jan 69, Apple; take 27
           the basic take for both released versions
       The Long And Winding Road (Lennon-McCartney) (3:43)
           31 Jan 69, Apple; take 19
           the basic take for the commercial release
       Get Back (reprise) (Lennon-McCartney) (0:37)
           28 Jan 69, Apple; laughing version (excerpt)
DISC TWO
Side C
       Not Guilty (Harrison) (3:19)
           8/9/12 Aug 68, EMI; take 102
           SESSIONS remix; excellent stereo
       Besame Mucho (Velazquez-Skylar) (2:34)
           6 Jun 62, EMI; excellent mono
       Catswalk (Lennon-McCartney) (1:02)
           Spring 62 rehearsal? (excerpt)
       Here We Go Again (Lennon-Spector) (1:18)
           73-74, source unknown
           Lennon, solo acoustic; very good mono
       While My Guitar Gently Weeps (Harrison) (3:23)
           25 Jul 68, EMI; take 1 (acoustic); excellent mono

Suicide (McCartney) (1:28)
> *One Hand Clapping sessions*, very good mono
> see **ONE HAND CLAPPING**

Mailman, Bring Me No More Blues (Roberts-Katz-Clayton) (1:50)
> 29 Jan 69, Apple; excellent stereo

Thank You Guru Dev/**Happy Birthday To You** (McCartney-?/Hill-Hill) (2:13)
> 15 Mar 68, Rishikesh, India; with the Beach Boys; very good mono

The Inner Light (Harrison) (2:32)
> 11 Jan 68, Bombay & 6 Feb 68, EMI
> excellent, true stereo; from UK EP

Shout! (Isley-Isley-Isley) (2:00)
> 19 Apr 64, IBC; for broadcast on *Around The Beatles*
> excellent mono

Side D

I'm Looking Through You (Lennon-McCartney) (2:53)
> 24 Oct 65, EMI; take 1

Strawberry Field Forever (Lennon-McCartney) (2:31)
> 24 Nov 66, EMI; take 1

Strawberry Fields Forever (Lennon-McCartney) (3:04)
> 28 Nov 66, EMI; takes 3 (false start) & 4

Strawberry Fields Forever (Lennon-McCartney) (3:13)
> 15 Dec 66, EMI; overdub onto take 25
> George Martin conducts his score

Strawberry Fields Forever (Lennon-McCartney) (3:17)
> 8/9/15/21 Dec 66, EMI; take 26

A Day In The Life (Lennon-McCartney) (5:05)
> 19/20 Jan & 3/10/22 Feb 67, EMI; edit of takes 6 & 7
> commercial version, with clean intro

I Want You (She's So Heavy) (Lennon-McCartney) (0:54)
> late Mar 69, John, Amsterdam Hilton
> from Israeli interview; good mono

SOURCE:
> DISC ONE is a copy of the original **GET BACK** LP, as produced by George Martin.
DISC TWO varies; see individual entries.

SOUND QUALITY:
> Excellent stereo, unless otherwise stated.

COMMENTS:
> Another boring Boxtop reissue. DISC ONE is a copy of any of a number of **GET BACK** boots; DISC TWO is either a copy or repackaging of **FILE UNDER: BEATLES, VOLUME TWO**. Note: some copies may have come with two DISC TWOs.

MONKEY BUSINESS
THE BEATLES
Rock Solid Records, RSR 76001-2
2 disc set in 2-color jacket, with song listing and recording information on the back; labels say "Amazing Stork Records;" song info matches.

DISC ONE
Side A

25 May 63, *Saturday Club*
> **I Saw Her Standing There** (McCartney-Lennon) (2:41)
> **Do You Want To Know A Secret** (McCartney-Lennon) (1:39)
> **Boys** (Dixon-Farrell) (2:29)
> **Long Tall Sally** (Johnson-Penniman-Blackwell) (1:39)
> **From Me To You** (McCartney-Lennon) (1:42)
> **Money (That's What I Want)** (Gordy-Bradford) (2:03)

24 Jun 63, *Side By Side*
   Side By Side (Wood) (0:48)
   The Beatles with the Karl Denver Trio
   Too Much Monkey Business (Berry) (1:56)
   Boys (Dixon-Farrell) (2:21)
   I'll Be On My Way (Lennon-McCartney) (1:51)
   From Me To You (McCartney-Lennon) (1:48)
Side B
23 Jun 63, *Easy Beat*
   Some Other Guy (Leiber-Stoller-Barrett) (1:53)
   A Taste Of Honey (Marlow-Scott) (1:48)
   Thank You Girl (McCartney-Lennon) (1:53)
   From Me To You (McCartney-Lennon) (1:42)
18 Apr 63, *Swinging Sound '63*
   Twist And Shout (Russell-Medley) (1:56)
   From Me To You (McCartney-Lennon) (1:43)
3 Jun 63, *Steppin' Out*
   Please Please Me (McCartney-Lennon) (1:48)
   I Saw Her Standing There (McCartney-Lennon) (2:41)
DISC TWO
Side C
29 Jun 63, *Saturday Club*
   I Got To Find My Baby (Berry) (1:47)
   Memphis (Berry) (2:08)
   From Me To You (McCartney-Lennon) (1:44)
   Roll Over Beethoven (Berry) (2:16)
13 May 63, *Side By Side*
   Long Tall Sally (Johnson-Penniman-Blackwell) (1:41)
   A Taste Of Honey (Marlow-Scott) (1:56)
   Chains (Goffin-King) (2:15)
   Thank You Girl (McCartney-Lennon) (1:53)
   Boys (Dixon-Farrell) (1:45)
Side D
11 Jun 63, *Pop Go The Beatles #2*
   Too Much Monkey Business (Berry) (1:40)
   I Got To Find My Baby (Berry) (1:49)
   Young Blood (Leiber-Stoller-Pomus) (1:49)
   Till There Was You (Willson) (2:03)
   Baby It's You (David-Bacharach-Williams) (2:31)
   Love Me Do (McCartney-Lennon) (2:15)
4 Jun 63, *Pop Go The Beatles #1*
   Everybody's Trying To Be My Baby (Perkins) (1:57)
   Do You Want To Know A Secret (McCartney-Lennon) (1:41)
   You Really Got A Hold On Me (Robinson) (2:44)

SOURCE:
   Various BBC radio broadcasts.

SOUND QUALITY:
   Very good mono except for *Swingin Sound '63* (fair mono) and *Steppin' Out* (good mono).

COMMENTS:
   This is a reissue of **THE BEATLES AT THE BEEB, VOLUMES ONE** and **TWO**. For a list of songs missing from these shows, see the corresponding entries in *Do You Want To Know A Secret?*
   As copied here, the cuts are noticeably too fast and the sound quality is worse.

MORE FROM THE TOUR
GEORGE HARRISON
Instant Analysis, 1048
Insert cover; labels are generic Instant Analysis.

Side A (22:43)
      Hari's On Tour (Express) (Harrison)
      While My Guitar Gently Weeps (Harrison)
      Something (Harrison)
      Sue Me Sue You Blues (Harrison)
      For You Blue (Harrison)
Side B (19:45)
      introducing the band
      Give Me Love (Harrison)
      Sound Stage Of Mind (Harrison)
      In My Life (Lennon-McCartney)
      Dark Horse (Harrison)

SOURCE:
      22 Nov 74, Fort Worth, Texas (excerpts)

SOUND QUALITY:
      Audience tape, good to very good mono.

COMMENTS:
      This was recently reissued as **A DARK HOARSE IN '74**.

NASHVILLE DIARY (EP)
PAUL McCARTNEY & WINGS
No manufacturer listed, PRO-1234
7-inch EP in brown & white picture sleeve, with song titles; label info matches.

Side A
      My Love (McCartney) (4:19)
      One Hand Clapping (McCartney) (1:20)
Side B
      Hi, Hi, Hi (McCartney) (2:45)
      Soily (McCartney) (2:58) (excerpt)

SOURCE:
      One Hand Clapping sessions; labels say 75, Nashville; see **ONE HAND CLAP-
PING** for a discussion of possible dates.

SOUND QUALITY:
      Very good stereo.

COMMENTS:
      This was the first appearance of *One Hand Clapping* material. This and more is available on **ONE HAND CLAPPING**. The title is that of Linda McCartney's 1975 MPL desk diary.

A NIGHTMARE IS ALSO A DREAM
THE BEATLES
No manufacturer listed, B3+B4
2-disc set, in full color jacket, ©1985 (unlikely), with song listing and recording information on the back; label info matches.

DISC ONE
Side A
    I Don't Want To Do It (Dylan) (2:48)
        85, George; from the soundtrack of *Porky's Revenge* (45 mix)
        excellent stereo
    Every Man Has A Woman Who Loves Him (Ono) (3:28)
        Aug 80, John; from the LP **EVERY MAN HAS A WOMAN**
        excellent stereo
    We All Stand Together (McCartney) (4:17)
        84, Paul; from the 45; excellent stereo
    In My Car (Starkey-Walsh-Foster-Goody) (3:04)
        mid-82, Ringo; from the German 45 (Bellaphon 100.16.012)
        excellent stereo
    Save The World (Harrison) (4:55)
        late 84, George; from the LP **GREENPEACE**; excellent stereo
    Pretty Little Head (McCartney) (3:41)
        Paul, 45 mix; excellent stereo
Side B
    Goodnight Vienna (Lennon) (2:55)
        Jun 74, John; demo for Ringo; very good stereo
    Ode To A Koala Bear (McCartney) (3:38)
        81? Paul; from the **Say Say Say** 12-inch; excellent stereo
    Ob-La-Di, Ob-La-Da (Lennon-McCartney) (2:40)
        3/4/5 Jul 68, EMI; take 5; very good stereo
        Calypso version, from the cancelled **SESSIONS** 45
    Press (McCartney) (4:16)
        85, Paul; 10-inch mix; excellent stereo
    Paul McCartney's Theme For *The Honorary Consul* (McCartney) (3:36)
        John Williams, 83, from the film *The Honorary Consul*
        excellent stereo
DISC TWO
Side C
    King Of Fuh (Friedland) (2:57)
        69, Brute Force, from rare 45 (UK) Apple 8; excellent mono
Holding On To A Dream (?) (2:52)
        unknown; possibly some Wings involvement
        good to very good mono
    Ob-La-Di, Ob-La-Da (Lennon-McCartney) (2:55)
        8/11/15 Jul 68, EMI; take 23; excellent mono
        the usual version, OOPSed; for a discussion of OOPSing, see the section
            "Making Sense Of Beatles Rarities" in *Do You Want To Know A Se-*
            cret?
    It's All Too Much (Harrison) (6:25)
        25/26 May & 2 Jun 67, De Lane Lea; take 196 [really 2]
        excellent mono; the usual version, OOPSed
excerpts from the radio special *Sergeant Pepper's Lonely Hearts Club Band: The His-*
tory Of The Beatle Years 1962-1970 (2:32)
        Beatles In The Studio
            snippets of EMI chat, countdowns; excellent mono/stereo
        I Wanna Be Your Man (Lennon-McCartney)
            29 Aug 66, Candlestick Park, San Francisco; excellent mono
            becomes background for an interview with Brian
Side D
    Here We Go Again (Lennon-Spector) (1:18)
        73-74? Lennon acoustic demo; very good mono
    Suicide (McCartney) (1:28)
        Fall 75? *One Hand Clapping* sessions
        video soundtrack; excellent mono

The Pirate Song (Harrison-Idle) (2:05)
>26 Dec 75, *Rutland Weekend Television Christmas Show*
>In 1975-6, Eric Idle (of Monty Python) and Neil Innes (of the Bonzo Dog Band) teamed up to produce *Rutland Weekend Television* for BBC-2. There were two series (12 May-16 Jun 75, 12 Nov-24 Dec 76) and a special (26 Dec 75). (On one of those a bogus pop-group called the "Rutland Stones" sang a Beatles parody written by Neil Innes. When Idle appeared in the U.S. on *Saturday Night Live*, he showed the clip, renaming the group "The Rutles.") The Christmas special featured this song co-written by George and Eric Idle; excellent mono

Johnny B. Goode (Berry) (3:39)
>15 Mar 86, Birmingham; *Heartbeat '86* charity gig
>George, with Denny Laine & Robert Plant
>a line recording, from the video; very good mono

Radio One Jingle (McCartney) (0:16)
>83? excellent mono

O Kristelighed (Grundtvig) (0:23)
>late Dec 69? Thy, Denmark? John & Yoko; good mono
>This is a century-old Danish Christmas carol, Wiener reports in his 3 Jun 88 *Goldmine* article. John & Yoko were in Aalborg visiting Kyoko. While John was in Denmark, Paul, George and Ringo held the final Beatles recording session at EMI, on 4 Jan 70.

Beatle intro's (0:45)
>24 Oct 63, *Karlaplansstudion*; broadcast on *Pop '63*; excellent mono
>the group introduces themselves by imitating their instruments

Lucille (Collins-Penniman) (8:33)
>14 Dec 84, Sydney, Australia
>George, as "Arnold Grove from Liverpool," with Deep Purple
>an audience tape, fair to good mono; *Hot Wacks Book XII* lists a supposedly excellent stereo bootleg from this performance

SOURCE:
>Varied; see individual entries.

SOUND QUALITY:
>Varied; see individual entries.

COMMENTS:
>There are a number of interesting items here, mixed in with the usual reissues. The OOPSed tracks are intriguing, if you haven't heard them before. The alternate commercial mixes of **Press** and **Pretty Little Head** are nice to have for those who thought that Paul was rich enough, and would rather see their money go to bootleggers instead. **Paul McCartney's Theme For *The Honorary Consul*** has had no US release that I am aware of but, while a pretty tune, is about as important a composition as his theme for *The Family Way*. One listen to **King Of Fuh** is all anyone needs. George's contribution to **Lucille** is negligible.

9 MM. AUTOMATIC
PAUL McCARTNEY & WINGS
ZAP, 7878
Insert cover with song listing; labels are "World Records."

Side A (26:48)
>13 Nov 75, Myer Music Bowl, Melbourne, Australia
>>**Venus And Mars** (McCartney)
>>**Rock Show** (McCartney)
>>**Jet** (McCartney)
>>**Let Me Roll It** (McCartney)
>>**Maybe I'm Amazed** (McCartney)
>>**I've Just Seen A Face** (Lennon-McCartney)

Blackbird (Lennon-McCartney)
Waltzing Matilda (Paterson-Cowan)
joke intro into:
Yesterday (Lennon-McCartney)
Listen To What The Man Said (McCartney)
Side B (28:20)
15 May 76, Capitol Center, Largo, Maryland
Beware My Love (McCartney)
introducing the band
Letting Go (McCartney)
Band On The Run (McCartney)
Hi, Hi, Hi (McCartney)
Soily (McCartney)

SOURCE:
Varied; see individual entries.

SOUND QUALITY:
Side A is a line recording, good to very good mono; Side B is an audience recording, very good mono.

COMMENTS:
More of the Melbourne concert, presumably from the television broadcast, is available (in better sound) on **ONE HAND CLAPPING**. The rest of the Capitol Center concert is available on **LIGHT AS A FEATHER** (ZAP, 7875) and **WINGS OVER AMERICA— LANDING GEAR DOWN** (ZAP, 7876).

1967
THE BEATLES
"Parlophone," PCS 1967
Full color jacket (**PEPPER** outtake photo), with song listing, lyrics and recording information on the back; label info matches.

Side A
SERGEANT PEPPER Inner Groove (0:03)
21 Apr 67, EMI
A Day In The Life #1 (Lennon-McCartney) (4:16)
19/20 Jan 67, EMI; take 6
from acetate; no orchestra & alternate vocals for Paul
Strawberry Fields Forever (Lennon-McCartney) (1:01)
late 66; John's acoustic demo
Lost Lennon Tapes 3-hour special
Only A Northern Song (Harrison) (3:16)
13/14 Feb & 20 Apr 67, EMI; synchronous mix of takes 3 & 11
This is a flat mono mix; all stereo versions so far are just "simulated" stereo (reprocessed mono).
Penny Lane (Lennon-McCartney) (2:51)
29/30 Dec 66 & 4/5/6/9/10/12/17 Jan 67, EMI
take 9 (mono remix #11), with trumpet ending
All You Need Is Love (Lennon-McCartney) (3:38)
14 Jun 67, Olympic & 19/23/24/25 Jun 67, EMI; take 58
broadcast version, from the *Our World* tv special
It's All Too Much (Harrison) (2:25)
25/26 May & 2 Jun 67, De Lane Lea; take 32 (mono remix #1)
with extra verse, from the *Yellow Submarine* soundtrack
A Day In The Life (Lennon-McCartney) (5:00)
19/20 Jan & 3/10/22 Feb 67, EMI; edit of takes 6 & 7
commercial version, with clean intro; excellent stereo

Side B
    Magical Mystery Tour (Lennon-McCartney) (2:35)
        25/26/27 Apr & 3 May 67; take 9 (mono remix #7)
        from the *MMT* soundtrack; extra effects, some different vocals and slightly
            different mix
    The Fool On The Hill (Lennon-McCartney) (2:42)
        6 Sep 67, EMI; demo
    Instrumental   (Lennon-Starkey?) (0:40)
        Sep 67; tape loops; from the *MMT* soundtrack
    Blue Jay Way (Harrison) (3:43)
        6/7 Sep & 6 Oct 67, EMI; take 3; mono mix
    Your Mother Should Know (Lennon-McCartney) (2:15)
        22 Aug 67, Chappell; take 8? the basic tracks
        no bass or organ, different backing vocals; very good mono
        with commercial ending tacked on
    I Am The Walrus (Lennon-McCartney) (4:23)
        6/7 Sep 67, EMI; take 17 (mono remix #4); the basic tracks
    Christmas Time (Is Here Again) (Lennon-McCartney-Harrison-Starkey) (6:29)
        28 Nov 67, EMI; very good mono, off speakers
        from the "EMI board room" tape

SOURCE:
    Varies; see individual entries.

SOUND QUALITY:
    Very good to excellent mono unless otherwise stated.

COMMENTS:
    Basically a theme reissue in a nice jacket, but nothing special here. There were two different covers, both alternate **SERGEANT PEPPER** cover photos.

OFF WHITE
THE BEATLES
No manufacturer listed, WHT 868
2-color embossed jacket with song listing on the back; labels say "Hawk Records, Test Pressing."

Side A
    The Continuing Story Of Bungalow Bill (Lennon-McCartney) (3:01)
        late May 68, Kinfauns; acoustic demo
        with stupid jet sound effects added
    Cry Baby Cry (Lennon-McCartney) (2:29)
        late May 68, Kinfauns; acoustic demo
        with stupid crying baby sound effects added
    Sexy Sadie (Lennon-McCartney) (2:20)
        late May 68, Kinfauns; acoustic demo
        with stupid organ added
    Yer Blues (Lennon-McCartney) (0:28)
        11 Dec 68, ad-lib with Mick Jagger (*Rock And Roll Circus*)
    Yer Blues (Lennon-McCartney) (3:21)
        late May 68, Kinfauns; acoustic demo
    Dear Prudence (Lennon-McCartney) (4:31)
        late May 68, Kinfauns; acoustic demo
    Julia (Lennon-McCartney) (3:37)
        late May 68, Kinfauns; acoustic demo
        with stupid clock sound effects added
    I'm So Tired (Lennon-McCartney) (3:00)
        late May 68, Kinfauns; acoustic demo

Side B
> **Child Of Nature** (Lennon) (2:34)
>> late May 68, Kinfauns; acoustic demo
>> with stupid animal noises added
> **While My Guitar Gently Weeps** (Harrison) (3:17)
>> 25 Jul 68, EMI; take 1 (acoustic)
>> excellent stereo; from **SESSIONS**
> **Lady Madonna** (Lennon-McCartney) (2:02)
>> 3/6 Feb 68, EMI; take 4
>> the basic track (take 3) was recorded on 3 Feb; the backing vocals, handclaps
>>> and a second lead vocal were added on 6 Feb, as were the brass
>>> overdubs; this take would appear to be from this 6 Feb overdubbing
>>> session, prior to the addition of the brass.
>> off speakers, from *The Beatles Live At Abbey Road*
> **Everybody's Got Something To Hide Except Me And My Monkey**
> (Lennon-McCartney) (3:00)
>> late May 68, Kinfauns; acoustic demo
>> with stupid monkey noises added
> **Goodbye** (McCartney) (2:20)
>> late 68? Dick James; Paul's demo; excellent mono
> **Honey Pie** (Lennon-McCartney) (1:59)
>> 1/2/4 Oct 68, Trident (the commercial version)
>> outfake of somebody singing along with the record
> **What's The New Mary Jane** (Lennon) (2:14)
>> late May 68, Kinfauns; acoustic demo
> **Revolution** (Lennon-McCartney) (3:53)
>> late May 68, Kinfauns; acoustic demo
>> with stupid dog barking added at the end

SOURCE:
> Varies; see individual entries.

SOUND QUALITY:
> Very good to excellent mono.

COMMENTS:
> What is it that drives a bootlegger to screw up some great material with really stupid sound effects? Six of these Kinfauns demos (**The Continuing Story Of Bungalow Bill**, **Cry Baby Cry**, **Dear Prudence**, **I'm So Tired**, **Sexy Sadie**, **Yer Blues**) had not, as of this collection's appearance, been broadcast on *The Lost Lennon Tapes*. The rest of the material is merely padding.
> Some copies were available on white vinyl. There was also a CD release with additional padding.

ONE TO ONE CONCERT AND MORE
JOHN LENNON & YOKO ONO
Wizardo, WRMB 301
Insert cover with song titles; labels are generic Wizardo.

Side A
> 30 Aug 72, Madison Square Garden, evening show (21:50)
>> intro
>> **Imagine** (Lennon)
>> **Come Together** (Lennon-McCartney)
>> **Instant Karma!** (Lennon)
>> **Cold Turkey** (Lennon) (excerpt)
>> **Mother** (Lennon)
>> **Give Peace A Chance** (Lennon-McCartney)

Side B
> 10 Dec 71 Ann Arbor, Michigan; John Sinclair benefit (12:14)
>> **Attica State** (Lennon)
>> **The Luck Of The Irish** (Lennon-Ono)
>> **John Sinclair** (Lennon-Ono)
> **Do The Oz** (Lennon-Ono) (3:06)
>> Jun 71, from 45 (US) Apple 1835
> **God Save Us** (Lennon-Ono) (3:07)
>> Jun 71, from 45 (US) Apple 1835
> **Power To The People** (Lennon) (3:12)
>> Feb 71, from 45 (UK) Apple R 5892

SOURCE:
> Varied; see individual entries.

SOUND QUALITY:
> Very good to excellent mono.

COMMENTS:
> Yet another collection of John's bits and pieces. Probably the the most interesting thing here is the **Imagine** from the One To One concert—it has the children's voices in it, from the actual tv broadcast, instead of the cleaner version from the FM broadcast.

...ONE, TWO, THREE, FOUR!

THE BEATLES
Big Jolly Records, JR008
2-disc set in full color jacket, with track listing and recording information on the back; labels have title, side numbers and artwork only.

DISC ONE
Side A
> **Paperback Writer** (Lennon-McCartney) (2:15)
>> 13/14 Apr 66, EMI; take 2 (echoless mix); very good stereo
> **I'm Down** (Lennon-McCartney) (2:22)
>> 14 Jun 65, EMI; take 7
>> commercial version; very good stereo
> **Don't Pass Me By** (Starkey) (3:31)
>> 5/6 Jun & 12/22 Jul 68, EMI; take 7 (w/edit piece #4)
>> UK mono LP mix, very good mono
> **Money (That's What I Want)** (Bradford-Gordy) (2:39)
>> 18 Jul 63, EMI; edit of takes 6 & 7; "true mono" mix
> **I'm Looking Through You** (Lennon-McCartney) (2:21)
>> 10/11 Nov 65, EMI; take 4
>> US stereo LP mix with 2 false starts; excellent stereo
> "movie medley" (Lennon-McCartney) (3:49)
>> 82? source unknown, fairly well done; very good stereo
>> not the commercial release; includes: **Magical Mystery Tour, All You Need Is Love, You've Got To Hide Your Love Away, I Should Have Known Better, A Hard Day's Night, Ticket To Ride** and **Get Back**.
> It's Gonna Be All Right (?) (2:40)
>> unknown; no Beatles involvement; very good stereo
>> The jacket says "Smyle," supposedly a Swedish group
>> a good song, sounds a bit like Lennon.

Side B
> _The Beatles Decade_ (0:57)
>> Feb 74, Capitol radio spot; excellent stereo (long version)
>> Celebrating, as Wiener puts it so well, "ten years of releasing shabby, truncated, poorly mixed pressings of Beatles records in the U.S."

The Beatles Decade (0:30)
>Feb 74, Capitol radio spot; excellent stereo (short version)

World Records mail order flexi (3:31)
>Fall 77, for **THE BEATLES COLLECTION**
>in English, excellent mono

World Records mail order flexi (6:08)
>Nov 80; for **THE BEATLES BOX**
>in English, excellent mono

World Records mail order flexi (3:50)
>Nov 80; for **THE BEATLES BOX**
>in German, excellent mono

World Records mail order flexi (5:13)
>Nov 80; for **THE BEATLES BOX**
>in French, excellent mono

DISC TWO
Side C

It's All Too Much (Harrison) (2:29)
>25/26 May & 2 Jun 67, De Lane Lea; take 32 (mono remix #1)
>with extra verse, from the *Yellow Submarine* soundtrack
>good to very good mono

I Forgot To Remember To Forget (Kesler-Feathers) (2:00)
>18 May 64, BBC; fair to good mono

Dream Baby (Walker) (0:50)
>8 Mar 62, BBC; very good mono (excerpt)

A Picture Of You (Beveridge-Oakman) (1:17)
>15 Jun 62, BBC; good mono (excerpt)

Happy Birthday To You (Hill-Hill) (0:26)
>5 Oct 63, BBC; very good mono

Ooh! My Soul (Penniman) (1:00)
>27 Aug 63, BBC; very good mono (excerpt)

Too Much Monkey Business (Berry) (1:44)
>11 Jun 63, BBC; very good mono
>2 different tapes (same date) spliced together

I Got To Find My Baby (Berry) (1:05)
>11 Jun 63, BBC; very good mono (excerpt)

Young Blood (Leiber-Stoller-Pomus) (1:24)
>11 Jun 63, BBC; very good mono (excerpt)

That's All Right Mama (Crudup) (2:47)
>16 Jul 63, BBC very good mono

Sweet Little Sixteen (Berry) (2:14)
>23 Jul 63, BBC; very good mono

Shout! (Isley-Isley-Isley) (2:13)
>6 May 64, *Around The Beatles*; good to very good mono

Side D

Savoy Truffle (Harrison) (2:27)
>3/5 Oct 68, Trident & 11/14 Oct 69, EMI (the commercial version)
>outfake of somebody singing along with the record

Honey Pie (Lennon-McCartney) (1:58)
>1/2/4 Oct 68, Trident (the commercial version)
>outfake of somebody singing along with the record (again)

I Saw Her Standing There (McCartney-Lennon)
>good mono; source unknown
>John's "Okay George, take it" at the beginning is unrelated to the rest of the
>>tape, and comes from "Feedback Guitar" (Jan 69, **GB** sessions). *You
>>Can't Do That!* suggests that this may be the Who (presumably based
>>on the guitar work).

Instrumental (improvisation) (2:38)
>Jan 69, **GET BACK** sessions; good mono
>This is from the jam which usually follows Watching Rainbows.

You Never Give Me Your Money (Lennon-McCartney) (5:34)
6 May, Olympic & 1/11 Jul 69, EMI; take 30
The basic tracks had been recorded 6 May at Olympic Studios; the vocals were added on 1 Jul and the bass on this date.
Something (Harrison) (5:15)
2 May, EMI & 5 May, Olympic & 11 Jul 69, EMI; take 37; extended
This is a tape reduction of take 36, the basic take of the commercial version; it was intended (but never used) for overdubs.

SOURCE:
Varies; see individual entries.

SOUND QUALITY:
Varies; see individual entries.

COMMENT:
ONE TWO THREE FOUR was supposedly a working title for **SESSIONS**, and this LP might have expected to cash in on that. Aside from its really great jacket illustration, there is not much here of interest. **I Saw Her Standing There** is uncommon, although available elsewhere; the radio and flexi ads on Side B are also uncommon, but of little value. The first four cuts on Side D are taken from **FROM A WHISPER TO A SHOUT!**

ORIENTAL NIGHTFISH
PAUL McCARTNEY WITH WINGS
Reading Railroad Records, HAR 169
2-disc set, on colored vinyl, in black-on-yellow jacket with track listing and recording information; label info matches.

DISC ONE
Side A
Summer 72 European tour, venue unknown (20:23)
an audience recording, poor to fair mono
Eat At Home (McCartney)
with long intro
Mumbo (P. McCartney-L. McCartney)
Best Friend (McCartney)
1882 (McCartney)
I Would Only Smile (Laine)
Oriental Nightfish (L. McCartney) (2:12)
Sep 73, Lagos, **BAND ON THE RUN** sessions
poor to fair mono (its first appearance)
Side B
16 Aug 72, Wings in Hanover, Germany? (21:08)
an audience recording (edited), fair to good mono
Bip Bop (P. McCartney-L. McCartney)
Smile Away (P. McCartney-L. McCartney)
chat
Give Ireland Back To The Irish (McCartney)
The Mess (McCartney)
Paul gives the title as "The Mess I'm In, for the gentleman with the microphone." (excerpt)
Mary Had A Little Lamb (P. McCartney-L. McCartney)
DISC TWO
Side C
16 Jun 76, Wings live at the Sports Arena, San Diego (23:35)
an audience recording (edited), very good stereo
Jet (McCartney)
Magneto And Titanium Man (McCartney)
My Love (McCartney)

Beware My Love (McCartney)
Soily (McCartney)
Side D
Mine For Me (McCartney) (0:28)
  Rod Stewart, with Paul & Linda; very good mono (excerpt)
  recorded 27 Nov 74, live at the Odeon Cinema, Lewisham? (*TV Guide* says
    recorded at Kilburn State Theatre, London)
  broadcast 25 Apr 75, *Midnight Special* (US tv)
Jet (McCartney) (2:38)
  Sep 73; from US 45 (Apple 1871) edit; very good mono
Zoo Gang (McCartney) (1:58)
  Jun 76; from the 45; excellent stereo
Country Dreamer (McCartney) (3:08)
  Oct 72; from the 45; excellent stereo
I Lie Around (McCartney) (5:00)
  Oct 72 from the 45; excellent stereo
16 Apr 73, from *James Paul McCartney*
  excellent mono
  Mary Had A Little Lamb (P. McCartney-L. McCartney) (2:34)
    73; live, but not in concert (excerpts)
  Uncle Albert (McCartney) (2:13)
    Jan-Mar 71; commercial version, with clean ending

SOURCE:
  Varies; see individual entries.

SOUND QUALITY:
  Varies; see individual entries.

COMMENTS:
  This is an rather rare piece, and most of this material appears nowhere else.
  The live material on Side A has resisted identification for a long time. Because I have versions to compare, I'm sure that it is not from Montreux (22 Jul), Lund (11 Aug), Hanover (16 Aug), Rotterdam (17 Aug), Amsterdam (21 Aug) or Antwerp (22 Aug).
  However, the following additional tapes are known to be around (in one form or another), although I have not heard them yet, and the material might be from any one of them: Copenhagen (1 Aug), Gothenberg (10 Aug), Groningen (19 Aug) and Amsterdam (20 Aug)
  Side B may not be from Hanover (see **LIVE IN HANOVER GERMANY, 1972**), but tradition and *Hot Wacks* say that it is. Since none of the songs are duplicated we cannot be certain. Interestingly, the *James Paul McCartney* excerpts on Side D are precisely those which do not appear on **MY LOVE**.

PAUL McCARTNEY IN SCOTLAND
PAUL McCARTNEY & WINGS
Wizardo, 302
Insert cover with song titles; labels are generic Wizardo.
Side A (26:42)
Soily (McCartney)
Big Barn Bed (McCartney)
When The Night (McCartney)
Wild Life (P. McCartney-L. McCartney)
Seaside Woman (L. McCartney)
Little Woman Love/C Moon (P. McCartney-L. McCartney)
Side B (20:22)
Maybe I'm Amazed (McCartney)
My Love (McCartney)
Go Now (Banks-Bennett)
Say You Don't Mind (Laine)
The Mess (McCartney) (excerpt)

SOURCE:
   23 Jul 73, The Odeon, Edinburgh, Scotland

SOUND QUALITY:
   Good mono audience tape.

COMMENTS:
   Wings played two nights in Edinburgh, the 22nd and the 23rd; it is uncertain which this one is, but the 23rd is the traditional date. This concert is also available as **SCOT-LAND—73** (Instant Analysis) with **Hi, Hi, Hi** listed as the last song.

PAUL McCARTNEY AND WINGS FLY SOUTH
PAUL McCARTNEY & WINGS
Wonderland Records, WL49000
2-disc set in black & white jacket, with song listing on the back; labels are blank.

DISC ONE
Side A
   13 Nov 75, Myer Music Bowl, Melbourne, Australia (19:30)
      Venus And Mars (McCartney)
      Rock Show (McCartney)
      Jet (McCartney)
      Let Me Roll It (McCartney)
      Maybe I'm Amazed (McCartney)
      I've Just Seen A Face (Lennon-McCartney)
Side B
   13 Nov 75, Myer Music Bowl, Melbourne, Australia (18:02)
      Blackbird (Lennon-McCartney)
      Waltzing Matilda (Paterson-Cowan)
            joke intro to:
      Yesterday (Lennon-McCartney)
      Listen To What The Man Said (McCartney)
      Call Me Back Again (McCartney)
      Letting Go (McCartney)

DISC TWO
Side C
   1 Nov 75, Entertainment Center, Perth, Australia (14:48)
      [narration (0:15)]
      The Long And Winding Road (Lennon-McCartney)
      Yesterday (Lennon-McCartney)
      Band On The Run (McCartney)
      [narration (0:09)]
      Hi, Hi, Hi (McCartney)
      [station ID]
Side D
   1 Nov 75, Entertainment Center, Perth, Australia (7:40)
      My Love (McCartney)
      [narration (0:08)]
      Paul's announcement
      Blackbird (Lennon-McCartney)
   interview by John O'Donnell (2:18)
         1 Nov 75, backstage at Perth
   Letting Go (McCartney) (4:35)
         1 Nov 75, Entertainment Center, Perth, Australia
   interview (0:54)
         Nov 75, Australia, exact date and place unknown

SOURCE:
    Varies; see individual entries.

SOUND QUALITY:
    Line recordings, very good to excellent mono; the concert tapes have been edited.

COMMENTS:
    The Melbourne Australia material is from a television broadcast; the Perth material is
from a 2 Nov 75 radio broadcast on station 3XY.

PISS OFF PETE!
THE BEATLES
No manufacturer listed, B-5
Full color jacket, which says ©1985 and "made in Belgium" (sorry, neither), with song titles
and recording information on the back; label info matches.

Side A
        interview with Pete Best (0:45)
                about getting the sack, part one
                82, from Backstage Records, BSR-1111
        24 Oct 63, *Karlaplannstudion*, Stockholm (17:54)
                broadcast on *Pop '63*, Swedish radio
                I Saw Her Standing There (McCartney-Lennon)
                From Me To You (McCartney-Lennon)
                Money (That's What I Want) (Bradford-Gordy)
                Roll Over Beethoven (Berry)
                You Really Got A Hold On Me (Robinson)
                She Loves You (Lennon-McCartney)
                Twist And Shout (Medley-Russell)
        interview with Pete Best (0:20)
                about getting the sack, part two
                82, from Backstage Records, BSR-1111
Side B
        interview with Pete Best (0:22)
                about getting the sack, part three
                82, from Backstage Records, BSR-1111
        Nothin' Shakin' (But The Leaves On The Trees)
        (Fontaine-Colacrai-Lampert-Gluck) (2:52)
                23 Jul 63, BBC
        Lonesome Tears In My Eyes (Burnette-Burnette-Burlison-Mortimer) (2:34)
                23 Jul 63, BBC
        So How Come (No One Loves Me) (Bryant) (1:45)
                23 Jul 63, BBC
        Please Mr. Postman (Holland-Bateman-Gordy) (1:59)
                30 Jul 63, BBC
        Crying, Waiting, Hoping (Holly) (2:06)
                6 Aug 63, BBC
        Ticket To Ride (Lennon-McCartney) (1:34)
                7 Jun 65, BBC; the short version
        Rock And Roll Music (Berry) (2:04)
                26 Dec 64, BBC
        Kansas City/Hey-Hey-Hey-Hey! (Leiber-Stoller/Penniman) (2:44)
                26 Dec 64, BBC
        This Boy (Lennon-McCartney) (2:08)
                30 Mar 64, BBC
        interview with Pete Best (0:06)
                about getting the sack, part four
                82, from Backstage Records, BSR-1111

Boys (Dixon-Farrell) (2:14)
> Pete Best; Summer 65, from US Cameo 391

interview with Pete Best (0:26)
>> about getting the sack, part five
>> 82, from Backstage Records, BSR-1111

SOURCE:
> The music on Side A was recorded the night before the beginning of the Beatles' brief Swedish tour. It is a line recording of the complete performance, with some different songs from their established line-up for that tour.
> The music on Side B is from various BBC radio shows, 63-65, except for the last cut, which is Pete Best solo.

SOUND QUALITY:
> All material is very good to excellent mono.

COMMENTS:
> This is basically a reissue of **JOHNNY AND THE MOONDOGS: SILVER DAYS**. The last cut (**Can't Buy Me Love**) has been replaced by a Pete Best solo recording, and the interview segments have been added.
> The jacket has fun at Pete Best's expense—but it *is* funny, in a cruel, sad way.

PLEASE RELEASE ME
THE BEATLES
"Apple Records," SAPCOR 29
2-disc set in full color jacket, with track listing and recording information on the back, says "Made In New Zealand;" labels say "Rubber Soul" and have song titles.

DISC ONE
Side A
> **I Saw Her Standing There** (McCartney-Lennon) (2:33)
>> 24 Sep 63, BBC
> **Misery** (McCartney-Lennon) (1:46)
>> 17 Sep 63, BBC
> **Anna (Go To Him)** (Alexander) (2:55)
>> 25 Jun 63, BBC
> **Chains** (Goffin-King) (2:11)
>> 17 Sep 63, BBC
> **Boys** (Dixon-Farrell) (2:29)
>> 24 Jun 63, BBC
> **Ask Me Why** (McCartney-Lennon) (1:49)
>> 24 Sep 63, BBC
> **Please Please Me** (McCartney-Lennon) (1:53)
>> 13 Aug 63, BBC
Side B
> **Love Me Do** (McCartney-Lennon) (2:22)
>> 10 Sep 63, BBC
> **P.S. I Love You** (McCartney-Lennon) (1:56)
>> 25 Jun 63, BBC
> **Baby It's You** (David-Bacharach-Williams) (2:37)
>> 11 Jun 63, BBC
> **Do You Want To Know A Secret** (McCartney-Lennon) (1:42)
>> 30 Jul 63, BBC
> **A Taste Of Honey** (Marlow-Scott) (1:53)
>> 18 Jun 63, BBC
> **There's A Place** (McCartney-Lennon) (1:46)
>> 16 Jul 63, BBC
> **Twist And Shout** (Medley-Russell) (2:28)
>> 24 Sep 63, BBC

DISC TWO
Side C
I Got To Find My Baby (Berry) (1:57)
  11 Jun 63, BBC
I Just Don't Understand (Wilkin-Westberry) (2:42)
  20 Aug 63, BBC
I'm Gonna Sit Right Down And Cry (Over You) (Thomas-Biggs) (1:57)
  6 Aug 63, BBC
I'm Talking About You (Berry) (1:58)
  16 Mar 63, BBC; good mono
Keep Your Hands Off My Baby (Goffin-King) (2:35)
  26 Jan 63, BBC
Lend Me Your Comb (Twomey-Wise-Weisman) (1:47)
  16 Jul 63, BBC
Lonesome Tears In My Eyes (Burnette-Burnette-Burlison-Mortimer) (2:37)
  23 Jul 63, BBC
Side D
Beatleviews (17:07)
  Lots of interview snippets, primarily from other bootlegs, most relating to their early musical influences. This side includes Paul's 12 Sep 84 *Arena* appearance, where he talks about Buddy Holly's influence and plays brief acoustic versions of
  Love Me Do (McCartney-Lennon) (0:06) and
  Words Of Love (Holly) (0:50)

SOURCE:
  Varies; see individual listings.

SOUND QUALITY:
  Very good to excellent mono unless otherwise stated.

COMMENTS:
  This is the second in the SAPCOR series.
  The front cover is a shot from what Dezo Hoffman said (in his book) was to have been the original cover photo concept for **PLEASE PLEASE ME**. DISC ONE presents alternate versions of every song on that LP; Side C continues the list of unreleased BBC songs (in alphabetical order). Except for a few slightly early fades and tempo changes which are not too noticeable to the casual listener, the BBC tracks seem to have been lifted directly from **THE BEATLES AT THE BEEB** series, with a slight loss of quality.

POWER BROKERS
THE BEATLES
Wizardo, WRMB 392
Insert cover with song listing; labels have side numbers only.

Side A
Nowhere Man (Lennon-McCartney) (2:21)
  30 Jun 66, Nippon Budokan Hall, Tokyo
Get Back (Lennon-McCartney) (3:39)
  Jan 69, **GET BACK** sessions; "No Pakistanis" version
What's The New Mary Jane (Lennon) (3:07)
  14 Aug 68, EMI; take 4 (stereo remix #4)
  very good stereo (excerpt)
All My Loving (Lennon-McCartney) (2:20)
  23 Aug 64, Hollywood Bowl
The Walk (McCracklin-Gorlic) (0:52)
  27 Jan 69, Apple; very good stereo
Teddy Boy (McCartney) (5:35)
  24 Jan 69, Apple; very good stereo

excerpt from *Let It Be* (3:16)
      Maxwell's Silver Hammer (Lennon-McCartney)
      Besame Mucho (Velazquez-Skylar)
          29 Jan 69, Apple

Side B
      Let It Be (Lennon-McCartney) (7:45)
          Jan 69, **GET BACK** session; first rehearsal
      Dizzy Miss Lizzie (Williams) (2:45)
          7 Jun 65, BBC
      Sie Liebt Dich (Lennon-McCartney) (2:14)
          29 Jan 64, Paris; take 14
      Honey Don't (Perkins) (2:06)
          3 Sep 63, BBC
      Sure To Fall (In Love With You) (Perkins-Claunch-Cantrell) (1:17)
          24 Sep 63, BBC (excerpt)
      I Need You (Harrison) (2:49)
          15/16 Feb 65, EMI; take 5; from *Help!* with dialogue
      For You Blue (Harrison) (2:52)
          25 Jan 69, Apple

SOURCE:
    Varies; see individual listings.

SOUND QUALITY:
    Very good to excellent mono unless otherwise stated.

COMMENTS:
    All material copied from other sources. Side A is a reissue of Side A of **NO OBVI-OUS TITLE—FIRST AMMENDMENT** (ZAP, 7853); Side B is a reissue of Side B of **BACK UPON US ALL—FOURTH AMMENDMENT** (ZAP, 76864).

THE QUARRYMEN REHEARSE WITH STU SUTCLIFF SPRING 1960
THE QUARRY MEN
Pre Beatle Records, VD 16
Full color jacket, with track listing on the back; labels match.

Side A
      Hallelujah! I Love Her So (Charles) (2:16)
          vocals: Paul
          This is the same version as is on **LIVERPOOL MAY 1960**.
      One After 909 (Lennon-McCartney) (2:24)
          vocals: John & Paul
          This is the same version as is on **LIVERPOOL MAY 1960**.
      I Will Always Be In Love With You (Ruby-Green-Stept) (2:18)
          vocals: John
    You'll Be Mine (?) (1:41)
          vocals: John & Paul
    unknown (?) (0:06)
          an unknown and probably unidentifiable snippet; leads right into:
      Matchbox (trad. arr. Perkins) (0:58)
          vocals: Stu?
      Wildcat (Schroeder-Gold) (2:25)
          vocals: Paul
    Some Days (Lennon-McCartney?) (1:33)
          vocals: Paul
    Instrumental (?) (2:20)
          The jacket says this is **Thinking Of Linking**, but if it is a Lennon-McCartney
             original, it's much more likely to be **Looking Glass** or **Winston's Walk**, as **Thinking of Linking** is supposed to have had vocals.

Side B
 I'll Follow The Sun (Lennon-McCartney) (1:45)
   vocals: Paul
   This is the same version as is on **LIVERPOOL MAY 1960**.
 One After 909 (Lennon-McCartney) (1:25)
   vocals: John & Paul
   This is a different version from that on **LIVERPOOL MAY 1960**.
 Well Darling (Lennon-McCartney?) (3:19)
   vocals: Paul & John
 You Must Write Every Day (Lennon-McCartney?) (2:30)
   vocals: Paul
 Moovin' And Groovin' (Eddy-Hazelwood) (2:11)
   instrumental
   The jacket calls this "Guitar Bop;" an excerpt from the longer cut on **LIVER-POOL MAY 1960**.
 That's When Your Heartaches Begin (Raskin-Hill-Fisher) (1:13)
   vocals: Paul
   Originally recorded by Elvis Presley.
 Hello Little Girl (Lennon-McCartney) (1:52)
   vocals: Paul & John
   At this point, the song has a different "middle eight" and shows very strong Everly Brothers influences.
 That'll Be The Day (Holly-Allison-Petty) (0:42)
   12 Sep 84; Paul plays the shellac on the *Arena* special

SOURCE:
 Except for the last cut, Quarry Men rehearsals, Spring 1960.

SOUND QUALITY:
 Good to very good mono. Some of these are excerpts from longer cuts (on **LIVERPOOL MAY 1960**), and all have been faded.

COMMENTS:
 This is a domestic reissue of a European piece, **THE QUARRYMEN AT HOME** (Blackshop, BS007); about half this material appeared on **LIVERPOOL MAY 1960**. Rumor has it that there are still a few tracks left unbooted, although they are said to be primarily instrumental jams.
 The jacket back reproduces Stu's striking self-portrait (sold at Sotheby's 30 Aug 84, for £1500).

RABBI SAUL
THE BEATLES
"Apple Records," SAPCOR 34
Full color jacket (front) with track listing on the back, says "Manufactured In New Zealand;" labels say "Rubber Soul" and have song titles.

Side A
 Norwegian Wood (Lennon-McCartney) (1:09)
   12 Oct 65, EMI; take 1; very good stereo
   off speakers, from *The Beatles At Abbey Road*
 Nowhere Man (Lennon-McCartney) (2:13)
   30 Jun 66, Nippon Budokan Hall, Tokyo
   excellent mono
 Michelle (Lennon-McCartney) (1:10)
   73, from *James Paul McCartney*
   excellent mono
 Michelle (Lennon-McCartney) (1:07)
   73, outtake from *James Paul McCartney*
   very good mono

I'm Looking Through You (Lennon-McCartney) (0:04)
10/11 Nov 65, EMI; take 4; excellent stereo
with false start, from US stereo LP
I'm Looking Through You (Lennon-McCartney) (3:02)
24 Oct 65, EMI; take 1; excellent stereo
Think For Yourself (Harrison) (0:09)
8 Nov 65, EMI; acapella rehearsal
from *Yellow Submarine*; very good mono
If I Needed Someone (Harrison) (2:31)
30 Jun 66, Nippon Budokan Hall, Tokyo
excellent mono
Catswalk (McCartney) (1:06)
Spring 62, rehearsal? excellent mono, with countdown
If You've Got Trouble (Lennon-McCartney) (2:27)
18 Feb 65, EMI; take 1; excellent stereo
Day Tripper (Lennon-McCartney) (3:05)
30 Jun 66, Nippon Budokan Hall, Tokyo
excellent mono
Pantomime: Everywhere It's Christmas (5:45)
aka **The Beatles' Fourth Christmas Record**
25 Nov 66, Dick James; excellent mono (excerpt)

Side B

Beatleviews (7:20)
bits and pieces from various interviews
good to excellent mono
As It Happened (13:31)
Murray The K's fan club record, Fairway OV 526-1
very good to excellent mono
includes John reading "I Sat Belonely" (Apr 64?)

SOURCE:
Varies; see individual entries.

SOUND QUALITY:
Varies; see individual entries. Many cuts are noticeably slow.

COMMENTS:
As with so many of the SAPCOR series, there is really nothing here (aside from a well-executed cover) to warrant its existence.

RE-INTRODUCING THE BEATLES
THE BEATLES
"Apple Records," SAPCOR 28
2-disc set in full color jacket, with track listing and recording information on the back, says "Manufactured In New Zealand;" labels say "Rubber Soul" and have song titles.

DISC ONE
Side A

Quarry Men rehearsals, Spring 60; fair to good mono
Note that I have used the titles which are consistent with the listing for
LIVERPOOL MAY 1960 (from which these are copied) in *Do You Want To Know A Secret?*
I'll Follow The Sun (Lennon-McCartney) (1:39)
vocal: Paul
Hallelujah! I Love Her So (Charles) (2:19)
vocal: Paul
One After 909 (Lennon-McCartney) (2:22)
vocal: Paul

Wildcat (Schroeder-Gold) (1:21)
> vocals: Paul (excerpt)
> Originally recorded by Gene Vincent, and released in the UK in Jan 60.
> A new identification, this cut was listed as "Oh No, Not Me" in *Do You Want To Know A Secret?*

I Don't Know (?) (5:53)
> vocal: Paul; backing: John
> The jacket identifies this as "Gonna Move Out Of Town."

R&B jam #3 (5:52)
> vocal: Paul; backing: John
> A slow R&B progression, almost dirge-like, built along the lines of **Kansas City**; Paul seems to be making the lyrics up as he goes; among others: "Be-bop-a-lula," and "Don't be cold as ice." The jacket identifies this as **Winston's Walk**, another long-lost song, but it too was an instrumental.

Side B

That'll Be The Day (Holly-Allison-Petty) (1:18)
> The Quarry Men; Buddy Holly *Arena* special, 12 Sep 84
> Paul plays the shellac, but begins to talk over it after about 40 seconds. The tape is noticeably slow.

My Bonnie (trad. arr. Sheridan) (0:39)
> mid-May 61, Hamburg; German intro only

Sweet Georgia Brown (Bernie-Pinkard-Casey) (2:04)
> Apr 62, Hamburg? with original, pre-Beatles lyrics
> A May 62 *Mersey Beat* article claims that this was recorded during Apr 62, while Bill Harry's Jan 85 liner notes for **THE BEATLES - FIRST** CD, (apparently based on the session notes) claims that this was recorded 21 Dec 61 in Hamburg. However, Mark Lewisohn (*The Beatles Live!*) points out that the Beatles were not in Hamburg then.

Red Hot/Reminiscing (Emerson/Curtis) (1:00)
> Dec 75, *Earth News Radio*?
> music: good mono; interview: excellent mono
> George talks over the music, which has been edited. The source of the live music is probably Star-Club Dec 62, as it was mentioned in connection with these tapes before they were released (77) on LP (Guzek, 76). This song does not appear on any legitimate release of the Star-Club material.

Dream Baby (Walker) (0:57)
> 8 Mar 62, BBC; good mono

1 Jan 62, Decca audition
> **Hello Little Girl** (Lennon-McCartney) (1:34)
> **Love Of The Loved** (Lennon-McCartney) (1:46)
> **Like Dreamers Do** (Lennon-McCartney) (2:27)
> **Three Cool Cats** (Leiber-Stoller) (2:15)
> **September In The Rain** (Warren) (1:48)
> **The Sheik Of Araby** (Snyder-Wheeler-Smith) (1:32)
> **Take Good Care Of My Baby** (Goffin-King) (2:16)

DISC TWO
Side C

first radio interview, by Monty Lister (7:17)
> 27 Oct 62, Hulme Hall, Port Sunlight, The Wirral
> from the flexi in *The Beatles Live!*

Weekend World (British Forces Network) interview (5:23)
> 24 Jan 64, Paris
> Exact broadcast date of this interview is unknown, but it should be late Jan/early Feb 64; Lewisohn says it was broadcast for British forces in Germany. There are edits in this tape.

Beatleviews (6:46)
> Interview snippets, all lifted from the *Sergeant Pepper's Lonely Hearts Club Band: A History Of The Beatle Years* radio series.

Side D

Side By Side (Wood) (0:48)
  The Karl Denver Trio with the Beatles
  63, BBC; two bits edited together
Pop Go The Beatles (trad. arr. Patrick) (1:04)
  63, BBC; two bits edited together
From Us To You (McCartney-Lennon) (0:28)
  63, BBC
Happy Birthday To You (Hill-Hill) (0:28)
  5 Oct 63, BBC; as "Happy Birthday, Saturday Club"
Beautiful Dreamer (Foster) (1:53)
  26 Jan 63, BBC; good mono
Carol (Berry) (2:38)
  16 Jul 63, BBC
Clarabella (Pingatore) (2:41)
  16 Jul 63, BBC
Crying, Waiting, Hoping (Holly) (2:11)
  6 Aug 63, BBC
Don't Ever Change (Goffin-King) (2:02)
  27 Aug 63, BBC
Glad All Over (Bennett-Tepper-Schroeder) (1:50)
  20 Aug 63, BBC
Sure To Fall (In Love With You) (Perkins-Claunch-Cantrell) (2:18)
  24 Sep 63, BBC

SOURCE:
  Varies; see individual entries.

SOUND QUALITY:
  Very good to excellent mono unless otherwise stated.

COMMENTS:
  The liner notes proclaim that this is the first of a sixteen record set which will "embark on a nostalgic trip through *all* the unreleased songs ever available." The emphasis is on titles rather than performances. Some of the cuts, the notes promise (or threaten?), have been processed, equalized, edited and spliced "in order to restore these recordings to their original sound quality."
  Oh boy. Regardless of good intentions, I can find no justification in amateur (or professional, for that matter) screwing around with the original source material.
  Some of the splices are obvious. However, except for a few slightly early fades and tempo changes which are not too noticeable to the casual listener, most of the BBC tracks seem to have been lifted directly from **THE BEATLES AT THE BEEB** series, with a slight loss of quality.

READY STEADY GO!
THE BEATLES
Wind Records, 001
Full color jacket with song listing; labels are generic Wind.

Side A

27 Apr 64, *Ready Steady Go!*
  You Can't Do That (Lennon-McCartney) (2:25)
  Cathy McGowan interviews George (1:52)
  Can't Buy Me Love (Lennon-McCartney) (2:04)
27 Nov 64, *Ready Steady Go!*
  She's A Woman (Lennon-McCartney) (2:49)
  Baby's In Black (Lennon-McCartney) (1:57)
  Kansas City/Hey-Hey-Hey-Hey! (Leiber-Stoller-Penniman) (2:17)

4 Oct 63, *Ready Steady Go!*
        She Loves You (Lennon-McCartney) (2:11)
Side B
        6 May 64, *Around The Beatles*
                Twist And Shout (Medley-Russell) (2:35)
                Roll Over Beethoven (Berry) (1:47)
                I Wanna Be Your Man (Lennon-McCartney) (1:41)
                Long Tall Sally (Johnson-Penniman-Blackwell) (1:39)
                Medley (McCartney-Lennon) (3:53)
                        Love Me Do
                        Please Please Me
                        From Me To You
                        She Loves You
                        I Want To Hold Your Hand
                Can't Buy Me Love (Lennon-McCartney) (2:01)
                Shout! (Isley-Isley-Isley) (1:54)

SOURCE:
        See individual entries. All of the performances here are lip-synched, although the recordings on Side B are not the usual commercial versions.

SOUND QUALITY:
        Very good to excellent mono.

COMMENTS:
        Much of this material is now commonly available on commercial video, and the studio sessions for *Around The Beatles* (IBC, 19 Apr 64) have appeared as well (on **NOT GUILTY**).

THE REALLY BIG SHEW (EP)
THE BEATLES
"CBS," SP910
7-inch EP with black & white picture sleeve, with track listing on the back; label info matches.

Side A
        First set (7:03)
                Introduction
                All My Loving (Lennon-McCartney)
                Till There Was You (Willson)
                She Loves You (Lennon-McCartney)
Side B
        Second set (5:28)
                Introduction
                I Saw Her Standing There (McCartney-Lennon)
                I Want To Hold Your Hand (Lennon-McCartney)

SOURCE:
        9 Feb 64, *The Ed Sullivan Show*.

SOUND QUALITY:
        Very good to excellent mono.

COMMENTS:
        A nicely-done piece, but the material is no longer rare.

RENAISSANCE MINSTRELS
THE BEATLES
Renaissance Records, 725
Black and white insert cover with song titles; label info matches.

Side A
>**From Me To You** (McCartney-Lennon) (2:36)
>>16 Feb 64, *The Ed Sullivan Show* (edit)
>>This version is not as broadcast; the tape has been edited so that one verse and one chorus repeat.

>**Twist And Shout** (Medley-Russell) (3:32)
>>23 Feb 64, *The Ed Sullivan Show* (edit)
>>This version is not as broadcast; the tape has been edited so that one verse and one chorus repeat, and audience clapping has been dubbed on.

>**This Boy** (Lennon-McCartney) (3:40)
>>16 Feb 64, *The Ed Sullivan Show* (edit)
>>This version is not as broadcast; the tape has been edited so that one verse and one chorus repeat.

>**I Saw Her Standing There** (McCartney-Lennon) (2:37)
>>9 Feb 64, *The Ed Sullivan Show*

>**She Loves You** (Lennon-McCartney) (2:48)
>>16 Feb 64, *The Ed Sullivan Show* (edit)
>>This version is not as broadcast; the tape has been edited so that one verse and one chorus repeat.

Side B
>**I Want To Hold Your Hand** (Lennon-McCartney) (3:14)
>>16 Feb 64, *The Ed Sullivan Show* (edit)
>>This version is not as broadcast; the tape has been edited so that one verse and one chorus repeat.

>**Please Please Me** (McCartney-Lennon) (3:15)
>>23 Feb 64, *The Ed Sullivan Show* (edit)
>>This version is not as broadcast; the tape has been edited so that one verse and one chorus repeat.

>**All My Loving** (Lennon-McCartney) (2:57)
>>16 Feb 64, *The Ed Sullivan Show* (edit)
>>This version is not as broadcast; the tape has been edited so that one verse and one chorus repeat.

>**She Loves You** (Lennon-McCartney) (2:20)
>>9 Feb 64, *The Ed Sullivan Show*

SOURCE:
>Various *Ed Sullivan Shows*.

SOUND QUALITY:
>Good to very good mono, edited and with added echo and applause.

COMMENTS:
>Echo has been added to all tracks and audience clapping had been dubbed over the music in places—my guess is someone was trying to construct a bogus "live" tape (longer versions, no duplicate songs, different order and Sullivan's intros cut), along the lines of **FOREST HILLS TENNIS STADIUM**. The editing is remarkably good. The material here from the 16th is the actual broadcast, not the more common rehearsal of the previous day (see **THE BEATLES CONQUER AMERICA**), but in this condition (mediocre sound and edited), although the title is a classic of sorts, it is hardly worth having.

RENAISSANCE MINSTRELS 2
THE BEATLES
Renaissance Records, RR-1001
Insert cover with song titles; labels have side numbers only.

Side A
The Walk (McCracklin-Gorlic) (0:53)
27 Jan 69, Apple; the usual version
Teddy Boy (McCartney) (5:35)
24 Jan 69, Apple; the usual version
Two Of Us (Lennon-McCartney) (3:38)
24 Jan 69, Apple; "good-bye" version with two false starts
I've Got A Feeling (Lennon-McCartney) (2:46)
24 Jan 69, Apple; "on your what?" version
The Long And Winding Road (Lennon-McCartney) (3:33)
31 Jan 69, Apple; & 30 Apr 69, EMI; take 19; very good stereo
this is the basic version of that which would later appear on **LET IT BE**
For You Blue (Harrison) (2:26)
25 Jan 69, Apple; with two false starts and laugh (edited)
chat
Dig A Pony (Lennon-McCartney) (3:32)
24 Jan 69, Apple; laughing version, with one false start
Side B
Across The Universe (Lennon-McCartney) (3:38)
4/8 Feb 68 & 2 Oct 69 EMI; take 8 (WWF version)
from the LP
The Inner Light (Harrison) (2:29)
12 Jan 68, Bombay & 6/8 Feb 68, EMI; take 6
excellent mono, from the 45
Let It Be (Lennon-McCartney) (3:44)
31 Jan 69, Apple & 30 Apr 69/4 Jan 70, EMI; take 30
from the 45
Don't Let Me Down (Lennon-McCartney) (3:28)
28 Jan 69, Apple; from the 45
Get Back (Lennon-McCartney) (3:06)
28 Jan 69, Apple; from the 45
I'm Down (Lennon-McCartney) (2:28)
14 Jun 65, EMI; take 7; excellent mono, from the 45
Instant Karma! (Lennon) (3:10)
27 Jan 70, Apple? from the 45

SOURCE:
Side A: Jan 69, **GET BACK** sessions (excerpted from early **GET BACK** bootlegs).
Side B varies; see individual entries.

SOUND QUALITY:
Excellent stereo, except as noted.

COMMENTS:
This is one of a number of reissues of this title.

RENAISSANCE MINSTRELS 3
THE BEATLES (INDIVIDUALLY)
Berkeley, 2033
One-color printed and folded jacket, with song titles; labels are blank.

Side A

It Don't Come Easy (Starkey) (2:54)
8 Mar 70; from the 45
Cold Turkey (Lennon) (4:58)
30 Sep 69; from the 45
Deep Blue (Harrison) (3:36)
Jul 71; from the 45
Another Day (P. McCartney-L. McCartney) (3:37)
Jan 71; from the 45
Instant Karma! (Lennon) (3:07)
27 Jan 70, Apple? from the 45
Back Off Boogaloo (Starkey) (3:10)
Sep 71; from the 45

Side B

Blindman (Starkey) (2:38)
Sep 71; from the 45
Happy Xmas (War Is Over) (Lennon-Ono) (3:26)
28-29 Oct 71; from the 45
Bangla Desh (Harrison) (3:48)
Jul 71; from the 45
Give Ireland Back To The Irish (P. McCartney-L. McCartney) (3:27)
1 Feb 72; from the 45
Give Peace A Chance (Lennon-McCartney) (4:46)
Montreal, 1 Jun 69; from the 45
Early 1970 (Starkey) (2:14)
8 Mar 70; from the 45

SOURCE:
Various uncollected (at the time) commercially released 45s.

SOUND QUALITY:
Excellent mono.

COMMENTS:
Because these are all commercially released tracks, this is technically a pirate and not a bootleg. There is another album of the same title (Contra Band), with a slightly different lineup.

RENAISSANCE MINSTRELS 4
THE BEATLES (COLLECTIVELY & SOLO) & OTHERS
Cumquat/Contra Band, 5020
Insert cover with song titles; labels are generic Contra Band.

Side A

I'm Down (Lennon McCartney) (2:30)
14 Jun 65, EMI; take 7; from the 45, excellent mono
Coochy-Coochy (Starkey) (4:30)
30 Jun-1 Jul 70, Nashville; from the 45, excellent stereo
Step Inside Love (Lennon-McCartney) (2:14)
Cilla Black; 28 Feb 68, EMI; from the 45, excellent mono
You've Got To Hide Your Love Away (Lennon-McCartney) (2:06)
The Silkie; 9 Aug 65; from the 45, excellent mono
That Means A Lot (Lennon-McCartney) (2:29)
P. J. Proby; 7 Apr 65, EMI; from the 45, excellent mono

Side B

Happy Xmas (War Is Over) (Lennon-Ono) (3:32)
28-29 Oct 71, from the 45, excellent stereo
Bangla Desh (Harrison) (3:53)
Jul 71, from the 45, excellent stereo

You Know My Name (Lennon-McCartney) (4:18)
   17 May & 7/8 Jun 67 & 30 Apr 69, EMI; take 30
   from the 45, excellent mono
Sie Liebt Dich (Lennon-McCartney) (2:15)
   29 Jan 64, Paris; take 14; from the 45, excellent mono
Give Peace A Chance (Lennon-McCartney) (4:49)
   1 Jun 69, Montreal; from the 45, excellent stereo
Cold Turkey (Lennon) (5:01)
   30 Sep 69, from the 45, excellent stereo

SOURCE:
   Various commercially released 45s.

SOUND QUALITY:
   Varies; see individual entries. A noisy pressing.

COMMENTS:
   Technically, this is a pirate and not a bootleg, as all of the material has been commercially released. Probably the most interesting cut is the Silkie version of **You've Got To Hide Your Love Away**, produced by John and on which Paul (guitar) and George (tambourine) play.

REVOLTING
THE BEATLES
"Apple Records," SAPCOR 35
2-disc set in full color jacket, with track listing and recording information on the back, says "Made In New Zealand;" labels say "Rubber Soul" and have song titles.

DISC ONE
Side A
   There Once Was A Beautiful Girl (?) (1:00)
     vocals: George, John, Paul
     Although he is supposed to have worked on it as early as 69, this is not
      George's later song, **Beautiful Girl.**
   I'm Talking About You (Berry) (0:51)
     vocals: George, Paul & John
   Great Balls Of Fire (Blackwell-Hammer) (1:43)
     vocals: Paul
   Don't Let The Sun Catch You Cryin' (Greene) (2:24)
     includes **Sexy Sadie** (Lennon-McCartney) (0:02)
   Suicide (McCartney) (0:45)
   Strawberry Fields Forever (Lennon-McCartney) (1:31)
     vocals: Paul
   Rainy Day Woman #12 And 35 (Dylan) (0:40)
     vocals: John
   Moving Along The River Rhine/**The Long And Winding Road (Blues)**
   (improvisation?/Lennon-McCartney) (5:04)
     vocals: Paul
   The Inner Light (Harrison) (0:38)
     vocals: John
   Let It Down (Harrison) (1:20)
     vocals: George, Paul
   Maybe Baby (Holly-Petty) (2:25)
     vocals: John
   Hot As Sun (McCartney) (1:22)
     some working vocals
   Every Night (McCartney) (1:11)

Side B

Mailman, Bring Me No More Blues (Roberts-Katz-Clayton) (1:46)
29 Jan 69, Apple; vocals: John, George
Suzy Parker (Lennon-McCartney-Harrison-Starkey) (2:28)
the usual version
Tennessee (Perkins) (1:48)
vocals: John, Paul, George
House Of The Rising Sun (trad.) (2:35)
vocals: John, Paul
Commonwealth (improvisation) (3:40)
vocals: Paul, John
White Power (Get Off!) (improvisation) (3:29)
vocals: Paul, John
Honey Hush (Turner) (2:09)
vocals: John, George, Paul
Enoch Powell (improvisation) (0:22)
vocals: Paul
Child Of Nature (Lennon) (1:40)
the early version of **Jealous Guy**
I Shall Be Released (Dylan) (1:48)
vocals: George

DISC TWO
Side C

All Shook Up/Your True Love (Blackwell-Presley/Perkins) (2:55)
vocals: Paul, George, John
Blue Suede Shoes (Perkins) (1:32)
vocals: George, John, Paul
Three Cool Cats (Leiber-Stoller) (2:09)
vocals: George, Paul, John
Blowing' In The Wind (Dylan) (0:33)
vocals: George, Paul, John (excerpt)
Harry Lime (*Third Man* Theme) (Karas) (1:42)
instrumental
Negro In Reserve (?) (0:38)
vocals: Paul, John
Wake Up In The Morning (Lennon-McCartney?) (2:33)
vocals: Paul, John
The jacket calls this "Early In The Morning"
If Tomorrow Ever Comes (Lennon-McCartney?) (1:01)
vocals: Paul, John
The jacket calls this "Tomorrow Never Comes"
Won't You Please Say Goodbye (Lennon-McCartney?) (0:48)
vocals: Paul, John
This song is not listed on the jacket.
Bring It On Home To Me (Cooke) (1:49)
vocals: George, Paul
Hitchhike (Gaye-Paul-Stevenson) (1:49)
vocals: Paul, George
Short Fat Fannie (Williams) (2:43)
vocals: George, Paul
Midnight Special (trad.) (2:07)
vocals: John, Paul
Gimme Some Truth (Lennon) (0:37)
vocals: Paul, John

Side D

Almost Grown (Berry) (1:27)
vocals: John; the jacket calls this cut "Round And Round."
Hi Heel Sneakers (Higginbottom) (1:26)
vocals: John, Paul (excerpts)

Penina (McCartney) (0:50)
> vocals: Paul

Shakin' In The Sixties (improvisation?) (0:39)
> vocals: John

Move It/Good Rockin' Tonight (Samwell/Brown) (1:44)
> vocals: John

All Things Must Pass (Harrison) (3:14)
> nearly finished version

Fools Like Me (Clement-Maddux) (1:57)
> vocals: John, George, Paul

You Win Again (Williams) (0:51)
> vocals: John, George, Paul

Watching Rainbows (Lennon) (3:03)
> vocals: John (excerpt)

Early In The Morning/**Honey Hush** (improv.?/Turner) (2:22)
> vocals: Paul, George
> The jacket calls this track **The Right String But The Wrong Yo-Yo** which, although it has repeatedly been listed on **GET BACK** sessions albums, has yet to appear.

Stand By Me (King-Glick)
> vocals: Paul

She Said She Said (Lennon-McCartney) (0:20)
> vocals: John

Too Bad About Sorrows (Lennon-McCartney) (0:59)
> vocals: John

You've Got Me Thinking (Lomax) (0:56)
> vocals: Paul, John

Diggin' My Potatoes/Rock Island Line (Brown/trad. arr. Donegan) (1:36)
> vocals: John, Paul

SOURCE:
> Jan 69, **GET BACK** sessions; all of these tracks are copied from other bootlegs.

SOUND QUALITY:
> Very good to excellent mono; most track fade.

COMMENTS:
> This is the eighth album in the SPACOR series. All of the tracks, which have appeared before, have been edited to eliminate most of the between-song chat and leave only the music which, while annoying to the purist, is surprisingly entertaining for the casual listener.
> I don't think much of the title, though; keeping in mind the retrogressive nature of the material, something like **DEVOLVER** would have been more appropriate. Oh well.

RIZZ OFF!
RINGO STARR
Wibble Records, RS-70740
Full color jacket, with song listing and recording information on the back; labels match.

Side A

Nonsense (Allen) (2:22)
> recorded May 85, broadcast 9 Dec 85
> from the tv film *Alice In Wonderland*; excellent stereo

Sun Country Classic Wine Cooler radio commercial #1 (0:58)
> Dec 86? excellent mono

Ringo/Sammy medley (3:55)
> 8 Dec 84, *Saturday Night Live*; excellent mono
> with Billy Crystal as Sammy Davis Jr.; includes:
> **With A Little Help From My Friends** (Lennon-McCartney)
> **What Kind Of Fool Am I?** (Newley-Bricusse)

Act Naturally (Russell-Morrison)
I've Gotta Be Me (Marks)
Octopus's Garden (Starkey)
Photograph (Starkey-Harrison)
Yellow Submarine (Lennon-McCartney)
With A Little Help From My Friends (Lennon-McCartney)
Dead Giveaway (Starkey-Wood) (5:05)
Jul 80, Paris? excellent stereo
These appear to be the basic tracks for the recording on **STOP AND SMELL THE ROSES**; longer, lacking some overdubs and with slightly different vocals in spots.
Back In The USSR (Lennon-McCartney) (3:05)
4 Jul 85, Washington DC; the Beach Boys, with Ringo
line recording, excellent stereo
This cut was included on a limited (but legitimate) album released by the [Mike] Love Foundation For American Music, **FOURTH OF JULY: A ROCKIN' CELEBRATION OF AMERICA**.
Sun Country Classic Wine Cooler radio commercial #2 (0:56)
Dec 86? excellent mono
Act Naturally (Russell-Morrison) (2:08)
25 Apr 71? *Cilla*; very good mono

Side B

Goodnight Vienna (Lennon) (3:02)
Summer 74; excellent stereo
the 45 version (which combines the album title track and the reprise), with a brief spoken intro by John.
Sun Country Classic Wine Cooler radio commercial #3 (1:01)
Dec 86? excellent mono
Movin' On Up (Barry-Du Bois) (0:22)
8 Dec 84, *Saturday Night Live*; excellent mono
Ringo and Jim Belushi sing along to the soundtrack
from *Blue Suede Shoes* (8:00)
21 Nov 85, Limehouse Studios; excellent stereo
introduction
Honey Don't (Perkins)
Matchbox (trad. arr. Perkins)
With A Little Help From My Friends (Lennon-McCartney) (4:21)
5-6 Jun 87, Prince's Trust
a line recording; excellent stereo
You Know It Makes Sense (Foskett) (2:02)
86, from the UK LP **IT'S A LIVE-IN WORLD**

SOURCE:
Varies; see individual entries.

SOUND QUALITY:
Varies; see individual entries.

COMMENTS:
Ringo's voice is actually getting better. Some okay stuff here, but a lot of padding as well. It's not clear exactly when Ringo recorded these radio commercials, but we know that their tv counterparts were filmed in Dec 86, so it's likely that they were recorded about the same time.

SERGEANT PEPPER'S LONELY HEARTS CLUB BAND: A HISTORY OF THE BEATLE YEARS 1962-1970
THE BEATLES
No manufacturer listed, BN-87

9-disc set in a box, with sticker on the front; includes information sheet with track listing and recording information; labels have appropriate year and say "The Pepper Band." This is a copy of a legitimate radio special; technically a pirate (as it is not trying to pass itself off as a legitimate copy) and not a bootleg.

NOTES:
—Each disc (show) begins with the same 90 second introduction in which Murray the K introduces the Beatles on stage at Wembley for the *NME* Annual Poll Winners' All-star Concert, 26 Apr 64; it also includes and excerpt from **Sergeant Pepper's Lonely Hearts Club Band** (Lennon-McCartney), and a brief interview excerpt, which varies.
—The material is listed in the order in which it begins; often, the narration or interview intrudes on the music (this is especially true of the outtake and live material).
—*Unless stated otherwise, songs are the commercial versions.*

DISC ONE [1962]
Side A
> Introduction (1:30)
>> The Beatles introduce themselves (0:18)
> Paul talks about fans at the Cavern (0:29)
>> 30 Jan 82, *Desert Island Discs*
> **Searchin'** (Leiber-Stoller) (2:53)
>> 1 Jan 62, Decca audition; excellent mono
> narration
> Brian talks about first seeing the Beatles (1:34)
> **Twist And Shout** (Medley-Russell) (2:05)
>> Dec 62, Star Club Hamburg; very good mono
> **My Bonnie** (Pratt) (2:01)
>> May 61, Hamburg; no intro
> narration
> Brian talks about their first business meeting (0:47)
> **Money (That's What I Want)** (Bradford-Gordy) (2:13)
>> 1 Jan 62, Decca audition; excellent mono
> narration
> —commercial break—
> narration
> **One After 909** (Lennon-McCartney) (3:14)
>> Spring 62 rehearsal? very good mono
> Paul chats about early songwriting, includes acapella: (0:57)
>> **Just Fun** (Lennon-McCartney) (0:09)
>> **One After 909** (Lennon-McCartney) (0:09)
>>> Jan 69, from *Let It Be*; very good mono
> **Catswalk** (McCartney) (1:20)
>> Spring 62 rehearsal? very good mono
> narration
> George Martin talks about first meeting the Beatles (2:27)
> **Ask Me Why** (McCartney-Lennon) (2:25)
>> Dec 62, Star Club, Hamburg; very good mono
> **Love Of The Loved** (Lennon-McCartney) (1:44)
>> 1 Jan 62, Decca audition; excellent mono
> narration
> George Martin talks about meeting the Beatles (0:32)
> narration
> *Besame Mucho* (Velazquez-Skylar) (2:30)
>> 6 Jun 62, EMI; unknown take #
> narration
Side B
> narration
> Brian talks about getting the Beatles into suits (0:28)

Some Other Guy (Leiber-Stoller-Barrett) (2:11)
          22 Aug 62, Cavern Club? very good mono
          A live version which appears to be the acetate auctioned at Sotheby's on 22
                    Dec 82 (but without the introduction by Bob Wooler).
An American in Liverpool (speaker unknown) (0:51)
Long Tall Sally (Johnson-Penniman-Blackwell) (0:45)
          Dec 62, Star Club, Hamburg; good mono (excerpt)
Paul talks about the Cavern (0:31)
Three Cool Cats (Leiber-Stoller) (2:15)
          1 Jan 62, Decca audition; excellent mono
narration
Pete Best recalls getting sacked (1:20)
          82, from Backstage Records, BSR-1111
Ringo recalls getting hired (1:19)
Carol (Berry) (2:34)
          16 Jul 63, BBC; excellent mono
narration
—commercial break—
narration
Love Me Do (McCartney-Lennon) (2:18)
          4 Sep 62, EMI; unknown take #; excellent mono
narration
P.S. I Love You (McCartney-Lennon) (1:59)
          11 Sep 62, EMI; take 10; excellent mono
narration
Paul talks about recording **How Do You Do It** (1:22)
How Do You Do It (Murray-Edmond) (1:53)
          4 Sep 62, EMI; take 2; excellent mono
narration
I Saw Her Standing There (McCartney-Lennon) (1:16)
          Dec 62, Star Club, Hamburg; good mono (excerpt)
narration
Paul talks about Hamburg (0:58)
I'm Gonna Sit Right Down And Cry (Over You) (Thomas-Biggs) (1:55)
          Dec 62, Star Club, Hamburg; good mono
George Martin talks about **Please Please Me** (1:01)
Brian talks about the Beatles sound (0:42)
narration
Another Beatles Christmas Record (0:30)
          26 Oct 64, EMI (excerpts)
Sweet Little Sixteen (Berry) (2:44)
          Dec 62, Star Club, Hamburg; good to very good mono
DISC TWO [1963]
Side C
          Introduction (1:30)
                    George talks about early influences (0:23)
                              mid-60s phone interview
narration
Please Please Me (McCartney-Lennon) (1:52)
          26 Nov 62, EMI; unknown take number; excellent mono
          All 45 and UK LP mono versions appear to be the original 30 Nov 62 mono
                    mix, with the correct lyrics. In all stereo versions to date, edited and
                    mixed on 25 Feb 63, John flubs a lyric toward the end. The Feb mono
                    edit appeared in the US on **EARLY BEATLES**.
Love Me Do (McCartney-Lennon) (1:12)
          11 Sep 62, EMI; take 10; excellent mono (excerpt)
narration
Helen Shapiro recalls the first UK tour (0:52)

I Saw Her Standing There (McCartney-Lennon) (2:24)
    24 Oct 63, *Karlaplannstudion*, Stockholm
    broadcast on *Pop '63*, Swedish radio; excellent mono
narration
Norman Smith remembers recording **Twist And Shout** (0:58)
    Summer 83, from *The Beatles At Abbey Road*
Twist And Shout (Medley-Russell) (2:27)
    11 Feb 63, EMI; take 1
    this tape includes in-studio chat and riffs from this session (apparently from
        the recording of **I Saw Her Standing There**), but the music is the
        usual take.
narration
Norman Smith about early stereo recording (0:43)
    Summer 83, from *The Beatles At Abbey Road*
Do You Want To Know A Secret (McCartney-Lennon) (1:55)
    11 Feb 63, EMI; take 6; excellent mono
    This tape is preceded and followed by in-studio chat and riffs (which may not
        belong there). This is the same basic take, but without echo; the mix
        replaces Ringo's sticks with clapping, and includes some extra backing
        vocals and the final chord (which is faded out on the commercial ver-
        sion, which is take 8).
narration
—commercial break—
Paul remembers the Chris Montez tour (0:44)
There's A Place (McCartney-Lennon) (1:43)
    11 Feb 63, EMI; take 13
narration
fan interview (very good mono) (0:30)
Paul talks about the Mersey Sound (0:36)
From Me To You (McCartney-Lennon) (1:51)
    5 Mar 63, EMI; edit of unknown take #s; excellent mono
    this cut is preceded by a countdown which, because it is stereo, may not be-
        long there
John talks about the second single (0:11)
narration
From Me To You (McCartney-Lennon) (1:13)
    24 Oct 63, *Karlaplannstudion*, Stockholm (excerpt)
    broadcast on *Pop '63*, Swedish radio; excellent mono
Paul, Ringo and George talk about touring (1:07)
Boys (Dixon-Farrell) (2:19)
    11 Feb 63, EMI; take 1
narration

Side D

Baby It's You (David-Bacharach-Williams) (1:05)
    11 Feb 63, EMI; take 5 (excerpt)
narration
Brian talks about hits (0:55)
narration
Bad To Me (Lennon-McCartney) (1:24)
    Feb 63? Dick James; demo
    from acetate, very good mono
Brian talks about working with George Martin (0:47)
She Loves You (Lennon-McCartney) (2:11)
    24 Oct 63, *Karlaplannstudion*, Stockholm
    broadcast on *Pop '63*, Swedish radio; excellent mono
fan interview (0:47)
    31 Oct 63, London Airport
I'll Get You (Lennon-McCartney) (1:58)
    1 Jul 63, EMI; unknown take #; fake stereo
narration

Money (That's What I Want) (Bradford-Gordy) (2:32)
            24 Oct 63, *Karlaplannstudion*, Stockholm
            broadcast on *Pop '63*, Swedish radio; excellent mono
narration
News report: the Beatles return from Sweden (1:17)
            31 Oct 63, London Airport
Roll Over Beethoven (Berry) (1:59)
            24 Oct 63, *Karlaplannstudion*, Stockholm
            broadcast on *Pop '63*, Swedish radio; excellent mono
narration
—commercial break—
I Saw Her Standing There (McCartney-Lennon) (1:29)
            11 Feb 63, EMI; edit of takes 9 & 12 (excerpt)
narration
The Beatles talk about success (1:08)
I Want To Hold Your Hand (Lennon-McCartney) (2:18)
            17 Oct 63, EMI; take 17; fake stereo
I Saw Her Standing There (McCartney-Lennon) (1:57)
            64, the George Martin Orchestra; excellent mono
narration
George Martin discusses cracking the American market (2:32)
Ringo's Theme (This Boy) (Lennon-McCartney) (2:03)
            64, the George Martin Orchestra; excellent mono
The Beatles' Christmas Record (0:50)
            20 Oct 63, EMI (excerpts)
This Boy (Lennon-McCartney) (2:08)
            17 Oct 63, EMI; take 5; fake stereo
DISC THREE [1964]
Side E
Introduction
            The Beatles introduce themselves (0:18)
                        same as for DISC ONE
Not A Second Time   (Lennon-McCartney) (1:12)
            11 Sep 63, EMI; take 9 (excerpt)
narration
George Martin remembers hitting Number One In America (0:29)
Medley (McCartney-Lennon) (3:50)
            Love Me Do
            Please Please Me
            From Me To You
            She Loves You
            I Want To Hold Your Hand
                        19 Apr 64, IBC; for *Around The Beatles*
                        excellent mono
narration
Brian Epstein remembers hitting Number One In America (1:01)
British news report on the Beatles' arrival in New York (1:44)
            includes first US press conference and excerpts from **THE
                        BEATLES STORY** (Capitol LP)
Paul remembers arriving in New York (0:52)
George Martin on Beatlemania (1:02)
narration
Brian Epstein on timing (0:20)
All My Loving (Lennon-McCartney) (1:59)
            30 Jul 63, EMI; take 14
A New York fan's complaint (0:15)
            outside The Plaza, New York City
narration
—commercial break—
narration

Press conference back in England (1:43)
      22 Feb 64
We Love You Beatles (Adam-Strouse) (2:15)
      64, The Carefrees; excellent mono
narration
Billy Joel remembers the Beatles on *Ed Sullivan* (0:40)
Don't Bother Me (Harrison) (2:18)
      12 Sep 63, EMI; take 15
      It's interesting how, when you start to examine the commercial releases very
            closely, you hear things you never knew were there (like the choking at
            the end of **Twist And Shout**). Here, right after the vocals start,
            George seems to say "Too fast."
George recalls writing **Don't Bother Me** (0:28)
narration
The Beatles accept the Variety Club award (0:47)
      19 Mar 64, Dorchester Hotel, London
Can't Buy Me Love (Lennon-McCartney) (2:04)
      29 Jan 64, Paris; take 4; fake stereo
narration
George Martin on the Beatles' development (0:54)
You Can't Do That (Lennon-McCartney) (2:26)
      25 Feb 64, EMI; take 9; excellent mono
narration

Side F

Shout! (Isley-Isley-Isley) (1:42)
      19 Apr 64, IBC; for *Around The Beatles*
      excellent mono
narration
messages to Australia (0:11)
      12 Sep 63, EMI
Beatles' arrival at Adelaide and press conference (1:08)
      12 Jun 64
Long Tall Sally (Johnson-Penniman-Blackwell) (1:54)
      1 Mar 64, EMI; take 1; excellent mono
narration
And I Love Her (Lennon-McCartney) (2:10)
      the George Martin Orchestra; excellent mono
narration
Fab Four On Film (1:41)
      Apr 64? (excerpts)
      Wiener gives the date of this interview as 26 May 64, but this must be incor-
            rect as Paul and Ringo were out of the country on holiday between 2-
            27 May.
I Should Have Known Better (Lennon-McCartney) (2:34)
      26 Feb 64, EMI; take 22
Fab Four On Film (0:53)
      Apr 64? (excerpts)
A Hard Day's Night (Lennon-McCartney) (2:24)
      16 Apr 64, EMI; take 9 (with countdown)
narration
—commercial break—
narration
John is interviewed in Los Angeles (1:17)
      23-25 Aug 64, from **HEAR THE BEATLES TELL ALL**
23 Aug 64, Hollywood Bowl (2:55)
      Things We Said Today (Lennon-McCartney)
      Roll Over Beethoven (Berry) (excerpt)
Fab Four On Film (0:50)
      Apr 64? (excerpts)

I Feel Fine (Lennon-McCartney) (2:22)
    18 Oct 64, EMI; take 9
    a less powerful mix than on the commercial version; this also features extra
        feedback at the beginning, no echo on the vocals, and continues to
        the end of the take instead of fading
narration
Another Beatles Christmas Record (0:29)
    26 Oct 64, EMI; (excerpts, includes outtakes)
She's A Woman (Lennon-McCartney) (2:51)
    12 Oct 64, EMI; take 6
DISC FOUR [1965]
Side G
    Introduction (1:30)
        George: Around the world in a box (0:17)
    Paul introduces Peter & Gordon (0:14)
        64, from promo 45
    I Don't Want To See You Again (Lennon-McCartney) (1:55)
        64, Peter & Gordon
    narration
    Ringo talks about his marriage (0:45)
        12 Feb 65, David Jacobs' garden
    Honey Don't (Perkins) (2:49)
        26 Oct 64, EMI; take 5
    Ringo talks about Country-Western music (1:02)
    Eight Days A Week (Lennon-McCartney) (2:35)
        6/18 Oct 64, EMI; take 13 (& edit piece, as take 15)
    narration
    Paul talks about making plans (0:30)
    I'm A Loser (Lennon-McCartney) (2:25)
        14 Aug 64, EMI; take 8; brief studio chat at the beginning
    narration
    —commercial break—
    Ticket To Ride (Lennon-McCartney) (3:07)
        15 Feb 65, EMI; take 2
        essentially the same mix as the commercial version, but with no echo on the
            vocals; also, the tape plays out to the end of the take rather than
            fading
    narration
    Ringo talks about skiing in *Help!* (1:18)
    Yes It Is (Lennon-McCartney) (2:35)
        16 Feb 65, EMI; take 14
    narration
    M.B.E. announcement interview (2:21)
        12 Jun 65? from a newsreel
    No Reply (Lennon-McCartney) (2:10)
        30 Sep 64, EMI; take 8
    narration
Side H
    The National Health Cow (0:29)
        Jun 65? BBC; John reads his poem
    narration
    Help! (Lennon-McCartney) (2:14)
        13 Apr 65, EMI; take 12 (with countdown)
    John reviews *Help!* (0:36)
    narration
    15 Aug 65, Shea Stadium (2:55)
        I Feel Fine (Lennon-McCartney)
        Dizzy Miss Lizzie (Williams) (excerpt)
    George and John about Shea Stadium (1:14)

remarkable audience interview (0:46)
>   15 Aug 65, Shea Stadium
a frantic introduction (0:10)
>   19 Aug 65, Sam Houston Coliseum, Houston; afternoon
30 Aug 65, Hollywood Bowl (4:05)
>   **Twist And Shout** (Medley-Russell)
>   **She's A Woman** (Lennon-McCartney)
>   (both tracks commercially available)
interviews:
>   George says they could keep going for ages (0:38)
>   George knows where he is (0:29)
>   22 Aug 65, Portland
>   Ringo—the safest one on stage? (0:24)
>   31 Aug 65, San Francisco
narration
John reacts to the San Francisco madness (1:45)
>   31 Aug 65, San Francisco
narration
—commercial break—
Yesterday (Lennon-McCartney) (2:00)
>   14 Jun 65, EMI; take 2
narration
Newsreel report on M.B.E. awards (0:39)
>   26 Oct 65?
I Feel Fine (Lennon-McCartney)
>   18 Oct 64, EMI; take 9 (excerpt)
Paul remembers getting his M.B.E. (0:50)
narration
We Can Work It Out (Lennon-McCartney) (2:14)
>   20/29 Oct 65, EMI; take 2
>   with countdown and extended ending
narration
Paul responds to *Time* (0:33)
>   28 Aug 66, Los Angeles press conference
Day Tripper (Lennon-McCartney) (2:53)
>   16 Oct 65, EMI; take 3
>   This is a noticeably different mix from the commercial stereo version. The gui-
>   tars and vocals are much more toward the center, and there is no
>   echo on the vocals.
The Beatles' Third Christmas Record (2:30)
>   8 Nov 65, EMI; excellent mono (excerpts)
DISC FIVE [1966]
Side I
>   Introduction (1:30)
>   Paul on the difficulties of playing live (0:23)
>   **Run For Your Life** (Lennon-McCartney) (2:31)
>   12 Oct 65, EMI; take 5; includes extensive pre-song chat
>   narration
>   **In My Life** (Lennon-McCartney) (2:17)
>   18 Oct 65, EMI; take 3
>   John on folk influences (0:31)
>   Seattle?
>   **Norwegian Wood** (Lennon-McCartney) (1:57)
>   21 Oct 65, EMI; take 4
>   narration
>   —commercial break—
>   **Paperback Writer** (Lennon-McCartney) (2:27)
>   13/14 Apr 66, EMI; take 2; no echo, extended ending
>   narration

John talks about the butcher cover (0:49)
        28 Sep 74, WNEW
Rain (Lennon-McCartney) (2:49)
        14/16 Apr 66, EMI; take 7
narration
Paperback Writer (Lennon-McCartney) (0:50)
        30 Jun 66, Nippon Budokan Hall, Tokyo (excerpt)
narration
And Your Bird Can Sing (Lennon-McCartney) (1:53)
        26 Apr 66, EMI; edit of takes 6 & 10
narration

Side J

Love You To (Harrison) (0:56)
        11/13 Apr 66, EMI; take 7 (excerpt)
narration
George Martin on encouraging musical variety (0:48)
Eleanor Rigby (Lennon-McCartney) (1:59)
        28/29 Apr & 6 Jun 66, EMI; take 15
narration
Dr. Robert (Lennon-McCartney) (2:07)
        17/19 Apr 66, EMI; take 7
John's apology (2:14)
        11 Aug 66, Astor Towers Hotel, Chicago
Rock And Roll Music (Berry) (0:54)
        30 Jun 66, Nippon Budokan Hall, Tokyo (excerpt)
Fan interview (0:50)
Got To Get You Into My Life (Lennon-McCartney) (2:19)
        8/11 Apr & 18 May & 17 Jun 66, EMI; take 9
Paul talks about **REVOLVER** (1:09)
        Aug 66
For No One (Lennon-McCartney) (1:51)
        9/16/19 Apr 66, EMI; take 14
Audience interview and report (0:37)
        18 Aug 66, Suffolk Downs Racetrack, Boston
        includes **Long Tall Sally** in the background
Report on leaving Mid-South Coliseum (0:33)
        19 Aug 66, Memphis, Tennessee
Good Day Sunshine (Lennon-McCartney) (1:54)
        8/9 Jun 66, EMI; take 1
George talks about them changes (0:52)
        Summer 66
Audience interview (0:10)
        includes excerpt of **I Feel Fine** (Lennon-McCartney)
I'm Only Sleeping (Lennon-McCartney) (2:51)
        27/29 Apr & 5/6 May 66, EMI; take 13
narration
I Wanna Be Your Man (Lennon-McCartney) (1:03)
        29 Aug 66, Candlestick Park (excerpt)
        This would appear, despite better sound quality, to be taken from Tony Bar-
            row's cassette tape of the event.
Brian talks about the 66 tour (0:35)
narration
—commercial break—
narration
George Martin on **Tomorrow Never Knows** (0:30)
Tomorrow Never Knows (Lennon-McCartney) (2:48)
        6/7/22 Apr 66, EMI; take 3
John on **Tomorrow Never Knows** (1:00)
        interview with Kenny Everett (date unknown)

Yellow Submarine (Lennon-McCartney) (2:30)
    26 May & 1 Jun 66, EMI; take 5
narration
Pantomime: Everywhere It's Christmas (0:48)
    aka **The Beatles' Fourth Christmas Record**
    25 Nov 66, Dick James; excellent mono (excerpts)
DISC SIX [1967]
Side K
Introduction (1:30)
    George Martin on drugs (0:18)
narration
George Martin remembers the **PEPPER** sessions (1:09)
Penny Lane (Lennon-McCartney) (2:52)
    29/30 Dec 66 & 4/5/6/9/10/12/17 Jan 67, EMI; take 9
narration
Strawberry Fields Forever (Lennon-McCartney) (1:35)
    28 Nov 66, EMI; take 2 (excerpt)
    with George Martin's voice-over; excellent mono
George Martin talks about **Strawberry Fields Forever** (1:53)
Strawberry Fields Forever (Lennon-McCartney) (3:57)
    24/28/29 Nov & 8/9/15/21 Dec 66, EMI; edit of takes 7 & 26
narration
—commercial break—
narration
Paul on **PEPPER** influences (1:58)
Sergeant Pepper's Lonely Hearts Club Band (Lennon-McCartney) (1:46)
    1/2 Feb & 3/6 Mar 67, EMI; take 10
With A Little Help From My Friends (Lennon-McCartney) (2:19)
    29/30 Mar 67, EMI; take 11 (excerpt)
George Martin on the **PEPPER** sessions (1:04)
Lucy In The Sky With Diamonds (Lennon-McCartney) (0:44)
    1/2 Mar 67, EMI; take 8 (excerpt)
Paul on **PEPPER** (0:36)
    67
Being For The Benefit Of Mr. Kite! (Lennon-McCartney) (2:30)
    17/20 Feb & 28/29/31 Mar 67, EMI; take 9
John on **PEPPER** (0:30)
A Day In The Life (Lennon-McCartney) (4:16)
    19/20 Jan & 3/10/22 Feb 67, EMI; edit of takes 6 & 7
    with countdown and no final chord; otherwise the commercial version, with
        clean intro; excellent stereo
George Martin on **A Day In The Life** (0:42)
Within You, Without You (Harrison) (0:37)
    15/22 Mar & 3 Apr 67, EMI; take 2 (excerpt)
final chord from **A Day In The Life** (0:13)
narration
Side L
narration
George Martin on **All You Need Is Love** (1:28)
All You Need Is Love (Lennon-McCartney) (4:17)
    14 Jun 67, Olympic & 19/23/24/25 Jun 67, EMI; take 58
    broadcast version, from the *Our World* tv special
    excellent mono, includes in-studio chat
Paul on **All You Need Is Love** (1:14)
    He mentions that he and John each wrote a song for *Our World*. John's
    song, **All You Need Is Love**, was to be recorded first, and during
    the recording they realized that it was the song to use. His song, he
    says, will no doubt be used later. He is probably referring to **Hello
    Goodbye**.

Beneath the interview is an apparent edit of the song, with the "Love, love love" refrain repeating. It is unlikely that these are backing vocal tracks, as they go on too long and appear where the chorus would be. It is unknown as to whether this was present in the original interview.

narration
Blue Jay Way (Harrison) (3:07)
      6/7 Sep & 6 Oct 67, EMI; take 3
The Maharishi talks about TM and the Beatles (1:24)
      26 Aug 67; University College, Bangor, North Wales
narration
—commercial break—
narration
The Beatles on Brian's death (0:54)
      27 Aug 67; Wales
Flying (Harrison-Lennon-McCartney-Starkey) (1:57)
      8 Sep 67, EMI; take 8 (mono remix #4); excellent mono
      This is the "Aerial Tour Instrumental" acetate, sold at Sotheby's in 81. Buried under dialogue, this version is quite different; while the beginning is basically the same—with the noticeable addition of a flute—the similarity ends where the commercial version turns into dreamy loops. Here, it becomes an entirely different tune, an upbeat, almost-skiffle little foot-stomper.
      After more overdubs on 28 Sep, **Flying** was 9:36; it was then edited down that day to a more commercial length, a little over two minutes, and all of this extra music was deleted. The "Aerial Tour Instrumental" acetate was aired complete and with no voice-over in a Sep 88 broadcast of *The Lost Lennon Tapes*.
      The deleted material from **Flying**, it must be noted, bears an extreme resemblence to the cut **In The Park**, recorded by George Dec 67 at EMI for **WONDERWALL MUSIC**. Could parts of the deleted material have been cannibalized for **WONDERWALL**?

narration
George Martin on Brian (0:44)
narration
Paul on making films (0:34)
      interview with Brian Matthew?
I Am The Walrus (Lennon-McCartney) (3:50)
      5/6/27/28 Sep 67, EMI; take 17
narration
Hello Goodbye (Lennon-McCartney) (3:18)
      2/19/20/25 Oct & 2 Nov 67, EMI; take 22
narration
Christmas Time (Is Here Again) (1:38)
      aka **The Beatles' Fifth Christmas Record**
      28 Nov 67, EMI (excerpts)
DISC SEVEN [1968]
Side M
Introduction (1:30)
      Paul talks about Rishikesh (0:21)
Magical Mystery Tour (Lennon-McCartney) (2:38)
      25/26/27 Apr & 3 May & 7 Nov 67, EMI; take 9
narration
Paul talks about *Magical Mystery Tour* (1:25)
Your Mother Should Know (Lennon-McCartney) (2:20)
      22 Aug 67, Chappell; take 8? the basic tracks
      no bass or organ, different backing vocals; very good mono
      the narration claims—incorrectly—that this is "Paul McCartney's original demo."
narration

Lady Madonna (Lennon-McCartney) (2:08)
    3/6 Feb 68, EMI; take 5
narration
—commercial break—
The Fool On The Hill (Lennon-McCartney) (2:48)
    6/25/26/27 Sep & 20 Oct 67, EMI; take 6
narration
Paul talks about Rishikesh (0:43)
    a longer version of the interview in the Introduction
narration
John and Paul explain Apple (1:14)
    15 May 68, *Tonight Show* (with Joe Garagiola)
Yellow Submarine (Lennon-McCartney) (0:45)
    67, The George Martin Orchestra (excerpt)
narration
Hey Bulldog (Lennon-McCartney) (3:01)
    11 Feb 68, EMI; take 10
narration
Derek Taylor remembers Apple (1:00)
Those Were The Days (Raskin) (4:54)
    Mary Hopkin; mid-Jul 68, Trident
narration

Side N

narration
Hey Jude (Lennon-McCartney) (6:52)
    31 Jul & 1 Aug 68, Trident; take 1
Paul talks about writing **Hey Jude** (1:29)
Revolution (Lennon-McCartney) (3:16)
    10/11/12 Jul 68, EMI; take 16
narration
—commercial break—
narration
While My Guitar Gently Weeps (Harrison) (3:44)
    5/6 Sep 68, EMI; take 25
George talks about The White Album (0:50)
Paul talks about The White Album and **Helter Skelter** (0:54)
Helter Skelter (Lennon-McCartney) (3:30)
    9/10 Sep 68, EMI; take 21
Paul talks about **Glass Onion** (1:14)
Glass Onion (Lennon-McCartney) (2:04)
    11/12/13/16 Sep & 10 Oct 68, EMI; take 33
narration
Yer Blues (Lennon-McCartney) (3:51)
    11 Dec 68, from *Rock And Roll Circus*
The Beatles' Sixth Christmas Record (1:31)
    Nov 68; excellent mono (excerpts)

DISC EIGHT [1969]
Side O

Introduction
    Paul remembers trying to motivate the others (0:18)
Back In The USSR (Lennon-McCartney) (2:33)
    22/23 Aug 68, EMI; take 6
narration
Paul talks to John about films, audiences and nerves (1:40)
    Jan 69, from *Let It Be*
Rocker (McCartney) (0:31)
    aka "Link Track" & "Instrumental 42"
    22 Jan 69, Apple; from **GET BACK** LP

Don't Let Me Down (Lennon-McCartney) (3:40)
     22 Jan 69, Apple; from **GET BACK** LP
     includes between-song chat and one false start
narration
All Together Now (Lennon-McCartney) (2:03)
     12 May 67, EMI; take 9
narration
—commercial break—
narration
Alistair Taylor recalls the rooftop concert (0:41)
One After 909 (Lennon-McCartney) (2:38)
     30 Jan 69, Apple rooftop; with **Danny Boy** (Weatherly) (0:05)
narration
Derek Taylor talks about the coming of Allen Klein (0:31)
Dig A Pony (Lennon-McCartney) (3:30)
     30 Jan 69, Apple rooftop
narration
John and Yoko on Bed Peace (1:19)
     26 Mar 69, Amsterdam Hilton?
narration
John remembers bagism (2:11)
     28 Sep 74, WNEW?
Get Back (Lennon-McCartney) (2:58)
     28 Jan 69, Apple (45 version)
narration
George Martin on Paul Is Dead (0:54)
Revolution 9 (Lennon-McCartney) (0:51)
     10/11/20/21 Jun 68, EMI
narration

Side P

narration
Paul remembers Allen Klein (0:55)
I Me Mine (Harrison) (1:23)
     3 Jan & 1 Apr 70, EMI; take 18 (excerpt)
narration
George on problems at Apple (1:09)
     69 or 70
The Ballad Of John And Yoko (Lennon-McCartney) (2:52)
     14 Apr 69, EMI; take 10
narration
Give Peace A Chance (Lennon-McCartney) (4:03)
     1 Jun 69, Montreal; with countdown (excerpt)
narration
—commercial break—
John on **ABBEY ROAD** (0:14)
     28 Sep 74, WNEW?
Come Together (Lennon-McCartney) (2:58)
     21/22/23/25/29/30 Jul 69, EMI; take 9 (excerpt)
George on **Something** (1:05)
     8 Oct 69, interview with David Wigg
     from **THE BEATLES TAPES**
Something (Harrison) (1:45)
     2 May & 5 May, Olympic & 11/16 Jul & 15 Aug 69, EMI; take 39 (excerpt)
George on **Here Comes The Sun** (0:49)
     8 Oct 69, interview with David Wigg
     from **THE BEATLES TAPES**
Here Comes The Sun (Harrison) (1:43)
     7/8/16 Jul & 6/11/15/19 Aug 69, EMI; take 15 (excerpt)
Paul remembers **ABBEY ROAD** (0:20)

Mean Mr. Mustard (Lennon-McCartney) (1:04)
        24/25/29 Jul 69, EMI; take 35
Polythene Pam (Lennon-McCartney) (1:17)
        25/28/30 Jul 69, EMI; take 40
George Martin on **ABBEY ROAD** (0:16)
She Came In Through The Bathroom Window (Lennon-McCartney) (1:47)
        25/28/30 Jul 69, EMI; take 40
narration
Across The Universe (Lennon-McCartney) (2:54)
        4/8 Feb 68 & 2 Oct 69 EMI; take 8 (WWF version) (excerpt)
The Beatles' Seventh Christmas Record (1:29)
        Nov 69? (excerpts); excellent mono
DISC NINE [1970]
Side Q
Introduction
        George on the future of the Beatles (0:23)
Golden Slumbers/Carry That Weight (Lennon-McCartney) (3:07)
        2/3/4/30/31 Jul & 15 Aug 69, EMI; take 17
The End (Lennon-McCartney) (2:02)
        23 Jul & 5/7/8/15/18 Aug 69, EMI; take 7
Paul on the future of the Beatles (0:18)
narration
John on **Instant Karma!** (0:23)
        18 Feb 70, David Wigg interview (?)
Instant Karma! (Lennon) (3:10)
        27 Jan 70, Apple?
narration
—commercial break—
John on the future of the Beatles (0:39)
        18 Feb 70, David Wigg interview
Let It Be (Lennon-McCartney) (3:46)
        31 Jan, Apple & 30 Apr 69 & 4 Jan 70, EMI; take 30
        45 version
narration
Sentimental Journey (Green-Brown-Homer) (3:15)
        Nov-Dec 69, Apple?
Ringo on **SENTIMENTAL JOURNEY** (0:18)
        from an interview with Anne Nightengale
narration
George on solo projects (1:20)
narration
Paul remembers the breakup (2:30)
Maybe I'm Amazed (McCartney) (3:44)
        Nov-69-Mar 70, EMI?
narration
Side R
I've Got A Feeling (Lennon-McCartney) (3:19)
        30 Jan 69, Apple Rooftop
George talks about *Let It Be* (3:07)
For You Blue (Harrison) (2:25)
        25 Jan 69, Apple; from **GET BACK** LP
George talks about **LET IT BE** (0:40)
Paul wants out of the contract (0:23)
The Long And Winding Road (Lennon-McCartney) (3:25)
        31 Jan 69, Apple; take 19; from **GET BACK** LP
Ringo on the future of the Beatles (0:51)
narration
—commercial break—
narration
George talks about **ALL THINGS MUST PASS** (0:14)

Awaiting On You All (Harrison) (2:42)
    May-Aug 70, Trident/EMI
George on Phil Spector (0:54)
My Sweet Lord (Harrison) (4:32)
    May-Aug 70, Trident/EMI
narration
news report on the filing of the lawsuit (0:23)
    30 Dec 70
Paul remembers having to sue the Beatles (0:49)
Working Class Hero (Lennon) (0:46)
    Oct 70, EMI (excerpt)
news report on Paul's court appearance (0:39)
    Feb 71
All Those Years Ago (Harrison) (3:39)
    Jan 81, AIR?
credits
Ringo: best of luck from the Beatles (0:05)
final chord from **A Day In The Life** (Lennon-McCartney) (0:40)
    22 Feb 67, EMI; take 9

SOURCE:
    This a copy of a series of legitimate radio shows from the Fall of 84.

SOUND QUALITY:
    Unless otherwise stated, all music is excellent stereo and all interviews are generally very good to excellent mono (except for the George Martin segments which appear to be stereo).

COMMENTS:
    This is piece is rather rare, mostly due to its price. This remarkable radio special marked the first appearances of may important individual items, as well as the broadcast premiere of raw EMI tapes. It made good use of them, and of large chunks of the 72 BEEB production, *The Beatles Story.*

SHEA—THE GOOD OLD DAYS
THE BEATLES
Contra Band, 2315
Full color jacket, with title; back is blank; labels have title.

Side A (17:42)
    I'm Down (Lennon-McCartney)
        This song was only performed once, but appears twice.
  dialogue
  Murray The K greets the crowd
  dialogue
  Ed Sullivan introduces the group
    Twist And Shout (Medley-Russell)
    I Feel Fine (Lennon-McCartney)
    Dizzy Miss Lizzie (Williams)
    Ticket To Ride (Lennon-McCartney)
Side B (13:15)
    Can't Buy Me Love (Lennon-McCartney)
    Baby's In Black (Lennon-McCartney)
    A Hard Day's Night (Lennon-McCartney)
        this song has dialogue on top of it
    Help! (Lennon-McCartney)
    I'm Down (Lennon-McCartney)
        this song has dialogue on top of it and fades early

SOURCE:
Excerpts from the soundtrack of *The Beatles At Shea Stadium*, filmed 15 Aug 65.

SOUND QUALITY:
Good to very good mono, significantly better than on **SHEA!**

COMMENTS;
The Beatles' show at Shea Stadium was a cultural event and arguably their most famous concert. Filmed by Ed Sullivan Productions, Inc., in association with NEMS Enterprises Ltd. and Subafilms Ltd., the 50-minute film premiered on the BBC on 1 Mar 66, and is occasionally shown on PBS. It's much better to see than to listen to, and the incessant screaming gives new meaning to the expression "wall of sound."

In late Feb 66 the Beatles admitted to having overdubbed some of the music for the film. This is most obvious with **Act Naturally** (not on this record but on **SHEA!**), which seems to have been lifted intact from **HELP!**

Also performed, but not in the film, were **She's A Woman** and **Everybody's Trying To Be My Baby**.

SOLDIER OF LOVE
THE BEATLES
Contra Band, TB-1022
Insert cover with song listing; labels have side numbers only.

Side A
I'll Be On My Way (Lennon-McCartney) (1:50)
24 Jun 63, BBC; good mono
Till There Was You (Willson) (2:02)
9 Feb 64, *The Ed Sullivan Show*; very good mono
Do The Oz (Lennon) (2:45)
Jun 71; from the 45, very good mono
Sentimental Journey (Green-Brown-Homer) (3:13)
15 Mar 70, soundtrack of promotional video
broadcast *The Ed Sullivan Show*, 17 May 70
different mix with some different vocals; very good mono
I Got A Woman (Charles-Richards) (1:25)
4 Apr 64, BBC; good mono (excerpt)
Soldier Of Love (Cason-Moon) (1:52)
16 Jul 63, BBC; very good mono
recorded off a US radio station playing a boot copy
Side B
As It Happened (15:15)
mid 64, very good mono
from Murray The K's fan club record, (US) Fairway OV 526-1
reissued 76 as (US) IBC F4KM-0082,83
bits and pieces of various interviews from early 64

SOURCE:
Varies; see individual entries.

SOUND QUALITY:
Varies; see individual entries.

COMMENTS:
Probably quite an interesting compilation for its time.

SOME LIKE IT HOT
THE BEATLES
Idle Mind, OC-595
Insert cover with barely literate track listings; labels are generic Idle Mind.

Side A
>set up at Twickenham
>**Paul's Piano Theme** (McCartney?) (1:23)
>>I have played this track for a number of people extremely familiar with classical piano music, and no one has been able to identify it; most suggest that it is an original (excerpt)
>**Don't Let Me Down** (Lennon-McCartney) (0:49)
>>with wah-wah (excerpt)
>chat
>**Maxwell's Silver Hammer** (Lennon-McCartney) (2:05)
>>movie edit; one early & one late (with anvil)
>**Two Of Us** (Lennon-McCartney) (1:38)
>>"Oo-oo" version (excerpt)
>**Oh! Darling** (Lennon-McCartney) (0:12)
>>Paul with piano
>chat about early songwriting; includes acapella:
>>**Just Fun** (Lennon-McCartney) (0:09)
>>**One After 909** (Lennon-McCartney) (0:09)
>**One After 909** (Lennon-McCartney) (0:59)
>>(excerpts)
>**Jazz Piano Song** (McCartney-Starkey) (0:56)
>>Paul & Ringo; vocals: Paul
>Paul doesn't annoy George (excerpt)
>**Across The Universe** (Lennon-McCartney) (1:21)
>>(excerpt)
>**Dig A Pony** (Lennon-McCartney) (0:57)
>>"killed a hound dog" version (excerpt)
>**Suzy Parker** (Lennon-McCartney-Harrison-Starkey) (0:50)
>>the usual version
>**I Me Mine** (Harrison) (2:25)
>>two versions edited together; first performance/"I-I-Me-Me-Mine"
>**For You Blue** (Harrison) (2:47)
>>long intro, with slide guitar (edited)
>*Besame Mucho* (Velazquez-Skylar) (1:56)
>>29 Jan 69, Apple; vocals: Paul, John
>**Octopus's Garden** (Starkey) (3:04)
>>George helps Ringo and everybody joins in

Side B
>**The Long And Winding Road** (Lennon-McCartney) (0:37)
>>cha-cha version
>**The Long And Winding Road** (Lennon-McCartney) (0:24)
>>Paul vamps
>**Shake, Rattle And Roll** (Calhoun) (2:06)
>>26 Jan 69, Apple; vocals: Paul, John
>**Kansas City/Miss Ann/Lawdy Miss Clawdy**
>(Leiber-Stoller/Dolphy/Price) (2:33)
>>26 Jan 69, Apple;vocals: John, Paul
>**Dig It** (Lennon-McCartney) (3:26)
>>26 Jan 69, Apple
>Paul talks to John about films, audiences and nerves
>**Let It Be** (Lennon-McCartney) (4:03)
>>31 Jan 69, Apple; a finished version
>**The Long And Winding Road** (Lennon-McCartney) (3:37)
>>31 Jan 69, Apple; a finished version ("always known")

SOURCE:
>Excerpts from the *Let It Be* soundtrack; recorded from another boot.

SOUND QUALITY:
>Good mono, recorded off a speaker.

COMMENTS:
>Nothing worthwhile here; an historical curiosity, if that.

SOMEWHERE IN UTOPIA
GEORGE HARRISON
Loka Productions, WX-124
2 disc set in 2-color jacket ©1988 with track listings and recording information.

DISC ONE
Side A
>**Got My Mind Set On You** (Clark) (5:16)
>>extended version from UK 12-inch (Dark Horse, WB8178T)
>**Zig Zag** (Harrison-Lynne) (2:42)
>>from UK 12-inch (Dark Horse, W8131T)
>6 Jun 87, *Prince's Trust All-Star Benefit Concert* (8:21)
>>**While My Guitar Gently Weeps** (Harrison)
>>**Here Comes The Sun** (Harrison)
>>A pair of truly outstanding live cuts at Wembley Arena, featuring Eric
>>Clapton on **While My Guitar**. The arrangements were excel-
>>lent and George's voice was stronger and more confident
>>than it'd been since the early '60s. (The group had rehearsed
>>for several days at the Academy in Brixton prior to the show.
>>Do you suppose the rehearsals were taped?)
>>George (with Ringo, Jeff Lynne, Elton John and Clapton) played the
>>same set on both Friday (5 Jun) and Saturday (6 Jun); on
>>Saturday Phil Collins also drummed. This should be available on
>>video, but seems to be hard to find.
>**When We Was Fab** (Harrison-Lynne) (5:15)
>>with reverse ending, from UK 12-inch (Dark Horse, WB8131T)

Side B
>The following four cuts are taken from the 7-inch 45 (SGH 777; also available as a
>CD, SGHCD 777), **SONGS BY GEORGE HARRISON**, which accompa-
>nied George's second book from Genesis Publications. Hand made, auto-
>graphed and limited to 2500 copies, the retail price (new) was £230 (about
>$460, 1988).
>**For You Blue** (Harrison) (4:09)
>>13 Dec 74, Capitol Center, Largo, Maryland
>>excellent mono; a vastly superior version to anything previously avail-
>>able from the tour; the mix makes them sound like a small band
>>performing in an intimate little club somewhere
>**Flying Hour** (Harrison-Ralph) (4:32)
>>original recording Oct 79-Oct 80, remixed 87
>>intended for **SOMEWHERE IN ENGLAND** but dropped
>>main differences: countdown, extended, end vocals moved around
>**Sat Singing** (Harrison) (4:25)
>>original recording Oct 79-Oct 80, remixed 87
>>intended for **SOMEWHERE IN ENGLAND** but dropped
>>very similar to commercial version; mostly just punched up
>**Lay His Head** (Harrison) (3:50)
>>original recording Oct 79-Oct 80, remixed 87
>>intended for **SOMEWHERE IN ENGLAND** but dropped
>>appears to be identical to the version on the UK 12-inch (**Got My
>>Mind Set On You**, Dark Horse, W8178T)

That's The Way It Goes (Harrison) (3:29)
original recording May-Aug 82 for **GONE TROPPO**
remixed 87, for UK 12-inch (**When We Was Fab**, Dark Horse, WB121T)

DISC TWO
Side C

10 Feb 88, *Rockline*, live at KLOS, Los Angeles (9:04)
George and acoustic guitar, with Jeff Lynne
a few riffs (0:04)
may or may not be **Drive My Car**, as the jacket claims
chat & riffs
Here Comes The Sun (Harrison) (0:16)
chat
medley (2:14)
Here Comes The Sun (Harrison)
The Bells Of Rhymey (Davies-Seeger)
Mr. Tambourine Man (Dylan)
Here Comes The Sun (Harrison)
chat
Take Me As I Am (Or Not At All) (Bryant) (0:04)
acapella
chat
That's All Right, Mama (Crudup) (0:25)
chat
Let It Be Me (Becaud-Delanoe-Curtis) (1:51)
chat
Something (Harrison) (0:41)
chat
Every Grain Of Sand (Dylan) (1:52)
Miss O'Dell (Harrison) (2:25)
Jan-Apr 73; from 45 (US) Apple 1862
Deep Blue (3:39)
Jul 71; from 45 (US) Apple 1836
I Don't Care Anymore (2:35)
Sep-Oct 74; from 45 (US) Apple 1877
Johnny B. Goode (Berry) (3:29)
15 Mar 86, Birmingham; *Heartbeat '86* charity gig
George, with Denny Laine & Robert Plant

Side D

87 Xmas message (0:07)
from **YULESVILLE**, Warner Brothers promo sampler
excellent mono
Ding Dong Ding Dong (Harrison) (3:38)
Sep-Oct 74; demo; very good stereo
Dark Horse (Harrison) (1:52)
Fall 74, A&M? very good mono
The jacket claims this is a live 74 version from an unreleased film of the tour. I
have been told that it was a live performance filmed at A&M for a
trailer for the unreleased film; I have not seen the trailer.
18 Nov 76, *Saturday Night Live* (6:42)
George with Paul Simon; excellent mono
intro
Here Comes The Sun (Harrison)
Homeward Bound (Simon)
16 Nov 76, NBC; rehearsal with Paul Simon for *SNL* (4:53)
from a portable recorder
Rock Island Line (trad.); very good stereo
includes brief versions of **Yesterday** (Lennon-McCartney) and
Bridge Over Troubled Water (Simon)
Bye Bye Love (Bryant-Bryant); very good mono

21 Dec 75? radio broadcast of *Rock Around The World*
recording date unknown; George interviewed by Alan Freeman
acoustic, excellent mono
Awaiting On You All (Harrison) (excerpt) (0:42)
Far East Man (Harrison) (excerpt) (0:30)
10 Feb 88, *Rockline*, live at KLOS, Los Angeles (0:36)
chat about **Got My Mind Set On You**
Got My Mind Set On You (Clark) (1:48)
62, James Ray; excellent mono

SOURCE:
Varies; see individual entries.

SOUND QUALITY:
Excellent stereo unless otherwise stated.

COMMENTS:
About one disc of new material and one of reissue. This is the first time all of the *Saturday Night Live* material has been collected in one place; the jacket seems to claim that the rehearsal took place on the 18th, the same day as the broadcast (which is possible).

STARS OF '63 (SUPER LIVE CONCERT SERIES)
THE BEATLES
Gamma Alpha Records, 4749/4750
2-disc set with insert cover and song listing; labels are generic Shalom.

DISC ONE
Side A (14:25)
I Saw Her Standing There (McCartney-Lennon)
Roll Over Beethoven (Berry)
The Hippy Hippy Shake (Romero)
Sweet Little Sixteen (Berry)
Lend Me Your Comb (Twomey-Wise-Weisman)
Your Feet's Too Big (Benson-Fisher)
Side B (14:33)
Twist And Shout (Medley-Russell)
Mr. Moonlight (Johnson)
A Taste Of Honey (Marlow-Scott)
Besame Mucho (Velazquez-Skylar)
Reminiscing (Curtis)
Kansas City/Hey-Hey-Hey-Hey! (Leiber-Stoller/Penniman)
DISC TWO
Side C (18:10)
Nothin' Shakin' (But The Leaves On The Trees)
(Fontaine-Colacrai-Lampert-Gluck)
To Know Her Is To Love Her (Spector)
Little Queenie (Berry)
Falling In Love Again (Lerner-Hollander)
Ask Me Why (McCartney-Lennon)
Be-Bop-A-Lula (Vincent-Davis)
vocal by Horst Obber
Hallelujah! I Love Her So (Charles)
vocal by Horst Obber
Side D (16:10)
Red Sails In The Sunset (Kennedy-Grosz)
Everybody's Trying To Be My Baby (Perkins)
Matchbox (trad. arr. Perkins)
I'm Talking About You (Berry)
I Wish I Could Shimmy Like My Sister Kate (Piron)

Long Tall Sally (Johnson-Penniman-Blackwell)
I Remember You (Mercer-Schertzinger)

SOURCE:
This is a pirate (an unauthorized copy which does not try to pass itself off as an original) of the Bellaphon commercially-released set from 77. The original recordings are, of course, from late Dec 62, The Star-Club, Hamburg.

SOUND QUALITY:
Very good to excellent mono (rechannelled as stereo); comparable to the original.

COMMENTS:
This set possibly has its origin in the short time between the initial German release and the subsequent American edition, when it looked as if the Beatles might quash it. It's hard to imagine any other reason for copying such an easily-available piece.

THE STEREO WALK
THE BEATLES
No manufacturer listed, B4
Full color jacket, ©1985 ("Made in Belgium") with track listing; labels say "Rubber Soul" and have track listing.

Side A
Suicide (McCartney) (0:46)
Jan 69, **GET BACK** sessions
Bad To Me (Lennon-McCartney) (1:28)
Feb 63? Dick James; demo
I'll Be On My Way (Lennon-McCartney) (2:01)
24 Jun 63, BBC
Catswalk (McCartney) (1:07)
Spring 62? rehearsal (early fade)
Goodbye (McCartney) (2:24)
late 68, Dick James? Paul's demo; excellent stereo
All Together On The Wireless Machine (McCartney?) (0:58)
unknown; possibly Fall 67, Paul with Kenny Everett
fair to good mono
Step Inside Love (Lennon-McCartney) (2:20)
Feb 68, Dick James? demo for Cilla Black? fair mono
from a British radio broadcast (source unknown, but possibly Kenny
Everett)
The Walk (McCracklin-Gorlic) (1:00)
27 Jan 69, Apple
excellent stereo (switches to mono at the very end; stereo **Walk** indeed!)
Back Seat Of My Car (McCartney) (2:24)
Jan 69, **GET BACK** sessions
Commonwealth (improvisation) (3:38)
Jan 69, **GET BACK** sessions
Thank You Guru Dev/**Happy Birthday To You** (McCartney-?/Hill-Hill) (2:18)
15 Mar 68, Rishikesh, India, with the Beach Boys
Wolfman Jack's voice-over has been edited out
Suzy Parker (Lennon-McCartney-Harrison-Starkey) (1:58)
Jan 69, **GET BACK** sessions
Side B
Back In The U.S.S.R. (Lennon-McCartney) (3:14)
4 Jul 85, Washington DC; the Beach Boys with Ringo
line recording, excellent stereo
This cut was included on a limited (but legitimate) album released by the [Mike]
Love Foundation For American Music, **FOURTH OF JULY: A
ROCKIN' CELEBRATION OF AMERICA.**

Ding Dong Ding Dong (Harrison) (3:46)
 Sep-Oct 74; demo; very good stereo?
Dark Horse (Harrison) (3:42)
 Sep-Oct 74; demo; very good stereo?
Hello Little Girl (Lennon-McCartney) (1:39)
 1 Jan 62; Decca audition
Beatles in the studio (1:06)
 bits and pieces of studio chat (and lots of countdowns) lifted mostly from
   SPLHCB: A History Of The Beatle Years; excellent mono and excel-
   lent stereo
Some Other Guy (Leiber-Stoller-Barrett) (1:55)
 22 Aug 62, Cavern Club (acetate)
 good to very good mono (excerpt)
Oct 74, KHJ-AM, Los Angeles (0:32)
 John fields a question about **What's The New Mary Jane**; a foretaste of a
   great interview.
JOHN LENNON ON RONNIE HAWKINS
 Dec 69; from 45 Cotillion PR 104/105
  The Long Rap (1:22)
  The Short Rap (0:06)
John & Yoko at the Everson (3:57)
 8 Oct 71, Everson Museum, Syracuse, New York; press conference (excerpt)
 from **THE HISTORY OF SYRACUSE MUSIC, VOLS. VIII & IX,**
   ECEIP PSLP 1015/1017
3 Mar 73, *The Grammy Award Show* ? (1:31)
 introductions
 Ringo & Harry Nilsson present an award
3 Mar 73, *The Grammy Award Show* (1:52)
 Ringo accepts the Album Of The Year Award for **THE CONCERT FOR
   BANGLA DESH**

SOURCE:
 Varies; see individual entries.

SOUND QUALITY:
 Very good to excellent mono, unless otherwise noted.

COMMENTS:
 The jacket makes a really big deal about **The Walk** being in stereo—as if it hadn't been
in stereo all along. The last few tracks on Side B are of modest interest.

STUDIO OUTTAKE RECORDINGS 1962-4
THE BEATLES
Wizardo, WRMB 326
Insert cover with song listing; generic Wizardo labels.

Side A
 Love Me Do (McCartney-Lennon) (2:20)
  23 Jul 63, BBC
 Please Please Me (McCartney-Lennon) (1:53)
  13 Aug 63, BBC
 From Me To You (McCartney-Lennon) (1:46)
  29 Jun 63, BBC
 I Saw Her Standing There (McCartney-Lennon) (1:23)
  24 Sep 63, BBC (excerpt)
 Misery (McCartney-Lennon) (1:42)
  4 Jun 63, BBC
 Do You Want To Know A Secret (McCartney-Lennon) (1:44)
  4 Jun 63, BBC

There's A Place (McCartney-Lennon) (1:45)
3 Sep 63, BBC
Anna (Go To Him) (Alexander) (2:45)
27 Aug 63, BBC
Chains (Goffin-King) (2:12)
17 Sep 63, BBC; some static in this cut
Boys (Dixon-Farrell) (2:03)
17 Sep 63, BBC; some static in this cut

Side B

She Loves You (Lennon-McCartney) (2:17)
20 Aug 63, BBC
Till There Was You (Willson) (2:07)
29 Jun 63, BBC
Roll Over Beethoven (Berry) (2:07)
29 Jun 63, BBC
You Really Got A Hold On Me (Robinson) (2:53)
4 Jun 63, BBC
(There's A) Devil In Her Heart (Drapkin) (2:09)
20 Aug 63, BBC
Money (That's What I Want) (Bradford-Gordy) (2:37)
3 Sep 63, BBC
Long Tall Sally (Johnson-Penniman-Blackwell) (1:51)
13 Aug 63, BBC
Honey Don't (Perkins) (2:06)
3 Sep 63, BBC; vocals: John
Kansas City/Hey-Hey-Hey-Hey! (Leiber-Stoller/Penniman) (2:33)
6 Aug 63, BBC
Words Of Love (Holly) (1:50)
20 Aug 63, BBC

SOURCE:
63, BBC.

SOUND QUALITY:
Very good mono.

COMMENTS:
This LP contains 20 of the 24 cuts from the 2-LP set **STUDIO SESSIONS** (and its reissue as **DECCA AUDITION OUTTAKES—SUPER STUDIO SERIES 2,** both Contra Band, 3640, 3641). Missing are **The Hippy Hippy Shake**, **Sure To Fall (In Love With You)**, **Lucille**, and the second **Money (That's What I Want)**.

SUNDAY NIGHT AT THE LONDON PALLADIUM
THE BEATLES
Shalom, E-3687
Insert cover with song titles; labels have matching info.

Side A

13 Oct 63? the London Palladium (14:38)
Val Parnell's *Sunday Night At The London Palladium*
transmitted live on ATV
I Want To Hold Your Hand (Lennon-McCartney)
This Boy (Lennon-McCartney)
chat
All My Loving (Lennon-McCartney)
screaming
Money (That's What I Want) (Bradford-Gordy)
Twist And Shout (Medley-Russell)
bows

Side B
> 29 Feb 64, *Big Night Out*
>> filmed 23 Feb 64, Teddington Studios, London
>>> **Please Mr. Postman** (Holland-Bateman-Gordy) (0:39)
>>>> excerpt, under titles
>>> intro & commercial (0:09)
>>> skits, etc. (5:48)
>>> **All My Loving** (Lennon-McCartney) (2:09)
>>> **I Wanna Be Your Man** (Lennon-McCartney) (1:57)
>>> skit (1:03)
>>> **Till There Was You** (Willson) (1:26)
>>> **Please Mr. Postman** (Holland-Bateman-Gordy) (2:34)
>>> **I Want To Hold Your Hand** (Lennon-McCartney) (0:37)
>>>> (excerpt)

SOURCE:
> Varies; see individual entries.

SOUND QUALITY:
> Line recordings, from speakers; very good mono.

COMMENTS:
> This disc is the same as **LONDON** (Contra Band, 3687).
> Both of these tapes come from video (or film) soundtracks; the *Big Night Out* is fairly common, but the *London Palladium* is less so. It is interesting because (if the dating is correct), the Beatles performed **I Want To Hold Your Hand** and **This Boy** before they were recorded (17 Oct 63, EMI) and released (29 Nov 63). Although all sources give this date and song listing, this may actually be the 12 Jan 64 show.
> *Big Night Out* was sometimes known as *Blackpool Night Out* (when it was filmed in Blackpool, but this one was filmed in London), and this particular show was also broadcast in the US on WOR (New York) on 14 Aug 65. This tape is obviously from the American broadcast. The songs on *Big Night Out* are the com-mercial versions, lip-synched. Of moderate interest, however, is the edit of **Till There Was You**—one verse and the ending.

SUPERTRACKS 1
THE BEATLES
Contra Band, 3922
Insert cover with song listing; labels are generic Contra Band.

Side A
> **You Really Got A Hold On Me** (Robinson) (3:01)
>> This cut begins with the intro and performance from the *Pop '63* Swedish radio show and ends with the commercial version. From *The Beatles Story* (BBC 72).
> **Have You Heard The Word** (Kipner-Groves) (3:12)
>> 74, the Fut; no Beatles involvement
> **You Really Got A Hold On Me** (Robinson) (2:25)
>> 26 Jan 69, Apple; from *Let It Be*
> **What's The New Mary Jane** (Lennon) (3:20)
>> 14 Aug 68, EMI; take 4 (stereo remix #4)
>> Possibly from the unreleased Apple 45
> **Teddy Boy** (McCartney) (5:48)
>> 24 Jan 69, Apple; very good stereo; the usual version

Side B
> **Dig It** (Lennon-McCartney) (4:51)
>> 26 Jan 69, Apple; from *Let It Be*
> **L.S. Bumble Bee** (Moore) (2:32)
>> 66, Peter Cook & Dudley Moore; no Beatles involvement
>> from UK Decca 45 F12551 (Jan 67); excellent mono

Maxwell's Silver Hammer (Lennon-McCartney) (2:13)
   Jan 69, **GET BACK** sessions; movie edit, from *Let It Be*
Besame Mucho (Velazquez-Skylar) (1:04)
   29 Jan 69, Apple; from *Let It Be* (excerpt)
Crying, Waiting, Hoping (Holly) (2:02)
   6 Aug 63, BBC
Shake, Rattle And Roll (Calhoun) (2:06)
   26 Jan 69, Apple; from *Let It Be*

SOURCE:
   Varies; see individual entries.

SOUND QUALITY:
   Very good mono, except as noted.

COMMENTS:
   Yet another typical early compilation; good stuff (perhaps) at the time, but worthless today. This may also have been available as **BYE BYE BYE** (with a printed jacket, and possibly also as a picture disc), perhaps with "Bye Bye Bye" on it.

TEXAN TROUBADOURS
THE BEATLES
No manufacturer listed, TX
2-disc set in blue & white printed jacket, with song listing on the back; labels are blank.

DISC ONE [afternoon show]
Side A (18:45)
   Announcements and introductions
   Twist And Shout (Medley-Russell)
   She's A Woman (Lennon-McCartney)
   I Feel Fine (Lennon-McCartney)
   Dizzy Miss Lizzie (Williams)
   Ticket To Ride (Lennon-McCartney)
   Everybody's Trying To Be My Baby (Perkins)
Side B (18:17)
   Can't Buy Me Love (Lennon-McCartney)
   Baby's In Black (Lennon-McCartney)
   I Wanna Be Your Man (Lennon-McCartney)
   A Hard Day's Night (Lennon-McCartney)
   crowd control
   Help! (Lennon-McCartney)
   I'm Down (Lennon-McCartney)
   Announcements
DISC TWO [evening show]
Side C (19:34)
   Announcements and introductions
   Twist And Shout (Medley-Russell)
   She's A Woman (Lennon-McCartney)
   I Feel Fine (Lennon-McCartney)
   Dizzy Miss Lizzie (Williams)
   Ticket To Ride (Lennon-McCartney)
   Everybody's Trying To Be My Baby (Perkins)
Side D (17:04)
   Can't Buy Me Love (Lennon-McCartney)
   Baby's In Black (Lennon-McCartney)
   I Wanna Be Your Man (Lennon-McCartney)
   A Hard Day's Night (Lennon-McCartney)
   Help! (Lennon-McCartney)
   I'm Down (Lennon-McCartney)

Announcements

SOURCE:
        19 Aug 65; Sam Houston Coliseum, Houston, Texas; both shows.

SOUND QUALITY:
        Excellent mono, line recording.

COMMENTS:
        Among the best live recordings, these were also available as a 2-disc set entitled
LIVE FROM THE SAM HOUSTON COLOSSEUM; the evening show was available
separately under the same title (as covered in *Do You Want To Know A Secret?*). Video of at
least one of these performances is allegedly making the rounds (although I have yet to hear
from anyone who has seen it).

TOP OF THE POPS (LP)
THE BEATLES
No manufacturer listed, 111
Insert cover with song listing; discs have no labels.

Side A
        People Say (Szigeti-Lichterman) (2:47)
                "John & Paul," 65, from US 45 Tip 1021
                good mono; no Beatles involvement
        I'm Walkin' (Szigeti-Lichterman) (2:14)
                "John & Paul," 65, from US 45 Tip 1021
                good mono; no Beatles involvement
        Hey Jude (Lennon-McCartney) (7:23)
                The video performance consists of new vocals (4 Sep 68, Twickenham) per-
                        formed to pre-recorded backing tracks (for the commercial version:
                        31 Jul & 1 Aug 68, Trident; take 1). This was done because of strict
                        Musician's Union rules about miming.
                very good mono
        Revolution (Lennon-McCartney) (3:36)
                The video performance consists of new vocals (4 Sep 68, Twickenham) per-
                        formed to pre-recorded backing tracks (10/11/12 Jul 68, EMI; take
                        16).
                very good mono
        16 Jul 64, *Top Gear* (3:07)
                [*Top Of The Pops* intro]
                Long Tall Sally (Johnson-Penniman-Blackwell)
Side B
        16 Jul 64, *Top Gear* (continued) (7:16)
                interview
                A Hard Day's Night (Lennon-McCartney)
                Things We Said Today (Lennon-McCartney)
                [*Top Of The Pops* closing]
                        very good mono
        Shout! (Isley-Isley-Isley) (0:42)
                6 May 64, *Around The Beatles* (excerpt)
                from **As It Happened**, with Murray The K's voice-over
        23 Aug 64, Hollywood Bowl (15:00)
                screaming
                intro
                Twist And Shout (Russell-Medley)
                You Can't Do That (Lennon-McCartney)
                All My Loving (Lennon-McCartney)
                She Loves You (Lennon-McCartney)
                Things We Said Today (Lennon-McCartney)

Roll Over Beethoven (Berry)

SOURCE:
Varies; see individual entries.

SOUND QUALITY:
Very good mono, except as noted. An extremely noisy pressing which is also mastered too slow.

COMMENTS:
People Say and **I'm Walking** appeared on a number of early Beatles bootleg albums, presumably due to rumor and curiosity about the names of the artists. One listen dispels any doubts, however.

The appearance here of the *Top Gear* material masquerading as a *Top Of The Pops* tv appearance is interesting, but the question has been settled with the release of BEEB11.

TOUR YEARS (63-66)
THE BEATLES
Honeysuckle Productions, ENG 4001
2-disc set in full color jacket with song listing on the back; labels say "Eva Records," but info matches.

DISC ONE
Side A
7 Dec 63, Empire Theatre, Liverpool (19:52)
From the 7 Dec 63 BBC-TV broadcast, *It's The Beatles!*
Recorded off a tv speaker, good mono.
From Me To You (McCartney-Lennon)
I Saw Her Standing There (McCartney-Lennon)
Roll Over Beethoven (Berry)
Boys (Dixon-Farrell)
Till There Was You (Willson)
This Boy (Lennon-McCartney)
I Want To Hold Your Hand (Lennon-McCartney)
Money (That's What I Want) (Bradford-Gordy)
Side B
16 Jun 64, Festival Hall, Melbourne, Australia (18:43)
From the 1 Jul 64 Australian TV broadcast, *The Beatles Sing For Shell.*
This is a line recording, very good mono.
You Can't Do That (Lennon-McCartney)
All My Loving (Lennon-McCartney)
She Loves You (Lennon-McCartney)
Can't Buy Me Love (Lennon-McCartney)
Twist And Shout (Russell-Medley)
Long Tall Sally (Johnson-Penniman-Blackwell)
broadcast credits (twice)
DISC TWO
Side C
19 Aug 65, Sam Houston Coliseum, Houston, Texas, evening (19:26)
This is a line recording, excellent mono.
She's A Woman (Lennon-McCartney)
Dizzy Miss Lizzie (Williams)
Ticket To Ride (Lennon-McCartney)
Everybody's Trying To Be My Baby (Perkins)
I Wanna Be Your Man (Lennon-McCartney)
A Hard Day's Night (Lennon-McCartney)
Help! (Lennon-McCartney)

Side D
    2 Jul 66, Nippon Budokan Hall, Tokyo, afternoon (19:22)
    This is a line recording, excellent mono.
        introduction & tuning
        Rock And Roll Music (Berry)
        Day Tripper (Lennon-McCartney)
        Baby's In Black (Lennon-McCartney)
        I Feel Fine (Lennon-McCartney)
        Yesterday (Lennon-McCartney)
        Nowhere Man (Lennon-McCartney)
        I'm Down (Lennon-McCartney)
        announcements

SOURCE:
    Varied; see individual entries. This Budokan show is traditionally dated 2 Jul 66, but may be 1 Jul 66.

SOUND QUALITY:
    See individual entries.

COMMENTS:
    These concert performances are commonly available, and several songs have been edited out of these three sets:
    7 Dec 63; Empire Theatre, Liverpool
        All My Loving (Lennon-McCartney)
        She Loves You (Lennon-McCartney)
        Twist And Shout (Medley-Russell)
        From Me To You (McCartney-Lennon)
            instrumental
    19 Aug 65; Sam Houston Coliseum, Houston, Texas; evening
        Twist And Shout (Medley-Russell)
        I Feel Fine (Lennon-McCartney)
        Can't Buy Me Love (Lennon-McCartney)
        Baby's In Black (Lennon-McCartney)
        I'm Down (Lennon-McCartney)
    2 Jul 66; Nippon Budokan Hall, Tokyo; afternoon
        She's A Woman (Lennon-McCartney)
        If I Needed Someone (Harrison)
        I Wanna Be Your Man (Lennon-McCartney)
        Paperback Writer (Lennon-McCartney)

TRAGICAL HISTORY TOUR/DR. PEPPER
THE BEATLES
"Apple Records," SAPCOR 36/37
2-disc set in full color gatefold jacket, with track listings on the inside; labels say "Rubber Soul" and have track listing.

DISC ONE [**DR. PEPPER**, SAPCOR 36]
Side A
    introduction (0:07)
        The first 2 seconds of **SERGEANT PEPPER** edited onto the concert in-
            troduction from *Ringo*; excellent stereo/mono (but who cares?)
    With A Little Help From My Friends (Lennon-McCartney) (1:55)
        26 Apr 78, *Ringo* tv special; excellent mono
    When I'm Sixty-four (Lennon-McCartney) (0:42)
        Jan 69, **GET BACK** sessions; very good mono

Sergeant Pepper's Lonely Hearts Club Band (reprise)
(Lennon-McCartney) (1:24)
    1 Apr 67, EMI; take 9; mono mix; excellent mono
A Day In The Life (Lennon-McCartney) (5:09)
    19/20 Jan 67, EMI; take 6; very good stereo?
    from acetate; no orchestra & alternate vocals for Paul
    very good mono; clean intro and final chord edited on
SERGEANT PEPPER Inner Groove
(Lennon-McCartney-Harrison-Starkey) (0:21)
    21 Apr 67, EMI; take 1; excellent mono
Christmas Time (Is Here Again) (Lennon-McCartney-Harrison-Starkey) (6:53)
    28 Nov 67, EMI; very good mono, off speakers
    from the "EMI board room" tape
Christmas Time (Is Here Again) (6:08)
    aka **The Beatles' Fifth Christmas Record**
    28 Nov 67, EMI; excellent mono
Side B
Strawberry Fields Forever (Lennon-McCartney) (2:08)
    29 Nov 66, EMI; take 2
    with George Martin's voice-over; excellent mono
    this cut from *SPLHCB: A History Of The Beatle Years*
Strawberry Fields Forever (Lennon-McCartney) (2:40)
    24 Nov 66, EMI; take 1, excellent stereo
Strawberry Fields Forever (Lennon-McCartney) (3:12)
    28 Nov 66, EMI; takes 3 (false start) & 4; excellent stereo
Strawberry Fields Forever (Lennon-McCartney) (3:29)
    15 Dec 66, EMI; overdub onto take 25; excellent stereo
    George Martin conducts his score
Strawberry Fields Forever (Lennon-McCartney) (3:27)
    8/9/15/21 Dec 66, EMI; take 26; excellent stereo
Strawberry Fields Forever (Lennon-McCartney) (4:10)
    24/28/29 Nov & 8/9/15/21 Dec 66, EMI; edit of takes 7 & 26
    completed master; excellent stereo, alternate (non-U.S.) mix
unknown (1:30)
    collage of music and sound effects; excellent stereo
    From Lewisohn's description, this would not appear to be the "Carnival of
        Light" tape. Too bad.
DISC TWO [**TRAGICAL HISTORY TOUR**, SAPCOR 37]
Side C
Magical Mystery Tour (Lennon-McCartney) (2:33)
    25/26/27 Apr & 3 May 67; take 9 (mono remix #7)
    from the *MMT* soundtrack; extra effects, some different vocals and slightly
        different mix; good mono
The Fool On The Hill (Lennon-McCartney) (2:53)
    6 Sep 67, EMI; demo; excellent mono
Instrumental (Lennon-Starkey?) (0:51)
    Sep 67; tape loops; from the *MMT* soundtrack; good mono
Blue Jay Way (Harrison) (3:54)
    6 Sep 67, EMI; mono mix; excellent mono
Your Mother Should Know (Lennon-McCartney) (2:22)
    22 Aug 67, Chappell; take 8? the basic tracks
    no bass or organ, different backing vocals; excellent mono
I Am The Walrus (Lennon-McCartney) (4:43)
    6/7 Sep 67, EMI; take 17 (mono remix #4)
    the basic tracks; excellent mono
Strawberry Fields Forever (Lennon-McCartney) (2:55)
    29 Nov 66, EMI; take 7 (mono remix #3)
    from acetate; very good mono

Jessie's Dream (McCartney-Starkey-Harrison-Lennon) (3:33)
Oct-Nov 67; from *MMT* soundtrack; good mono
music, dialogue and effects

Side D

24 Nov 67, BBC *Where It's At* (6:33)
Kenny Everett's prerecorded interview with John about *Magical Mystery Tour* (excerpts). There is a short piece of studio chat featuring Paul, which (session) could be the source of All Together On The Wireless Machine; fair to good mono.

9 Jun 68, BBC *The Kenny Everett Show* (9:44)
Recorded 5 or 6 Jun 68, EMI. This is not the raw interview (as on **GOLDEN BEATLES**), but a tape of the actual broadcast and contains extra material and some interesting effects; fair to good mono.

Una Sensazionale Intervista (6:34)
5-6 Jun 68, EMI; from (Italian) Apple DPR-108; excellent mono
The Kenny Everett interview, with lots of fooling around and vocal improvisations; includes **Cottonfields**, Goodbye Jingle, Tiny Tim For President, and so on.

Kenny Everett (0:49)
5 or 6 Jun 68, EMI? excellent mono

SOURCE:
Varies; see individual entries.

SOUND QUALITY:
Varies; see individual entries.

COMMENTS:
Only one thing of interest is on DISC ONE, the uncommon mono **Pepper (Reprise)**. The title of DISC TWO is, of course, stolen from the Rutles. A number of the music pieces which went into the *Magical Mystery Tour* soundtrack (Side C) were not recorded at EMI, and little is known about them. Side D has two terrific Kenny Everett pieces, neither of which have appeared before (in this form, to my knowledge).

TUG OF WAR DEMOS AND MORE
PAUL McCARTNEY
Sandwich Records, TOW 1980
Printed black and white jacket, ©1987, with song listing on the back; labels have LP title only.

Side A

Ballroom Dancing (McCartney) (1:53)
Take It Away (McCartney) (3:58)
Keep Under Cover (McCartney) (3:32)
Dress Me Up As A Robber (McCartney) (1:02)
acoustic
Dress Me Up As A Robber (McCartney) (1:53)
Dress Me Up As A Robber (McCartney) (0:28)
intro (instrumental)
The Pound Is Sinking (McCartney) (2:24)
At this point, it lacks the second melody (see Side B)
Sweetest Little Show (McCartney) (2:50)
Ebony And Ivory (McCartney) (1:37)

Side B

The Pound Is Sinking (McCartney) (2:10)
The second melody, probably a separate song at this point; the jacket, reasonably enough, calls it "Hear Me Lover"
Wanderlust (McCartney) (1:35)
Take Her Back, Jack (McCartney?) (1:27)
Unbelievable Experience (McCartney?) (1:42)

We All Stand Together (McCartney) (3:51)
Boil Crisis (McCartney) (3:59)
      written in 78; "Paul McCartney's concession to punk."
Give Us A Chord, Roy (McCartney?) (3:51)
Seems Like Old Times (McCartney) (4:05)

SOURCE:
      Probably home demos, circa Fall 80.

SOUND QUALITY:
      Excellent stereo, and greatly superior to **WAR AND PEACE**, which has much of this material.

COMMENTS:
      The most remarkable McCartney boot since—well, maybe since ever; or maybe, since **COLD CUTS** (either one). Five of these songs have never been officially released in any form. Of the five, only **Seems Like Old Times** drags a bit; the others are full of fun and hooks—the kind of thing one assumes McCartney can knock off on a rainy afternoon (and the kind of thing, it should be noted, that most critics seem to loathe, which is probably why they never get released).

21
THE BEATLES
Melvin Records, MM-002
Printed, 1-color front jacket and insert back with tracking listing; labels have artwork and title.

Side A
      The Hippy Hippy Shake (Romero) (1:35)
            4 Jun 63, BBC
      To Know Her Is To Love Her (Spector) (2:33)
            6 Aug 63, BBC; good to very good mono
      I'm Gonna Sit Right Down And Cry (Over You) (Thomas-Biggs) (1:50)
            6 Aug 63, BBC; good to very good mono
      Some Other Guy (Leiber-Stoller-Barrett) (1:47)
            22 Aug 62, Cavern Club (film); good to very good mono
      Love Of The Loved (Lennon-McCartney) (1:47)
            1 Jan 62, Decca audition; good to very good mono
      Crying, Waiting, Hoping (Holly) (1:58)
            6 Aug 63, BBC; good to very good mono
      A Shot Of Rhythm And Blues (Thompson) (2:05)
            27 Aug 63, BBC; good to very good mono
      Sure To Fall (In Love With You) (Perkins-Claunch-Cantrell) (2:03)
            24 Sep 63, BBC; good to very good mono
      Shout! (Isley-Isley-Isley) (2:16)
            6 May 64, *Around The Beatles*; good to very good mono
Side B
      Have You Heard The Word (Kipner-Groves) (4:17)
            74, the Fut; no Beatles involvement
      Honey Hush (Turner) (2:00)
            Jan 69, **GET BACK** sessions
      Commonwealth (improvisation) (3:21)
            Jan 69, **GET BACK** sessions
      Enoch Powell (improvisation) (0:23)
            Jan 69, **GET BACK** sessions
      White Power (Get Off!) (improvisation) (4:52)
            Jan 69, **GET BACK** sessions
            a version with the two parts edited together

Why Don't We Do It In The Road (Lennon-McCartney) (0:05)
  Jan 69, **GET BACK** sessions
  as "Why Don't You Put It On The Toast"
Suzy Parker (Lennon-McCartney-Harrison-Starkey) (1:44)
  Jan 69, **GET BACK** sessions
Besame Mucho (Velazquez-Skylar) (1:47)
  29 Jan 69, Apple
Cottonfields (Ledbetter) (0:18)
  5-6 Jun 68, EMI; excerpt from *Una Sensazionale Intervista*, (Italian)
    Apple DPR-108; very good mono
Move It/Good Rockin' Tonight (Samwell/Brown) (1:33)
  Jan 69, **GET BACK** sessions
Jazz Piano Song (McCartney-Starkey) (0:47)
  Jan 69, **GET BACK** sessions
The Walk (McCracklin-Gorlic) (0:51)
  27 Jan 69, Apple
What's The New Mary Jane (Lennon) (2:43)
  14 Aug 68, EMI; take 4 (stereo remix #4); (excerpt)
  Possibly from the unreleased Apple 45

SOURCE:
  Varies; see individual entries. Primarily copied from **AS SWEET AS YOU ARE (YELLOW MATTER CUSTARD)** and **SWEET APPLE TRAX**.

SOUND QUALITY:
  Very good to excellent mono, unless otherwise noted; most cuts are far too fast.

COMMENTS:
  Reportedly, only 400 copies of this album were made, but the content is nothing worth seeking out. The entries in *Hot Wacks* appear to have both the label numbers and content of **21** and **21 BIG ONES** reversed. It is correct as it appears here.

TWICE IN A LIFETIME
JOHN LENNON & PAUL McCARTNEY (SOLO)
No manufacturer listed, B-7
Color jacket with song listing on the back; label info matches

Side A
  Twice In A Lifetime (McCartney) (2:15)
    84, from the film of the same name
  Write Away (McCartney) (2:52)
    86, from the **PRESS TO PLAY** CD
    excellent stereo, some distortion
  Tough On A Tightrope (McCartney) (4:30)
    86, from the **PRESS TO PLAY** CD
    excellent stereo, some distortion
  It's Not True (McCartney) (5:34)
    86, from the **PRESS TO PLAY** CD
    excellent stereo, some distortion
  Wanderlust (McCartney) (3:52)
    84, from the soundtrack of *Give My Regards To Broad Street*
    excellent stereo
Side B
  12 Sep 84, from the *Arena* Buddy Holly special (4:44)
    That'll Be The Day (Holly-Petty-Allison) (1:10)
      Paul plays the Quarry Men shellac disc, but begins to talk over it after 37 seconds.

Paul talks about Buddy Holly and his influence on the Beatles, and plays brief acoustic versions of
Love me Do (McCartney-Lennon) (0:06) and
Words Of Love (Holly) (0:50)
tv spot for *Let It Be* (0:14)
very good mono
Give Peace A Chance (Lennon-McCartney) (0:34)
1 Jun 69, Montreal; rehearsal, excerpt; good mono
pieces of the commercial version are tacked on the end
The KYA 1969 Peace Talk (9:39)
29 May 69, Montreal; very good mono
John on the phone, during the bed-in, talking about peace, Billy Preston, Beatles projects, and peace. This was pressed and sold as a 45 by San Francisco radio station KYA.
30 Dec 69, *Man Of The Decade* (8:54)
excerpts from the UK tv special; some music (common), but primarily interviews at Tittenhurst; John's segment ran about 20 minutes and is traded on video
The show, hosted by Desmond Morris, was an examination of three men who had helped shaped the 60s: John Kennedy, Mao Tse-Tung, and John Lennon; in a public poll, John Kennedy was chosen as most influential.

SOURCE:
Varies; see individual entries.

SOUND QUALITY:
Excellent mono unless otherwise stated.

COMMENTS:
The only cut of real interest is the unreleased **Twice In A Lifetime**; this is probably its first appearance on a bootleg. Although previously available, the two Lennon interviews are also worthwhile.
The jacket deserves special mention—it's a great photo composite of John and Paul together on stage circa 72; very nicely done.

TWICKENHAM JAMS (LP)
THE BEATLES
Smilin' Ears, SE 7702
2-tone green printed jacket ©1977 with track listing; label info matches.

Side A
Early In The Morning/**Honey Hush** (improv?/Turner) (2:15)
vocals: Paul, George (excerpt)
Stand By Me (King-Glick) (1:58)
vocals: Paul
riffs & chat
Hare Krishna (improvisation?) (0:57)
vocals: Paul (excerpt)
riffs & chat
unknown (?) (0:06)
vocals: Paul
All Things Must Pass (Harrison) (3:03)
nearly finished version
riffs & chat
Fools Like Me (Clement-Maddux) (1:47))
vocals: John, George, Paul
riffs

You Win Again (Williams) (0:48)
vocals: John, George, Paul (excerpt)
Side B
Slippin' And Slidin' (Penniman-Bocage-Collins-Smith) (2:13)
18 Apr 75, *Old Grey Whistle Test*
"And the roof almost came down when..." (1:32)
source unknown
This appears to be a piece of a television show, possibly a tribute to Ed Sullivan. It contains brief statements by Dick Cavett and Sullivan, as well
as excerpts from various *Ed Sullivan Shows*. A longer piece of this is
on **THE BEST OF TOBE MILO.**
Una Sensazionale Intervista (6:30)
5-6 Jun 68, EMI; from (Italian) Apple DPR-108
The Kenny Everett interview, with lots of fooling around and vocal improvisations; includes **Cottonfields**, Goodbye Jingle, Tiny Tim For President, and so on.
Kenny Everett (0:46)
Summer 68, EMI
Kenny Everett describes the Beatles at work in the studio, as they fool around
in the background; this is not part of *Intervista*.
Every Time Somebody Comes To Town (Dylan-Harrison) (1:25)
late Nov 68? George and Bob Dylan, possibly recorded at Nat Weiss's
(Dylan's manager) home in Woodstock, about the same time George
recorded his segment for the 68 Christmas message with Tiny Tim.

SOURCE:
Side A is from the Jan 69, **GET BACK** sessions; Side B varies; see individual entries.

SOUND QUALITY:
Side A is very good mono; Side B is good to very good mono.

COMMENTS:
Side A duplicates the **TWICKENHAM JAMS** (EP) which, interestingly enough, has
much shorter versions than those on **THE BLACK ALBUM.**

ULTRA RARE TRAX, VOL. 1
THE BEATLES
The Swingin' Pig, TSP-CD-001
Compact disc; back has track listing and some recording information.

I Saw Her Standing There (McCartney-Lennon) (2:44)
11 Feb 63, EMI; take 2
One After 909 (Lennon-McCartney) (2:41)
5 Mar 63, EMI; take 2
She's A Woman (Lennon-McCartney) (3:08)
8 Oct 65, EMI; take 2, with false start
I'm Looking Through You (Lennon-McCartney) (2:50)
4 Oct 65, EMI; take 1
If You've Got Trouble (Lennon-McCartney) (2:12)
18 Feb 65, EMI; take 1
How Do You Do It (Murray-Edmond) (1:51)
4 Sep 62, EMI; take 2; excellent mono
Penny Lane (Lennon-McCartney) (2:46)
17 Jan 67, EMI; take 9 (mono remix #9); excellent mono
The US promo 45 was mono remix #11 from 17 Jan 67, but the trumpet ending was eliminated on 25 Jan 67 and mono remix #14 became the
commercial version; this mix is different from both other versions.

Strawberry Fields Forever (Lennon-McCartney) (3:09)
    24/28/29 Nov & 8/9/15/21 Dec 66, EMI; excellent stereo
    take 26, vocals with new score
From Me To You (McCartney-Lennon) (1:39)
    5 Mar 63, EMI; unknown take
Besame Mucho (Velazquez-Skylar) (2:23)
    6 Jun 62, EMI; unknown take; excellent mono
The Fool On The Hill (Lennon-McCartney) (2:37)
    6 Sep 67, EMI; Paul's piano demo; excellent mono
Paperback Writer (Lennon-McCartney) (2:27)
    13/14 Apr 66, EMI; take 2 (commercial version, raw take)

SOURCE:
    EMI studio outtakes, 1962-67.

SOUND QUALITY:
    Excellent stereo, except as noted

COMMENTS:
    Mind-blowing. Much of this material had already appeared on **SESSIONS**, and there is some question as to whether the appearances here are really from acetates (as claimed) or just from disc (but note that **How Do You Do It** is the original version, not the **SESSIONS** edit). Regardless, the new material here is simply amazing. My favorite is the *Besame Mucho*, but **I Saw Her Standing There** is also terrific. Despite the price (volumes 1 & 2 were reissued on CD in the USA as **BACK-TRACK**, with two extra cuts—probably your best bet; they were also available on LP), absolutely essential.

ULTRA RARE TRAX, VOLUME TWO
THE BEATLES
The Swingin' Pig, TSP-CD-002
Compact disc; back has track listing and some recording information.

Can't Buy Me Love (Lennon-McCartney) (2:04)
    29 Jan 64, Paris; take 1
There's A Place (McCartney-Lennon) (0:06)
    11 Feb 63, EMI; take 3; false start
There's A Place (McCartney-Lennon) (1:46)
    11 Feb 63, EMI; take 4
That Means A Lot (Lennon-McCartney) (2:15)
    20 Feb 65, EMI; take 2; very good mono
Day Tripper (Lennon-McCartney) (0:21)
    16 Oct 65, EMI; take 2; instrumental, false start
Day Tripper (Lennon-McCartney) (2:55)
    16 Oct 65, EMI; take 3
I Am The Walrus (Lennon-McCartney) (4:10)
    5/6 Sep 67, EMI; take 17 (mono remix #4); excellent mono
Misery (McCartney-Lennon) (1:40)
    11 Feb 63, EMI; take 1; excellent mono
Leave My Kitten Alone (Turner-McDougall) (2:42)
    5 Aug 64, EMI; take 5
We Can Work It Out (Lennon-McCartney) (2:03)
    20 Oct 65, EMI; take 2
A Hard Day's Night (Lennon-McCartney) (2:25)
    16 Apr 64, EMI; unknown take; excellent mono
Norwegian Wood (Lennon-McCartney) (2:09)
    21 Oct 65, EMI; take 4, with two false starts

SOURCE:
    EMI studio outtakes, 1963-67.

SOUND QUALITY:
        Excellent stereo, except as noted. Some tape hiss is evident

COMMENTS:
        For my money, the best cut on here is the killer take **1** of **Can't Buy Me Love**, with its (later) abandoned backing vocals. Despite **I'm Looking Through You** and **Norwegian Wood**, I rate it as the best alternate version of a Beatles song available.
        EMI is, of course, just a trifle miffed that this material leaked out and is reportedly conducting a Big Investigation. The rumor that these have been in private hands for many years is probably true, and I would expect the trail is too cold to be followed.

ULTRA RARE TRAX, VOLUME 3 & 4
THE BEATLES
The Swinging Pig Records, TR 2190 S
2-disc set in full color jacket with track listing; labels are "Beeb Transcription Records" and have track listing.

DISC ONE
Side A
        12-Bar Original (Lennon-McCartney-Harrison-Starkey) (3:48)
                4 Nov 65, EMI; excellent mono (excerpt) from acetate
        Help! (Lennon-McCartney) (0:13)
                13 Apr 65, EMI; take 1; instrumental, false start
        Help! (Lennon-McCartney) (0:16)
                13 Apr 65, EMI; take 2; instrumental, false start
        Help! (Lennon-McCartney) (0:55)
                13 Apr 65, EMI; take 3; instrumental, false start
        Help! (Lennon-McCartney) (2:22)
                13 Apr 65, EMI; take 5; instrumental, complete
        I Feel Fine (Lennon-McCartney (2:32)
                18 Oct 64, EMI; take 6; instrumental, complete
        I Feel Fine (Lennon-McCartney (2:28)
                18 Oct 64, EMI; take 9 (overdubs onto take 7?)
Side B
        Day Tripper (Lennon-McCartney) (1:55)
                16 Oct 65, EMI; take 1; instrumental, false start
        Day Tripper (Lennon-McCartney) (0:22)
                16 Oct 65, EMI; take 2; instrumental, false start
        Day Tripper (Lennon-McCartney) (3:05)
                16 Oct 65, EMI; take 3
        We Can Work It Out (Lennon-McCartney) (1:36)
                20 Oct 65, EMI; take 1; instrumental, false start
        We Can Work It Out (Lennon-McCartney) (2:18)
                20 Oct 65, EMI; take 2
        Yes It Is (Lennon-McCartney) (2:39)
                16 Feb 65, EMI; take 1? with rough vocal
        Yes It Is (Lennon-McCartney) (1:09)
                16 Feb 65, EMI; take 2; false start, with rough vocal
DISC TWO
Side C
        One And One Is Two (Lennon-McCartney) (1:50)
                64? from Dick James acetate; good mono; demo, Paul & acoustic guitar
                This song, given to The Strangers with Mike Shannon, probably does not exist as a Beatles version.
        Do You Want To Know A Secret (McCartney-Lennon) (1:57)
                11 Feb 63, EMI; take 8; excellent mono
                overdubbing backing vocals for the commercial version

She's A Woman (Lennon-McCartney) (5:28)
> 8 Oct 64, EMI; take 7; with false start, extended into a jam
> The released version was take 6; this was an extra attempt which, while interesting because of the extended jam (as Ringo says, "We've got a song and an instrumental."), was not as good as the previous take.

Hold Me Tight (Lennon-McCartney) (2:31)
> 12 Sep 63, EMI; unknown take
> This song was first recorded on 11 Feb 63; however, as Lewisohn says that the tape no longer exists (and due to its similarity to the released version), this should be from the later session.

Ticket To Ride (Lennon-McCartney) (3:17)
> 15 Feb 65, EMI; take 2
> complete take of commercial version

Side D

Yes It Is (Lennon-McCartney) (2:43)
> 16 Feb 65, EMI; take 14, the commercial version
> vocal overdubs onto instrumental take 14

There's A Place (Lennon-McCartney) (2:01)
> 11 Feb 63, EMI; unknown take
> There were 10 basic takes of this song, of which 3, 5 & 7 were false starts (3 & 4 are on **ULTRA RARE TRAX VOL. 2**). The commercial version utilized an overdubbed take 10. This is either 1, 2, 6, 8 or 9; judging from the weak performance, it may be 1 or 2.

A Taste Of Honey (Marlow-Scott) (2:01)
> 11 Feb 63, EMI; take 7; excellent mono
> Takes 1-5 were for the basic tune, and Paul's vocal was double-tracked as takes 6 & 7 onto take 5; take 7 was used for the commercial version.

There's A Place (McCartney-Lennon) (1:51)
> 11 Feb 63, EMI; take 11; excellent mono
> ...takes 11-13 being harmonica overdubs onto take 10. The released version was take 13, although this take is virtually identical to it.

I Saw Her Standing There (McCartney-Lennon) (2:50)
> 11 Feb 63, EMI; take 10; excellent mono
> Takes 1-9 were the basic song.
> Takes 1 & 2 were complete. Take 3 was an edit piece (possibly the guitar solo), never used. Takes 4 & 5 were complete. Takes 6, 7 & 8 were false starts. Take 9 was complete.
> Take 10 was an overdub onto take 9 (not used, and it's not clear exactly what was overdubbed as there are no handclaps here); take 11 was a false start; take 12 was a successful handclapping overdub onto take 1.
> The released version is an edit of takes 9 & 12 (overdubs onto take 1). It is unclear just how it is broken down. One would expect everything with handclaps to be from take 12, but the only part of the commercial version without them seems to be the guitar solo, which does not match the solo from this tape.

Misery (McCartney-Lennon) (0:32)
> 11 Feb 63, EMI; take 2, false start; excellent mono

Misery (McCartney-Lennon) (0:15)
> 11 Feb 63, EMI; take 3, false start; excellent mono

Misery (McCartney-Lennon) (0:33)
> 11 Feb 63, EMI; take 4, false start; excellent mono

Misery (McCartney-Lennon) (0:32)
> 11 Feb 63, EMI; take 5, false start; excellent mono

Misery (McCartney-Lennon) (1:47)
> 11 Feb 63, EMI; take 6; excellent mono
> There were 11 basic takes of **Misery** altogether (take 1 is on **ULTRA RARE TRAX VOL. 2**; takes 2, 3, 4, 5, 8 & 9 were false starts), with take 11 being the best; on 20 Feb 63, George Martin (alone) overdubbed piano as takes 12-16 onto take 11, of which take 16 was chosen for the commercial version.

SOURCE:
    EMI studio outtakes, 1963-65, except as noted.

SOUND QUALITY:
    Excellent stereo, except as noted, but not as good as the CDs of volumes 1 & 2.

COMMENTS:
    Take 4 of **Help!**, listed on the jacket, does not really appear here, although it is announced on the tape; it may be that the tape was rewound over it.
    This marks the first appearance of the actual **12-Bar Original** and **One And One Is Two**, both from acetates bought at auction in the last few years, and they are undoubtedly the most important tracks in the set.

ULTRA RARE TRAX, VOLUME 5 & 6
THE BEATLES
The Swinging Pig Records, TR 2191 S
2-disc set in full color jacket with track listing; labels are "Beeb Transcription Records" and have track listing.

DISC ONE
Side A
    Lady Madonna (Lennon-McCartney) (2:10)
        3 Feb 68, EMI; take 3 (with overdubs)
        More overdubs on 6 Feb would complete the track.
    Rain (Lennon-McCartney) (3:02)
        14/16 Apr 66, EMI; take 7
        the basic take for the commercial version
    A Day In The Life (Lennon-McCartney) (0:21)
        19/20 Jan & 3/10/ 22 Feb 67, EMI; edit of takes 6 & 7 (stereo remix #5)
    A Day In The Life (Lennon-McCartney) (2:28)
        19/20 Jan & 3/10/22 Feb 67, EMI; edit of takes 6 & 7 (stereo remix #6)
        It's not clear whether these are excerpts or not; one would expect that a mix
            would be completed, but possibly not, and the tapes do sound as if
            they were actually stopped, rather than edited. If this is so, it adds an
            important point to our knowledge: the idea that all of the alternate
            mixes may not exist complete.
        Both have clean intros with countdowns, but the differences between these
            two mixes mostly have to do with the placement of the various tracks.
            Brief as it is, RS 5 sounds very much like the commercial version.
            However, there are one or two interesting points about RS 6.
        First, the bass is much more prominent. Second, the tape switches to mono
            after about 45 seconds and remains that way from "He blew his mind
            out in a car..." to "Nobody was really sure if he was from the House of
            Lords," before reverting to stereo. Because of the timing, this was
            certainly intentional, but the reason for it is a puzzle.
    What's The New Mary Jane (Lennon) (6:44)
        14 Aug 68, EMI; take 4
        The sound is a bit muddy, but this version does seem to be lacking some of
            the things on the common (take 4, stereo remix #4) version—
            George's vocals, for example—and may be the basic take 4 before any
            mixing.
Side B
    All You Need Is Love (Lennon-McCartney) (6:57)
        14 Jun 67, Olympic & 19/23/24/25 Jun 67, EMI; take 58
        broadcast version, from the *Our World* tv special
        excellent mono, includes in-studio chat
        the most complete version available

Norwegian Wood (Lennon-McCartney) (1:57)
> 12 Oct 65, EMI; take 1
> This is a finished, alternate version; the remake of 21 Oct 65 became the commercial release.

Not Guilty (Harrison) (4:20)
> 8/9/12 Aug 68; take 102
> This, the basic take 102 with all overdubs, is the longest and best-sounding version available to date. Although a mono mix was made on 12 Aug and an acetate cut of it (available on **NOT GUILTY**), there was no stereo mix until summer 84, when **SESSIONS** was produced. That version was also edited and rearranged, and probably ought not be considered authentic.

Because (Lennon-McCartney) (2:13)
> 1/4 Aug 69, EMI; vocals only
> John's guitar riff can be heard faintly on this tape, probably from the Beatles' headphones.

DISC TWO
Side C

Hello Goodbye (Lennon-McCartney) (4:36)
> 2 Oct 67, EMI; take 1; instrumental; excellent mono

Paperback Writer (Lennon-McCartney) (0:28)
> 13 Apr 66, take 1; instrumental, false start

Paperback Writer (Lennon-McCartney) (2:36)
> 13/14 Apr 66, EMI; take 2
> basic take for commercial version (echoless mix)

Hey Jude (Lennon-McCartney) (5:30)
> 30 Jul 68, EMI; take 9
> Parts of this take are featured in the *Experiment In Television* rehearsal film.

I Hate To See The Evening Sun Go Down (improvisation?) (0:35)
> 30 Jul 68, EMI
> Another brief piece of this appears in the complete *Experiment In Television* rehearsal film. It may be an improvisation, or it may be based on **In The Evening (When The Sun Goes Down)** (Carr), which was recorded by Ray Charles.

Side D

Strawberry Fields Forever (Lennon-McCartney) (2:35)
> 24 Nov 66, EMI; take 1, with vocals; excellent stereo

Strawberry Fields Forever (Lennon-McCartney) (2:41)
> 28 Nov 66, EMI; take 2; instrumental,
> they stop but resume the song and finish it

Strawberry Fields Forever (Lennon-McCartney) (011)
> 28 Nov 66, EMI; take 3; excellent stereo
> instrumental, false start (John says it's too loud)

Strawberry Fields Forever (Lennon-McCartney) (3:07)
> 28 Nov 66, EMI; take 4, with vocals; excellent stereo

Strawberry Fields Forever (Lennon-McCartney) (0:18)
> 29 Nov 66, EMI; take 5; excellent stereo
> instrumental, false start (just a few riffs)

Strawberry Fields Forever (Lennon-McCartney) (3:51)
> 29 Nov 66, EMI; take 6; excellent stereo

Strawberry Fields Forever (Lennon-McCartney) (3:09)
> 29 Nov 66, EMI; take 7; excellent stereo
> this is a remix of take 6 with additional overdubs

Strawberry Fields Forever (Lennon-McCartney) (3:24)
> 15 Dec 66, EMI; overdub onto take 25; excellent stereo
> George Martin conducts his score

Strawberry Fields Forever (Lennon-McCartney) (3:22)
> 24/28/29 Nov & 8/9/15/21 Dec 66, EMI; excellent stereo
> take 26, vocals with new score

SOURCE:
    EMI studio outtakes, 1965-69, except as noted.

SOUND QUALITY:
    Excellent stereo, except as noted, but not as good as the CDs of volumes 1 & 2.

COMMENTS:
    More amazing material. The **Not Guilty** cannot be topped, and who ever thought we'd hear take 1 of **Hello Goodbye**? Side D clears up a lot of problems about **Strawberry Fields Forever** and gives us just about every important version needed to follow the development of the song. The stereo **Hey Jude**, with the original arrangement is also fantastic. And yet another **What's The New Mary Jane** (remember when there was only one, and it was mono and only 2&1/2 minutes?)!
    How much longer can this go on? Beatles fans, collectors and scholars never dared dream they'd have access to treasure like this. And rumors have it that the source of these tapes has many more hours, and one wonders whether this is the best of it, or just some chosen at random. Perhaps someday we will get the long **Helter Skelter** and **Revolution 1** as well.

THE VERY BEST OF THE BEATLES RAREST, VOLUME ONE
THE BEATLES
Kornyfone, TKRWM 1985 (BEAT 01)
Insert cover with song listing and recording information; labels have side numbers only.

Side A
    Let It Be (Lennon-McCartney) (7:52)
        first rehearsal? with chord changes
    Penina (McCartney) (0:52)
        vocals: Paul
    Shakin' In The Sixties (improvisation?) (0:35)
        vocals: John
    Move It/Good Rockin' Tonight (Samwell/Brown) (1:38)
        vocals: John
    Across The Universe (Lennon-McCartney) (3:24)
        vocals: John, Paul
    Two Of Us (Lennon-McCartney) (1:50)
        fast version, with backing vocals
    bass improvisation (0:45)
        Paul
    Ramblin' Woman (Dylan?) (1:59)
        George, solo acoustic
    I Threw It All Away/Mama You Been On My Mind (Dylan) (3:58)
        George, solo acoustic
Side B
    Tennessee (Perkins) (1:59)
        vocals: John, Paul, George
    Across The Universe (Lennon-McCartney) (0:10)
        the last version
    House Of The Rising Sun (trad.) (2:30)
        vocals: John, Paul
    Commonwealth (improvisation) (3:56)
        vocals: Paul, John
    Enoch Powell (improvisation) (0:20)
        vocals: Paul
    White Power (Get Off!) (improvisation) (6:48)
[189]   vocals: Paul, John (excerpts); includes:
        Why Don't We Do It In The Road (Lennon-McCartney) (0:03)
            as "Why Don't You Put It On The Toast"

Honey Hush (Turner) (2:05)
          vocals: John, George, Paul
For You Blue (Harrison) (1:59)
          all-electric version
Let It Be (Lennon-McCartney) (2:35)
          Record Mirror version

SOURCE:
        Jan 69, **GET BACK** sessions.

SOUND QUALITY:
        Excellent mono.

COMMENTS:
        Side A consists of material from **SWEET APPLE TRAX VOL. 2**, Side B; Side B is the same as Side A of **SWEET APPLE TRAX VOL. 1** (and all subsequent reissues).

THE VERY BEST OF THE BEATLES RAREST, VOLUME TWO
THE BEATLES
Kornyfone, TKRWM 1986 (BEAT 02)
Insert cover with song listing and recording information; labels have side numbers only.

Side A
        23 Aug 64, the Hollywood Bowl (13:30)
                Twist And Shout (Medley-Russell)
                You Can't Do That (Lennon-McCartney)
                All My Loving (Lennon-McCartney)
                She Loves You (Lennon-McCartney)
                Things We Said Today (Lennon-McCartney)
                Roll Over Beethoven (Berry)
        Love Me Do (McCartney-Lennon) (2:23)
                23 Jul 63, BBC
        Please Please Me (McCartney-Lennon) (1:53)
                13 Aug 63, BBC
Side B
        23 Aug 64, the Hollywood Bowl (continued) (15:53)
                Can't Buy Me Love (Lennon-McCartney)
                If I Fell (Lennon-McCartney)
                I Want To Hold Your Hand (Lennon-McCartney)
                Boys (Dixon-Farrell)
                A Hard Day's Night (Lennon-McCartney)
                Long Tall Sally (Johnson-Penniman-Blackwell)
        17 Jun 64, Festival Hall, Melbourne, Australia (5:22)
                Till There Was You (Willson)
                I Saw Her Standing There (McCartney-Lennon)

SOURCE:
        Varied; see individual entries.

SOUND QUALITY:
        Very good to excellent mono.

COMMENTS:
        The 64 Hollywood Bowl concert, with a few extra tracks thrown in.

THE VERY BEST OF THE BEATLES RAREST, VOLUME SIX
THE BEATLES
Kornyfone, TKRWM 1995 (BEAT 06)
Insert cover with track listing; labels have side numbers only.

Side A
        Rocker (McCartney) (0:29)
                22 Jan 69, Apple; aka "Link Track" & "Instrumental 42"
        Save The Last Dance For Me/Don't Let Me Down
        (Pomus-Shuman/Lennon-McCartney) (0:50)
                22 Jan 69, Apple
        Don't Let Me Down (Lennon-McCartney) (3:33)
                22 Jan 69, Apple
        Dig A Pony (Lennon-McCartney (3:41)
                24 Jan 69, Apple; laughing version
        I've Got A Feeling (Lennon-McCartney) (2:44)
                24 Jan 69, Apple; cocked-up version
        Get Back (Lennon-McCartney) (3:12)
                28 Jan 69, Apple; the 45 version
        One After 909 (Lennon-McCartney) (2:47)
                30 Jan 69, Apple rooftop; with **Danny Boy** (Weatherly) (0:02)
Side B
        For You Blue (Harrison) (2:28)
                25 Jan 69, Apple; with false start and laughing
        Teddy Boy (McCartney) (3:39)
                24 Jan 69, Apple; the usual version
        Two Of Us (Lennon-McCartney) (3:27)
                24 Jan 69, Apple; "good-bye" version
        Maggie Mae (trad. arr. Lennon-McCartney-Harrison-Starkey) (0:37)
                24 Jan 69, Apple; same as commercial release
        Dig It (Lennon-McCartney) (3:52)
                26 Jan 69, Apple; longer version of commercial take
        Let It Be (Lennon-McCartney) (4:00)
                31 Jan 69, Apple; take 27
                the basic take for both released versions
        The Long And Winding Road (Lennon-McCartney) (3:56)
                31 Jan 69, Apple; take 19
                the basic take for the commercial release
        Get Back (Reprise) (Lennon-McCartney) (0:41)
                28 Jan 69, Apple; laughing version (excerpt)

SOURCE:
        Jan 69, for the **GET BACK** album.

SOUND QUALITY:
        Very good stereo; some glitches.

COMMENTS:
        A **GET BACK** album for the working man; see **LET IT BE** for discussion of this lineup.

VIRGIN + 3
THE BEATLES
TMOQ 71068
Printed jacket with song listing; labels are generic TMOQ.

Side A

Maxwell's Silver Hammer (Lennon-McCartney) (2:06)
movie edit; one early & one late (with anvil)
Besame Mucho (Velazquez-Skylar) (1:02)
29 Jan 69, Apple; vocals: Paul, John (excerpt)
chat
Two Of Us (Lennon-McCartney) (0:13)
John is off-mic
One After 909 (Lennon-McCartney) (0:57)
(excerpts)
Rip It Up/Shake, Rattle And Roll (Blackwell-Marascalco/Calhoun) (2:02)
vocals: Paul, John
Get Back (Lennon-McCartney) (3:00)
30 Jan 69, Apple rooftop
Dig A Pony (Lennon-McCartney) (3:40)
30 Jan 69, Apple rooftop

Side B

Jazz Piano Song (McCartney-Starkey) (0:58)
Paul & Ringo; vocals: Paul
Suzy Parker (Lennon-McCartney-Harrison-Starkey) (0:47)
the usual version
I Me Mine (Harrison) (1:40)
"I-I-Me-Me-Mine" version
I've Got A Feeling (Lennon-McCartney) (1:17)
"Good morning!" version (excerpt)
Paul talks to John about films, audiences and nerves
Let It Be (Lennon-McCartney) (3:57)
31 Jan 69, Apple; a finished version

SOURCE:
Jan 69, *Let It Be* soundtrack.

SOUND QUALITY:
Good to very good mono.

COMMENTS:
This is the same as **GET BACK SESSION II**. Aside from a cute cover, it is of absolutely no interest. Artist William Stout (now working in Hollywood) apparently depicted every Fab but George as pigs (presumably to reflect the TMOQ mascot): John (and Yoko) here, Paul on TMOQ 71065 (**HOLLYWOOD BOWL, 1964**), and Ringo on TMOQ 71076 (**SPICY BEATLES SONGS**). *Good Lord!* Choke...

VISIT TO MINNEAPOLIS (EP)
THE BEATLES
Melvin Records, MMEP001A
7-inch EP, in blue & white picture sleeve, with track listing on the back; labels are blue & white Melvin.

Side A

Press conference (4:49)
the usual dumb questions (excerpts)
She's A Woman (Lennon-McCartney) (2:51)

Side B

Twist And Shout (Medley-Russell) (1:34)
Jerk with a badge (4:02)
Lock up your daughters! A classic. This is also available commercially on video on *Fun With The Fab Four* (Goodtimes, 9015).
Everybody's Trying To Be My Baby (Perkins) (2:27)

SOURCE:
>The concert was at Twin Cities' Metropolitan Stadium, Minneapolis, 21 Aug 65; the press conference would have been 21 Aug also; the interview with the police inspector would have been 22 or 23 Aug.

SOUND QUALITY:
>Good to very good mono, the concert material is recorded off a monitor.

COMMENTS:
>An interesting little document.

WHY SHOULD I COMPLAINT?
PAUL McCARTNEY & WINGS
No manufacturer listed, MC
12-inch color picture disc, limited to 500 copies, with title and song listing on a sticker; says "Made in USA."

Side A
>chat and riffs
>**Band On The Run** (McCartney) (5:12)
>>take 6, with "Hand on the buns" intro
>**1985** (McCartney) (6:12)
>>new vocals to the backing tracks from the album
>chat
>**Live And Let Die** (McCartney) (3:06)
>>take 3; features fully orchestrated backing tracks, but with a final crescendo which does not appear on the commercial release, or the performance on *James Paul McCartney*, and does not appear to be part of the arrangement used on the tour.
>chat
>**Go Now** (Banks-Bennett) (3:33)
>>vocals: Denny Laine
>chat
>**One Hand Clapping** (McCartney) (1:18)
>**Soily** (McCartney) (3:45)
>>take 7

Side B
>**My Love** (McCartney) (3:57)
>**Little Woman Love** (P. McCartney-L. McCartney) (0:09)
>chat
>**Little Woman Love/C Moon** (P. McCartney-L. McCartney) (4:15)
>tuning
>**Maybe I'm Amazed** (McCartney) (4:30)
>>with "novel opening"
>chat
>**Bluebird** (McCartney) (3:08)
>chat
>**Blackbird** (Lennon-McCartney) (2:22)
>>74, from Paul's unreleased *Backyard* film
>>3 takes, "dedicated to Edie"
>**Jet** (McCartney) (3:38)

SOURCE:
>*One Hand Clapping* sessions (sticker says Elstree, May 75), except for **Blackbird**.

SOUND QUALITY:
>Very good stereo.

COMMENTS:
       The title listed is correct. The A-Side photo is of Paul from the cover session for **PIPES OF PEACE**; the B-Side photo is Bo Derek (!) from *Tarzan The Ape Man*. Side B is the same as Side B of **FROM A WHISPER TO A SHOUT**, and all of this material has been previously available.

WILLOWBROOK REHEARSALS
JOHN LENNON & YOKO ONO WITH ELEPHANT'S MEMORY BAND
No manufacturer listed, L-27229
2-disc set in 2-color jacket, with track listing on the back; labels are generic (3 different).

DISC ONE
Side A
       recording the commercial for added matinee (10:31) (excerpt)
              John, Yoko, Geraldo Rivera & the band; includes:
              New York City (Lennon) (0:49)
              New York City (Lennon) (0:23)
              New York City (Lennon) (1:06) (excerpt)
       Unchained Melody/It's Only Make Believe (North-Zaret/Twitty-Nance) (2:58)
              (excerpt)
       Come Together (Lennon-McCartney) (0:26)
              instrumental
       chat & tuning & piano lessons
       "Tequila" (improvisation) (2:10)
              instrumental
       New York City (Lennon) (4:37)
Side B
       It's So Hard (Lennon) (2:47)
       chat
       Back Off Boogaloo (Starkey) (0:08)
       false start
       Woman Is The Nigger Of The World (Lennon-Ono) (5:19)
       Give Peace A Chance (Lennon-McCartney) (10:07)
       chat
       Instrumental (improvisation) (6:53)
DISC TWO
Side C
       Unchained Melody/It's Only Make Believe (North-Zaret/Twitty-Nance) (3:45)
       chat & riffs
       Well Well Well (Lennon) (5:05)
       chat & riffs
       false start
       Instant Karma (Lennon) (3:06)
       chat
       Instant Karma (Lennon) (0:23)
              instrumental
       Mother (Lennon) (4:08)
       Mother (Lennon) (0:14)
       chat
       Come Together (Lennon-McCartney) (3:39)
Side D
       Cold Turkey (Lennon) (4:09)
       Instrumental (4:15)
       Instrumental (4:12)
       Roll Over Beethoven (Berry) (3:16)
       Give Peace A Chance (Lennon-McCartney) (7:30)
              with chorus

SOURCE:
Rehearsals for the two benefit concerts for the Willowbrook School For Children at Madison Square Garden, 30 Aug 72. *The Lost Lennon Tapes* dated this rehearsal as 18 Aug at Butterfly Studio.

SOUND QUALITY:
Very good to excellent mono; the tape has a few glitches and has been edited to eliminate Yoko's songs (and other material) and fade the instrumental jams early.

COMMENTS:
The band consisted of John (guitar, vocals), Yoko (vocals), Stan Bronstein (sax); Gary Van Scyox (bass), Adam Ippolito (keyboards), Richard Frank Jr. (drums) and Wayne "Tex" Gabriel (guitar). This material (excluding the recording of the commercial on Side A), with Yoko's songs, is also available on the 3-volume set, **ONE AND ONE AND ONE IS THREE**.

WINGS—L.A. FORUM
PAUL McCARTNEY & WINGS
Kornyfone, TKRWM 2805
2-disc set with insert cover and song titles; labels have side numbers only.

DISC ONE
Side A (22:39)
Venus And Mars (McCartney)
Rock Show (McCartney)
Jet (McCartney)
Let Me Roll It (McCartney)
Spirits Of Ancient Egypt (McCartney)
Medicine Jar (McCulloch-Allen)
Side B (23:48)
Maybe I'm Amazed (McCartney)
Call Me Back Again (McCartney)
Lady Madonna (Lennon-McCartney)
The Long And Winding Road (Lennon-McCartney)
Live And Let Die (McCartney)
DISC TWO
Side C (23:53)
Listen To What The Man Said (McCartney)
Let 'Em In (McCartney)
Time To Hide (Laine)
Silly Love Songs (McCartney)
Beware My Love (McCartney)
Side D (18:49)
Letting Go (McCartney)
Band On The Run (McCartney)
Hi, Hi, Hi (McCartney)
Soily (McCartney)

SOURCE:
21 Jun 76, L.A. Forum

SOUND QUALITY:
Very good audience tape, stereo.

COMMENTS:
Excerpts from this concert (a good one) are also on **ZOO GANG** and **LASER BEAMS**.

WINGS LIVE AT NEWCASTLE
PAUL McCARTNEY & WINGS
Cassette tape (52:27)

Intro, tuning
Soily (McCartney)
Big Barn Bed (McCartney)
When The Night (McCartney)
Seaside Woman (L.McCartney)
Wild Life (P. McCartney-L. McCartney)
Little Woman Love/C Moon (P. McCartney-L. McCartney)
Maybe I'm Amazed (McCartney)
My Love (McCartney)
Live And Let Die (McCartney)
The Mess (McCartney)
Hi, Hi, Hi (McCartney)
Long Tall Sally (Johnson-Penniman-Blackwell)
    with Brinsley Schwartz

SOURCE:
    10 Jul 73, Newcastle City Hall, Newcastle, England.

SOUND QUALITY:
    A line recording, excellent stereo.

COMMENTS:
    This tape sounds as if it might be taken from an acetate, as there is considerable surface noise and several obvious breaks. Several shows on this tour may have been filmed (possibly for the now-shelved *Bruce McMouse Show* project), and at least one fully-produced concert video (in stereo) is now said to be around. An LP from this tape, **NEWCASTLE 1973**, appeared just before we went to press.

WINGS LIVE IN ANTWERP, 22 AUG 72
PAUL McCARTNEY & WINGS
Cassette tape (1:23:53)

Eat At Home (P. McCartney-L. McCartney)
    with long rock intro
Smile Away (P. McCartney-L. McCartney)
Bip Bop (P. McCartney-L. McCartney)
Mumbo (P. McCartney-L. McCartney)
Blue Moon Of Kentucky (Monroe)
1882 (McCartney)
I Would Only Smile (Laine)
The Mess (McCartney)
break
Best Friend (McCartney)
Soily (McCartney)
I Am Your Singer (P. McCartney-L. McCartney)
Seaside Woman (L. McCartney)
Say You Don't Mind (Laine)
Henry's Blue (McCullough)
Give Ireland Back To The Irish (McCartney)
Cottonfields (Ledbetter)
My Love (McCartney)
Mary Had A Little Lamb (P. McCartney-L. McCartney)
Maybe I'm Amazed (McCartney)

Hi, Hi, Hi (McCartney)
applause & encore
Long Tall Sally (Johnson-Penniman-Blackwell)

SOURCE:
      22 Aug 72, *Cine Roma*, Antwerp, Belgium.

SOUND QUALITY:
      Audience tape, good to very good stereo (so good in places it almost seems to be a line recording—presumably the worst aspects of the sound result from repeated copying).

COMMENTS:
      This show, unbooted to date, contains the only known (to me) recording of Wings performing **Cottonfields**. The performance was a very good one, making this the best and most complete (unbooted) show available.

WINGS OVER AMERICA—LANDING GEAR DOWN
PAUL McCARTNEY & WINGS
ZAP, 7876
Insert cover with song titles; labels say "World Records" and have wrong titles.

Side A (22:23)
      Live And Let Die (McCartney)
      Picasso's Last Words (McCartney)
      Richard Corey (Simon)
      Bluebird (McCartney)
      I've Just Seen A Face (Lennon-McCartney)
      Blackbird (Lennon-McCartney)
      Yesterday (Lennon-McCartney)
Side B (26:23)
      You Gave Me The Answer (McCartney)
      Magneto And Titanium Man (McCartney)
      My Love (McCartney)
      Listen To What The Man Said (McCartney)
      Let 'Em In (McCartney)
      Silly Love Songs (McCartney)

SOURCE:
      15 May 76, Capitol Center, Largo, Maryland

SOUND QUALITY:
      An audience recording, very good mono.

COMMENTS:
      The first part of this show appears on **LIGHT AS A FEATHER** (ZAP, 7875); the last part appears on Side B of **9 MM. AUTOMATIC** (ZAP, 7878).

WINGS OVER ATLANTA
PAUL McCARTNEY & WINGS
Melvin Records, MM03
Printed jacket with song titles on the back; labels are black on purple and have album title and typical Melvin "artwork."

Side A (20:51)
      Venus And Mars (McCartney)
      Rock Show (McCartney)
      Jet (McCartney)

Let Me Roll It (McCartney)
The Long And Winding Road (Lennon-McCartney)
Live And Let Die (McCartney)
Side B (20:14)
The Star Spangled Banner (trad. arr. Key)
        brief, joke intro to:
Yesterday (Lennon-McCartney)
Silly Love Songs (McCartney)
Beware My Love (McCartney)
Soily (McCartney)

SOURCE:
19 May 76, the Omni, Atlanta, Georgia (excerpts)

SOUND QUALITY:
An audience recording, good to very good mono; there is considerable tape drag at the beginning of Side B.

COMMENTS:
Like many Melvin pieces, this one is hard to find—and hardly worth finding.

WINGS OVER SWITZERLAND, LIVE IN MONTREUX 1973
PAUL McCARTNEY & WINGS
No Manufacturer listed, ST-ZZYZX 020/1
Full color jacket ("Made In Western Germany") with track listing; labels are generic.

DISC ONE
Side A (20:30)
Bip Bop (P. McCartney-L. McCartney)
Smile Away (P. McCartney-L. McCartney)
Mumbo (P. McCartney-L. McCartney)
Give Ireland Back To The Irish (McCartney)
1882 (McCartney)
Side B (21:55)
I Would Only Smile (Laine)
Blue Moon Of Kentucky (Monroe)
The Mess (McCartney)
break
Best Friend (McCartney)
Soily (McCartney)
DISC TWO
Side C (22:27)
I Am Your Singer (P. McCartney-L. McCartney)
Say You Don't Mind (Laine)
Henry's Blue (McCullough)
Seaside Woman (L. McCartney)
Wild Life (P. McCartney-L. McCartney)
Side D (19:43)
My Love (McCartney)
Mary Had A Little Lamb (P. McCartney-L. McCartney)
Maybe I'm Amazed (McCartney)
Hi, Hi, Hi (McCartney)
Long Tall Sally (Johnson-Penniman-Blackwell)

SOURCE:
22 Jul 72, Wings live at the Pavillion, Montreux, Switzerland

SOUND QUALITY:
An audience tape, good to very good mono (loud songs are distorted).

COMMENTS:
    The best (and most complete) 72 Wings show available on disc to date—too bad it wasn't a better performance. This may be a copy of **LIVE IN MONTREUX, SWITZER-LAND 1972** (and possibly **WINGS OVER SCOTLAND**).

WITH LOVE FROM US TO YOU
THE BEATLES
Oro RECORDS 6365
Color jacket with track listings on the back and "bonus poster."

Side A
    Please Mr. Postman (Holland-Bateman-Gordy) (2:02)
        30 Jul 63, BBC
    I'll Be On My Way (Lennon-McCartney) (1:52)
        24 Jun 63, BBC
    Crying, Waiting, Hoping (Holly) (2:07)
        6 Aug 63, BBC
    Don't Ever Change (Goffin-King) (1:55)
        27 Aug 63, BBC
    A Shot Of Rhythm And Blues (Thompson) (2:18)
        27 Aug 63, BBC
    Lonesome Tears In My Eyes (Burnette-Burnette-Burlison-Mortimer) (2:35)
        23 Jul 63, BBC
    Nothin' Shakin' (But The Leaves On The Trees)
    (Fontaine-Colacrai-Lampert-Gluck) (2:51)
        23 Jul 63, BBC
    All My Loving (Lennon-McCartney) (2:05)
        30 Mar 64, BBC
    Roll Over Beethoven (Berry) (2:15)
        30 Mar 64, BBC
    I Wanna Be Your Man (Lennon-McCartney) (2:08)
        30 Mar 64, BBC
Side B
    Can't Buy Me Love (Lennon-McCartney) (2:05)
        30 Mar 64, BBC
    This Boy (Lennon-McCartney) (2:16)
        21 Dec 63, BBC
    Rock And Roll Music (Berry) (2:01)
        26 Dec 64, BBC
    And I Love Her (Lennon-McCartney) (2:18)
        16 Jul 64, BBC
    A Hard Day's Night (Lennon-McCartney) (2:38)
        16 Jul 64, BBC
    Things We Said Today (Lennon-McCartney) (2:16)
        16 Jul 64, BBC
    Kansas City/Hey-Hey-Hey-Hey! (Leiber-Stoller/Penniman) (2:41)
        26 Dec 64, BBC
    Honey Don't (Perkins) (2:23)
        7 Jun 65, BBC
    Dizzy Miss Lizzie (Williams) (2:41)
        7 Jun 65, BBC
    Ticket To Ride (Lennon-McCartney) (2:55)
        7 Jun 65, BBC
    From Us To You (McCartney-Lennon) (0:28)
        30 Mar 64, BBC

SOURCE:
Various BBC radio broadcasts, 63-65, copied from **THE BEATLES AT THE BEEB** radio special.

SOUND QUALITY:
Very good mono.

COMMENTS:
Because this is copied from the radio special, a number of the broadcast dates on the jacket are wrong (correct dates are listed above) and some cuts have been truncated to eliminate voice-over intros and outros.

WITHERED BEATLES
THE BEATLES
"Apple Records," SAPCOR 30
2-disc set in black & white jacket, with song listing on the back; says "Made In New Zealand;" labels say "Rubber Soul" and have song titles.

DISC ONE
Side A

How Do You Do It (Murray-Edmond) (1:56)
4 Sep 62, EMI; take 2
Thank You Girl (McCartney-Lennon) (1:59)
13 May 63, BBC
All My Loving (Lennon-McCartney) (2:09)
30 Mar 64, BBC
Don't Bother Me (Harrison) (0:14)
11 Sep 63, EMI; take 11 (false start)
from *The Beatles Live At Abbey Road* show
One After 909 (Lennon-McCartney) (3:01)
5 Mar 63, EMI; unknown take
Till There Was You (Willson) (2:16)
30 Mar 64, BBC
Please Mr. Postman (Holland-Bateman-Gordy) (2:21)
30 Mar 64, BBC

Side B

Roll Over Beethoven (Berry) (2:19)
30 Mar 64, BBC
I'll Be On My Way (Lennon-McCartney) (2:00)
24 Jun 63, BBC
You Really Got A Hold On Me (Robinson) (2:48)
17 Sep 63, BBC
I Wanna Be Your Man (Lennon-McCartney) (2:12)
30 Mar 64, BBC
(There's A) Devil In Her Heart (Drapkin) (2:18)
24 Sep 63, BBC
Besame Mucho (Velazquez-Skylar) (2:32)
6 Jun 62, EMI; unknown take
The easiest way to tell this version from the Decca version is by the lack of backing vocals.
Money (That's What I Want) (Bradford-Gordy) (2:37)
18 Jun 63, BBC

DISC TWO
Side C

Memphis (Berry) (2:22)
29 Jun 63, BBC
Nothin' Shakin' (But The Leaves On The Trees)
(Fontaine-Colacrai-Lampert-Gluck) (3:02)
23 Jul 63, BBC

Ooh! My Soul (Penniman) (1:37)
      27 Aug 63, BBC
      Two different tapes edited together; first is only good mono.
A Shot Of Rhythm And Blues (Thompson) (2:09)
      18 Jun 63, BBC
So How Come (No One Loves Me) (Bryant) (1:52)
      23 Jul 63, BBC
Soldier Of Love (Cason-Moon) (2:06)
      16 Jul 63, BBC
Some Other Guy (Leiber-Stoller-Barrett) (2:02)
      23 Jun 63, BBC

Side D

The Beatles Christmas Record (5:01)
      20 Oct 63, EMI; excellent mono
KFWBeatles (1:39)
      Good mono; this is a copy of Capitol Custom RB-2637, released on 5 Jun 64
            in Los Angeles by KFWB and includes:
      KFWB music spot #1
            to the tune of **She Loves You**; no Beatles involvement
      greetings
            to Wink Martindale & Jolly Joe Yoakum
      KFWB music spot #2
            to the tune of **It Won't Be Long**; no Beatles involvement
8 Feb 64, *Saturday Club* (4:22)
      telephone interview from NYC with Brian Matthew; good mono
Beatleviews (9:11)
      Interview snippets, many far too slow, generally from or dealing with 1964.
      Good to excellent mono.

SOURCE:
      Varied; see individual entries.

SOUND QUALITY:
      Very good to excellent mono unless otherwise stated.

COMMENTS:
      This is the third album in the "SAPCOR" series.

Y'ORITE WACK
THE BEATLES
Shogun, 13113
2-disc set, on colored vinyl, in full color jacket, with song titles on the back; label info
matches.

DISC ONE
Side A [duplicates **GET BACK JOURNALS**, Side S]
      George chats about John's 1969 diary, watching tv, and the inspiration for his new
          song.
I Me Mine (Harrison) (1:00)
      (excerpts)
      George and Ringo talk about watching tv and Hamburg. George plays his new song
          for Paul.
I Me Mine (Harrison) (1:34)
      George worries about grammar.
Let It Be (Lennon-McCartney) (0:47)
      playback
Maybe I'm Amazed/That Would Be Something (McCartney) (2:16)
      Paul on guitar

Discussion about the difficulties of playing live in Arabia, scheduling
    the sunrise, looking nice, good vibes, a boat full of Beatlemaniacs,
[167]   and bedtime.
    Don't Let Me Down (Lennon-McCartney) (0:10)
    Get Back (Lennon-McCartney) (0:45)
        jam
Side B [duplicates **GET BACK JOURNALS**, Side F]
    Too Bad About Sorrows (Lennon-McCartney) (0:12)
        vocals: John
    Just Fun (Lennon-McCartney) (0:12)
        vocals: Paul
    She Said She Said (Lennon-McCartney) (0:30)
        vocals: John
    Mean Mister Mustard (Lennon-McCartney) (3:21)
        "sister Shirley" runthrough, with middle 8
    Don't Let Me Down (Lennon-McCartney) (0:32)
        middle 8 only
    All Things Must Pass (Harrison) (3:07)
        nearly finished version
    Fools Like Me (Clement-Maddux) (2:02)
        vocals: John, George, Paul
    You Win Again (Williams) (1:31)
        vocals: John, George, Paul
    improvisation (0:30)
        piano, bass, rhythm
    She Came In Through The Bathroom Window (Lennon-McCartney) (1:40)
        early rehearsal with chord changes (excerpt)
    Watching Rainbows/jam (Lennon/all) (5:55)
        vocals: John (excerpts)
DISC TWO
Side C [duplicates **GET BACK JOURNALS**, Side P]
    All I Want Is You (improvisation?) (0:57)
        vocals: Paul, John (excerpt)
        At this point, it seems that **Dig A Pony** was being called "All I Want Is You."
            This piece is not related to that song.
[263] Paul reads the news about the Beatles.
    Look Out! (?) (0:42)
        vocals: Paul, John
    Roll Over Beethoven (Berry) (0:18)
        vocals: Paul, John
    riffs
    Paul reads the news while the band plays:
[261] **Blue Suede Shoes** (Perkins) (1:43)
        improvisation (excerpt); vocals: John
    Thirty Days (Berry) (1:05)
        (excerpt) vocals: Paul, John
    Too Bad About Sorrows (Lennon-McCartney) (0:57)
        vocals: Paul, John
    Dig A Pony (Lennon-McCartney) (2:40)
[265]   "I hit a roadhog" version (excerpts)
    You Got The Message (?) (0:03)
        vocals: John
    chat & riffs
    I'm Ready (King-Durand-Obichaux) (0:07)
        vocals: Paul
        lyrics from this song (recorded by Fats Domino) also appear in **Rocker** on
            the various versions of **GET BACK**
    Dig A Pony (Lennon-McCartney) (0:08)
    chat & riffs

Papa's Got A Brand New Bag (Brown) (0:04)
      vocals: Paul
Dig A Pony (Lennon-McCartney) (1:23)
      "Girl" version (excerpt)
You're Going To Lose That Girl/Shout!
(Lennon-McCartney/Isley-Isley-Isley) (0:17)
      sung as "You're going to shag that girl" and "Shag!"
      vocals: Paul, John
chat & John talks about lyrics
The William Smith Boogie (improvisation?) (0:23)
      vocals: John; effects: Paul
weirdness & riffs
You Gotta Get Back (improvisation) (0:21)
      vocals: Paul (excerpt)
chat
Dig A Pony (Lennon-McCartney) (0:06)
      (excerpt)
You've Got Me Thinking (Lomax) (1:02)
      vocals: Paul, George, John
more about lyrics & riffs
I've Got A Feeling (Lennon-McCartney) (0:32)
      (excerpt)
Side D [duplicates **GET BACK JOURNALS**, Side R]
Let It Be (Lennon-McCartney) (8:07)
      extended rehearsal, heavy drum mix
Maxwell's Silver Hammer (Lennon-McCartney) (1:34)
      rehearsal with piano and whistling (excerpt)
Time Is Tight (Jones) (0:44)
      George works on the bass riff while Paul improvises at the piano
When I'm Sixty-four (Lennon-McCartney) (1:15)
      Paul recites and sings to George's **Time Is Tight** (Jones) bass riff and
         comes awfully close to writing **Oh My My** (Poncia-Starkey)
(There's A) Devil In Her Heart (Spector) (0:16)
      vocals: John (excerpt)
Don't Let Me Down (Lennon-McCartney) (1:16)
      rehearsal with chat & riffs (excerpt)
Thirty Days (Berry) (0:13)
      vocals: John (excerpt)
Rock And Roll Music (Berry) (0:51)
      vocals: John (excerpt)
I Me Mine (Harrison) (7:25)
      rehearsal, "I-I-Me-Me-Mine" version

SOURCE:
    GET BACK sessions; jacket says 16 Jan-20 Jan 69.

SOUND QUALITY:
    Very good to excellent mono.

COMMENTS:
    More **GET BACK JOURNALS** reissue. And until somebody can tell me what
"Y'orite Wack" is supposed to mean, it also gets my vote for stupidest bootleg title ever, too.
So there.

ZOO GANG
PAUL McCARTNEY & WINGS
Idle Mind, IMP 1117
Insert cover with song listing and some recording information; labels are generic Idle Mind.

Side A
> 23 Jun 76, L.A. Forum (11:30)
>> **Spirits Of Ancient Egypt** (McCartney)
>> **Lady Madonna** (Lennon-McCartney)
>> **The Long And Winding Road** (Lennon-McCartney)
>
> 21 Jun 76, L.A. Forum (5:53)
>> **Live And Let Die** (McCartney)
>> **Picasso's Last Words** (McCartney)
>
> 14 Jun 76, Cow Palace, San Francisco (1:56)
>> **You Gave Me The Answer** (McCartney)
>
> 21 Jun 76, L.A. Forum (8:09)
>> **Magneto And Titanium Man** (McCartney)
>> **Go Now** (Banks-Bennett)

Side B
> 14 Jun 76, Cow Palace, San Francisco (20:54)
>> **My Love** (McCartney)
>> **Let 'Em In** (McCartney)
>> **Silly Love Songs** (McCartney)
>> **Beware My Love** (McCartney)
>
> 23 Jun 76, L.A. Forum (5:38)
>> **Soily** (McCartney)
>
> **Zoo Gang** (McCartney) (1:53)
>> Sep 73, from the 45

SOURCE:
> Various 76 tour concerts (and one 45 B-side); see individual entries.

SOUND QUALITY:
> The concert material consists of very good to excellent audience tapes (the 23 Jun tape appears to be stereo, the others mono); all tapes have been edited. **Zoo Gang** is excellent stereo.

COMMENTS:
> Idle MInd is the label responsible for the 3-disc set of the L.A. show of 23 Jun, **WINGS FROM THE WINGS**. The 21 Jun material is taken from the same tape as **LASER BEAMS** (WRMB, 382), but is not copied from that disc.

INDEX TO DISCOGRAPHY
(VERSION 2.0)

      This index operates a little differently from most. First, it indexes primarily the music from the discography portion of the book. Second, rather than giving the page number of the reference, it gives the record on which the cut or artist appears; since the discography is in alphabetical order, it's a simple matter to proceed from there. I've found this form to be much more useful for quick reference, and no slower for involved work.

      Due to space limitations, a simple (and in most cases self-obvious) code is used to represent the title. This index is cumulative and has been updated to include all corrections to *Do You Want To Know A Secret?* Those titles listed below in **boldface** are from the previous book. Those in regular type are from *Fixing A Hole*. The abbreviation "(cv)" means that this is the commercial version.

BBC	**BBC**
BEAT	**THE BEATLES**
BEAUT	**BEAUTIFUL DREAMER**
BEEB	**THE BEATLES AT THE BEEB**
BEEB1	**THE BEATLES AT THE BEEB VOLUME ONE**
BEEB2	**THE BEATLES AT THE BEEB VOLUME TWO**
BEEB3	**THE BEATLES AT THE BEEB VOLUME THREE**
BEEB4	**THE BEATLES AT THE BEEB VOLUME FOUR**
BEEB5	**THE BEATLES AT THE BEEB VOLUME FIVE**
BEEB6	**THE BEATLES AT THE BEEB VOLUME SIX**
BEEB7	THE BEATLES AT THE BEEB, VOLUME SEVEN
BEEB8	THE BEATLES AT THE BEEB, VOLUME EIGHT
BEEB9	THE BEATLES AT THE BEEB, VOLUME NINE
BEEB10	THE BEATLES AT THE BEEB, VOLUME TEN
BEEB11	THE BEATLES AT THE BEEB, VOLUME ELEVEN
BEEBCD	**THE BEATLES AT THE BEEB** (CD)
BEFORE	**BEFORE PLAY**
BELGIUM	BELGIUM 1972
BLACK	**(THE BLACK ALBUM)**
BLASTS	ED'S REALLY BIG BEATLE BLASTS
BOTH	**BOTH SIDES**
BROAD	**BROADCASTS**
BUDO	**THE BEATLES IN BUDOKAN** 1966.6.30/7.1
BUG	BUG CRUSHER "LIVE"
BWORD	BUMBLE WORDS (SUPER STUDIO SERIES 3)
BYEBYE	BYE BYE LOVE
BYGEO	**BY GEORGE!**
CANDLE	**CANDLESTICK PARK**
CASTS	BROADCASTS (LENNON)
CASUAL	**CASUALTIES**
CAVERN	CAVERN DAYS
CHIC	CHICAGO 11 30 74
CIRCUIT	CIRCUIT SONGS
CLASS2	CLASSIFIED DOCUMENT, VOLUME TWO
CLASS3	CLASSIFIED DOCUMENT, VOLUME THREE
COLD	**COLD CUTS**
COMMON	COMMONWEALTH
COMPL	COMPLETE ITALY & PARIS
CONF	**CONFIDENTIAL DOCUMENT**
CONQ	**THE BEATLES CONQUER AMERICA**
CRONE	LIVE AT THE CIRCUS CRONE
CUTS	**COLD CUTS—ANOTHER, EARLY VERSION**
DARK	**A DARK HOARSE IN '74**
DEC63	**DECEMBER 63**
DECCA	**THE DECCA TAPES**
DEMO	**DEMO SESSION**
DIGIT	**DIG IT!**
DOCTOR	DOCTOR WINSTON O'BOOGIE ON THE TOMORROW SHOW
DOLL'S	A DOLL'S HOUSE
DON'T	DON'T PASS ME BY
EGGS	**EGGS UP**
ELVIS	ELVIS MEETS...THE BEATLES
EMIOUT	EMI OUTTAKES
ENGL	**SOMEWHERE IN ENGLAND**
EXTEN	EXTENDED SESSIONS
FALCON	FALCONER
FANS	**300,000 BEATLE FANS CAN'T BE WRONG**
FCK	FUCK!
FEATHER	LIGHT AS A FEATHER
FHILLS	FOREST HILLS TENNIS STADIUM

LOOK	LOOK BACK
LOOKING	LOOKING BACK ON ABBEY ROAD
LOST1	*THE LOST LENNON TAPES*, VOL. 1
LOST2	*THE LOST LENNON TAPES*, VOL. 2
LOST3	*THE LOST LENNON TAPES*, VOL. 3
LOST4	*THE LOST LENNON TAPES*, VOL. 4
LOST5	*THE LOST LENNON TAPES*, VOL. 5
LOST6	*THE LOST LENNON TAPES*, VOL. 6
LOST7	*THE LOST LENNON TAPES*, VOL. 7
MAGTR	MAGTRAX
MAIL	MAILMAN BLUES
MAPLE	MAPLE LEAF GARDENS
MARY	"MARY JANE"
MAY60	**LIVERPOOL MAY 1960**
MAYP	**THE MAY PANG TAPES**
MEET	MEET THE BEEB
MELB	LIVE IN MELBOURNE, AUSTRALIA
MELLO	MELLOW YELLOW
MIEUX	***"JE SUIS LE PLUS MIEUX"***
MINN	VISIT TO MINNEAPOLIS (EP)
MIXED	MIXED BLESSING
MONKEY	MONKEY BUSINESS
MOON	**JOHNNY MOONDOG**
MORE	MORE FROM THE TOUR
MUNICH	THE LIVE BEATLES: RECORDED LIVE IN MUNICH, WEST GERMANY, JUNE 24TH, 1966
MYLO	**MY LOVE**
NASH	NASHVILLE DIARY (EP)
NASSAU	LIVE AT NASSAU COLISSEUM
NEWCAS	WINGS LIVE AT NEWCASTLE
NIGHT	A NIGHTMARE IS ALSO A DREAM
NO3	**NO. 3 ABBEY ROAD**
NOT4	**NOT FOR SALE**
NOTG	**NOT GUILTY**
NOTH	**NOTHING IS REAL**
OBLA45	**OB-LA-DI, OB-LA-DA** (EP)
OBLADI	**OB-LA-DI, OB-LA-DA** (LP)
OFF	OFF WHITE
OGNIR	**OGNIR RRATS GREATEST HITS**
ONCE	**ONCE UPON A TIME**
ONEH	**ONE HAND CLAPPING**
ONLY	**ONLY LIVE SHOW**
ONOT	**OHNOTHIMAGEN**
ORIENT	ORIENTAL NIGHTFISH
PARL	**FROM US TO YOU: A PARLOPHONE REHEARSAL SESSION**
PETE	PISS OFF PETE!
PLAY	**IN A PLAY ANYWAY**
PLEASE	PLEASE RELEASE ME
PLOP	**PLOP PLOP ... FIZZ FIZZ**
POPS	**TOP OF THE POPS** (EP)
POWER	POWER BROKERS
PREC	**SOMETHING PRECIOUS AND RARE**
PREV	LIVE TRACKS—PREVIOUSLY ITALIAN E.P.
QUEEN	**COMPLAINT TO THE QUEEN**
R'N'R	A COLLECTION OF ROCK'N'ROLL REHEARSALS
RABBI	RABBI SAUL
RARER	**RARER THAN RARE**
RAREST1	THE VERY BEST OF THE BEATLES RAREST, VOLUME ONE
RAREST2	THE VERY BEST OF THE BEATLES RAREST, VOLUME TWO
RAREST6	THE VERY BEST OF THE BEATLES RAREST, VOLUME SIX

THIS	**THIS IS NOT HERE**
THOSE	**THOSE WERE THE DAYS**
TOBE	THE BEST OF TOBE MILO PRODUCTIONS
TOKIO	THE LIVE BEATLES: TOKIO JULY 2, 1966 (CD)
TOKYO	**LIVE IN TOKYO**
TOP	TOP OF THE POPS (LP)
TORON	**GET BACK TO TORONTO**
TOUR	TOUR YEARS (63-66)
TRAGIC	TRAGICAL HISTORY TOUR/DR. PEPPER
TRAX3	**SWEET APPLE TRAX, VOLUME 3**
TUG	TUG OF WAR DEMOS
TWICE	TWICE IN A LIFETIME
TWICK	TWICKENHAM JAMS (LP)
ULTRA1	ULTRA RARE TRAX, VOLUME 1 (CD)
ULTRA2	ULTRA RARE TRAX, VOLUME 2 (CD)
URT34	ULTRA RARE TRAX, VOLUMES 3 & 4 (LP)
URT56	ULTRA RARE TRAX, VOLUMES 5 & 6 (LP)
UTOPIA	SOMEWHERE IN UTOPIA
VANC	**VANCOUVER**
VIENNA	**GOODNIGHT VIENNA**
VIRGIN	VIRGIN+3
W/PETE	THE BEATLES AT THE BEEB W/ PETE BEST
WALK	THE STEREO WALK
WALLS	**OFF THE WALLS**
WAR	**WAR AND PEACE**
WATCH	**WATCHING RAINBOWS**
WEMB	**WINGS OVER WEMBLEY**
WHEN	**WHEN IT SAYS BEATLES...**
WHISP	FROM A WHISPER TO A SHOUT!
WHY	WHY SHOULD I COMPLAINT?
WILLOW	WILLOWBROOK REHEARSALS
WINGS	**WINGS FROM THE WINGS**
WINSTON	**WINSTON O'BOOGIE**
WITHER	WITHERED BEATLES
WLOVE	WITH LOVE FROM US TO YOU
WOND	**WONDERFUL PICTURE OF YOU**
WORK	**WORKING CLASS HERO**
Y'ORITE	Y'ORITE WACK
YEARS	**IT WAS TWENTY YEARS AGO TODAY**
YELL	**YELLOW MATTER CUSTARD**
YIN	**YIN YANG**
YOUNG	**YOUNGBLOOD**
ZOO	ZOO GANG

A

Abandoned Love
  84 demo? George
    LIFT, ONOT
ABBEY ROAD REVISITED (LP)
  — see THOSE
Abilene
  63 BBC? probably no B. involvement
    MEET
Ach Du Lieber (Balls For Mr. Benglestein)
  Jan 69, **GB** sessions
    GRAVE, JOURN, MAGTR
Across The Universe

4/8 Feb 68, EMI; take 8 (acetate of 5 Jan 70 remix?)
    DIGIT, EXTEN
4/8 Feb 68, EMI; take 8 (no maracas?)
    SOME
4/8 Feb 68 & 2 Oct 69 EMI; take 8 (cv, WWF)
    EXTEN, HEAD, HOMOG, ITEMS, REN2, SPLHCB
4&8 Feb 68, EMI; take 8 (Hum's Wild)
    ARCH3, LOST3
Jan 69, **GB** sessions (various)
    ALMO, BLACK, BWORD, CIRCUIT, COMMON, FS2S, GBSESS, HEAD, HIHO, HOT, JOURN, LETEND, MAGTR, PLAY, RAREST1, RUSSIA

SCOUSE
And I Love Her
  16 Jul 64, BBC
    BBC, BEEB, BEEB11, KNIGHT,
    WLOVE
  64, The George Martin Orchestra (cv)
    SPLHCB
"And the roof almost came down when..."
unknown, tv show?
    TOBE, TWICK
And Your Bird Can Sing
  26 Apr 66, EMI; edit of takes 6 & 10
  (cv)
    SPLHCB
Angel Baby
  Oct-Dec 73, from **ROOTS**
    CASTS, FS2S, 1970S, SHOTS,
    SHOULD, WORK
Anna (Go To Him)
  25 Jun 63, BBC
    BEEB3, PLEASE
  27 Aug 63, BBC
    LBEEB, STUDIO, STUD2
Another Beatles Christmas Record
  26 Oct 64, EMI
    KNIGHT, SPLHCB
  26 Oct 64, EMI (outtakes)
    SPLHCB
Another Day
  Jan 69, **GB** sessions
    RUSSIA
  Jan 71 (cv, from the 45)
    MYLO, REN3
Around And Around
  Jan 69, **GB** sessions
    ALMO, GOLDM, JOURN
Around The World
unknown, Paul, home rehearsal
    HOME
Arrow Through Me
  mid-Jul 78, alternate version
    EGGS, SUIT
  25 Nov 79, Wings, Liverpool
    TOKYO
  7 Dec 79, Wings, Wembley
    WEMB
  29 Dec 79, Hammersmith
    KAMP
As It Happened
  Murray The K fan club record
    RABBI, SOLDIER
As Time Goes By
  Jan 76? John, *Earth News Radio*
    LIMIT
Ask Louey
  77, from **SCOUSE THE MOUSE**
  (cv)
    SCOUSE
Ask Me Why
  15 Jun 62, BBC

LBEEB, MEET, W/PETE
  Dec 62, Star-Club, Hamburg (cv)
    SPLHCB, STARS
  24 Sep 63, BBC
    BEEB6, PLEASE
Aspen flexi disc
  Spring/Summer 69
    LIFE, THIS
Attica State
  10 Dec 71, Ann Arbor
    ARCH4, LIFT, LOST4, 1TO1
  Feb 72, *Mike Douglas*
    TELE
Average Person
  Paul, home demo, circa Fall 80
    WAR
Awaiting On You All
  May-Aug 70, Trident/EMI (cv)
    SPLHCB
  21 Dec 75? *Rock Around The World*
    BYGEO, UTOPIA

B

Baa Baa Black Sheep
  Jan 69, **GB** sessions
    BLACK, GBSESS, GOLDM, JOURN,
    SOUND
Baby Face
  7 Dec 79, Wings at Wembley
    WEMB
**(You're So Square) Baby I Don't
Care**
  Jan 69, **GB** sessions
    RUSSIA
Baby It's You
  11/20 Feb 63, EMI; take 5 (cv)
    SPLHCB
  11 Jun 63, BBC
    BEEB2, BEEBCD, MONKEY,
    PLEASE
Baby You're A Rich Man
  11 May 67, Olympic; take 2 (cv, mono)
    JUDY
  11 May 67, Olympic; take 2 (cv, true
stereo)
    ITEMS
Baby's In Black
  27 Nov 64, *Ready Steady Go* (cv, lip-
synch)
    RSG!
  20 Jun 65, Paris, evening
    HOTW, SINGLES
  27 Jun 65, Rome
    ARRIV, ROMA
  15 Aug 65, Shea Stadium
    FHILLS, GOOD, SHEA
  19 Aug 65, Houston, afternoon
    AUCTION, TEXAN
  19 Aug 65, Houston, evening
    HOUST, TEXAN

DON'T, JULIAN, LALB, NASSAU,
SPLHCB
The Beatles' Sixth Christmas Record
Nov 68
DON'T, RED, SPLHCB
The Beatles' Third Christmas Record
8 Nov 65, EMI
AUCTION, DON'T, SPLHCB
THE BEATLES VS. DON HO (LP)
— see LINING
Beautiful Boy (Darling Boy)
summer 80, acoustic unknown, take 1
ARCH1, LOST3
Jul 80, Bermuda demo
ARCH1, CONFI, LOST1
Aug 80, DF sessions
LOST3
30 Jan 82, *Desert Island Discs* (Paul sings along)
GREAT
Beautiful Dreamer
26 Jan 63, BBC
BEAUT, MEET, REINTRO, WOND, W/PETE
Because
1/4 Aug 69, EMI; vocals only
URT56
1/4/5 Aug 69, EMI; take 16; harpsicord, vocals & synthesizer
BOTH, B-ROAD, INAB, LIVEAT, RETURN
Beef Jerky
Jul 74, **W&B** sessions
PREC, WINSTON
Being For The Benefit Of Mr. Kite!
17/20 Feb & 28/29/31 Mar 67; take 9 (cv)
SPLHCB
The Bells Of Rhymey
10 Feb 88, George, *Rockline*
UTOPIA
Besame Mucho
1 Jan 62, Decca audition
DECCA
6 Jun 62, EMI (unknown take)
FILE2, MIXED, SESS, SPLHCB, ULTRA1, WITHER
15 Jun 62, BBC
LBEEB, MEET, W/PETE
Dec 62, Star-Club, Hamburg (cv)
B4TIME, STARS
29 Jan 69, Apple (from *Let It Be*)
BWORD, CIRCUIT, HEARD, HOT, PLAY, POWER, SUPER1, THEIR, 21, VIRGIN
Best Friend
72, Wings, European tour, unknown
COLD

72, Wings, European tour, unknown (another)
ORIENT
22 Jul 72, Wings, Montreux
SWITZ
16 Aug 72, Wings, Hanover
HANOV
17 Aug 72, Wings, Rotterdam
QUEEN
22 Aug 72, Wings, Antwerp
ANTW
THE BEST OF THE BEATLES AND JETHRO TULL (LP) — see DON'T
Beware My Love
3 May 76, Wings, Fort Worth
FORTW
15 May 76, Wings, Largo
9MM
19 May 76, Wings, Atlanta
ATLAN
14 Jun 76, Wings, San Francisco
ZOO
16 Jun 76, Wings, San Diego
ORIENT
21 Jun 76, Wings, L.A. Forum
FORUM
23 Jun 76, Wings, L.A. Forum
WINGS
Beyond The Sea
date unknown, John, Dakota
ARCH3, LOST4
Big Barn Bed
18 Mar 73, Borehamwood, for *JPMcC*
LIFT, MYLO
19 Jun 73, Wings, Leeds
LEEDS
10 Jul 73, Wings, Newcastle
NEWCAS
23 Jul 73, Wings, Edinburgh
SCOT
Bip Bop
71? *Wings Over The World*
1970S
11 Feb 72, Wings, Hull
BELGIUM, SPRING
22 Jul 72, Wings, Montreux
SWITZ
16 Aug 72, Wings, Hanover
ORIENT
2 Aug 72, Wings, Antwerp
ANTW
Birthday
18 Sep 68, EMI; take 22 (cv, OOPSed)
EXTEN, NOT4, RED
BITS & PIECES III: LET'S DO IT (EP) — see YEARS
Blackbird
Nov 69-Jan 69, **PCARD** sessions
NO3, RARER, SUN, 20X4
73, *James Paul McCartney*

LIFT, MYLO
74, from Paul's unreleased *Backyard* film
RED, WATCH, WHISP, WHY
75-6 tour, Wings (unknown)
4SIDES
1 Nov 75, Wings, Perth
FLY
13 Nov 75, Wings, Melbourne
FLY, 9MM, ONEH
15 May 76, Wings, Largo
GEAR
23 Jun 76, Wings, L.A. Forum
LASER, WINGS
Bless You
Jul 74, **W&B** sessions
PREC, WALLS
Blindman
Sep 71, from 45 (cv)
1970S, OGNIR, REN3
Blowin' In The Wind
Jan 69, **GB** sessions
COMMON, JOURN, REVOLT, TRAX3
Blue Jay Way
6/7 Sep & 6 Oct 67, EMI; take 3 (cv,
mono remix 27)
EMIOUT, 1967, TRAGIC
6/7 Sep & 6 Oct 67, EMI; take 3 (cv,
stereo remix 12)
SPLHCB
Blue Moon
date unknown, John, Dakota
ARCH3, LOST4
Blue Moon Of Kentucky
11 Feb 72, Wings, Hull
BELGIUM, SPRING
22 Jul 72, Wings, Montreux
SWITZ
17 Aug 72, Wings, Rotterdam
HANOV, QUEEN
22 Aug 72, Wings, Antwerp
ANTW
21 Nov 85, *Blue Suede Shoes*
LOOK, ONOT
Blue Suede Shoes
Jan 69, **GB** sessions (various)
COMMON, FILE1, JOURN, LETEND,
ONCE, REVOLT, SING, TRAX3,
Y'ORITE
8 Oct 82, *Parkinson In Australia* (Ringo)
CLASS2, MAIL
21 Nov 85, *Blue Suede Shoes*
LOOK, ONOT
Bluebird
73, *James Paul McCartney* (outtake)
LIFT, 20X4
73, *James Paul McCartney*
LIFT, MYLO
Fall 75, *One Hand Clapping* sessions
ONEH, WHISP, WHY
13 Nov 75, Wings, Melbourne

ONEH
9 May 76, Wings, Toronto
MAPLE
15 May 76, Wings, Largo
GEAR
23 Jun 76, Wings, L.A. Forum
LASER, WINGS
Blues In The Night
Aug 80, **DF** sessions
BEFORE
Bo Diddley
Jan 69, **GB** sessions
FILE1, OBLADI
14 Sep 79, Paul, Hammersmith
LOOK, RAVING
Boat Ride
77, from **SCOUSE THE MOUSE**
(cv)
LIFT, RICHIE, SCOUSE
Boil Crisis
Paul, home demo, circa Fall 80
TUG, WAR
Born In A Prison
18 Aug 72, One-To-One rehearsals
1AND2
Borrowed Time
Jul 80, Bermuda demo
ARCH2, CONFI
Boys
11 Feb 63, EMI; take 1 (cv, stereo)
SPLHCB
13 May 63, BBC
BEEB2, MONKEY
25 May 63, BBC
BEEB1, BEEBCD, MONKEY
24 Jun 63, BBC
BEEB1, BEEBCD, MONKEY, PLEASE
25 Jun 63, BBC
BEEB3
17 Sep 63, BBC
BEEB6, SOME, STUDIO, STUD2
7 Dec 63, Liverpool
DEC63, TOUR, YOUNG
26 Dec 63, BBC
BEEB8
session for BBC 3 Aug 64
PARL
3 Aug 64, BBC
BEEB11
23 Aug 64, Hollywood Bowl
COMPL, 8ARMS, ONLY, RAREST2,
ROMA, STONE
22 Aug 64, Vancouver
VANC
2 Sep 64, Philadelphia?
FLATS
3 Oct 64, Granville Theatre (*Shindig*)
CONQ
Summer 65, Pete Best
PETE

Bravo Award, 23 Jun 66, Munich
  CRONE, 4EVER, MUNICH
Breath Away From Heaven
  86, from *Shanghai Surprise*
  LIFT, ONOT
Bridge Over Troubled Water
  16 Nov 76, George, rehearsal for
  Saturday Night Live
  ROUGH, UTOPIA
Bring It On Home To Me
  Jan 69, **GB** sessions
  JOURN, MAGTR, REVOLT, TRAX3
  Oct-Dec 73, **R&R** sessions
  MAYP, R'N'R, SHOULD
Bring It To Jerome
  Jan 69, **GB** sessions
  COMMON, GRAVE, JOURN
Broad Street Music
  14 Oct 84, *Southbank*
  GREAT
The Broadcast
  mid-Sep 78, alternate vocals
  EGGS
Brown-eyed Handsome Man
  Jan 69, **GB** sessions
  RUSSIA
  date unknown, John, Dakota
  ARCH3, LOST4
BRUNG TO EWE BY HAL SMITH
  May 71, Paul, Apple promo
  DOLL'S, 1970S, TOBE
Bubbles
  Summer 79, **McII** home sessions
  RAVING
Bunny Hop jam
  18 Aug 72, One-To-One rehearsals
  CLASS3, VIENNA
BYE BYE BYE (LP) — see SUPER1
Bye Bye Bye
  unknown, possibly no Beatles
  involvement
  CAVERN, THEIR, THOSE
Bye Bye Love
  25 Jan 69, Apple (brief excerpt)
  BYEBYE
  16 Nov 76, George, rehearsal for
  Saturday Night Live
  RARER, 20X4, UTOPIA

C

C Moon
  73, *James Paul McCartney*
  MYLO
  Fall 75, *One Hand Clapping* sessions
  ONEH
  5 Nov 75, Wings, Adelaide
  DOLL'S
Cage
  78, Wings, outtake
  EGGS

  78, Wings, outtake (remix)
  COLD
Call Me Back Again
  13 Nov 75, Wings, Melbourne
  FLY
  9 May 76, Wings, Toronto
  MAPLE
  15 May 76, Wings, Largo
  FEATHER
  21 Jun 76, Wings, L.A. Forum
  FORUM
  23 Jun 76, Wings L.A. Forum
  WINGS
  unknown, Paul, home rehearsal
  HOME
Can You Dig It — see **Dig It**, 24 Jan 69
Can't Buy Me Love
  29 Jan 64, Paris; take 1
  ULTRA2
  29 Jan 64, Paris; take 4 (cv, fake stereo)
  SPLHCB
  30 Mar 64, BBC
  BEEB, BEEB9, KNIGHT, 1964,
  SILVER, WLOVE
  4 Apr 64, BBC
  BEEB10
  19 Apr 64, IBC (for *ATB*)
  CAVERN, DIGIT, EMIOUT, NOTG
  27 Apr 64, *Ready Steady Go!* (cv, lip-
  synch)
  RSG!
  6 May 64, *Around The Beatles*
  RSG!
  18 May 64, BBC
  BEEB10
  12 Jun 64, Adelaide
  DOLL'S, FANS, 1964
  16 Jun 64, Melbourne
  CANDLE, FANS, HOTW, TOUR
  17 Jun 64, Melbourne
  MELB, GREAT
  22 Aug 64, Vancouver
  VANC
  23 Aug 64, Hollywood Bowl
  8ARMS, ONLY, RAREST2, ROMA
  2 Sep 64, Philadelphia?
  FLATS
  20 Jun 65, Paris, afternoon
  HOTW
  20 Jun 65, Paris, evening
  BEAT, COMPL, HOTW, SINGLES
  27 Jun 65, Rome
  COMPL, ROMA
  15 Aug 65, Shea Stadium
  GOOD, SHEA
  19 Aug 65, Houston, afternoon
  TEXAN
  19 Aug 65, Houston, evening
  HOUST, TEXAN
A Candle Burns

— see Peace Of Mind
Carol
  16 Jul 63, BBC
    BBC, BEEB, BEEB3, BEEBCD,
    BROAD, DEMO, LINING, REINTRO,
    SPLHCB
Carry That Weight
— see **Golden Slumbers/ Carry That Weight**
A Case Of The Blues
  Jan 69, **GB** sessions
    ALMO
Caterwaul
  77, **SCOUSE THE MOUSE**
    RICHIE, SCOUSE
Cathy's Clown
  Jan 69, **GB** sessions
    GOLDM, JOURN
Catswalk
  Spring 62? rehearsal
    FILE2, MIXED, NOT4, RABBI,
    SPLHCB, WALK
Caveman jam
  81, from *Caveman*
    RICHIE
CAVERN CLUB (LP) — see CAVERN
Chains
  11 May 63, BBC
    BEEB2, MONKEY
  25 Jun 63, BBC
    BEEB3
  17 Sep 63, BBC
    BEEB6, PLEASE, STUDIO, STUD2
Cheese And Onions
  23 Apr 77, *Saturday Night* (Rutles)
    ROPE
Child Of Nature
  late-May 68, Kinfauns; acoustic demo
    ARCH1, LOST2, OFF
  Jan 69, **GB** sessions
    BOTH, CASTS, 4SIDES, GOLDM,
    JOURN, MAGTR, ONCE, REVOLT,
    SHOTS, TRAX3, WOND
Chinese Laundry Blues
  date unknown, John, Dakota
    ARCH2, LOST2
Chopsticks
  Jan 69, **GB** sessions
    COMMON, JOURN, LETEND, TRAX3
Christmas message
  21 Dec 63,*Thank Your Lucky Stars*
    LINING
Christmas Song (John & Yoko) — see *O Kristelighed*
Christmas Time (Is Here Again)
  28 Nov 67, EMI (long, EMI boardroom tape)
    EXTEN, FILE1, 1967, NOTH, TRAGIC
  28 Nov 67, EMI (short, **SESSIONS** /45)

DIGIT, OBLA45, OBLADI, SESS
Christmas Time (Is Here Again) aka
The Beatles' Fifth Christmas Record
  28 Nov 67, EMI
    DON'T, LALB, NASSAU, SPLHCB,
    TRAGIC
CINELOGUE ONE (LP) — see PLAY
Clarabella
  16 Jul 63, BBC
    BBC, BEEB, BEEB3, BEEBCD,
    BROAD, REINTRO
CLASSIFIED DOCUMENT (LP) —
see CONFI
Cleanup Time
  80, Dakota, piano demo
    ARCH1, LOST1
  80, Dakota; piano run-through
    LOST7
  Aug 80, DF sessions, mostly chat
    LOST3
  Aug 80, DF session, alternate mix
    LOST4
C'Mon Everybody
  Oct-Dec 73, **R&R** sessions
    SHOULD, VIENNA
  Aug 80, **DF** sessions
    BEFORE, WINSTON
COLD TURKEY FOR KAMPUCHEA
(LP) — see KAMP
Cold Turkey
  Sep 69, acoustic demo
    LOST6
  30 Sep 69, alternate take (from acetate)
    LOST7
  30 Sep 69 (cv)
    REN3, REN4
  18 Aug 72, One-To-One rehearsals
    1AND3, WILLOW
  30 Aug 72, MSG, evening
    1TO1, PLOP, SHOTS, TEDDY
Come And Get It
  24 Jul 69 EMI, Paul, demo
    BOTH, EXTEN, FILE1, JULIAN, SESS
  Sep 69, Badfinger, basic take
    CLASS2, DOLL'S
  Sep 69, Badfinger (cv)
    FS2S
COME BACK JOHNNY! (LP) — see
TEDDY
Come On, People
  Spring 60, Quarry Men rehearsals
    MAY60
Come Together
  21/22/23/25/29/30 Jul 69, EMI; take 9 (cv)
    SPLHCB
  Aug, 72, One-To-One rehearsals (instrumental)
    1AND1, WILLOW

18 Aug 72, One-To-One rehearsals
  B-ROAD, 1AND2, WILLOW
30 Aug 72, MSG, evening
  ARW1, HARD, JOSHUA, 1TO1,
  PLOP, TEDDY, WORK
Comin' Home
12 Dec 69, Copenhagen; D&B
  w/George
  FALCON
Coming Up
25 Nov 79, Wings, Liverpool
  TOKYO
7 Dec 79, Wings, Wembley
  WEMB
29 Dec 79, Wings, Hammersmith
  KAMP
commercials, promos, radio & tv spots:
  BAND ON THE RUN
  GREAT, RARER
  The Beatles Decade (long)
  GREAT, 1234, RARER
  The Beatles Decade (short)
  1234, GREAT
  THE BEATLES COLLECTION
  1234
  THE BEATLES BOX (English)
  1234
  THE BEATLES BOX (French)
  1234
  THE BEATLES BOX (German)
  1234
  BRUNG TO EWE BY HAL SMITH
  DOLL'S, 1970S, TOBE
  Concert For Bangla Desh
  GREAT, RARER
  GOODNIGHT VIENNA
  LIFT, TEDDY
  A Hard Day's Night (trailer)
  RECO
  A Hard Day's Night promo
  LINING
  Help!
  LINING, WHEN
  Hi Hi Hi/C Moon
  4SIDES, LIFT, MAIL, 20X4
  I Love My Suit #1
  OGNIR
  I Love My Suit #2
  20X4, SNAPS
  McCARTNEY II
  GREAT
  Let It Be
  TWICE
  One To One (outtakes)
  LOST3, WILLOW
  Simple Life
  OGNIR
  Sun Country Wine Cooler (3 diff.)
  RIZZ
  WALLS AND BRIDGES

LIFT, TEDDY
WHK (radio, 3 diff.)
  WHEN
WINGS GREATEST
  GREAT
Commonwealth
Jan 69, **GB** sessions
  BLACK, COMMON, GBSESS, HEAD,
  HIHO, JOURN, RAREST1, REVOLT,
  21, WALK
Complain To The Queen
20 Aug 72, Paul, Dutch radio
  4SIDES, QUEEN, SUIT
**COMPLETE CHRISTMAS
COLLECTION** (LP) — see DON'T
concerts and performances:
22 Aug 62, Cavern Club (film)
  BEAT, RARER, SOME, WOND
Dec 62, Star-Club, Hamburg (diff. from
  cv)
  REICH
Dec 62, Star-Club, Hamburg (cv)
  B4TIME, STARS
13 Oct 63, London Palladium
  ABC, BEAT, SUNDAY
24 Oct 63, Stockholm
  PETE, SILVER, STAGE, STOCK
4 Nov 63, Royal Variety Show
  ROYAL
20 Nov 63, Manchester
  ABC, RECO
7 Dec 63, Liverpool
  DEC63, TOUR, YOUNG
19 Jan 64, Paris
  HOTW
11 Feb 64, Washington DC
  BEAT, FIRST
4 Jun 64, Copenhagen
  LINING
12 Jun 64, Adelaide
  DOLL'S, FANS, 1964
16 Jun 64, Melbourne (*Sing For Shell*)
  CANDLE, FANS, HOTW, TOUR
17 Jun 64, Melbourne
  8ARMS, GREAT, MELB, RAREST2
22 Aug 64, Vancouver
  VANC
23 Aug 64, Hollywood Bowl
  BACK, COMPL, 8ARMS, ONLY,
  PREV, RAREST2, ROMA, SPLHCB,
  STONE, TOP
2 Sep 64, Philadelphia?
  FLATS, SINGLES
3 Oct 64, Granville Theatre (*Shindig*)
  CONQ
11 Apr 65, Empire Pool, Wembley
  DIGIT
20 Jun 65, Paris, afternoon
  HOTW
20 Jun 65, Paris, evening

78, for filming of *Ringo* tv special
  4SIDES, OGNIR
14 Sep 79, Paul, Hammersmith
  LOOK, RAVING
25 Nov 79, Wings, Liverpool
  TOKYO
7 Dec 79, Wings, Wembley
  WEMB
29 Dec 79, Wings, Hammersmith
  KAMP
4 Jul 84, Beach Boys w/Ringo,
Washington DC
  OBLA45, RED, RIZZ
14 Dec 84, Deep Purple (w/ George),
Sydney
  NIGHT
21 May 85, Julian, Sydney
  MAIL
20 Jun 85, Paul, Prince's Trust
  OBLA45
21 Nov 85, Ringo & George w/Carl
Perkins (*Blue Suede Shoes*)
  LOOK, ONOT, RIZZ
15 Mar 86, George, *Heartbeat '86*
  NIGHT, OBLA45, UTOPIA
6 Jun 86, George & Ringo, Prince's
Trust
  UTOPIA

**The Continuing Story Of Bungalow
Bill**
  late May 68, Kinfauns; acoustic demo
  OFF
Coochy Coochy
  Jun 30/1 Jul 70, Nashville (cv)
  1970S, OGNIR, REN4
Cook Of The House
  7 Dec 79, Wings, Wembley
  WEMB
  29 Dec 79, Wings, Hammersmith
  KAMP
Cookin' (In The Kitchen Of Love)
  Spring 76, John, Dakota, demo
  ATCH3, LOST3
Corrine, Corrina
  1 May 70, CBS Nashville (Dylan
  w/George)
  CLASS3
Corridor Music
  14 Oct 84, *Southbank* (alternate)
  GREAT
Cottonfields
  5-6 Jun 68? EMI; from *Intervista*
  BUG, CAVERN, RECO, THEIR,
  THOSE, 21
  22 Aug 72, Wings, Antwerp
  ANTW
Country Dreamer
  Oct 72, commercial version
  ORIENT
Crackin' Up

Jan 69, **GB** sessions
  COMMON, JOURN, TRAX3
"Crimble medley"
  21 Dec 63, BBC
  BEEB8
Cry Baby Cry
  late May 68, Kinfauns; acoustic demo
  OFF
Cry For A Shadow
  May 61, Hamburg (cv)
  HOWDO
Crying, Waiting, Hoping
  1 Jan 62, Decca audition
  DECCA
  6 Aug 63, BBC
  BEEB, BEEB4, DEMO, DON'T, PETE,
  REINTRO, SILVER, SUPER1, THEIR,
  21, WLOVE, YEARS, YELL, YOUNG
  Jan 69, **GB** sessions
  SOUND

D

Da-Doo-Run-Run
  Jan 69, **GB** session (*Let It Be*)
  CIRCUIT, GREAT, PLAY
Daddy's Little Sunshine Boy
  67? John & Ringo
  ARCH2, LOST2
Dance The Do
  74, Mike McCartney w/Paul (cv)
  GREAT
Danny Boy
  30 Jan 69, Apple rooftop
  GBCD, GETB, JOURN, LETBE,
  MIXED, RAREST6, SPLHCB
Dark Horse
  Sep-Oct 74, acoustic demo
  DOLL'S, ONOT
  Sep-Oct 74, electric demo
  BYGEO, 4SIDES, ROUGH
  Fall 74, A&M? from unreleased trailer?
  GREAT, UTOPIA
  2 Nov 74, Vancouver
  LIVAN
  22 Nov 74, Fort Worth
  DARK, MORE
  26 Nov 74, Baton Rouge
  BATON
  30 Nov 74, Chicago
  CHIC
  15 Dec 74, Nassau
  LAST
The David Frost Theme
  4 Sep 68, for *Frost on Sunday*
  JULIAN, SFF
A Day In The Life
  19/20 Jan 67, EMI; take 6 (acetate)
  CONFI, FORE, HEAD, 1967, YEARS,

19/20 Jan & 3/10/22 Feb 67, EMI; edit
of takes 6 & 7 (cv, with clean intro);
stereo remix 5
  URT56
19/20 Jan & 3/10/22 Feb 67, EMI; edit
of takes 6 & 7 (cv, with clean intro);
stereo remix 6
  URT56
19/20 Jan & 3/10/22 Feb 67, EMI; edit
of takes 6 & 7 (cv, with clean intro)
  EXTEN, FILE2, HEAD, LIVEAT,
  MIXED, NOT4, 1967, SPLHCB,
  TRAGIC, YEARS
Day Tripper
  16 Oct 65, EMI; take 1 (instr., false
  start)
    URT34
  16 Oct 65, EMI; take 2 (instr., false
  start)
    ULTRA2, URT34
  16 Oct 65, EMI; take 3 (basic take)
    ULTRA2, URT34
  16 Oct 65, EMI; take 3 (echoless mix)
    SPLHCB
  16 Oct 65, EMI; take 3 (cv, UK stereo)
    CASUAL
  2 Dec 65, *Top Of The Pops*
    FHILLS, STAGE
  30 Jun 66, Tokyo
    BACK, BUDO, 8ARMS, FIVE, HOTW,
    JAPAN64, RABBI, ROMA, TOBE,
    TOKIO
  2 Jul 66, Tokyo, afternoon
    BUDO, JAPAN64, TOUR
  29 Aug 66, Candlestick Park
    CANDLE, SINGLES
  24 Dec 67, Hendrix, *Top Gear*
    GUITAR, WORK
  21 May 85, Julian, Sydney
    MAIL
Daytime Nighttime Suffering
  Jan 79? early mix
    CLASS2
Dead Giveaway
  Jul 80, Paris? basic take
    RIZZ
Dear John
  late Nov 80, John, Dakota
    ARCH3, LOST3
Dear Prudence
  late May 68, Kinfauns; acoustic demo
    LOST5, OFF
  28/29/30 Aug 68; Trident, take 1 (fewer
  vocals)
    LOST6
  Fall 68, John, instrumental
    DOLL'S, REN3
Dear Yoko
  Jul 80, Bermuda; acoustic
    LOST7

**DECCA AUDITION OUTTAKES —
SUPER STUDIO SERIES 2** (LP) —
see STUD1, STUD2
Deep Blue
  Jul 71 (cv)
    BYGEO, 1970S, UTOPIA
(There's A) Devil In Her Heart
  20 Aug 63, BBC
    BEEB5, STUDIO, STUD2
  24 Sep 63, BBC
    BEEB6, YOUNG, WITHER
  Jan 69, **GB** sessions
    JOURN, RUSSIA, Y'ORITE
Dialogue From The Film *Let It Be*
  70, promo 45
    GREAT
Did We Meet Somewhere Before?
  78, Paul outtake
    CUTS
  78, Paul, outtake (remix)
    COLD
Dig A Pony
  Jan 69, **GB** sessions (various)
    BWORD, CIRCUIT, COMMON, FILE1,
    GRAVE, HOT, IHAD, LETEND, PLAY,
    Y'ORITE
  24 Jan 69, Apple (from **GET BACK**)
    GBCD, GETB, HEAD, HOMOG,
    JOURN, LETBE, MIXED, RAREST6,
    REN2, TORON
  30 Jan 69, Apple rooftop (cv & from *Let
  It Be*)
    PLAY, SPLHCB, VIRGIN
Dig It
  24 Jan 69, Apple? (different tune, as
  "Can You Dig It?")
    CLASS3, SOUND
  26 Jan 69, Apple (various lengths)
    BACK, BYEBYE, CIRCUIT, DIGIT,
    DON'T, EXTEN, GBCD, GETB, HOT,
    JOURN, LETBE, LETEND, MIXED,
    OBLADI, PLAY, RAREST6, SOUND,
    SUPER1
Diggin' My Potatoes
  Jan 69, **GB** sessions
    REVOLT, SING, WOND
Ding Dong Ding Dong
  Sep-Oct 74, demo
    4SIDES, ROUGH, UTOPIA, WALK
Dizzy Miss Lizzie
  7 Jun 65, BBC
    BACK, BBC, BEEB, BUG, CAVERN,
    8ARMS, FCK,HEARD, HOWDO,
    POWER, RECO, THOSE, WLOVE
  15 Aug 65, Shea Stadium
    FHILLS, GOOD, SHEA, SPLHCB
  19 Aug 65, Houston, afternoon
    TEXAN
  19 Aug 65, Houston, evening
    HOUST, TEXAN, TOUR

Do The Oz
  Jun 71 (cv)
    LIMIT, MOON, 1TO1, SOLDIER,
    WORK
Do You Want To Dance?
  Oct-Dec 73, **R&R** sessions
    MAYP, R'N'R, SHOULD
Do You Want To Know A Secret
  11 Feb 63, EMI; take 6
    NOT4, SESSCD, SPLHCB
  11 Feb 63, EMI; take 8
    URT34
  25 May 63, BBC
    BEEB1, BEEBCD, MONKEY
  4 Jun 63, BBC
    BEEB2, COMPL, MONKEY, STONE,
    STUDIO, STUD1
  30 Jul 63, BBC
    BEEB, BEEB4, BROAD, PLEASE
Domino
  Jan 69, **GB** sessions
    BLACK, JOURN, LETEND, MAGTR
Don't Be Cruel
  Jan 69, **GB** sessions
    RUSSIA
Don't Be Crazy
  Dakota, piano demo
    LOST5
Don't Bother Me
  11 Sep 63, EMI; take 11 (false start)
    INAB, LIVEAT, WITHER
  11 Sep 63, EMI; take 12
    INAB, LIVEAT
  11 Sep 63, EMI; take 15 (cv)
    SPLHCB
Don't Ever Change
  27 Aug 63, BBC
    BBC, BEEB, BEEB5, DEMO, DON'T,
    REINTRO, THEIR, YELL, WLOVE
Don't Know Why
  12 Dec 69, Copenhagen; D&B
  w/George
    FALCON
Don't Let Me Down
  Jan 69, **GB** sessions (various)
    BLACK, BWORD, CIRCUIT, CLASS3,
    COMMON, FS2S, GBSESS, GOLDM,
    GRAVE, HIHO, HOT, JULIAN,
    JOURN, MAGTR, PLAY, RECO,
    RUSSIA, SOUND, TRAX3, 2MUCH,
    WATCH, WHISP, Y'ORITE
  22 Jan 69, Apple (from **GET BACK**)
    GBCD, GETB, JOURN, LETBE,
    MIXED, RAREST6, SPLHCB, TORON
  28 Jan 69, Apple (cv, from 45)
    HEAD, HOMOG, REN2
  30 Jan 69, Apple roof (from *Let It Be*)
    HEARD, PLAY
  Spring 69, bed-in? Amsterdam 21-28
  Mar 69?

    BUG, CAVERN, RECO, THEIR,
    THOSE
**Don't Let The Sun Catch You
Crying**
  Jan 69, **GB** sessions
    REVOLT, SOUND
Don't Pass Me By
  5/6 Jun & 12/22 Jul 68, EMI; take 7 (cv,
  mono mix)
    1234
Don't Worry Kyoko
  21-22 Nov 68, hospital? (*Aspen* flexi)
    LIFE, THIS
  18 Aug 72, One-To-One rehearsals
    1AND3
Down And Out
  Mar-Jul 73 (cv)
    4SIDES, OGNIR
Down In Eastern Australia I Met Her
  unknown, John
    LOST2
Dr. Robert
  17/19 Apr 66, EMI; take 7 (cv)
    SPLHCB
Dream Away
  late 80, from *Time Bandits*
    BYGEO, ONOT
Dream Baby
  8 Mar 62, BBC
    BEEB, LBEEB, MEET, 1234,
    REINTRO, WOND, W/PETE
Dream Lover
  Aug 80, **DF** sessions
    BEFORE, WINSTON
Dress Me Up As A Robber
  home demos, circa fall 80
    TUG, WAR

E

Early In The Morning
  Jan 69, **GB** sessions
    BYEBYE
Early In The Morning (improvisation)
  Jan 69, **GB** sessions
    BLACK, COMMON, JOURN,
    REVOLT, TWICK, WATCH
Early 1970
  8 Mar 70 (cv)
    REN3
Eat At Home
  72, Wings tour, unknown
    ORIENT
  2 Aug 72, Wings, Antwerp
    ANTW
Ebony And Ivory
  home demo, circa Fall 80
    TUG, WAR
  82 (cv, solo version, from 12")
    SUIT
Eight Days A Week

6/18 Oct 64, EMI; edit of takes 13 & 15 (cv)
SPLHCB
1882
summer 72, live, unknown
DOLL'S
summer 72, live, unknown (another)
ORIENT
22 Jul 72, Wings, Montreux
SWITZ
16 Aug 72, Wings, Hanover
HANOV
17 Aug 72, Wings, Rotterdam
QUEEN
22 Aug 72, Wings, Antwerp
ANTW
Eleanor Rigby
28/29 Apr & 6 Jun 66, EMI; take 15 (cv)
SPLHCB
The End
23 Jul & 5/7/8/15/18 Aug 69, EMI; take 7 (cv)
ARW1, SPLHCB
23 Jul & 5/7/8/15/18 Aug 69, EMI; take 7 (cv, outfake)
TALKS
The End Of Another Day
73, from *James Paul McCartney*
MYLO
Enoch Powell
Jan 69, **GB** sessions
BLACK, COMMON, GBSESS, HEAD, HIHO, JOURN, RAREST1, REVOLT, 21
Every Grain Of Sand
10 Feb 88, George, *Rockline*
UTOPIA
Every Little Thing
30 Sep 64, EMI; take 9, (cv, outfake)
20X4
Jan 69, **GB** sessions
RUSSIA
Every Man Has A Woman
Aug 80, **DF** sessions, duet
ARCH2, LOST2
Aug 80, **DF** sessions (cv)
NIGHT
Every Night
Jan 69, **GB** sessions
COMMON, GRAVE, JOURN, REVOLT, WOND
25 Nov 79, Wings, Liverpool
TOKYO
7 Dec 79, Wings, Wembley
WEMBLEY
29 Dec 79, Wings, Hammersmith
KAMP
Every Time Somebody Comes To Town
late Nov 68? George with Dylan

LIFT, 20X4, TWICK
Everybody Had A Hard Year
Fall 68, Kenwood, John
ARCH3, LOST4
Everybody's Got Something To Hide Except Me And My Monkey
late May 68, Kinfauns; acoustic demo
ARCH3, LOST4, OFF
Everybody's Trying To Be My Baby
Dec 62, Star-Club, Hamburg (cv)
REICH, STARS
4 Jun 63, BBC
BEEB2, MONKEY
4 Apr 64, BBC
BEEB10
26 Nov 64, BBC
DEC63
26 Dec 64, BBC
AUCTION, BEEB, BROAD, LINING, WHEN
20 Jun 65, Paris, evening
HOTW
19 Aug 65, Houston, afternoon
TEXAN
19 Aug 65, Houston, evening
HOUST, TEXAN, TOUR
21 Aug 65, Minneapolis
MINN
27 Jun 65, Rome
ARRIV, ROMA
21 Nov 85, *Blue Suede Shoes*
LOOK, ONOT

F

Fab Four On Film
Capitol promo P-B-5100 (1982)
CONQ, GREAT, SPLHCB
Falling In Love Again
Dec 62, Star-Club, Hamburg (cv)
STARS
Far East Man
21 Dec 75? *Rock Around The World*
BYGEO, UTOPIA
The Fat Budgie (poem)
3 Jul 65, BBC; *The World Of Books*
2MUCH, 4SIDES
Feedback Guitar
Jan 69, **GB** sessions
BYEBYE, LETEND, WATCH
Fiddle About
Sep 72, Ringo; from **TOMMY** (cv)
RICHIE
films:
Backyard
CONFI, RED, WATCH, WHISP, WHY
The Beatles At Shea Stadium
FHILLS, GOOD, SHEA
The Beatles Come To Town
ABC, RECO
Caveman

RICHIE
Cavern Club 22 Aug 62 — see **Some
    Other Guy**, Cavern Club (film)
Clock (John, NYC, Summer 71)
    ARCH1, LOST3
Eat The Document (Dylan)
    LIFT, TEDDY
Give My Regards To Broad Street
    GREAT
A Hard Day's Night (trailer)
    RECO
Help!
    SFF
Let It Be
    BWORD, CIRCUIT, HEARD, HOT,
PLAY
Magical Mystery Tour
    DIGIT, RARER, TRAGIC
MBE announcement newsreel (mid-Jun
65)
    ABC
The Music Lives On
    Paul, Hammersmith, 14 Sep 79
        LOOK, RAVING
One Hand Clapping
    Fall 75 (and other dates)
        ONEH
Porky's Revenge
    ONOT
Rape
    MOON
Rock And Roll Circus
    — see **Yer Blues**
Shanghai Surprise
    LIFT, ONOT
Ten For Two
    ARCH4, LIFT, LOST4
Time Bandits
    BYGEO, ONOT
Wings' first rehearsal
    1970S
Yellow Submarine
    LINING, MELLO, WHEN
*What's Happening: The Beatles In The
USA*
    LINING, WHEN
Flowing More Freely Than Wine
    Jan 69, **GB** sessions
        BLACK, JOURN, MAGTR
Flying
    Sep 67, EMI; alternate version
        SPLHCB
Flying Hour
    79-80, original, deleted version
        BYGEO, ENGL, ONOT
    87 remix for **SBGH**
        UTOPIA
The Fool On The Hill
    6 Sep 67, EMI; demo

1967, ULTRA1, RARER, SESSCD,
SFF, TRAGIC
6/25/26/27 Sep & 20 Oct 67, EMI; take
6 (cv)
    SPLHCB
demo/cv edit
    ROPE
25 Nov 79, Wings, Liverpool
    TOKYO
7 Dec 79, Wings, Wembley
    WEMB
29 Dec 79, Wings, Hammersmith
    KAMP
A Fool Was I
unknown, probably no Beatles
involvement
    VIENNA
Fools Like Me
    Jan 69, **GB** sessions
        BLACK, JOURN, REVOLT, TWICK,
        WATCH, Y'ORITE
For No One
    9/16/19 May 66, EMI; take 14 (cv)
        SPLHCB
    14 Oct 84, *Southbank* (documentary)
        CONFI, GREAT
For You Blue
    Jan 69, **GB** sessions (various)
        BACK, BLACK, BYEBYE, CIRCUIT,
        COMMON, GBCD, GBSESS, GETB,
        GOLDM, HEAD, HIHO, HOMOG,
        HOT, JOURN, LETBE, LETEND,
        MIXED, PLAY, POWER, RAREST1,
        RAREST6, REN2, SPLHCB, TORON,
    22 Nov 74, Fort Worth
        DARK, MOREF
    26 Nov 74, Baton Rouge
        BATON
    30 Nov 74, Chicago
        CHIC
    13 Dec 74, Largo
        UTOPIA
    15 Dec 74, Nassau
        LAST
Frank Cummings (poem)
    MOON
Frere Jacques
    Jan 69, **GB** sessions
        RUSSIA
From Me To You
    5 Mar 63, EMI; unknown take
        ULTRA1
    5 Mar 63, EMI (cv, with countdown)
        SPLHCB
    5 Mar 63, EMI (cv, original mono mix)
        ITEMS
    7 Apr 63, BBC
        MEET. W/PETE
    18 Apr 63, BBC
        BEEB1, MONKEY

LIVAN
10 Nov 74, Long Beach
STICK
22 Nov 74, Fort Worth
DARK, MOREF
26 Nov 74, Baton Rouge
BATON
30 Nov 74, Chicago
CHIC
15 Dec 74, Nassau
LAST

Give Peace A Chance
1 Jun 69, Montreal, rehearsal?
LIFT, LINING, TWICE
1 Jun 69, Montreal (cv)
LIMIT, REN3, REN4
1 Jun 69, Montreal (cv, with
countdown)
SPLHCB
Oct 69? John & Yoko, acoustic
CLASS2
18 Aug 72, One-To-One rehearsals
1AND1, 1AND3, WILLOW, YIN
30 Aug 72, MSG, evening
HARD, JOSHUA, 1TO1, PLOP,
WORK
6 Sep 72, MD Telethon
CLASS2

Give Us A Chord, Roy
Paul, home demo circa Fall 80
TUG

Givin' Grease A Ride
early 74, Mike McGear (cv)
GREAT

Glad All Over
20 Aug 63, BBC
BEAUT, BEEB5, DEMO, DON'T,
REINTRO, YELL
21 Nov 85, *Blue Suede Shoes*
LOOK, ONOT

Glass Onion
11/12/13/16 Sep & 10 Oct 68, EMI; take
33 (cv)
SPLHCB

Go Johnny Go
Jan 69, **GB** sessions
COMMON, JOURN, TRAX3

Go Now
19 May 73, Wings, Leeds
LEEDS
23 Jul 73, Wings, Edinburgh
SCOT
Fall 75, *One Hand Clapping* sessions
ONEH, WHY
21 Jun 76, Wings, L.A. Forum
ZOO
23 Jun 76, Wings, L.A. Forum
LASER, WINGS
25 Nov 79, Wings, Liverpool
TOKYO

7 Dec 79, Wings, Wembley
WEMB
29 Dec 79, Wings, Hammersmith
KAMP

Go Your Own Way
George, 74 WEA promo
CLASS2, GREAT

God
Fall 70? John, acoustic
ARCH1, LOST1

God Bless California
Jan 71, Thornton, Fradkin & Unger (cv)
GREAT

God Save Oz (see **God Save Us**)

God Save Us
71, acoustic demo (w/bongos)
LOST5
Jun 71, demo (John's vocals)
LOST1, MOON
Jun 71 (cv)
1TO1

Going Down On Love
Jul 74, **W&B** sessions
PREC,WALLS, WINSTON

Golden Slumbers/Carry That Weight
2 Jul 69, EMI; take13
B-ROAD, COMMON, EXTEN,
LOOKING, NO3, RARER, RETURN,
ROAD, TALKS, WATCH
2/3/4/30/31 Jul & 15 Aug 69, EMI; take
17 (cv)
SPLHCB

Die Goldenen OTTO — Sieger 1966
23 Jun 66; speech (German flexi)
CRONE, 4EVER, MUNICH

Gone, Gone, Gone
Jan 69, **GB** sessions
ALMO, LETEND
21 Nov 85, *Blue Suede Shoes*
LOOK, ONOT

Good Day Sunshine
8/9 Jun 66, EMI; take 1 (cv)
SPLHCB

Good Morning Good Morning
Feb 67? John's home demo
ARCH3, LOST4

Good Night
Mar-Apr 69, from **WEDDING ALBUM**
(cv)
LIMIT, RED

Good Night Tonight
29 Dec 79, Wings, Hammersmith
KAMP

Good Rockin' Tonight
Jan 69, **GB** sessions
BLACK, HIHO, JOURN, MAGTR,
RAREST1, REVOLT, 21

Goodbye
late 68, Paul, Dick James, demo
2MUCH, EXTEN, FILE1, NOT4, OFF,

RED, SESSCD, WALK
1-2 Mar 69, Mary Hopkin, basic take
  CLASS2, DOLL'S
Goodnight Lonely Princess
  83? cv from CD
    GREAT
Goodnight Tonight
  25 Nov 79, Wings, Liverpool
    TOKYO
  7 Dec 79, Wings, Wembley
    WEMB
Goodnight Vienna
  Jun 74, John, **W&B** sessions, demo
    ARCH2, LOST1, MOON, NIGHT,
    VIENNA
  Summer 74 (45, cv, with spoken intro)
    RIZZ
Got My Mind Set On You
  62, James Ray (cv)
    UTOPIA
  87, George (cv, extended)
    UTOPIA
Got To Get You Into My Life
  7/8/11 Apr & 18 May & 17 Jun 65, EMI;
  take 9
    SPLHCB
  25 Nov 79, Wings, Liverpool
    TOKYO
  7 Dec 79, Wings, Wembley
    WEMB
  29 Dec 79, Wings, Hammersmith
    KAMP
Gotta Sing, Gotta Dance
  73, from *James Paul McCartney*
    4SIDES, LIFT, MYLO
The Grand Old Duke Of York
  11 Feb 72, Wings, Hull
    SPRING
Great Balls Of Fire
  Jan 69, **GB** sessions
    REVOLT, SOUND
Grow Old With Me
  Aug 80, John, Dakota
    ARCH2, LOST2
Guitar Blues
  21 Feb 64, Miami
    LINING, WHEN

H

Hallelujah! I Love Her So
  Spring 60, Quarry Men
    MAY60, REINTRO, STU
  Dec 62, Star-Club, Hamburg (cv)
    STARS
Happiness Is A Warm Gun
  Jan 69, **GB** sessions
    TRAX3
Happy Birthday To You
  18 Jun 63, BBC
    BEEB3, BEEBCD

5 Oct 63, BBC
  BEAT, BEEB, BEEB7, 1234,
  REINTRO, WOND
18 MAY 64, BBC
  BEEB10
15 Mar 68, India, with Beach Boys
  FILE2, JULES, MIXED, ROPE, SFF,
  WALK, WHEN
Happy Xmas (War Is Over)
  Nov 71 (cv)
    LIMIT, REN3, REN4
A Hard Day's Night
  16 Apr 64, EMI; takes 2 & 3 (false
  starts)
    INAB, LIVEAT
  16 Apr 64, EMI; take 9 (cv, stereo,
  w/countdown)
    SPLHCB
  16 Apr 64, EMI; take 9 (cv, from LP)
    INAB
  16 Apr 64, EMI; take 9 (cv, from 45)
    LIVEAT
  16 Apr 64, EMI; take 9 (cv, true stereo)
    CASUAL
  16 Jul 64, BBC
    BEEB, BEEB11, BUG, KNIGHT,
    LALB, LOOKING, LONG, MARY,
    NASSAU, POPS, ROAD, TOP,
    WLOVE, YEARS
  session for BBC 3 Aug 64
    PARL
  3 Aug 64, BBC
    BEEB11
  22 Aug 64, Vancouver
    VANC
  23 Aug 64, Hollywood Bowl
    8ARMS, ONLY, RAREST2, ROMA
  2 Sep 64, Philadelphia?
    FLATS
  20 Jun 65, Paris, afternoon
    HOTW
  20 Jun 65, Paris, evening
    HOTW
  27 Jun 65, Rome
    ARRIV, ROMA, SINGLES
  15 Aug 65, Shea Stadium
    GOOD, SHEA
  19 Aug 65, Houston, afternoon
    TEXAN
  19 Aug 65, Houston, evening
    HOUST, TEXAN, TOUR
A Hard Rain's Gonna Fall
  Jan 69, **GB** sessions
    BYEBYE
Hard Times
  78, live, from the *Ringo* tv special
    4SIDES, OGNIR
Hare Krishna Mantra
  Jan 69, **GB** sessions

**BLACK, COMMON, JOURN, TWICK,
WATCH**
Hari's On Tour (Express)
22 Nov 74, Fort Worth
DARK, MOREF
26 Nov 74, Baton Rouge
BATON
15 Dec 74, Nassau
LAST
Harry Lime (Third Man Theme)
Jan 69, **GB** sessions
FILE1, GOLDM, JOURN, REVOLT,
TRAX3
Hava Nagila
Jan 69, **GB** sessions
SOUND
Mar 69, Amsterdam Hilton
MOON, VIENNA
Have You Heard The Word
74, the Fut; no Beatles involvement
BUG, BWORD, CAVERN, HEARD,
SUPER1, THEIR, THOSE, 21
He Said He Said
65-66, John, solo acoustic demo
ARCH2, LOST2
Hear Me Lord
Jan 69, **GB** sessions
RUSSIA
Heart Of The Country
73, *James Paul McCartney* (outtake)
LIFT, 20X4
73, from *James Paul McCartney*
LIFT, MYLO
Heart On My Sleeve
78, live, from the *Ringo* tv special
4SIDES, OGNIR
Heather
Nov 68-Jan 69, **PCARD** sessions
NO3, RED, SUN, 20X4
Hello Dolly
Jan 69, **GB** sessions
RUSSIA
Hello Goodbye
2 Oct 67, EMI; take 1 (instrumental)
URT56
2/19/20/25 Oct & 2 Nov 67, EMI; take
22 (cv)
CASUAL, LIVEAT, SPLHCB
Jan 69, **GB** sessions
SING
Hello Little Girl
Spring 60, Quarry Men
STU
1 Jan 62, Decca audition
DECCA, REINTRO, SESSCD, WALK
Hello Mudduh, Hello Fadduh
Jan 69, **GB** sessions
RUSSIA
Help!

13 Apr 65, EMI; take 1 (instr., false
start)
URT34
13 Apr 65, EMI; take 2 (instr., false
start)
URT34
13 Apr 65, EMI; take 3 (instr., false
start)
URT34
13 Apr 65, EMI; take 5 (instr., false
start)
URT34
13 Apr 65, EMI; take 8 (cv, rhythm
tracks only)
INAB, LIVEAT
13 Apr 65, EMI; take 12 (cv, stereo,
with countdown)
CLASS3, SPLHCB
13 Apr 65, EMI; take 12 (cv, from 45)
ITEMS
13 Apr 65, EMI; take 12 (cv, no electric
guitar —outfake)
20X4
17 Jul 65, Blackpool
STOCK
15 Aug 65, Shea Stadium
FHILLS, GOOD, RARER, SHEA
19 Aug 65, Houston, afternoon
SINGLES, TEXAN
19 Aug 65, Houston, evening
HOUST, TEXAN, TOUR
12 Sep 65, *Ed Sullivan*
CONQ, FCK
Jan 69, **GB** sessions
CASTS, FILE1, GOLDM, IHAD,
JOURN, SHOTS
late 70, John, Tittenhurst
ARCH2, LOST3
Help! open-ended interview
GOLDEN
Help Me
11 Feb 72, Wings, Hull
BELGIUM, SPRING
Helter Skelter
9/10 Sep 68, EMI; take 21 (cv, stereo)
SPLHCB
Henry's Blue
11 Feb 72, Wings, Hull
SPRING
22 Jul 72, Wings, Montreux
SWITZ
16 Aug 72, Wings, Hanover
HANOV
22 Jul 72, Wings, Antwerp
ANTW
Her Majesty
Jan 69, **GB** sessions, rehearsal
B-ROAD, WOND
2 Jul 69, EMI; take 3, with the final
chord

ARW1, CASUAL, EXTEN, LOOKING,
NO3, RETURN, ROAD, TALKS, 20X4,
2MUCH, WATCH, WHEN

Here Comes The Sun
7/8/16 Jul & 6/11/15/19 Aug 69, EMI;
take 15 (cv)
SPLHCB
18 Nov 76, *Saturday Night Live*
ARW1, B-ROAD, BYGEO, UTOPIA
6 Jun 87, George, Prince's Trust
UTOPIA
10 Feb 88, George, *Rockline*
UTOPIA

Here We Go Again
73? first complete acoustic demo
LOST6
74? Lennon acoustic, demo
FILE2, LOST1, MIXED, NIGHT

Hey Bulldog
11 Feb 68, EMI; take 10 (cv)
SPLHCB
11 Feb 68, EMI; take 10 (cv, outfake)
RECO, ROPE

Hey Diddle
71? *Wings Over The World*
1970S
74, Paul outtake
CUTS
74, Paul, outtake (remix)
COLD

Hey Jude
30 Jul 68, take 9
URT56
30 Jul 68, EMI; mostly take 9, for
Experiment In Television
INAB, LIVEAT, NOTH, RECO, RED,
TOBE
31 Jul/1 Aug 68 (Trident); take 1 (cv)
JUDY, SPLHCB
4 Sep 68, Twickenham; for *Frost On Sunday*
JULIAN, LALB, SFF, TOP

Hey Little Girl (In The High School Sweater)
Jan 69, **GB** sessions
FILE1, OBLA

Hi Heel Sneakers
Jan 69, **GB** sessions
BLACK, COMMON, GRAVE, JOURN,
REVOLT, RUSSIA

Hi, Hi, Hi
22 Jul 72, Wings, Montreux
SWITZ
19 Aug 72, Wings, Groningen
(soundcheck)
QUEEN
22 Aug 72, Wings, Antwerp
ANTW
Oct 72, from the 45
MYLO

10 Jul 73, Wings, Newcastle
NEWCAS
Fall 75, *One Hand Clapping* sessions
NASH, ONEH, SUIT
1 Nov 75, Wings, Perth
FLY
13 Nov 75, Wings, Melbourne
ONEH
3 May 76, Wings, Ft. Worth
FORTW
15 May 76, Wings, Largo
9MM
21 Jun 76, Wings L.A. Forum
FORUM
23 Jun 76, Wings L.A. Forum
LASER, WINGS

The Hippy Hippy Shake
Dec 62, Star-Club, Hamburg (cv)
B4TIME, STARS
16 Mar 63, BBC
MEET, W/PETE
4 Jun 63, BBC
DEMO, LBEEB, STUD1, THEIR, 21
30 Jul 63, BBC
BEEB, BEEB4, BROAD, FCK
10 Sep 63, BBC
BEEB6, YOUNG
15 Feb 64, BBC
BEEB9
Jan 69, **GB** sessions
JOURN, MAGTR, TRAX3

The History Of Rock And Roll
National Lampoon, no Beatles
involvement
CLASS3

**THE HISTORY OF SYRACUSE
MUSIC V.8/9** (LP) — see WALK

Hitchhike
Jan 69, **GB** sessions
JOURN, MAGTR, REVOLT, TRAX3

Hold Me Tight
12 Sep 63, EMI; unknown take (not cv)
URT34

Holding On To A Dream
unknown, possible Wings involvement
DOLL'S, NIGHT, 20X4

The Holdup
72, David Bromberg (cv)
GREAT

Homeward Bound
18 Nov 76, *Saturday Night Live*
BYGEO, UTOPIA

Honey Don't
3 Sep 63, BBC
BACK, BEEB5, BOTH, CASTS, FCK,
LINING, POWER, SHOTS, SNAPS,
STUDIO, STUD2
18 May 64, BBC
BEEB10
26 Oct 64, EMI; take 5 (cv)

SPLHCB
26 Oct 64, EMI; take 5 (cv, outfake?)
ROUGH
7 Jun 65, BBC
BEEB, WLOVE
Oct 70, **POB** sessions
LOST6
8 Oct 82, Ringo, _Parkinson In Australia_
CLASS2, MAIL
21 Nov 85, _Blue Suede Shoes_
LOOK, RIZZ

Honey Hush
Jan 69, **GB** sessions
BLACK, COMMON, GBSESS, HEAD,
HIHO, JOURN, RAREST1, REVOLT
21, TWICK

Honey Pie
1/2/4 Oct 68, Trident; take 1 (cv,
outfake)
CONFI, HEAD, OFF, 1234, WHISP,
YEARS

The Honeymoon Song
6 Aug 63, BBC
BEAUT, BEEB, BEEB4, DEMO,
DON'T, KNIGHT, THEIR, YELL

Hong Kong Blues
Oct 79-Oct 80, original mix
ENGL

Hot As Sun
Jan 69, **GB** sessions
REVOLT, WOND
25 Nov 79, Wings, Liverpool
TOKYO
7 Dec 79, Wings, Wembley
WEMB
29 Dec 79, Wings, Hammersmith
KAMP

Hound Dog
30 Aug 72, MSG, evening
HOUND, PLOP, TEDDY, SNAPS

House Of The Rising Sun
Jan 69, **GB** sessions
BLACK, COMMON, FS2S, GBSESS,
HEAD, HIHO, JOURN, RAREST1,
REVOLT

How Do You Do?
Nov 68-Jan 69, **PCARD** sessions
NO3, SUN

How Do You Do It
4 Sep 62, EMI; take 2 (original version)
BOTH, FS2S, HOWDO, LIVEAT,
LOOKING, NOT4, RECO, ROAD,
SPLHCB, 2MUCH, ULTRA1, WITHER
4 Sep 62, EMI; take 2 (**SESSIONS**
edit)
SESS, SESSCD

How Do You Sleep?
Jul 71, **POB** sessions; alternate take
ARCH2, LOST2

I

I Am The Walrus
6/7 Sep 67, EMI; take 17 (mono remix
#4); the basic tracks
CASUAL, 1967, RARER, SESSCD,
SFF, TRAGIC, ULTRA2
5/6/27/28 Sep 67, EMI; take 17 (cv)
SPLHCB
basic/cv edit (amateur)
ROPE
Sep 67, EMI; longest edit
ITEMS

I Am Your Singer
22 Jul 72, Wings, Montreux
SWITZ
16 Aug 72, Wings, Hanover
HANOV
20 Aug 72, Wings, Amsterdam
QUEEN
22 Aug 72, Wings, Antwerp
ANTW

I Call Your Name
4 Apr 64, BBC
BEEB10

I Do Like To Be Beside The Seaside
unknown; John, Dakota?
ARCH2, LOST2

I Don't Care Anymore
Sep-Oct 74, from 45
BYGEO, UTOPIA
21 Dec 75? _Rock Around The World_
BYGEO, ONOT

I Don't Know
Spring 60, Quarry Men
MAY60, REINTRO

I Don't Wanna Face It
Jul 80, Bermuda? acoustic demo
LOST7
Aug 80, **DF** sessions, alternate mix
ARCH2, CONFI

I Don't Want To Do It
84 demo?
LIFT, ONOT
85, from _Porky's Revenge_ (LP mix)
ONOT
85, from _Porky's Revenge_ (45 mix)
NIGHT, ONOT

I Don't Want To See You Again
64, Peter & Gordon (cv)
SPLHCB

I Feel Fine
18 Oct 64, EMI; take 6
URT34
18 Oct 64, EMI; take 9 (cv, basic take)
SPLHCB, URT34
18 Oct 64, EMI; take 9 (cv, stereo)
ITEMS, SPLHCB
26 Nov 64, BBC
BEEB, BROAD, FCK

20 Jun 65, Paris, evening
  BEAT
20 Jun 65, Paris, afternoon
  HOTW
27 Jun 65, Rome
  COMPL, ROMA
17 Jul 65, Blackpool
  STOCK
15 Aug 65, Shea Stadium
  FHILLS, GOOD, SHEA, SPLHCB
19 Aug 65, Houston, afternoon
  TEXAN
19 Aug 65, Houston, evening
  HOUST, TEXAN
12 Sep 65, *Ed Sullivan*
  CONQ, RECO
24 Jun 66, Munich, evening
  CRONE, 4EVER, MUNICH,
  SINGLES, STAGE
30 Jun 66, Tokyo
  BUDO, 8ARMS, FIVE, HOTW,
  JAPAN64, TOKIO
2 Jul 66, Tokyo, afternoon
  BUDO, TOKIO, TOUR
29 Aug 66, Candlestick Park
  CANDLE
I Forgot To Remember To Forget
18 May 64, BBC
  BEEB10, DEMO, FCK, HEARD,
  MAIL, 1234, RECO, YOUNG
I Found Out
Oct 70, longer (Australian pressing)
  ONCE, LIMIT
I Got A Woman
13 Aug 63, BBC
  BEEB5, DEMO, DON'T, FCK, YELL
4 Apr 64, BBC
  BEEB, BEEB10, BROAD, DEMO,
  HOWDO, SOLDIER, SNAPS
I Got To Find My Baby
11 Jun 63, BBC
  BEEB2, BEEBCD, MONKEY, 1234,
  PLEASE, WOND
29 Jun 63, BBC
  BEAUT, BEEB, BEEB2, MONKEY
I Hate To See The Evening Sun Go Down
30 Jul 68, EMI; improvisation?
  URT56
30 Jul 68, EMI; *Experiment In Television*
  RECO, RED
I Just Don't Understand
20 Aug 63, BBC
  BEEB, BEEB5, DEMO, DON'T,
  PLEASE, THEIR, YELL
I Know A Place
77, from **SCOUSE THE MOUSE**
(cv)
  LIFT, RICHIE, SCOUSE
I Lie Around
Oct 72 (cv)

ORIENT
I Like 'Em Heavy
unknown, Paul, home rehearsal
  HOME
I Lost My Little Girl
Oct 77, Melvin Bragg interview
  GREAT, SUN
unknown broadcast
  GREAT
Fall 80? Paul, home rehearsal
  CLASS3, HOME
I Love My Suit
  #1   OGNIR
  #2   20X4, SNAPS
I Love You Too
65, Fourmost (cv, no Beatles
involvement)
  ROPE
I Me Mine
Jan 69, **GB** sessions (various)
  BLACK, BWORD, CIRCUIT, GRAVE,
  HEARD, HOT, JOURN, LETEND,
  MAGTR, PLAY, SING, VIRGIN,
  Y'ORITE
3 Jan 70, EMI; take 16 (5 Jan 70
remix?)
  EXTEN, FILE1, NOT4, SESSCD
3 Jan & 1 Apr 70, EMI; take 18 (cv)
  SPLHCB
I Need You (Harrison)
15/16 Feb 65, EMI, take 5 (from *Help!*)
  BACK, POWER
I Need You (unknown)
unknown, no Beatles involvement
  ARW1, ROUGH
I Promise
late 70, John
  ARCH2, LOST2
I Remember You
Dec 62, Star-Club, Hamburg (cv)
  STARS
I Sat Belonely (poem)
  Apr 64? **As It Happened** (Murray the
  K)
  4SIDES, MOON, ONCE, RABBI,
  2MUCH
I Saw Her Standing There
Dec 62, Star-Club, Hamburg (cv)
  B4TIME, SPLHCB, STARS
11 Feb 63, EMI; take 2
  ULTRA1
11 Feb 63, EMI; take (6, 7 or 8)
  INAB, LIVEAT
11 Feb 63, EMI; take 10
  URT34
11 Feb 63, EMI; take 12
  INAB, LIVEAT
11 Feb 63, EMI; edit of takes 9 & 12
(cv)
  SPLHCB

16 Mar 63, BBC
MEET, W/PETE
25 May 63, BBC
BEEB1, BEEBCD, MONKEY
3 Jun 63, BBC
BEEB1, MONKEY
25 Jun 63, BBC
BEEB3
21 Jul 63, BBC
MEET, W/PETE
24 Sep 63, BBC
BEEB6, PLEASE, STUDIO, STUD2
5 Oct 63, BBC
BEEB7
20 Oct 63, BBC
BEEB7
24 Oct 63, Stockholm
FHILLS, PETE, SILVER, SPLHCB,
STAGE, STOCK
7 Dec 63, Empire Theatre, Liverpool
DEC63, TOUR, YOUNG
26 Dec 63, BBC
BEEB8
64? George Martin Orchestra
SPLHCB
9 Feb 64, *Ed Sullivan*
BLASTS, CONQ, REN1, SHEW,
THOSE
11 Feb 64, Washington
FIRST
15 Feb 64, *Ed Sullivan*, rehearsal
CONQ
16 Feb 64, *Ed Sullivan*
BLASTS
18 May 64, BBC
BEEB10
12 Jun 64, Adelaide
DOLL'S, FANS, 1964, SINGLES
17 Jun 64, Melbourne
8ARMS, GREAT, MELB, RAREST2
unknown (The Who?)
1234, WHISP
Nov 74, John, rehearsal w/ Elton
ONCE
28 Nov 74, MSG, John, w/ Elton
GUITAR, WORK
20 Jun 85, Paul, *Prince's Trust*
OBLA45
I Shall Be Released
Jan 69, **GB** sessions
GRAVE, JOURN, MAGTR, REVOLT,
TRAX3
I Should Have Known Better
26 Feb 64, EMI; take 22 (cv)
SPLHCB
16 Jul 64, BBC
BEEB11? (cv)
session for BBC 3 Aug 64
(false start) KNIGHT, PARL, RARER
(no harmonica) PARL, RARER

(final version) PARL
3 Aug 64, BBC
BEEB11
I Threw It All Away
Jan 69, **GB** sessions
BLACK, HIHO, JOURN, LETEND,
MAGTR, RAREST1
I Wanna Be Your Man
11 Feb 64, Washington
FIRST, SINGLES
15 Feb 64, BBC
BEEB9
29 Feb 64, *Big Night Out* (lip-synch)
SUNDAY
30 Mar 64, BBC
BBC, BEEB, BEEB9, BUG, RECO,
WITHER, WLOVE
19 Apr 64, IBC (for *ATB*)
DIGIT, NOTG
6 May 64, *Around The Beatles*
EMIOUT, RSG!, SOME
20 Jun 65, Paris, afternoon
HOTW
20 Jun 65, Paris, evening
HOTW
27 Jun 65, Rome
ARRIV, ROMA
19 Aug 65, Houston, afternoon
TEXAN
19 Aug 65, Houston, evening
HOUST, TEXAN, TOUR
30 Jun 66, Tokyo
8ARMS, BUDO, FIVE, JAPAN64,
TOKIO
2 Jul 66, Tokyo, afternoon
BUDO, JAPAN64
29 Aug 66, Candlestick Park
CANDLE, NIGHT, SPLHCB
I Want To Hold Your Hand
10 Oct 63, London Palladium
SUNDAY
17 Oct 63, EMI; take 17 (cv, fake
stereo)
SPLHCB
17 Oct 63, EMI; take 17 (cv, true
stereo)
ABC, CASUAL
7 Dec 63, Liverpool,
DEC63, TOUR, YOUNG
21 Dec 63, BBC
BEEB8
26 Dec 63, BBC
BEEB8
19 Jan 64, Paris
HOTW, KNIGHT, SINGLES
9 Feb 64, *Ed Sullivan*
BLASTS, CONQ, SHEW
11 Feb 64, Washington
BEAT, FIRST
15 Feb 64, BBC

BEEB9
15 Feb 64, *Ed Sullivan* rehearsal
  CONQ
16 Feb 64, *Ed Sullivan*
  BLASTS
16 Feb 64, *Ed Sullivan* (edit)
  REN1, THOSE
23 Feb 64 *Ed Sullivan*
  BLASTS, CONQ
29 Feb 64, *Big Night Out* (lip-synch)
  SUNDAY
12 Jun 64, Adelaide
  DOLL'S, FANS
23 Aug 64, Hollywood Bowl
  8ARMS, ONLY, PREV, RAREST2,
  ROMA
2 Sep 64, Philadelphia?
  FLATS
I Want You (She's So Heavy)
Jan 69, **GB** sessions
  CLASS3, SOUND
22 Feb 69, Trident; Paul vocals
  ARW1, BOTH, IHAD, ROUGH
Mar 69, John, Amsterdam Hilton
  DIGIT, FILE2, MIXED, VIENNA
I Will Always Be In Love With You
Spring 60, Quarry Men
  STU
I Would Only Smile
Summer 72 tour, unknown
  ORIENT
22 Jul 72, Wings, Montreux
  SWITZ
16 Aug 72, Wings, Hanover
  HANOV
17 Aug 72, Wings, Rotterdam
  QUEEN
22 Aug 72, Wings, Antwerp
  ANTW
Mar 73, Wings outtake
  CUTS
Mar 73, Wings, Denny's remix
  SUIT
I'd Have You Any Time
late Nov 68? George with Dylan
  LIFT, 20X4
I'll Be On My Way
24 Jun 63, BBC
  2MUCH, BEEB, BEEB1, BEEBCD,
  DIGIT, LINING, MONKEY, ROUGH,
  SOLDIER, WALK, WITHER, WLOVE,
  YEARS
I'll Cry Instead
1 Jun 64, EMI; edit of takes 6 & 8; (cv,
stereo, long)
  CASUAL
I'll Follow The Sun
Spring 60, Quarry Men
  CONFI, MAY60, STU
26 Nov 64, BBC

AUCTION, BBC, BEEB, BROAD,
  DEC63, RARER
I'll Get You
1 Jul 63, EMI; unknown take (cv)
  SPLHCB
13 Aug 63, BBC
  BEAUT, BEEB5
10 Sep 63, BBC
  BEEB6, KNIGHT
I'll Give You A Ring
78, Paul home rehearsal
  HOME
82, from the 45
  SUIT
I'm A Loser
14 Aug 64, EMI; take 8 (cv, with chat)
  SPLHCB
14 Aug 64, EMI; take 8 (cv)
  LIVEAT
3 Oct 64, Granville Theatre (*Shindig*)
  CONQ, RECO
26 Nov 64, BBC
  AUCTION, BEEB, BROAD
7 Jun 65, BBC
  CLASS2
20 Jun 65, Paris, evening
  COMPL, HOTW
20 Jun 65, Paris, afternoon
  HOTW
24 Jun 65, Milan?
  4EVER, ITALY
27 Jun 65, Rome
  ARIV, ROMA
I'm A Man (Bo Diddley)
Aug 80, **DF** sessions
  BEFORE, WINSTON
I'm Down
14 Jun 65, EMI; take 7 (cv, mono)
  HOMOG, HEAD, JUDY, REN2, REN4
14 Jun 65, EMI; take 7 (cv, true stereo)
  ITEMS, 1234
17 Jul 65, Blackpool
  STOCK
15 Aug 65, Shea Stadium
  FHILLS, GOOD, RARER, SHEA
19 Aug 65, Houston, afternoon
  SINGLES, TEXAN
19 Aug 65, Houston, evening
  HOUST, TEXAN
30 Aug 65, Hollywood Bowl?
  LINING
12 Sep 65, *Ed Sullivan*
  CONQ, FCK, RECO
24 Jun 66, Munich, evening
  CRONE, 4EVER, MUNICH, STAGE
30 Jun 66, Tokyo
  BUDO, 8ARMS, FIVE, HOTW
  JAPAN64, TOKIO
2 Jul 66, Tokyo, afternoon
  BUDO, JAPAN64, TOUR

I'm Gonna Love You Too
Paul, 74, from unreleased *Backyard* film
CONFI
I'm Gonna Sit Right Down And Cry (Over You)
Dec 62, Star-Club, Hamburg (cv)
SPLHCB
6 Aug 63, BBC
BEAUT, BEEB4, DEMO, DON'T, PLEASE, THEIR, 21, YELL
I'm Happy Just To Dance With You
session for BBC 3 Aug 64 (instrumental)
PARL
session for BBC 3 Aug 64 (final version)
PARL, KNIGHT
3 Aug 64, BBC
BEEB11
I'm Looking Through You
24 Oct 65, EMI; take 1
FILE2, INAB, LIVEAT, MIXED, RABBI, SESS, SESSCD, ULTRA1
10/11 Nov 65, EMI; take 4 (cv, w/ false starts)
1234, RABBI
I'm Losing You
80, Dakota?
ARCH1, LOST3
Aug 80, **DF** sessions, w/ slide guitar
ARCH1, BEFORE, WINSTON
I'm Only Sleeping
27/29 Apr & 5/6 May 66, EMI; take 13 (cv)
SPLHCB
27/29 Apr & 5/6 May 66, EMI; take 13 (cv, alternate mono mix)
CASUAL, NOTH
I'm Ready
Jan 69, **GB** sessions
JOURN, Y'ORITE
I'm So Tired
late May 68, Kinfauns; acoustic demo
OFF
Jan 69, **GB** sessions
EXTEN, FILE1, GOLDM, JOURN, RED, TRAX3, WHEN
I'm Stepping Out
Jul 80, Bermuda; acoustic & rhythm box
LOST7
I'm Talking About You
Dec 62, Star-Club, Hamburg (diff. from cv)
REICH
Dec 62, Star-Club, Hamburg (cv)
STARS
16 Mar 63, BBC
BEAUT, MEET, PLEASE, W/PETE
Jan 69, **GB** sessions
REVOLT, SOUND
I'm The Greatest
70, Tittenhurst? John, early

ARCH2, LOST2
71, studio demo
ARCH2, LOST2
10 Jul 73? John at **RINGO** sessions (various takes)
LIMIT, MIEUX, ONCE, SHOTS, SOUND
78, *Ringo* tv special
OGNIR
I'm Walkin'
65, "John and Paul" (no B. involvement)
LALB, MARY, NASSAU, TOP
I've Got A Feeling
Jan 69, **GB** sessions (various)
BLACK, BWORD, CIRCUIT, CLASS3, COMMON, GBSESS, GOLDM, GRAVE, HIHO, IHAD, JOURN, LETEND, MIXED, NOT4, PLAY, SING, SOUND, VIRGIN, Y'ORITE
24 Jan 69, Apple (from **GET BACK**)
GBCD, GETB, HEAD, HOMOG, JOURN, LETBE, RAREST6, REN2, TORON
30 Jan 69, Apple rooftop (cv & from *Let It Be*)
PLAY, SPLHCB
I've Got My Blue Fingers
Jan 69, **GB** sessions
COMMON, GRAVE, IHAD, JOURN
I've Gotta Be Me
8 Dec 84, *SNL*, Ringo & "Sammy"
RIZZ
I've Had Enough
25 Nov 79, Wings, Liverpool
TOKYO
7 Dec 79, Wings, Wembley
WEMB
29 Dec 79, Wings, Hammersmith
KAMP
I've Just Seen A Face
13 Nov 75, Wings, Melbourne
FLY, 9MM, ONEH
76 tour, Wings, unknown
4SIDES
15 Jun 76, Wings, Largo
GEAR
23 Jun 76, Wings, L.A. Forum
LASER, WINGS
If I Fell
16 Jul 64, BBC
BEEB11
session for BBC 3 Aug 64
KNIGHT, PARL
3 Aug 64, BBC
BEEB11
22 Aug 64, Vancouver
RARER, VANC
23 Aug 64, Hollywood Bowl
8ARMS, ONLY, PREY, RAREST2, ROMA, SINGLES

13 Jan 72, *David Frost*
JOSHUA, TELE
18 Aug 72, One-To-One rehearsals
1AND1, WILLOW
30 Aug 72, MSG, evening
TEDDY

J

Jambalaya
Jan 69, **GB** sessions
JOURN, MAGTR
Jazz Piano Song
Jan 69, **GB** sessions (*Let It Be*)
BWORD, CIRCUIT, HEARD, HOT,
JOURN, PLAY, 21, VIRGIN
Jealous Guy
Jul 71, alternate take
LOST5
Jenny Jenny
Jan 69, **GB** sessions
RUSSIA
12 Dec 69, Copenhagen; D&B
w/George
FALCON
Jerusalaim
Mar 69, John, Amsterdam Hilton
MOON, VIENNA
Jesse's Dream
Oct-Nov 67, from *MMT* soundtrack
TRAGIC
Jet
Sep 73, promo 45 edit?
ORIENT
Fall 75, *One Hand Clapping* sessions
ONEH, WHISP, WHY
13 Nov 75, Wings, Melbourne
FLY, 9MM
9 May 76, Wings, Toronto
MAPLE
15 May 76, Wings, Largo
FEATHER
19 May 76, Wings, Atlanta
ATLAN
16 Jun 76, Wings, San Diego
ORIENT
21 Jun 76, Wings, L.A. Forum
FORUM
23 Jun 76, Wings, L.A. Forum
WINGS
John Henry
70s, John, Dakota
ARCH1, LOST1
**JOHN LENNON ON RONNIE
HAWKINS** (promo 45) — see WALK
John Sinclair
10 Dec 71, Ann Arbor
ARCH4, LIFT, LOST4, 1TO1
13 Jan 72, John, *David Frost*
JOSHUA, TELE
Johnny B. Goode

15 Feb 64, BBC
BEAT, BEAUT, BEEB, BEEB9, FCK
Jan 69, **GB** sessions
GRAVE, JOURN, SING
16 Feb 72, John, *Mike Douglas*
JOSHUA, LOOK, TEDDY, TELE,
WORK
15 Mar 86, George, *Heartbeat 86*
NIGHT, OBLA45, UTOPIA
Josei Joi Banzai
73, Yoko (cv, from Japanese 45)
THIS
Josei Joi Banzai (Part 2)
73, Yoko (cv, from Japanese 45)
THIS
Julia
late-May 68, Kinfauns, acoustic demo
LOST3, OFF
Junior's Farm
Fall 75, *One Hand Clapping* sessions
CLASS3, ONEH
4 Nov 75, Wings, Adelaide
CONFI, DOLL'S
5 Nov 75, Wings, Adelaide
CLASS2, DOLL'S
Just A Dream
77 (cv, from the 45)
OGNIR
Just Because
Oct-Dec 73, **R&R** sessions
SHOULD, WINSTON
Just Fun
Jan 69, **GB** sessions
BLACK, BWORD, CIRCUIT, GREAT,
HOT, JOURN, PLAY, SPLHCB,
WATCH, WHEN, Y'ORITE

K

Kansas City
26 Jan 69, Apple
CIRCUIT, FILE1, HOT, LETEND,
PLAY, SING
Kansas City/Hey-Hey-Hey-Hey!
Dec 62, Star-Club, Hamburg (cv)
B4TIME, STARS
6 Aug 63, BBC
BEEB4, STUDIO, STUD1, YOUNG
18 May 64, BBC
BEEB10
session for BBC 3 Aug 64
PARL, RARER
3 Aug 64, BBC
BEEB11
3 Oct 64, Granville Theatre (*Shindig*)
CONQ, RARE
27 Nov 64, *Ready Steady Go!* (lip-
synch)
RSG!
26 Dec 64, BBC

AUCTION, BEEB, DEC63, 1964,
PETE, SILVER, WLOVE
Keep Right On To The End Of The Road
Summer 71, John, from *Oz* flexi
LOST1
Keep Under Cover
Paul, home demo, circa Fall 80
TUG, WAR
Keep Your Hands Off My Baby
26 Jan 63, BBC
BEAUT, CASTS, MEET, PLEASE,
SHOTS, WOND, W/PETE
Kenny Everett interview
5-6 Jun 68, EMI; from acetate?
GOLDEN
KFWBeatles
Jun 64
GOLDEN, GREAT, WHEN, WITHER
The King Of Fuh
Brute Force, from Apple 45
MAIL, NIGHT
Komm, Gib Mir Deine Hand
17 Oct 63, EMI & 29 Jan 64 Paris; edit
of takes 5 & 7 (cv)
KOMM
The KYA 1969 Peace Talk
29 May 69, from the 45
TWICE

L

L.S. Bumblebee
66, Cook & Moore; no B. involvement
BWORD, SUPER1
L.S. BUMBLEBEE (LP) — see BWORD
Lady Jane
Jan 69, **GB** sessions
JOURN
Lady Madonna
3 Feb 68, EMI; take 3 (w/overdubs)
URT56
3/6 Feb 68, EMI; take 4?
DIGIT, EXTEN, INAB, JULIAN,
LIVEAT, OFF
3/6 Feb 68, EMI; take 5 (cv)
JUDY, SPLHCB
Jan 69, **GB** sessions
RUSSIA
9 May 76, Wings, Toronto
MAPLE
15 May 76, Wings, Largo
FEATHER
25 May 76, Wings, MSG
CONFI
21 Jun 76, Wings, L.A. Forum
FORUM
23 Jun 76, Wings, L.A. Forum
ZOO, WINGS
Lady Marmalade
Mar 75 interview, NYC, John

CASTS, 4SIDES, GUITAR, ONCE,
SHOTS, WORK
Lalena (Donovan)
Nov 68-Jan 69, **PCARD** sessions
NO3, SUN
The Land Of Gisch (Donovan)
Nov 68-Jan 69, **PCARD** sessions
NO3, SUN
LAST LIVE SHOW (LP) — see ONLY
Lawdy Miss Clawdy
26 Jan 69, Apple
CIRCUIT, HOT, LETEND, PLAY,
SING
Lay His Head
Oct 79-Oct 80, original mix
BYGEO, BOTH, ENGL, ONOT
87 remix for **SBGH**
UTOPIA
Leaning On A Lamp Post
unknown, John
ARCH2, LOST2
Leave My Kitten Alone
14 Aug 64, EMI; take 4 (false start)
FILE1, NOT4
14 Aug 64, EMI; take 5
FILE1, INAB, LIVEAT, NOT4, SESS,
SESSCD, ULTRA2
Lend Me Your Comb
Dec 62, Star-Club, Hamburg (cv)
B4TIME, REICH, STARS
16 Jul 63, BBC
BBC, BEEB, BEEB3, BEEBCD,
BROAD, DEMO, LINING, PLEASE
Let 'Em In
15 May 76, Wings, Largo
GEAR
14 Jun 76, Wings, San Francisco
ZOO
21 Jun 76, Wings, L.A. Forum
FORUM
23 Jun 76, Wings, L.A. Forum
WINGS
Let It Be
Jan 69, **GB** sessions (various)
ALMO, BACK, BLACK, BYEBYE,
COMMON, FS2S, GBSESS, GRAVE,
HIHO, JOURN, LETEND, POWER,
RAREST1, SOUND, TORON, WOND,
Y'ORITE
31 Jan 69, Apple (finished take from *Let
It Be*)
EXTEN, HOT, OBLADI, PLAY, NOTG,
VIRGIN
31 Jan, Apple & 30 Apr 69, EMI; take 27
(from **GET BACK**, basic cv)
GBCD, GETB, JOURN, LETBE,
MIXED, RAREST6, REN2
31 Jan 69, Apple & 30 Apr 69 & 4 Jan
70, EMI; take 30 (cv, from 45, stereo)
HEAD, HOMOG, SPLHCB

31 Jan 69, Apple & 30 Apr 69 & 4 Jan
70, EMI; take 30 (cv, mono Japanese 45
mix)
  CASUAL
25 Nov 79, Wings, Liverpool
  TOKYO
7 Dec 79, Wings, Wembley
  WEMB
29 Dec 79, Wings, Hammersmith
  KAMP
Let It Be Me
10 Feb 88, George, *Rockline*
  UTOPIA
Let It Down
Jan 69, **GB** sessions
  REVOLT, SOUND
Let Me Roll It
Fall 75, *One Hand Clapping* sessions
  ONEH
13 Nov 75, Wings, Melbourne
  FLY, 9MM
9 May 76, Wings, Toronto
  MAPLE
19 May 76, Wings, Atlanta
  ATLAN
15 May 76, Wings, Largo
  FEATHER
21 Jun 76, Wings L.A. Forum
  FORUM
23 Jun 76, Wings L.A. Forum
  WINGS
Let's Go On Flying
21-22 Nov 68, hospital? (*Aspen* flexi)
  LIFE, THIS
Let's Love
Jun 74, Peggy Lee (cv)
  GREAT
Let's Twist Again
Jan 74, Bowie w/John?
  CLASS2
Letting Go
1 Nov 75, Wings, Perth
  FLY
13 Nov 75, Wings, Melbourne
  FLY
3 May 76, Wings, Ft. Worth
  FORTW
15 May 76, Wings, Largo
  9MM
21 Jun 76, Wings L.A. Forum
  FORUM
23 Jun 76, Wings, L.A. Forum
  WINGS
unknown, Paul, home rehearsal
  HOME
Life Begins At Forty
Fall 80, Dakota
  ARCH1, LOST1
Life Itself
the usual version

  ENGL
Like Dreamers Do
1 Jan 62, Decca audition
  DECCA, REINTRO
Listen To This Radio Spot
  LIFT, TEDDY
Listen To What The Man Said
13 Nov 75, Wings, Melbourne
  FLY, 9MM
15 May 76, Wings, Largo
  GEAR
21 Jun 76, Wings L.A. Forum
  FORUM
23 Jun 76, Wings, L.A. Forum
  WINGS
Listen, The Snow Is Falling
28/29 Oct 71 (cv)
  THIS
Little Queenie
Dec 62, Star-Club, Hamburg (cv)
  REICH, STARS
Jan 69, **GB** sessions
  COMMON, GRAVE, JOURN,
  LETEND
Little Woman Love
Oct 72 (cv)
  1970S
Fall 75, *One Hand Clapping* sessions
  ONEH, WHISP, WHY
Little Woman Love/C Moon
73, *James Paul McCartney*
  LIFT, MYLO
19 May 73, Wings, Leeds
  LEEDS
10 Jul 73, Wings, Newcastle
  NEWCAS
23 Jul 73, Wings, Edinburgh
  SCOT
Fall 75, *One Hand Clapping* sessions
  ONEH, WHISP, WHY
5 Nov 75, Wings, Adelaide
  DOLL'S
Little Yellow Pills
Jan 69, **GB** sessions
  SOUND
Live And Let Die
73, *James Paul McCartney*
  MYLO
19 May 73, Wings, Leeds
  LEEDS
10 Jul 73, Wings, Newcastle
  NEWCAS
Fall 75, *One Hand Clapping* sessions
  ONEH, WHY
9 May 76, Wings, Toronto
  MAPLE
15 May 76, Wings, Largo
  GEAR
19 May 76, Wings, Atlanta
  ATLAN

21 Jun 76, Wings, L.A. Forum
FORUM, ZOO
23 Jun 76, Wings, L.A. Forum
LASER, WINGS
LIVE AT THE PARIS OLYMPIA (LP)
— see COMPL
LIVE FROM GERMANY (LP)
— see NASSAU
LIVE FROM LIVERPOOL (45)
— see TOKYO
**LIVE FROM THE SAM HOUSTON
COLOSSEUM** (LP)
— see TEXAN
LIVE IN ANY TOWN (LP)
— see ROMA
LIVERPOOL LIVE (LP)
— see TOKYO
Living In A Pet Shop
77, from **SCOUSE THE MOUSE**
(cv)
LIFT, RICHIE, SCOUSE
LONDON (LP)
— see SUNDAY
London Bridge Is Falling Down
Jan 69, **GB** sessions
BYEBYE
Lonely Old People
unknown, Paul, home rehearsal
HOME
Lonesome Tears In My Eyes
23 Jul 63, BBC
BBC, BEEB, BEEB4, DEMO, DON'T,
PETE, PLEASE, SILVER, WLOVE,
YELL
The Long And Winding Road
Jan 69, **GB** sessions (various)
BWORD, CIRCUIT, CLASS3, HEARD,
JOURN, LETEND, PLAY
(blues) Jan 69, **GB** sessions
REVOLT, SOUND
31 Jan 69, Apple; finished, unknown
take (from *Let It Be*)
HOT, PLAY
31 Jan 69, Apple; take 19 (from **GET
BACK**)
GBCD, GETB, HEAD, HOMOG,
JOURN, LETBE, MIXED, RAREST6,
REN2, SPLHCB
31 Jan 69, Apple & 1 Apr 70, EMI; take
18 (cv; take 19 overdubbed for **LET IT
BE**)
ELVIS
1 Nov 75, Wings, Perth
FLY
9 May 76, Wings, Toronto
MAPL
15 May 76, Wings, Largo
FEATHER
19 May 76, Wings, Atlanta
ATLAN

21 Jun 76, Wings L.A. Forum
FORUM
23 Jun 76, Wings, L.A. Forum
WINGS, ZOO
The Long Rap
Dec 69, from 45, John for Ronnie
Hawkins
WALK
Long Tall Sally
Dec 62, Star-Club, Hamburg (cv)
SPLHCB, STARS
13 May 63, BBC
BEEB2, MONKEY
25 May 63, BBC
BEEB1, BEEBCD, MONKEY
13 Aug 63, BBC
AUCTION, BEEB5, STUDIO, STUD1
11 Feb 64, Washington
FIRST
1 Mar 64, EMI; take 1 (cv)
HEARD (tv lip-synch?), SPLHCB
4 Apr 64, BBC
BEEB10, BROAD
19 Apr 64, IBC (for *ATB*)
NOTG
6 May 64, *Around The Beatles*
CAVERN, EMIOUT, RSG!, SOME
12 Jun 64, Adelaide
DOLL'S, FANS
16 Jun 64, Melbourne
CANDLE, FANS, HOTW, TOUR
17 Jun 64, Melbourne
MELB
16 Jul 64, BBC
BEEB, BEEB11, LALB, LOOKING,
LONG, MARY, NASSAU, POPS,
ROAD, TOP
session for BBC 3 Aug 64
PARL
3 Aug 64, BBC
BEEB11
22 Aug 64, Vancouver
VANC
23 Aug 64, Hollywood Bowl
8ARMS, ONLY, RAREST2, ROMA
2 Sep 64, Philadelphia?
FLATS
11 Apr 65, NME Concert
DIGIT
20 Jun 65, Paris, afternoon
HOTW
20 Jun 65, Paris, evening
HOTW
27 Jun 65, Rome
ARRIV, ROMA
18 Aug 66, Boston (in background)
SPLHCB
29 Aug 66, Candlestick Park
CANDLE
Jan 69, **GB** sessions (recitation)

JOURN
12 Dec 69, Copenhagen; D&B
w/George
FALCON
22 Jul 72, Wings, Montreux
SWITZ
22 Aug 72, Wings, Antwerp
ANTW
18 Mar 73, Borehamwood, *JPMc*
MYLO
10 Jul 73, Wings, Newcastle
CONFI, NEWCAS
Look Out!
Jan 69, **GB** sessions
JOURN, Y'ORITE
Lord, Take This Makeup Off Me
date unknown, John, Dakota
ARCH3, LOST4
Love
82 remix (cv)
ARCH4, ONCE, YIN
Love Awake
79, alternate version
SUIT
A Love For You
outtake, unknown
COLD
Love Is
unknown, Paul, home rehearsal
HOME
Love Is A Swingin' Thing
Jan 69, **GB** sessions
GOLDM, JOURN
Love Is Like A Macaroni (improv.)
Jan 69, **GB** sessions
GOLDM, JOURN, TRAX3
Love Me Do
4 Sep 62, EMI; unknown take (cv, with
Ringo))
ITEMS, LIVEAB, SPLHCB
11 Sep 62, EMI; take 10 (cv, with Andy
White)
SPLHCB
11 Jun 63, BBC
BEEB2, MONKEY
23 Jul 63, BBC
8ARMS, LBEEB, RAREST2, RECO,
STUDIO, STUD1
10 Sep 63, BBC
BEEB6, PLEASE
20 Oct 63, BBC
BEEB7
Fall 84, Paul, *Arena* special
PLEASE, THAT'LL, TWICE
Love Of The Loved
1 Jan 62, Decca audition
DECCA, HOWDO, REINTRO,
SESSCD, SPLHCB, THEIR, 21,
2MUCH
1 Jan 62, Decca audition (edit)

DEMO
Love You To
11/13 Apr 66, EMI; take 7 (cv)
SPLHCB
Low-down Blues Machine
Jan 69, **GB** sessions (improv?)
RUSSIA
Lucille
17 Sep 63, BBC
BEEB6, DEMO, FHILLS, KNIGHT,
SOME, STUD2, THEIR
5 Oct 63, BBC
BEEB7, HEARD, RECO
Jan 69, **GB** sessions
COMMON, JOURN, TRAX3
early 72, Wings first rehearsal, from
Wings Over The World
1970S
11 Feb 72, Wings, Hull (twice)
BELGIUM, SPRING
unknown Wings rehearsal (video)
GREAT, SUN
29 Dec 79, Wings, Hammersmith
KAMP
14 Dec 84, Sydney; Deep Purple
w/George
NIGHT
The Luck Of The Irish
12 Nov 71, takes1 & 2
ARCH2, LOST2
10 Dec 71, Ann Arbor
ARCH4, LIFT, LOST4, 1TO1
13 Jan 72, *David Frost*
BOTH, TELE
Lucy In The Sky With Diamonds
1/2 Mar 67, EMI; take 8 (cv)
SPLHCB
28 Nov 74, MSG; John w/Elton John
GUITAR, WORK
Lunchbox-Odd Sox
Sep 75, Wings (basic take for cv)
CUTS
unknown, Paul home rehearsals
HOME

M

MACH SHAU (LP) — see REICH
Madman (various versions)
Jan 69, **GB** sessions
ALMO, CASTS, COMMON, GRAVE,
IHAD, JOURN, LETEND, SHOTS,
ROPE, WATCH
Maggie Mae
24 Jan 69, Apple
BACK, GBCD, GETB, GRAVE,
JOURN, LETBE, MAGTR, MIXED,
RAREST6, WOND
Aug 80, **DF** sessions
LOST6
Magical Mystery Tour

25/26/27 Apr & 3 May 67, EMI; take 9
(mono remix 7) from the *MMT*
soundtrack
   DIGIT, 1967, RARER, TRAGIC
25/26/27 Apr & 3 May & 7 Nov 67; take
9 (cv)
   SPLHCB
Magneto And Titanium Man
   15 May 76, Wings, Largo
      GEAR
   16 Jun 76, Wings, San Diego
      ORIENT
   21 Jun 76, Wings, L.A. Forum
      ZOO
   23 Jun 76, Wings, L.A. Forum
      LASER, WINGS
Mailman, Bring Me No More Blues
   29 Jan 69, **GB** sessions
      FILE2, MAIL, MIXED, REVOLT,
      SESS, SOUND, YEARS
Maisie
   79, Juber & Wings (cv, from Juber's LP)
      SUIT
Make Love, Not War
   70, John (early **Mind Games**)
      ARCH2, LOST2
Mama You Been On My Mind
   Jan 69, **GB** sessions
      BLACK, HIHO, JOURN, LETEND,
      MAGTR, RAREST1
A Man Like Me
   78, from the *Ringo* tv special
      4SIDES, OGNIR
Mannish Boy
   date unknown, John, Dakota
      ARCH3, LOST4
Mary Had A Little Lamb
   22 Jul 72, Wings, Montreux
      SWITZ
   16 Aug 72, Wings, Hanover
      ORIENT
   22 Aug 72, Wings, Antwerp
      ANTW
   73, *JPMc*
      LIFT, ORIENT
MARY JANE (LP) — see BUG
Matchbox
   Spring 60, Quarry Men
      STU
   Dec 62, Star Club, Hamburg (cv)
      REICH, STARS
   30 Jul 63, BBC
      AUCTION, BEEB, BEEB4, BROAD
   18 May 64, BBC
      BEEB10
   Oct 70, **POB** sessions
      LOST6
   21 Nov 85, Ringo, *Blue Suede Shoes*
      LOOK, RIZZ
Maxwell's Silver Hammer

Jan 69, **GB** sessions (various)
   BWORD, CIRCUIT, HEARD, HOT,
   JOURN, LINING, PLAY, POWER,
   RARER, SUPER1, VIRGIN, WHISP,
   WOND, Y'ORITE
9/10/11 Jul 69, EMI; take 21
   ARW1, B-ROAD, EXTEN, LOOKING,
   NO3, RETURN, ROAD, TALKS
Maya Love
   2 Nov 74, Vancouver
      LIVAN
   15 Dec 74, Nassau
      LAST
Maybe Baby
   Jan 69, **GB** sessions
      REVOLT, SOUND
   Summer 72, San Francsico; John,
   acoustic
      4SIDES, LIFT, TEDDY
Maybe I'm Amazed
   Jan 69, **GB** sessions
      GRAVE, JOURN, Y'ORITE
   Nov 69-Mar 70 (cv)
      SPLHCB
   22 Jul 72, Wings, Montreux
      SWITZ
   22 Aug 72, Wings, Antwerp
      ANTW
   73, *James Paul McCartney*
      MYLO
   19 May 73, Wings, Leeds
      LEEDS
   10 Jul 73, Wings, Newcastle
      NEWCAS
   23 Jul 73, Wings, Edinburgh
      SCOT
   Fall 75, *One Hand Clapping* sessions
      ONEH, WHISP, WHY
   13 Nov 75, Wings, Melbourne
      FLY, 9MM
   9 May 76, Wings, Toronto
      MAPLE
   15 May 76, Wings, Largo
      FEATHER
   21 Jun 76, Wings L.A. Forum
      FORUM
   23 Jun 76, Wings, L.A. Forum
      WINGS
   Oct 77, Melvin Bragg interview
      SUN
   25 Nov 79, Wings, Liverpool
      TOKYO
   7 Dec 79, Wings, Wembley
      WEMB
   29 Dec 79, Hammersmith
      KAMP
Mean Mister Mustard
   Jan 69, **GB** sessions (various)

ARW1, BLACK, B-ROAD, JOURN,
RETURN, ROPE, TALKS, WATCH,
Y'ORITE
Jul 69, EMI? (short, bouncy version;
possibly Kenny Everett with no Beatles
involvement)
   CAVERN, THOSE
24/25/29 Jul 69, EMI; take 35 (cv)
   SPLHCB
Medicine Jar
  9 May 76, Wings, Toronto
   MAPLE
 15 May 76, Wings, Largo
   FEATHER
 21 Jun 76, Wings L.A. Forum
   FORUM
 23 Jun 76, Wings, L.A. Forum
   WINGS
Medley (McCartney-Lennon)
 19 Apr 64, IBC (for *Around The Beatles*)
   FCK, 1964, NOT4, NOTG, SPLHCB
  6 May 64, *Around The Beatles*
   CAVERN, EMIOUT, RECO, RSG!
Melvin Bragg
 Oct 77, Paul, Melvin Bragg interview
   GREAT, SUN
Memphis
  1 Jan 62, Decca audition
   DECCA, WHEN
  8 Mar 62, BBC
   LBEEB, MEET, WOND, W/PETE
 18 Jun 63, BBC
   BEEB3, BEEBCD
 29 Jun 63, BBC
   BEEB2, MONKEY, WITHER
 30 Jul 63, BBC
   BEEB, BEEB4, BROAD
  5 Oct 63, BBC
   BEAT, BEEB7, WOND, YOUNG
 16 Feb 72, John, *Mike Douglas*
   LOOK, TELE, WORK
The Mess
 11 Feb 72, Wings, Hull (twice)
   BELGIUM, SPRING
 22 Jul 72, Wings, Montreux
   SWITZ
 16 Aug 72, Wings, Hanover
   ORIENT
 21 Aug 72, The Hague (audience)
   QUEEN
 21 Aug 72, The Hague (cv)
   1970S
 22 Aug 72, Wings, Antwerp
   ANTW
 18 Mar 73, Borehamwood, for *JPMc*
   LIFT, MYLO
 19 May 73, Wings, Leeds
   LEEDS
 10 Jul 73, Wings, Newcastle
   NEWCAS

23 Aug 73, Wings, Edinburgh
   SCOT
Michelle
 73, *James Paul McCartney* (outtake)
   LIFT, RABBI, 20X4
 73, *James Paul McCartney*
   LIFT, MYLO, RABBI
 Oct 77, Melvin Bragg interview
   SUN
Midnight Special
 Jan 69, **GB** sessions
   JOURN, MAGTR, REVOLT, TRAX3
Midsummer New York
 Feb 72, *Mike Douglas Show*
   TELE, THIS
Milk Cow Blues
 Jan 69, **GB** sessions
   COMMON, GRAVE, JOURN
Million Miles
 unknown, Paul, home rehearsal
   HOME
Mind Games
 Sep 73, alternate take
   LOST7
Mine For Me
 25 Apr 75? *Midnight Special*; Rod
 Stewart w/ Paul & Linda (recorded Nov
 74, Kilburn State Theatre, London?)
   ORIENT
Mirror Mirror
 Dakota, date unknown; piano take 1
   LOST6
 Dakota, date unknown; piano take 5
   LOST6
Misery
 11 Feb 63, EMI; take 1
   ULTRA2
 11 Feb 63, EMI; take 2 (false start)
   URT34
 11 Feb 63, EMI; take 3 (false start)
   URT34
 11 Feb 63, EMI; take 4 (false start)
   URT34
 11 Feb 63, EMI; take 5 (false start)
   URT34
 11 Feb 63, EMI; take 6
   URT34
 11/20 Feb 63, EMI; take 16 (cv, mono)
   8ARMS, 1964
 11/20 Feb 63, EMI; take 16 (cv, true
 stereo)
   HOWDO
 16 Mar 63, BBC
   MEET, W/PETE
  4 Jun 63, BBC
   COMPL, LBEEB, RECO, STONE,
   STUDIO, STUD1
 17 Sep 63, BBC
   BEEB6, PLEASE
Miss Ann

Jan 69, **GB** sessions
  CIRCUIT, HOT, LETEND, PLAY,
  SING
Miss O'Dell
  Jan-Apr 73 (cv)
  BYGEO, 1970S, UTOPIA
Momma's Little Girl
  72? brief version
  4SIDES
  72, outtake
  CUTS
  72, outtake (remix)
  COLD
  73, *James Paul McCartney* outtake
  LIFT, 20X4
Money (That's What I Want)
  1 Jan 62, Decca audition
  DECCA, ELVIS, SPLHCB
  25 May 63, BBC
  BEEB1, BEEBCD, MONKEY
  18 Jun 63, BBC
  BEEB3, WITHER
  29 Jun 63, BBC
  LBEEB, STUD1
  18 Jul 63, EMI; edit of takes 6 & 7 (cv,
  "true mono")
  CASUAL, HOWDO, 1234
  3 Sep 63, BBC
  LBEEB, STUDIO, STUD2
  13 Oct 63, London Palladium
  ABC, SUNDAY
  24 Oct 63, Stockholm
  FHILLS, PETE, SILVER, SPLHCB,
  STAGE, STOCK
  7 Dec 63, Empire Theatre, Liverpool
  DEC63, TOUR, YOUNG
  26 Dec 63, BBC
  BEEB8
  15 Feb 64, BBC
  BEEB9
  Jan 69, **GB** sessions (instr.)
  JOURN, MAGTR, TRAX3
Moovin' And Groovin'
  Spring 60, Quarry Men
  MAY60, STU
Mother
  18 Aug 72, One-To-One rehearsals
  1AND2, WILLOW
  30 Aug 72, MSG, evening
  HARD, JOHSUA, 1TO1, PLOP,
  SHOTS, TEDDY, WORK
A Mouse Like Me
  77, from **SCOUSE THE MOUSE**
  (cv)
  LIFT, SCOUSE, RICHIE
Move It
  Jan 69, **GB** sessions
  BLACK, HIHO, JOURN, MAGTR,
  RAREST1, REVOLT, 21
Move On Fast

18 Aug 72, One-To-One rehearsals
  1AND1
Move Over Ms. L
  Jul 74, **W&B** sessions
  PREC, WALLS, WINSTON
  Oct 74 (cv, from 45)
  1970S, LIMIT, PLOP
"Movie Medley"
  82? source unknown
  1234
Movin' On Up
  8 Dec 84, *SNL*, Ringo & "Sammy"
  RIZZ
Moving Along The River Rhine
  Jan 69, **GB** sessions (improv?)
  SOUND, REVOLT
Mr. H. Atom
  Summer 79, **McII** home sessions
  RAVING
Mr. Moonlight
  Dec 62, Star Club, Hamburg (cv)
  B4TIME, STARS
Mr. Tambourine Man
  10 Feb 88, George, *Rockline*
  UTOPIA
Mr. Wind (Donovan)
  Nov 68-Jan 69, **PCARD** sessions?
  NO3, SUN
Mucho Mungo
  Mar-May 74, **PUSSYCATS** sessions
  ARCH1, MOON, ONCE, YIN
  late 75-early76, John, Dakota
  LOST1
Mull Of Kintyre
  Oct, 77, Melvin Bragg interview
  GREAT, SUN
  unknown, Paul, home rehearsal
  HOME
  25 Nov 79, Wings, Liverpool
  TOKYO
  7 Dec 79, Wings, Wembley
  WEMB
  29 Dec 79, Wings, Hammersmith
  KAMP
Mumbo
  72, Wings tour, unknown
  ORIENT
  22 Jul 72, Wings, Montreux
  SWITZ
  22 Aug 72, Wings, Antwerp
  ANTW
My Baby Specializes
  12 Dec 69, Copenhagen; D&B
  w/George
  FALCON
My Bonnie
  May 61, Hamburg (cv, English intro)
  ELVIS, ROPE
  May 61, Hamburg (cv, German intro)
  REINTRO, ROPE

May 61, Hamburg (cv, no intro)
  DON'T, ROPE, SPLHCB
My Carnival
  12 Feb 75, New Orleans (for news)
    4SIDES, SNAPS, TOBE, 20X4
  12 Feb 75, New Orleans; unreleased mix
  #1
    CUTS
  12 Feb 75, New Orleans; unreleased mix
  #2
    COLD
My Life
  Dakota, piano demo, take 1
    LOST5
  Dakota, acoustic demo, take 3
    LOST5
My Love
  11 Feb 72, Wings, Hull
    BELGIUM, SPRING
  22 Jul 72, Wings, Montreux
    SWITZ
  22 Aug 72, Wings, Antwerp
    ANTW
  73, *James Paul McCartney*
    MYLO
  19 May 73, Wings, Leeds
    LEEDS
  10 Jul 73, Wings, Newcastle
    NEWCAS
  23 Jul 73, Wings, Edinburgh
    SCOT
  Fall 75, *One Hand Clapping* sessions
    NASH, ONEH, WHISP, WHY
  1 Nov 75, Wings, Perth
    FLY
  15 May 76, Wings, Largo
    GEAR
  14 Jun 76, Wings, San Francisco
    ZOO
  16 Jun 76, Wings, San Diego
    ORIENT
  23 Jun 76, Wings, L.A. Forum
    WINGS
My Old Man's A Dustman
  unknown, John
    ARCH2, LOST2
My Sweet Lord
  May-Aug 70, Trident/EMI (cv)
    SPLHCB
  2 Nov 74, Vancouver
    LIVAN
  26 Nov 74, Baton Rouge
    BATON
  30 Nov 74, Chicago
    CHIC
  15 Dec 74, Nassau
    LAST
Mystery Train
  Aug 80, **DF** sessions
    BEFORE, WINSTON

N

National Health Cow (poem)
  BBC Jun-Jul 65?
    2MUCH, 4SIDES, NOT4, SPLHCB
Negro In Reserve
  Jan 69, **GB** sessions
    FILE1, GOLDM, JOURN, REVOLT,
    TRAX3
The Neville Club (poem)
  10 Dec 63, Doncaster?
    LOST6
New Orleans
  Jan 69, **GB** sessions
    COMMON, GRAVE, IHAD, JOURN,
    LETEND
New York City
  18 Aug 72, One-To-One rehearsals
    1AND1, WILLOW
  30 Aug 72, MSG, evening
    TEDDY
News Of The Day (From Reuters)
  late Nov 78, John, Dakota
    ARCH3, LOST4
Night Out
  #1, Wings, studio outtake, unknown
    CUTS
  #2, Wings, studio outtake, unknown
    COLD
Night Train To Memphis
  21 Nov 75, *Blue Suede Shoes*
    LOOK, ONOT
1985
  Fall 75, *One Hand Clapping* sessions
    ONEH, ROUGH, WHY
No Bed For Beatle John
  21-22 Nov 68, hospital?
    LIFE
No No Song
  28 Apr 75, *Smothers Brothers*
    RICHIE
No Pakistanis—see **Get Back**
No Reply
  30 Sep 64, EMI; take 8 (cv)
    SPLHCB
No Values
  84, *Broad Street* soundtrack
    GREAT
No Words
  25 Nov 79, Wings, Liverpool
    TOKYO
  7 Dec 79, Wings, Wembley
    WEMB
  29 Dec 79, Wings, Hammersmith
    KAMP
**Nobody Loves You (When You're
Down And Out)**
  Jul 74, **W&B** sessions
    PREC, WALLS
Nonsense

May 85, Ringo, *Alice In Wonderland*
RIZZ

Norwegian Wood
12 Oct 65, EMI, take 1
INAB, LIVEAT, RABBI, URT56
21 Oct 65, EMI; take 4, w/2 false starts
ULTRA2
21 Oct 65, EMI; take 4 (cv)
SPLHCB
Jan 69, **GB** sessions (instrumental)
BLACK, JOURN, MAGTR

Not A Second Time
11 Sep 63, EMI; take 9 (cv)
SPLHCB

Not Fade Away
Jan 69, **GB** sessions
FILE1, OBLADI
John, Summer 71, St. Regis Hotel
LOST6

Not Guilty
8/9/12 Aug 68, EMI; take 102 (from tape)
URT56
8/9/12 Aug 68, EMI; take 102 (from acetate)
MAIL, NOTG, NOTH
8/9/12 Aug 68, EMI; take 102 (**SESSIONS** remix)
EXTEN, FILE2, MIXED, RED, SESS, SESSCD

Nothin' Shakin' (But The Leaves On The Trees)
Dec 62, Star Club, Hamburg (cv)
REICH, STARS
23 Jul 63, BBC
BBC, BEEB, BEEB4, DEMO, DON'T PETE, SILVER, YELL, WITHER, WLOVE

Nothing From Nothing (Preston)
2 Nov 74, Vancouver
LIVAN
15 Dec 74, Nassau
LAST

Now Hear This Song Of Mine
May 71, Paul, from **BRUNG TO YOU BY HAL SMITH**
DOLL'S, 1970S, TOBE

Nowhere Man
24 Jun 66, Munich, evening
BEAT, CRONE, 4EVER, MUNICH, SINGLES, STAGE
30 Jun 66, Tokyo
BUDO, 8ARMS, FIVE, HOTW, JAPAN64, POWER, RABBI, ROMA, TOKIO
2 Jul 66, Tokyo
JAPAN64, TOUR
29 Aug 66, Candlestick Park
CANDLE

O

O Kristelighed
70, Denmark; John & Yoko
BOTH, NIGHT

Ob-La-Di, Ob-La-Da
3/4/5 Jul 68, EMI; take 5; (Calypso version, from **SESSIONS** 45)
DIGIT, EXTEN, NIGHT, OBLA45, OBLADI, RED, YEARS
8/11/15 Jul 68, EMI; take 23 (cv, OOPSed)
NIGHT
Jan 69, **GB** sessions
CASTS, GOLDM, JOURN, SHOTS, TRAX3

Octopus's Garden
Jan 69, **GB** sessions (*Let It Be*)
BWORD, CIRCUIT, HEARD, HOT, JOURN, PLAY
26/29 Apr & 17 Jul 69, EMI; take 32
ARW1, B-ROAD, EXTEN, LOOKING, NO3, RETURN, ROAD, TALKS
78, from *Ringo* television special
OGNIR
8 Dec 84, *SNL*, Ringo & "Sammy"
RIZZ

Ode To A Koala Bear
81? (cv, from **Say Say Say** 12-inch)
NIGHT

Oh! Darling
27Jan 69, Apple?
B-ROAD, BWORD, CIRCUIT, CLASS3, HOT, PLAY, SOUND
20/26 Apr 69, EMI; take 26; alternate lead vocals
ARW1, EXTEN, LOOKING, NO3, RARER, RETURN, ROAD, TALKS, 20X4
17, 18 or 22 Jul 69, EMI; lead vocal only
B-ROAD, DIGIT, EXTEN, OBLADI

Oh My Love
72, The Wackers (cv, no B. involvement)
4SIDES, GUITAR, ONCE, RARER, WORK

Oh Woman Oh Why
Jan 71 (cv, from the 45)
MYLO
Jan 71, promo 45 mix? edited
1970S

Oi Gevalt
The Yeadles (cv, no B. involvement)
GOLDEN

Old Brown Shoe
16/18 Apr 69, EMI; take 4 (cv)
JUDY

Old Dirt Road
Jul 74, **W&B** sessions
PREC, WALLS

Old Siam Sir

late Jul 78, basic take
   DOLL'S
late Jul 78, alternate mix
   EGGS
25 Nov 79, Wings, Liverpool
   TOKYO
7 Dec 79, Wings, Wembley
   WEMB
29 Dec 79, Wings, Hammersmith
   KAMP

ON STAGE IN EUROPE (LP) — see
STAGE
Once Upon A Time
  Jan 69, **GB** sessions
   SOUND
The One After 909
  Spring 60, The Quarry Men (#1)
   MAY60, REINTRO, STU
  Spring 60, The Quarry Men (#2)
   STU
  Spring 62, rehearsal?
   NOT4, SPLHCB
  5 Mar 63, EMI; take 2
   ULTRA1
  5 Mar 63, EMI; unknown takes
   FILE1, INAB, LIVEAT, SESS,
   2MUCH, SESSCD, WITHER
  Jan 69, **GB** sessions (various)
   ALMO, BLACK, BWORD, CIRCUIT,
   COMMON, GBCD, GETB, GREAT,
   GOLDM, HOT, JOURN, LETBE,
   LETEND, MIXED, PLAY, RAREST6,
   ROUGH, RUSSIA, SOUND,
   SPLHCB, TRAX3, VIRGIN, WATCH
One And One Is Two
  64? from Dick James acetate
   URT34
One Hand Clapping
  Fall 75, *One Hand Clapping* sessions
   CONFI, DOLL'S, NASH, ONEH, WHY
One Of The Boys
  Dakota, acoustic take 2
   LOST7
Only A Northern Song
  13/14 Feb & 20 Apr 67, EMI;
  synchronous mix of takes 3 & 11 (cv,
  from 45)
   CASUAL, 1967
Only You
  Summer 74; John's demo w/Ringo
   CLASS3
Ooh! My Soul
  27 Aug 63, BBC
   BEAUT, BEEB5, 1234, WITHER,
   WOND, W/PETE
Open Your Box
  18 Aug 72, One-To-One rehearsals
   1AND2
Oriental Nightfish
  Sep 73, Lagos, Wings

   CUTS, 4SIDES, ORIENT, ROPE
**ORIGINAL AUDITION TAPE,
CIRCA 1962** (LP) — see DEMO
Outa-Space (Preston)
  2 Nov 74, Vancouver
   LIVAN
  15 Dec 74, Nassau
   LAST

P

P.S. I Love You
  11 Sep 62, EMI; take 10 (cn)
   8ARMS, SPLHCB
  25 Jun 63, BBC
   BEEB3, PLEASE
**Pantomime: Everywhere It's
Christmas** [aka **The Beatles Fourth
Christmas Record**]
  25 Nov 66, Dick James
   DON'T, LALB, NASSAU, RABBI,
   SPLHCB
Papa's Got A Brand New Bag
  Jan 69, **GB** sessions (very brief)
   JOURN, Y'ORITE
Paperback Writer
  13 Apr 66, EMI; take 1 (instr., false
  start)
   URT56
  13/14 Apr 66, EMI; take 2 (cv, basic
  take)
   SPLHCB, ULTRA1, URT56
  13/14 Apr 66, EMI; take 2 (cv, no echo)
   JULIAN, NOT4, NOTG, 1234,
   SESSCD
  13/14 Apr 66, EMI; take 2 (cv)
   LIVEAT
  30 Jun 66, Tokyo
   8ARMS, BUDO, FIVE, HOTW,
   JAPAN64, ROMA, SPLHCB, TOKIO
  2 Jul 66, Tokyo, afternoon
   BUDO, JAPAN64, SINGLES
  29 Aug 66, Candlestick Park
   CANDLE
PARIS AGAIN (LP) — see COMPL
PARIS '65 (LP) — see COMPL
Partners In Crime
  unknown, Paul, home rehearsal
   HOME
Passenger Pigeon
  77, from **SCOUSE THE MOUSE**
   SCOUSE
Paul McCartney's Theme For *The
Honorary Consul*
  83, John Williams
   NIGHT
Paul's Piano Theme
  Jan 69, **GB** sessions (*Let It Be*)
   CIRCUIT, HOT, PLAY
Peace Of Mind

unknown, possibly no Beatles
involvement
  JULIAN, SFF, 20X4
Peggy Sue
  Summer 71, NYC, from *Clock* ; John,
  acoustic
    ARCH1, LOST3
  Summer 72, San Francisco; John,
  acoustic
    4SIDES, LIFT, TEDDY
  Oct-Dec 73, **R&R** sessions
    MAYP, R'N'R, SHOULD
  Paul, 74, from unreleased *Backyard* film
    CONFI
Penina
  Jan 69, **GB** sessions
    BLACK, JOURN, MAGTR, RAREST1,
    REVOLT
Penny Lane EMI
  29/30 Dec 66 & 4/5/6/9/10/12/17 Jan
  67, EMI; take 9; trumpet ending (mono
  remix 9)
    ULTRA1
  29/30 Dec 66 & 4/5/6/9/10/12/17 Jan
  67, EMI; take 9; trumpet ending (mono
  remix 11, US promo 45)
    EMIOUT, EXTEN, 1967
  29/30 Dec 66 & 4/5/6/9/10/12/17 Jan
  67, EMI; take 9 (cv, mono or stereo)
    JUDY, LIVEAT, SPLHCB
  29/30 Dec 66 & 4/5/6/9/10/12/17 Jan
  67, EMI; take 9; trumpet ending (stereo,
  RARITIES remix)
    ITEMS
Penny O'Dell
  see Holding On To A Dream
People Say
  65, "John & Paul" no Beatles
involvement
    LALB, MARY, NASSAU, TOP
Photograph
  8 Dec 84, *SNL*, Ringo & "Sammy"
    RIZZ
Picasso's Last Words
  9 May 76, Wings, Toronto
    MAPLE
  15 May 76, Wings, Largo
    GEAR
  21 Jun 76, Wings, L.A. Forum
    ZOO
  23 Jun 76, Wings, L.A. Forum
    LASER, WINGS
A Picture Of You
  15 Jun 62, BBC
    LBEEB, MEET, 1234, WOND,
    W/PETE
(Take Another) Piece Of My Heart
  Jan 69, **GB** sessions
    RUSSIA, SOUND
Piggies

19/20 Sep & 10 Oct 68; take 12 (cv, UK
mono mix)
  RARER
Pipes Of Peace
  82, AIR? early version
    CLASS2
The Pirate Song
  26 Dec 75, *RWT Xmas Show*
    BYGEO, 4SIDES, NIGHT, ONOT,
    ROPE, SNAPS
Please Mr. Postman
  8 Mar 62, BBC
    LBEEB, MEET, W/PETE
  30 Jul 63, BBC
    BEEB, BEEB4, PETE, SILVER,
    WLOVE, YEARS
  29 Feb 64, *Big Night Out* (lip-synch)
    SUNDAY
  30 Mar 64, BBC
    BEEB9, ROUGH, WITHER
Please Mrs. Henry
  Jan 69, **GB** sessions
    RUSSIA
Please Please Me
  26 Nov 62, EMI; unknown take (cv,
  original mono mix, with "correct" lyrics)
    CASUAL, SPLHCB
  16 Mar 63, BBC
    MEET, W/PETE
  3 Jun 63, BBC
    BEEB1, MONKEY
  13 Aug 63, BBC
    BEEB5, COMPL, 8ARMS, PLEASE,
    RAREST2, STONE, STUDIO, STUD1
  20 Oct 63, BBC
    BEEB7
  11 Feb 64, Washington
    FIRST, SINGLES
  23 Feb 64, *Ed Sullivan*
    BLAST, CONQ
  23 Feb 64, *Ed Sullivan* (edit)
    REN1, THOSE
  Jan 69, **GB** sessions
    CASTS, GOLDM, IHAD, JOURN,
    SHOTS, SOUND
Polythene Pam
  Jan 69, **GB** sessions (various)
    ARW1, B-ROAD, GRAVE, JOURN,
    MAGTR, RETURN, SING, WOND
  25/28/30 Jul 69, EMI; take 40 (cv)
    SPLHCB
Poor Elijah
  12 Dec 69, Copenhagen; D&B
w/George
    FALCON
Pop Go The Beatles (theme)
  63, BBC (various)
    BEEB, BEEB2, BEEB3, BEEB4,
    BEEB5, BEEB6, BEEBCD, BROAD,
    REINTRO

POST CARD sessions — see
NO3, SUN, 20X4
Post Script — see **(Just Like) Starting
Over**
The Pound Is Sinking
Paul, home demo, circa Fall 80
TUG, WAR
Power To The People
Feb 71, alternate take
ARCH4, LOST4
Feb 71 (cv, rough mix)
ARCH1, LOST1
Feb 71 (cv)
1TO1
Press
85 (cv, 10-inch mix)
NIGHT
Pretty Little Head
85 (cv, 45 mix)
NIGHT
Proud Mum
mid-74, Paul, outtake
CUTS
Proud Mum (Reprise)
mid-74, Paul, outtake
CUTS

Q

Quarry Men rehearsals
MAY60, STU
THE QUARRYMEN AT HOME (LP)
— see STU
Queen Of The Hop
Jan 69, GB sessions
COMMON, GRAVE, JOURN
A Quick One While He's Away
Jan 69, **GB** sessions
LINING, WATCH

R

radio broadcasts:
(for BBC performances, see BBC index)
28 Oct 62
Hulme Hall, Port Sunlight (hospital radio)
REINTRO
30 Aug 63
Non Stop Pop
MEET
24 Oct 63
Pop '63, Sweden
BUG, CAVERN, GRAVE, HEARD,
PETE, STAGE, STOCK
16 Jan 64
ORTF; *Olympia Theatre,* Paris
HOTW
Jan-Feb 64
Weekend World (AFN)
REINTRO
Feb 64
WQAM, Beatles' farewell to Miami
RARER

8 Feb 64
Saturday Club
WITHER
18 Jun 65
John, BBC *Tonight*
LOST3
20 Jun 65
Palais des Sports, Paris, evening
BEAT, HOTW
24 Nov 67
John on *Where It's At*
TRAGIC
24 Dec 67
Jimi Hendrix on *Top Gear*
GUITAR, WORK
Summer 68
The Kenny Everett Show
TRAGIC
Jun 69
rehearsals, on French RTL
ROPE
2 Oct 69
John on BBC for **ABBEY ROAD**
TALKS
Summer 72, BBC
The Beatles Story
THOSE, TOBE, TWICK
20 Aug 72
Paul & Wings in Amsterdam
4SIDES, QUEEN
30 Aug 72
John at MSG, evening show
PLOP, ROAD, SNAPS, SHOTS,
TEDDY, THIS, WORK
28 Sep 74
John, WNEW-FM
LISTEN, RECO, SHOTS, TEDDY,
WHEN
Oct 74
John KHJ-AM
CASTS, SHOTS, WALK
2 Nov 75
Wings, Perth
FLY
Dec 75
George on *Earth News Radio*
LINING, REINTRO
21 Dec 75?
George on *Rock Around The World*
BYGEO, ONOT, UTOPIA
Jan 76
John on *Earth News Radio*
LIMIT
30 Jan 82
Paul on *Desert Island Discs*
GREAT
7 Mar 82,
The Beatles At The Beeb
BEEB
late 83

Ringo's Yellow Submarine
  CLASS3, JULIAN, MELLO
Oct 84
  *SPLHCB: A History Of The Beatles
  Years*
  NIGHT, NOT4, TRAGIC, WALK
Jan 88-Dec 89
  The Lost Lennon Tapes
  ARCH1, ARCH2, ARCH3, ARCH4,
  LOST1, LOST2, LOST3, LOST4,
  LOST5, LOST6, LOST7
10 Feb 88
  Rockline (George)
  UTOPIA
Radio One Jingle
  83, Paul
  BOTH, NIGHT
Radio Peace
  26 Mar 69, Amsterdam
  YIN
Radio Play
  21-22 Nov 68, hospital?
  LIFE
Rain EMI
  14/16 Apr 66, EMI; take 7 (alternate mix
  w/ no tambourine?
  NOTG
  14&16 Apr 66, EMI; take 7 (alternate
  mix w/ early bw drums?)
  NOTG
  14/16 Apr 66, EMI; take 7 (cv, mono or
  stereo)
  JUDY, LIVEAT, SPLHCB
  14&16 Apr 66, EMI; take 7 (cv, outfake,
  one channel of stereo mix)
  NOTG
Rainclouds
  early 81; (cv, b-side)
  SUIT
Raining In My Heart
  14 Sep 79, Paul, Hammersmith
  LOOK, RAVING
Rainy Day Woman #12 & 35
  Jan 69, **GB** sessions
  REVOLT, SOUND
Ramblin' Woman
  Jan 69, **GB** sessions
  BLACK, JOURN, LETEND, MAGTR,
  RAREST1, RUSSIA
Reach Out, I'll Be There
  Jan 69, **GB** sessions
  IHAD, JOURN
Ready Teddy
  Oct-Dec 73, **R&R** sessions
  MAYP, R'N'R, SHOULD
**THE REAL CASE HAS JUST
BEGUN** (LP) — see SOUND
Real Life
  Dakota, piano demo
  ARCH4, LOST5

Real Love
  80, John, acoustic demo
  ARCH1, LOST1
Reception
  mid-Sep 78, longer, alternate version
  EGGS
Red Hot
  Dec 62, Star-Club, Hamburg?
  LINING, REINTRO, WHEN
Red Sails In The Sunset
  Dec 62, Star- Club, Hamburg (cv)
  STARS
Remember Love
  69 (cv from UK 45)
  THIS
Reminiscing
  Dec 62, Star-Club, Hamburg?
  LINING, REINTRO
  Dec 62, Star-Club, Hamburg (cv)
  B4TIME, STARS
Revolution
  late-May 68, Kinfauns; acoustic demo
  ARCH3, LOST2, OFF
  10 Jul 68, EMI; take 13 (basic take for
  cv)
  LOST4
  10/11/12 Jul 68, EMI; take 16 (cv,
  mono)
  CASUAL
  10/11/12 Jul 68, EMI; take 16 (cv,
  stereo)
  SPLHCB
  4 Sep 68, Twickenham (*Top Of The
  Pops*, 19 Sep 68)
  HOWDO, JULIAN, LALB, NOTH,
  RECO, TOP, 2MUCH
Revolution 9
  10/11/20/21 Jun 68, EMI (cv)
  SPLHCB
Richard Corey
  9 May 76, Wings, Toronto
  MAPLE
  15 May 76, Wings, Largo
  GEAR
  23 Jun 76, Wings, L.A. Forum
  LASER, WINGS
Ringo/"Sammy" (Billy Crystal) medley
  SNL, 8 Dec 84
  RIZZ
Ringo's Theme (This Boy)
  64, George Martin Orchestra (cv)
  SPLHCB
Rip It Up
  Jan 69, **GB** sessions
  FILE1, PLAY, SING, VIRGIN
  Aug 80, **DF** sessions
  BEFORE, WINSTON
  Oct-Dec 73, **R&R** sessions
  MAYP, R'N'R, SHOULD
The Rishikesh Song

unknown, John, acoustic
  ARCH1, LOST1
Robbers Ball
  unknown, Paul outtake
    COLD
Rock And Roll Music
  26 Dec 64, BBC
    AUCTION, BEEB, DEC63, PETE,
    SILVER, WLOVE
  20 Jun 65, Paris, afternoon
    HOTW
  20 Jun 65, Paris, evening
    BEAT, HOTW
  27 Jun 65, Rome
    ARRIV, SINGLES
  24 Jun 66, Munich, evening
    CRONE, 4EVER, MUNICH, STAGE
  30 Jun 66, Tokyo
    BUDO, 8ARMS, FIVE, HOTW,
    JAPAN64, SPLHCB, TOKIO
  2 Jul 66, Tokyo, afternoon
    BUDO, JAPAN64, TOUR
  29 Aug 66, Candlestick Park
    CANDLE
  Jan 69, **GB** sessions
    JOURN, RUSSIA, Y'ORITE
Rock And Roll People
  73? electric composing demo
    ARCH4, LOST5
  4 Aug 73, take 5 (alternate)
    ARCH4, LOST6
  Oct 74, Johnny Winter (cv)
    MAIL
Rock And Roller
  73, Billy Lawrie (cv)
    DOLL'S
Rock Island Line
  Jan 69, **GB** sessions
    SING, REVOLT, WOND
  Summer 72, San Francisco; John,
  acoustic
    4SIDES, LIFT, TEDDY
  John, acoustic, unknown
    ARCH1, LOST1
  John, electric, mid-70s, Dakota
    ARCH4, LOST5
  16 Nov 76, George, *SNL* (rehearsal)
    ROUGH, UTOPIA
Rock Show
  13 Nov 75, Wings, Melbourne
    FLY, 9MM
  9 May 76, Wings, Toronto
    MAPLE
  15 May 76, Wings, Largo
    FEATHER
  19 May 76, Wings, Atlanta
    ATLAN
  21 Jun 76, Wings, L.A. Forum
    FORUM
  23 Jun 76, Wings, L.A .Forum

WINGS
Rocker (aka "Link Track" & "Instrumental
42")
  22 Jan 69, Apple (from **GET BACK**)
    GBCD, GETB, JOURN, LETBE,
    MIXED, RAREST6, SPLHCB, 2MUCH
Rockestra Theme
  78 Paul, home rehearsals
    HOME
  3 Oct 78, alternate mix, no backing
    EGGS
  29 Dec 79, Hammersmith
    KAMP
Roll It Over
  Jun 70, George & Clapton (cv)
    4SIDES, ROUGH
Roll Over Beethoven
  Dec 62, Star-Club, Hamburg (diff. from
  cv)
    REICH
  Dec 62, Star -Club, Hamburg (cv)
    B4TIME, STARS
  29 Jun 63, BBC
    BEEB2, MONKEY, STUDIO, STUD1
  3 Sep 63, BBC
    BEEB5
  24 Oct 63, Stockholm, *Pop 63*
    HEARD, PETE, SILVER, SPLHCB,
    STAGE, STOCK
  7 Dec 63, Empire Theatre, Liverpool
    DEC63, TOUR, YOUNG
  21 Dec 63, BBC
    BEEB8
  26 Dec 63, BBC
    BEEB8
  11 Feb 64, Washington
    FIRST
  15 Feb 64, BBC
    BEEB9
  30 Mar 64, BBC
    BEEB, BEEB9, BUG, WITHER,
    WLOVE
  19 Apr 64, IBC (for *Around The Beatles*)
    DIGIT, NOTG
  6 May 64 *Around The Beatles*
    EMIOUT, RSG!, SOME
  12 Jun 64, Adelaide
    DOLL'S, FANS, 1964
  17 Jun 64, Melbourne
    MELB
  22 Aug 64, Vancouver
    VANC
  23 Aug 64, Hollywood Bowl
    8ARMS, ONLY, RAREST2, ROMA,
    SPLHCB, TOP
  2 Sep 64, Philadelphia?
    FLATS, SINGLES
  Jan 69, **GB** sessions
    CASTS, IHAD, JOURN, SHOTS,
    Y'ORITE

18 Aug 72, One-To-One rehearsals
  1AND3, WILLOW
Rudolph The Red-Nosed Reindeer
21 Dec 63, BBC
  BEEB8
Rumble
Oct-Dec 73, **R&R** sessions
  MAYP, R'N'R, SHOULD
Run For Your Life
12 Oct 65, EMI; take 5 (cv, with studio chat)
  SPLHCB
Running Free
77, from **SCOUSE THE MOUSE** (cv)
  BOTH, LIFT, RICHIE, SCOUSE

S

S.O.S.
77, from **SCOUSE THE MOUSE** (cv)
  LIFT, SCOUSE, RICHIE
Sabre Dance
Jan 69, **GB** sessions
  RUSIA
Sakura
Feb 72, *Mike Douglas*
  TELE, THIS
Same Time Next Year
Jul 78, Paul, outtake
  CUTS
Jul 78, Paul, outtake (remix)
  COLD
Sat Singing
Oct 79-Oct 80, from original
SOMEWHERE IN ENGLAND
  BYGEO, ENGL, ONOT
87 remix, for **SBGH**
  UTOPIA
(I Can't Get No) Satisfaction
Jan 69, **GB** sessions (riffs)
  GOLDM, JOURN
Save The Last Dance For Me
Jan 69, **GB** sessions
  GBCD, GETB, JOURN, LETBE,
  MIXED, RAREST6, 2MUCH
Save The World
79-80 (cv)
  ENGL
late 84 remix, from **GREENPEACE** (cv)
  NIGHT, ONOT
Savoy Truffle
3/5, Trident & 11/14 Oct 68, EMI; take 1
(cv, UK mono mix)
  RECO
3/5, Trident & 11/14 Oct 68, EMI; take 1
(cv, outfake, one channel of stereo mix)
  ROPE

3/5, Trident & 11/14 Oct 68, EMI; take 1
(cv, outfake, singalong)
  1234, WHISP
Say Darling
11 Feb 72, Wings, Hull
  BELGIUM, SNAPS, SPRING
Say You Don't Mind
22 Jul 72, Wings, Montreux
  SWITZ
16 Aug 72, Wings, Hanover
  HANOV
22 Aug 62, Wings, Antwerp
  ANTW
23 Jul 73, Wings, Edinburgh
  SCOT
Scared
Jul 74, **W&B** sessions
  PREC, WALLS
School Days
Jan 69, **GB** sessions
  GOLDM, JOURN
SCOTLAND (LP) — see SCOT
SCOUSE THE MOUSE (LP) — see
LIFT, RICHIE, SCOUSE
Scouse The Mouse
77, from **SCOUSE THE MOUSE** (cv)
  LIFT, RICHIE, SCOUSE
Scouse's Dream
77, from **SCOUSE THE MOUSE** (cv)
  LIFT, RICHIE, SCOUSE
Scousey
77, from **SCOUSE THE MOUSE** (cv)
  SCOUSE
SCRAMBLED EGG (EP) — see
DOLL'S, SUIT
Searchin'
1 Jan 62, Decca audition
  DECCA, SPLHCB
30 Jan 82, *Desert Island Discs*, (Paul
sings along with the Coasters)
  GREAT
Seaside Woman
11 Feb 72, Wings, Hull
  SPRING
22 Jul 72, Wings, Montreux
  SWITZ
16 Aug 72, Wings, Hanover
  HANOV
17 Aug 72, Wings, Rotterdam
  QUEEN
22 Aug 72, Wings, Antwerp
  ANTW
19 May 73, Wings, Leeds
  LEEDS
10 Jul 73, Wings, Newcastle
  NEWCAS
23 Jul 73, Wings, Edinburgh

SCOT
SECOND TO NONE (LP) — see
8ARMS
Seems Like Old Times
Paul, home demo, circa Fall 80
TUG
Send Me Some Lovin'
Oct-Dec 73, **R&R** sessions
MAYP, R'N'R, SHOULD
Send Me The Heart
74, Wings, outtake
CUTS
74, Wings, Denny's album (cv, remix)
SUIT
Una Sensazionale Intervista
5-6 Jun 68, EMI; with Kenny Everett
BUG, CAVERN, MAIL, RECO, TOBE,
TRAGIC, TWICK, WHEN
Sentimental Journey
Nov-Dec 69, EMI? (cv)
SPLHCB
15 Mar 70, promo video soundtrack
RICHIE, SOLDIER
September In The Rain
1 Jan 62, Decca audition
DECCA, REINTRO, WHEN
September Song
John, late Nov 80, Dakota
ARCH3, LOST3
SERGEANT PEPPER Inner Groove
21 Apr 67, EMI; take 1 (cv)
ITEMS, 1967, TRAGIC
21 Apr 67, EMI; take 1 (cv, backward)
FORE
**Sergeant Pepper's Lonely Hearts
Club Band**
1/2 Feb & 3/6 Mar 67, EMI; take 10 (cv)
SPLHCB
**Sergeant Pepper's Lonely Hearts
Club Band (Reprise)**
1 Apr 67, EMI; take 9 (cv, mono mix)
TRAGIC
Serve Yourself
Jul 80, Bermuda?
MOON, YIN
date unknown, piano
ARCH3, LOST4
SESSIONS (LP) — see SESS, SESSCD
Sexy Sadie
late may 68, Kinfauns; acoustic demo
OFF
Jan 69, **GB** sessions
REVOLT, SOUND
Shake, Rattle And Roll
26 Jan 69, Apple
CIRCUIT, FILE1, HOT, LETEND,
PLAY, SING, SUPER1, VIRGIN
Shakin' In The Sixties
Jan 69, **GB** sessions

BLACK, JOURN, MAGTR, RAREST1,
REVOLT
Shanghai Surprise
86, from *Shanghai Surprise*
LIFT, ONOT
Shazam! (riff)
21 Dec 63, BBC
BEEB8
**She Came In Through the Bath-
room Window**
Jan 69, **GB** sessions (various)
ARW1, BLACK, B-ROAD, IHAD,
JOURN, MAGTR, RETURN, SOUND,
SPLHCB, WATCH, Y'ORITE
She Loves You
13 Aug 63, BBC
BEEB5
20 Aug 63, BBC
BEEB5, STUDIO, STUD2
10 Sep 63, BBC
BEEB6, KNIGHT
24 Sep 63, BBC
BEEB6
4 Oct 63, *Ready Steady Go!* (lip-synch)
RSG!
20 Oct 63, BBC
BEEB7
24 Oct 63, Stockholm, *Pop 63*
PETE, SILVER, SPLHCB, STAGE,
STOCK
4 Nov 63, Royal Variety Show
BEEB7, 4EVER, ROYAL
20 Nov 63, ABC Manchester
ABC, RECO
7 Dec 63, Empire Theatre, Liverpool
DEC63, YOUNG
21 Dec 63, BBC
BEEB8
26 Dec 63, BBC
BEEB8
19 Jan 64, Paris
HOTW
9 Feb 64, *Ed Sullivan*
BLASTS, CAVERN, CONQ, REN1, SHEW
11 Feb 64, Washington
FIRST
15 Feb 64, *Sullivan* rehearsal
CONQ
16 Feb 64, *Ed Sullivan*
BLASTS
16 Feb 64, *Ed Sullivan* (edit)
THOSE, RECO, REN1
12 Jun 64, Adelaide
DOLL'S, FANS, 1964
16 Jun 64, Melbourne
CANDLE, FANS, HOTW, TOUR
17 Jun 64, Melbourne
MELB
22 Aug 64, Vancouver
SINGLES, VANC

23 Aug 64, Hollywood Bowl
  8ARMS, ONLY, RAREST2, ROMA,
  TOP
2 Sep 64, Philadelphia?
  FLATS
She Said She Said
  66? John solo acoustic
  ARCH2, LOST2
  Jan 69, **GB** sessions
  BLACK, JOURN, REVOLT, WATCH,
  Y'ORITE
She's A Woman
  8 Oct 64, EMI; take 1
  INAB, LIVEAT
  8 Oct 64, EMI; take 2 (w/ false start)
  ULTRA1
  8 Oct 64, EMI; take 6 (cv, true stereo)
  ITEMS, SPLHCB
  8 Oct 64, EMI; take 7
  URT34
  26 Nov 64, BBC
  BEEB, BROAD, FCK
  27 Nov 64, *Ready Steady Go!* (lip-
synch)
  RSG!
  11 Apr 65, NME Concert
  DIGIT
  20 Jun 65, Paris, evening
  BEAT, COMPL, HOTW
  24 Jun 65, Milan?
  4EVER, ITALY, PREV, SINGLES
  27 Jun 65, Rome
  ARRIV, ROMA
  19 Aug 65, Houston, afternoon
  TEXAN
  19 Aug 65, Houston, evening
  HOUST, TEXAN, TOUR
  21 Aug 65, Minneapolis
  MINN
  30 Aug 65, Hollywood Bowl (cv)
  SPLHCB
  24 Jun 66, Munich (very brief excerpt)
  CRONE, 4EVER, MUNICH, STAGE
  30 Jun 66, Tokyo
  BUDO, 8ARMS, FIVE, HOTW,
  JAPAN64, TOKIO
  2 Jul 66, Tokyo, afternoon
  BUDO, JAPAN64
  29 Aug 66, Candlestick Park
  CANDLE
Aug 80, **DF** sessions
  BEFORE, WINSTON
She's Got It Bad
  unknown, Paul, home rehearsal
  HOME
The Sheik Of Araby
  1 Jan 62, Decca
  DECCA, REINTRO
Shimmy Shake
  Dec 62, Star-Club, Hamburg (cv)

STARS
Short Fat Fannie
  Jan 69, **GB** sessions
  JOURN, MAGTR, REVOLT, TRAX3
The Short Rap
  Dec 69, John for Ronnie Hawkins (from
  promo 45)
  WALK
A Shot Of Rhythm And Blues
  18 Jun 63, BBC
  BEEB3, BEEBCD, WITHER, WOND,
  YOUNG
  21 Jul 63, BBC
  DEMO, MEET, WOND, W/PETE
  27 Aug 63, BBC
  BBC, BEEB, DEMO, DON'T, 21,
  LBEEB, WLOVE, YELL
  Jan 69, **GB** sessions
  RUSSIA
Shout!
  19 Apr 64, IBC (for *Around The
  Beatles*)
  FCK, FILE2, MONKEY, NOT4, NOTG,
  SESSCD, SPLHCB
  6 May 64, *Around The Beatles*
  BEAT, LALB, MARY, NASSAU, 1234,
  RSG!, SOME, TOP, 21
  Jan 69, **GB** sessions
  JOURN, RUSSIA, Y'ORITE
Side By Side
  63, BBC (program theme)
  BEEB1, BEEB2, BEEBCD, MONKEY,
  REINTRO, YEARS,
Sie Liebt Dich
  29 Jan 64, Paris; take 14
  BACK, EMIOUT, ITEMS, KOMM,
  LALB, MARY, NASSAU, POWER,
  REN4
Silly Love Songs
  3 May 76, Wings, Ft. Worth
  FORTW
  15 May 76, Wings, Largo
  GEAR
  19 Jun 76, Wings, Atlanta
  ATLAN
  14 Jun 76, Wings, San Francisco
  ZOO
  21 Jun 76, Wings, L.A. Forum
  FORUM
  23 Jun 76, Wings, L.A. Forum
  WINGS
Simple Life
  77, Japanese commercial
  OGNIR
Sing A Song For Tragopan
  77, from **SCOUSE THE MOUSE**
  (cv)
  SCOUSE
Singing The Blues
  Jan 69, **GB** sessions

LETEND, SING
12 Dec 81, Ringo, *Parkinson* (UK TV)
   CLASS2, MAIL
Sisters O Sisters
13 Jan 72, *David Frost*
   TELE
18 Aug 72, One-To-One rehearsals
   1AND1
30 Aug 72, MSG, evening
   THIS
Sitar play
  Dec 72, George, *David Frost*
   CLASS3, LINING
Six O'Clock
Mar-Jul 73 (cv, long)
   4SIDES, OGNIR
Slippin' And Slidin'
Jan 69, **GB** sessions
   RUSSIA
Oct-Dec 73, **R&R** sessions
   MAYP, R'N'R, SHOULD
18 Apr 75, *Old Grey Whistle Test*
   GUITAR, RARER, TWICK, WORK, YIN
13 Jun 75, *Salute To Sir Lew Grade*
   PLOP, SHOTS, VIENNA
21 May 85, Julian, Sydney
   MAIL
Slow Down
20 Aug 63, BBC
   AUCTION, BEEB5, DON'T, HOWDO,
   YELL
Smile Away
11 Feb 72, Wings, Hull
   BELGIUM, SPRING
22 Jul 72, Wings, Montreux
   SWITZ
16 Aug 72, Wings, Hanover
   ORIENT
17 Aug 72, Wings, Rotterdam
   QUEEN
22 Aug 72, Wings, Antwerp
   ANTW
Snow Is Falling All The Time
21-22 Nov 68, hospital? (*Aspen* flexi)
   LIFE, THIS
Snow Up Your Nose For Christmas
77, from **SCOUSE THE MOUSE**
(cv)
   SCOUSE
So Bad
84 (cv, from CD)
   GREAT
So Glad To See You Here
3 Oct 78, longer, alternate mix
   EGGS
So How Come (No One Loves Me)
23 Jul 63, BBC
   BBC, BEEB, BEEB4, DEMO, DON'T,
   PETE, SILVER, WITHER, YELL
Soily

22 Jul 72, Wings, Montreux
   SWITZ
22 Aug 72, Wings, Antwerp
   ANTW
19 May 73, Wings, Leeds
   LEEDS
10 Jul 73, Wings, Newcastle
   NEWCAS
23 Jul 73, Wings, Edinburgh
   SCOT
Fall 75, *One Hand Clapping* sessions
   NASH, ONEH, WHY
15 May 76, Wings, Largo
   9MM
19 May 76, Wings, Atlanta
   ATLAN
16 Jun 76, Wings, San Diego
   ORIENT
21 Jun 76, Wings, L.A. Forum
   FORUM
23 Jun 76, Wings, L.A. Forum
   LASER, WINGS, ZOO
Soldier Of Love
16 Jul 63, BBC
   BBC, BEEB, BEEB3, BEEBCD,
   BROAD, LINING, SOLDIER, THEIR,
   WITHER, YEARS
Jan 69, **GB** sessions
   GOLDM, JOURN
Solid Gold
74, Keith Moon, with Ringo (cv)
   RICHIE
Some Days
  Spring 60, Quarry Men
   STU
Some Other Guy
22 Aug 62, Cavern Club (film)
   BEAT, RARER, SOME, 21, 2MUCH,
   WITHER, WOND
22 Aug 62, Cavern Club (acetate)
   SPLHCB, WALK
26 Jan 63, BBC
   BEAUT, BEEB, CASTS, MEET,
   SHOTS, W/PETE
23 Jun 63, BBC
   BEEB1, BEEBCD, MONKEY, YEARS
Some People Never Know
11 Feb 72, Wings, Hull
   BELGIUM, SPRING
Someplace Else
86, *Shanghai Surprise*
   LIFT, ONOT
Something
2 May, EMI & 5 May, Olympic & 11 Jul
69, EMI; take 37 (extended)
   EXTEN, LOOKING, NO3, 1234,
   RETURN, ROAD, TALKS, 2MUCH
2 May, EMI & 5 May, Olympic & 11 Jul
69, EMI; take 37 (short)
   ARW1, BOTH, B-ROAD

2 May, EMI & 5 May, Olympic & 11/16
Jul & 15 Aug 69, EMI; take 39 (cv)
    SPLHCB
10 Nov 74, Long Beach
    STICK
22 Nov 74, Fort Worth
    DARK, MOREF
26 Nov 74, Baton Rouge
    BATON
30 Nov 74, Chicago
    CHIC
15 Dec 74, Nassau
    LAST
10 Feb 88, *Rockline*
    UTOPIA
SOMEWHERE IN ENGLAND
(original LP) — see BYGEO, ENGL
Song For John
21-22 Nov 68, hospital? (*Aspen* flexi)
    LIFE
SONGS BY GEORGE HARRISON
(EP) — see UTOPIA
Sound Stage Of Mind
74 tour, unknown
    SNAPS
2 Nov 74, Vancouver
    LIVAN
4 Nov 74, Seattle
    DOLL'S
22 Nov 74, Fort Worth
    DARK, MOREF
26 Nov 74, Baton Rouge
    BATON
15 Dec 74, Nassau
    LAST
SPICY BEATLES SONGS (LP) — see
BUG
Spin It On
23 Jul 78 (cv, alternate mix)
    EGGS
25 Nov 79, Wings, Liverpool
    TOKYO
7 Dec 79, Wings, Wembley
    WEMB
29 Dec 79, Wings, Hammersmith
    KAMP
Spirits Of Ancient Egypt
9 May 76, Wings, Toronto
    MAPLE
15 May 76, Wings, Largo
    FEATHER
21 Jun 76, Wings, L.A. Forum
    FORUM
23 Jun 76, Wings, L.A. Forum
    WINGS, ZOO
Stand By Me
Jan 69, **GB** sessions
    BLACK, COMMON, JOURN,
    REVOLT, TWICK, WATCH
Oct-Dec 73, **R&R** sessions

MAYP, R'N'R, SHOULD
18 Apr 75, *Old Grey Whistle Test*
    GUITAR, RARER, WORK, YIN
13 Jun 75, *Salute To Sir Lew Grade*
    SHOTS, VIENNA
21 May 85, Julian, Sydney
    MAIL
Star Spangled Banner
19 May 76, Wings, Atlanta
    ATLAN
23 Jun 76, Wings, L.A. Forum
    LASER, WINGS
(Just Like) Starting Over
Jul 80, Bermuda; demo take 3
    LOST5
Aug 80, Dakota, acoustic "take 3"
    ARCH2, LOST2
Aug 80, **DF** sessions; first vocal take (v.
only)
    LOST5
Aug 80, **DF** session; first vocal take
(rough mix)
    LOST5
Aug 80, **DF** sessions (studio outtakes)
    BEFORE, WINSTON
Aug 80, **DF** sessions (long promo
version)
    MAIL
**(Just Like) Starting Over (Post
Script)**
Aug 80, **DF** sessions (end of promo 12-
inch version)
    LIMIT
Stay
Aug 80, **DF** sessions
    BEFORE, WINSTON
Steel And Glass
Jul 74, **W&B** sessions
    PREC, WALLS
Step Inside Love
Feb 68, Dick James, demo?
    CAVERN, DOLL'S, JULIAN, RARER,
    THEIR, THOSE, WALK
68, Cilla Black (cv)
    REN4
Steppin' Out
Jul 80, Bermuda; acoustic & rhythm box
    ARCH4
Strawberry Fields Forever
Nov 66? acoustic demo
    ARCH1, 1967
Nov 66? electric demo
    LOST3
Nov 66 ? electric "arranging" demo
    ARCH1, LOST1
24 Nov 66, EMI; take 1
    FILE2, HEAD, MIXED, NOTH,
    TRAGIC, URT56
29 Nov 66, EMI; take 2
    URT56

29 Nov 66, EMI; take 2 with George Martin's voice-over
  NOTH, SPLHCB, TRAGIC
28 Nov 66, EMI; take 3, false start
  HEAD, FILE2, MIXED, NOTH, SESSCD, TRAGIC, URT56
28 Nov 66, EMI; take 4
  HEAD, FILE2, MIXED, NOTH, SESSCD, TRAGIC, URT56
29 Nov 66, EMI; take 5 (instr., false start)
  URT56
29 Nov 66, EMI; take 6
  URT56
29 Nov 66, EMI; take 7 (mono remix 3)
  NOTH, SFF, TRAGIC, URT56
15 Dec 66, EMI; orchestral overdub onto take 25
  HEAD, FILE2, MIXED, NOTH, SESSCD, TRAGIC, URT56
8/9/15/21 Dec 66, EMI; take 26
  HEAD, FILE2, MIXED, NOTH, SESSCD, TRAGIC, ULTRA1, URT56
24/28/29 Nov & 8/9/15/21 Dec 66, EMI; edit of takes 7 & 26 (cv, stereo "non-US" mix)
  CASUAL, NOTH, TRAGIC
24/28/29 Nov & 8/9/15/21 Dec 66, EMI; edit of takes 7 & 26 (cv, stereo)
  JUDY, SPLHCB
Nov-Dec 66, EMI (various, excerpts)
  INAB, LIVEAT
Jan 69, **GB** sessions
  REVOLT, SOUND
STUDIO OUTTAKES (EP) — see GUITAR, WORK
Sue Me Sue You Blues
72, demo
  LIFT, ONOT
22 Nov 74, Fort Worth
  DARK, MOREF
26 Nov 74, Baton Rouge
  BATON
30 Nov 74, Chicago
  CHIC
15 Dec 74, Nassau
  LAST
Suicide
Jan 69, **GB** sessions
  REVOLT, SOUND, WALK
75, *One Hand Clapping* sessions
  FILE2, JULIAN, MIXED, NIGHT, ONEH, YEARS
unknown, Paul, home rehearsal
  HOME
Summer's Day Song
Summer 79, **McII** home sessions
  RAVING
Sun King
Jan 69, **GB** sessions (instrumental)

ARW1, B-ROAD, COMMON, JOURN, MAGTR, RETURN, TRAX3
Sun Records Medley
21 Nov 75, *Blue Suede Shoes*
  LOOK, ONOT
The Sunshine In Your Hair
unknown, Paul, home rehearsal
  HOME
Sure To Fall (In Love With You)
1 Jan 62, Decca audition
  DECCA
18 Jun 63, BBC
  BEEB3, BEEBCD, YOUNG
24 Sep 63, BBC
  BACK, BEEB6, DEMO, DON'T, POWER, REINTRO, STUD2, 21, YELL
4 Apr 64, BBC
  BBC, BEEB, BEEB10, BROAD
8 May 64, BBC
  BEEB10
Surprise, Surprise (Sweet Bird Of Paradox)
Summer 74, Dakota? acoustic
  ARCH1, LOST1
Jul 74, **W&B** sessions
  PREC, WALLS, WINSTON
Suzy Parker
Jan 69, **GB** sessions
  BACK, BLACK, CIRCUIT, CLASS3, GBSESS, GOLDM, HOMOG, HOT, JOURN, PLAY, REVOLT, SOUND, THEIR, 21, VIRGIN, WALK
SWEET APPLE TRAX VOLS. 1 & 2
(LPs) — see BLACK, JOURN
Sweet Georgia Brown
Apr 62, Hamburg (cv, original lyrics)
  REINTRO
Apr 62, Hamburg/64 (cv, with Beatles ref.)
  ELVIS
Sweet Little Sixteen
Dec 62, Star -Club, Hamburg (cv)
  B4TIME, SPLHCB, STARS
23 Jul 63, BBC
  BEAUT, BEEB, BEEB4, KNIGHT, 1234, YOUNG
Jan 69, **GB** sessions
  ALMO, GOLDM, JOURN
John, 73, **R&R** sessions
  LOST6
Sweetest Little Show
Paul, home demo, circa Fall 80
  TUG, WAR

T

Take Good Care Of My Baby
1 Jan 62, Decca audition
  DECCA, REINTRO
Take Her Back, Jack
Paul, home demo, circa Fall 80

TUG, WAR
Take It Away
  Paul, home demo, circa Fall 80
    TUG, WAR
  Feb-Mar 81, (cv, with clean intro, from video?)
    SUIT
Take Me As I Am (Or Not At All)
  10 Feb 88, George, *Rockline*
    UTOPIA
Take This Hammer
  Jan 69, **GB** sessions
    BYEBYE, GRAVE, JOURN, LETEND, ONCE, SING
Takin' A Trip To Carolina
  Jan 69, **GB** sessions
    RUSSIA
A Taste Of Honey
  Dec 62, Star-Club, Hamburg (diff. from cv)
    REICH
  Dec 62, Star-Club, Hamburg (cv)
    B4TIME, STARS
  11 Feb 63, EMI; take 7 (basic take)
    URT34
  11 Feb 63, EMI; take 7 (cv)
    1964
  13 May 63, BBC
    BEEB2, MONKEY
  18 Jun 63, BBC
    BEEB3, PLEASE
  23 Jun 63, BBC
    BEEB1, BEEBCD, MONKEY
  10 Sep 63, BBC
    BEEB6
Tea For Two
  Jan 69, **GB** sessions
    COMMON, JOURN, LETEND, TRAX3
Tears Of The World
  79-80, original **SOMEWHERE IN ENGLAND**
    BYGEO, ENGL, ONOT
Teddy Boy
  Jan 69, **GB** sessions
    GBCD, GETB, GRAVE, HEAD, HOMOG, JOURN, LETBE, LETEND, MAGTR, MIXED, POWER, RAREST6, REN2, SUPER1, TORON
television broadcasts:
  Alice In Wonderland, 9 Dec 85 (Ringo)
    RIZZ
  Around The Beatles, 6 May 64
    BEAT, CAVERN, EMIOUT, LALB, NASSAU, RECO, SOME
  Arena Buddy Holly special, 12 Sep 84 (Paul)
    THAT'LL, TWICE
  Aspel And Company, 9 Jun 84 (Paul)
    BOTH, GREAT
  The Beatles, 10 Jun 64 (VARA)

LINING
  The Beatles In Adelaide, 13 Jun 64
    FANS, DOLL
  The Beatles Sing For Shell, 1 Jul 64
    CANDLE, HOTW, TOUR
  Big Beat '65, NME Poll Winners 65, 18 Apr 65
    DIGIT
  Big Night Out, 29 Feb 64
    SUNDAY
  Blackpool Night Out, 1 Aug 65
    STOCK
  Blue Suede Shoes, 5 Jan 86 (George & Ringo)
    LOOK, ONOT, RIZZ
  Cilla, 6 Feb 68 (Ringo)
    RARER, RIZZ, SNAPS, SOME
  Circus-Krone-Bau, Munich; 24 Jun 66
    BEAT, CRONE, MUNICH, STAGE
  The David Frost Show, 13 Jan 72 (John)
    JOSHUA, TELE, THIS
  The David Frost Show, 3 Dec 71 (George)
    CLASS3, LINING
  The Dick Cavett Show, 11 May 72 (John)
    JOSHUA, TELE
  The Ed Sullivan Show, 9 Feb 64
    BLASTS, CONQ, REN1, SHEW
  The Ed Sullivan Show, rehearsal, 15 Feb 64
    CONQ
  The Ed Sullivan Show, 16 Feb 64
    BLASTS, 8ARMS, REN1
  The Ed Sullivan Show, 16 Feb 64 (edit)
    RECO, REN1, THOSE
  The Ed Sullivan Show, 23 Feb 64
    BLASTS, CONQ
  The Ed Sullivan Show, 23 Feb 64 (edit)
    REN1, THOSE
  The Ed Sullivan Show, 12 Sep 65
    CONQ, RECO
  The Ed Sullivan Show, 5 Jun 66
    ABC
  The Ed Sullivan Show, 17 May 70 (Ringo)
    RICHIE, SOLDIER
  Experiment in Television, 29 Jul 68
    LIVEAT, NOTH, RECO, RED
  Eyewitness News, Summer 72
    4SIDES, LIFT, TEDDY
  Flip Wilson, 12 Oct 72 (?) (tribute & Paul int.)
    TOBE
  Frost on Sunday, 8 Sep 68
    JULIAN, LALB, NASSAU, SFF, TOP
  Goodnight America, 28 Jun 76 (Paul)
    FORTW

The Grammy Award Show, 3 Mar 73 (Ringo)
   WALK
The Grammy Award Show, 1 Mar 75 (John)
   1970S, PLOP
Hullabaloo, 3 Jan 66 (same as *TOTP*, 2 Dec 65)
   FHILLS, STAGE
It's The Beatles! 7 Dec 63
   DEC63, TOUR, YOUNG
James Paul McCartney, 16 Apr 73
   MYLO, LIFT, ORIENT
Jerry Lewis MD Telethon, 6 Sep 72
   CLASS2
Man Of The Decade, 30 Dec 69 (John)
   TWICE
Midnight Special, 25 Apr 75? (Rod Stewart w/ Paul & Linda)
   ORIENT
The Mike Douglas Show, 14-18 Feb 72 (John)
   JOSHUA, LOOK, TEDDY, TELE, THIS, WORK
The Mike Douglas Show, 17 Apr 78 (Ringo)
   ARW1, LINING
Monday Night Football, 9 Dec 74 (John)
   LIFT, TEDDY
The Music Lives On, 8 Sep 84 (Paul)
   LOOK, RAVING
Newsfront, 15 May 68 (John & Paul)
   RED
Old Grey Whistle Test, 18 Apr 75 (John)
   GUITAR, RARER, TWICK, WORK, YIN
The One-To-One Concert, 14 Dec 72,
   JOSHUA, 1TO1, PLOP, ROAD, SNAPS, SHOTS, TEDDY, THIS, WORK
Our World, 25 Jun 67
   MELLO, SFF, WHEN
Palais des Sports ; 20 Jun 65; evening
   BEAT, HOTW
Parkinson, 12 Dec 81 (Ringo)
   CLASS2, MAIL
Parkinson In Australia, 8 Oct 82 (Ringo)
   CLASS2, MAIL
People And Places, 11 Nov 62? (Cavern film)
   BEAT, RARER, SOME, WOND
The Prince's Trust, 20 Jun 85 (Paul)
   OBLA45
Ready Steady Go! 4 Oct 63
   RSG!
Ready Steady Go! 6 May 64
   RSG!
Ready Steady Go! 27 Apr 64
   RSG!
Ringo, 26 Apr 78

   4SIDES, MELLO, OGNIR, RICHIE, TRAGIC
Royal Variety Show, 10 Nov 63
   CASTS, BEEB7, 4EVER, ROYAL
Rutland Weekend Television Xmas Show, 26 Dec 75 (George)
   4SIDES, NIGHT, ROPE, SNAPS
A Salute To Sir Lew Grade, 13 Jun 75 (John)
   PLOP, RARER, SHOTS,20X4, VIENNA
Saturday Night Live (rehearsal) 16 Nov 76 (George)
   RARER, ROUGH, UTOPIA
Saturday Night Live, 18 Nov 76 (George)
   B-ROAD, BYGEO, UTOPIA
Saturday Night Live, 23 Apr 77 (Rutles)
   ROPE
Saturday Night Live, 8 Dec 84 (Ringo)
   RIZZ
Shindig, 20 Jan 65
   CONQ, RARER, RECO
The Smothers Brothers Comedy Hour, 28 Apr 75 (Ringo)
   RICHIE
The South Bank Show, 14 Jan 78 (Melvin Bragg interview, filmed Oct 77)
   GREAT, SUN
The South Bank Show, 14 Oct 84 (making *Broad Street*)
   CONF, GREAT
Sunday Night At The London Palladium, 13 Oct 63
   ABC, BEAT, SUNDAY
Thank Your Lucky Stars, 21 Dec 63
   LINING
Tomorrow, 28 Apr 75 (John)
   DOCTOR, 1970S
Tonight Show, 15 May 68 (John & Paul)
   RED, SPLHCB
Top Of The Pops, 2 Dec 65
   FHILLS, STAGE
Top Of The Pops, 19 Sep 68
   HOWDO, LALB, NASSAU, NOTH, RECO, TOP, 2MUCH
Top Of The Pops, 12 Feb 70 (John)
   DOLL'S, SOME
Wings Over The World, 16 Mar 79
   1970S
Wings, Melbourne, 13 Nov 75
   FLY, ONEH
Ten Years After On Strawberry Jam 74, Scaffold (cv)
   GREAT
Tennessee (Perkins)
 Jan 69, **GB** sessions
   BLACK, COMMON, GBSESS, HEAD, HIHO, JOURN, RAREST1, REVOLT
Tennessee (Lennon)

JUDY
17 Oct 63, EMI; take 15 (cv, true stereo)
   FCK, ITEM, SPLHCB, YEARS
7 Dec 63, Empire Theatre, Liverpool
   DEC63, SINGLES, TOUR, YOUNG
21 Dec 63, BBC
   BEEB, BEE8, KNIGHT, WLOVE
19 Jan 64, Paris
   HOTW
11 Feb 64, Washington
   FIRST
15 Feb 64, *Ed Sullivan* rehearsal
   CONQ
16 Feb 64, *Ed Sullivan*
   BLASTS, 8ARMS
16 Feb 64, *Ed Sullivan* (edit)
   REN1, THOSE
30 Mar 64, BBC
   BEEB9, 1964, PETE, ROUGH, SILVER, YEARS
12 Jun 64, Adelaide
   DOLL'S, FANS
17 Jun 64, Melbourne
   MELB
This Song Of Love
Jan 69, **GB** sessions
   JOURN, LETEND, SING
Those Were The Days
Jul 68, Apple; Mary Hopkin (cv)
   SPLHCB
Spring 69, bed-in?
   BUG, CAVERN, RECO, THEIR, THOSE
Three Cool Cats
1 Jan 62, Decca audition
   DECCA, REINTRO, SPLHCB, WHEN
Jan 69, **GB** sessions
   COMMON, JOURN, REVOLT, TRAX3
Ticket To Ride
15 Feb 65, EMI; take 2 (cv, basic take)
   SPLHCB, URT34
15 Feb 65, EMI; take 2 (cv)
   LIVEAT
15 Feb 65, EMI; take 2 (cv, UK stereo mix)
   CASUAL
11 Apr 65; NME concert
   DIGIT
7 Jun 65, BBC (long)
   BEEB, FCK, WLOVE
7 Jun 65, BBC (short)
   PETE, SILVER
20 Jun 65, Paris, afternoon
   HOTW
20 Jun 65, Paris, evening
   BEAT, COMPL, HOTW
27 Jun 65, Rome
   ARRIV, ROMA
17 Jul 65, Blackpool

STOCK
15 Aug 65, Shea Stadium
   GOOD, SHEA
19 Aug 65, Houston, afternoon
   TEXAN
19 Aug 65, Houston, evening
   HOUST, SINGLES, TEXAN, TOUR
12 Sep 65, *Ed Sullivan Show*
   CONQ, RECO
Tie Me Kangaroo Down, Sport
26 Dec 63, BBC; Rolf Harris w/Beatles
   BEEB8
Tight A$
73? electric composing demo
   ARCH4, LOST7
Till There Was You
1 Jan 62, Decca audition
   DECCA
Dec 62, Star-Club, Hamburg (diff. from cv)
   REICH
11 Jun 63, BBC
   BEEB2, MONKEY
29 Jun 63, BBC
   LBEEB, STUDIO, STUD1
30 Jul 63, BBC
   BEEB4, BROAD
4 Nov 63, Royal Variety
   BEEB7, 4EVER, ROYAL
7 Dec 63, Empire Theatre, Liverpool
   DEC63, TOUR, YOUNG
21 Dec 63, BBC
   BEEB8
26 Dec 63, BBC
   BEEB8
9 Feb 64, *Ed Sullivan*
   BLASTS, CONQ, SHEW, SOLDIER
11 Feb 64, Washington
   BEAT, FIRST
29 Feb 64, *Big Night Out* (lip-synch, edited)
   SUNDAY
30 Mar 64, BBC
   BEEB, BEEB9, WITHER
12 Jun 64, Adelaide
   DOLL'S, FANS, 1964
17 Jun 64, Melbourne
   8ARMS, MELB, RAREST2
Jan 69, **GB** sessions
   RUSSIA
Time Bandits
81, from *Time Bandits*
   ONOT
Time Is Tight
Jan 69, **GB** sessions (bass riff)
   JOURN, Y'ORITE
Time To Hide
21 Jun 76, Wings, L.A. Forum
   FORUM
23 Jun 76, Wings, L.A. Forum

14 Aug 68, EMI; take 4, stereo remix 4
BUG, EMIOUT, MARY, ONCE,
POWER, SHAME, SFF, SUPER1,
THEIR21, WHISP
14 Aug 68/26 Nov 69, EMI; take 4,
stereo remix 5
4SIDES, LIMIT, RED, SHAME,
SOME, 2MUCH
Jan 76? ad-lib on *Earth News Radio*
LIMIT
14 Aug 68, EMI; take 4, 84 **SES-
SIONS** remix
SESS, SESSCD

What's The Use Of Getting Sober?
Jan 69, **GB** sessions
JOURN, MAGTR, TRAX3

**Whatever Gets You Through The
Night**
Summer 74, NYC, composing tape
ARCH3, LOST3
Jul 74, **W&B** sessions
ONCE, PREC, SHOTS, WALLS,
WINSTON
28 Nov 77, MSG with Elton John
GUITAR, PLOP, WORK

Whatever Happened To...?
John, 80, Dakota; acoustic
LOST3
When I Was Young And In My Prime
unknown, John, Dakota
ARCH2, LOST2

When I'm Sixty-four
Jan 69, **GB** sessions
JOURN, WOND, Y'ORITE

When Irish Eyes Are Smiling
Jan 69, **GB** sessions
COMMON, GRAVE, JOURN

When The Night
19 May 73, Wings, Leeds
LEEDS
10 Jul 73, Wings, Newcastle
NEWCAS
23 Jul 73, Wings, Edinburgh
SCOT

When The Saints
May 61, Hamburg (cv)
DON'T

When We Was Fab
87 (cv, with reverse ending from 12-
inch)
UTOPIA
When You're Drunk You Think Of Me
Jan 69, **GB** sessions
JOURN, MAGTR, TRAX3

Where Have You Been All My Life?
Dec 62, Star-Club, Hamburg (diff. from
cv)
REICH
Jan 69, **GB** sessions
GOLDM, JOURN

**Where There's A Will, There's A
Way**
12 Dec 69, Copenhagen; D&B
w/George
FALCON

While My Guitar Gently Weeps
25 Jul 68, EMI; take 1 (acoustic)
EXTEN, FILE2, INAB, LIVEAT,
MIXED, NOTH, OFF, RED, SESS,
SESSCD
5/6 Sep 68, EMI; take 25 (cv)
SPLHCB
2 Nov 74, Vancouver
LIVAN
10 Nov 74, Long Beach
STICK
22 Nov 74, Fort Worth, Texas
DARK, MOREF
25 Nov 74, Baton Rouge
BATON
30 Nov 74, Chicago
CHIC
15 Dec 74, Nassau
LAST
6 Jun 87, Prince's Trust
UTOPIA
"White Album Jam"
unknown, no Beatles involvement
WHISP
White Power (Get Off!)
Jan 69, **GB** sessions
BLACK, COMMON, GBSESS, HEAD,
HIHO, JOURN, POWER, RAREST1,
21

Who Can See It?
2 Nov 74, George, Vancouver
CONFI, LIVAN

Who Has Seen The Wind?
70? (cv, from UK 45)
THIS

Whole Lotta Love
Oct-Dec 73, **R&R** sessions
MAYP, R'N'R, SHOULD

Whole Lotta Shakin' Goin' On
Jan 69, **GB** sessions (*Let It Be*)
COMMON, JOURN, THEIR, TRAX3
21 Nov 75,*Blue Suede Shoes*
LOOK, ONOT

Why Don't We Do It In The Road
Jan 69, **GB** sessions
BLACK, COMMON, GBSESS, HEAD,
JOURN, Y'ORITE

Wide Prairie
Oct 73, Paris? Wings outtake
CUTS

Wild Life
11 Feb 72, Wings, Hull
SPRING
22 Jul 72, Wings, Montreux
SWITZ

16 Feb 65, EMI; take 1? with rough vocal
    URT34
16 Feb 65, EMI; take 2; false start w/ rough v
    URT34
16 Feb 65, EMI; take 14; cv, basic take
    URT34
16 Feb 65, EMI; take 14 (cv, mono US 45 mix)
    CASUAL
16 Feb 65, EMI; take 14 (cv, true stereo)
    DIGIT, NOT4, SPLCHB, YEARS
16 Feb 65, EMI; take 14 (cv, outfake with bogus chat)
    FCK

Yesterday
14 Jun 65, EMI; take 2 (cv)
    SPLHCB
17 Jul 65, Blackpool
    STOCK
12 Sep 65, *Ed Sullivan*
    CONQ
24 Jun 66, Munich, evening
    BEAT, CRONE, 4EVER, MUNICH, STAGE
30 Jun 66, Tokyo
    BUDO, 8ARMS, FIVE, FS2S, HOTW, JAPAN64, ROMA, TOKIO
2 Jul 66, Tokyo, afternoon
    BUDO, JAPAN64, TOUR
29 Aug 66, Candlestick Park
    CANDLE, SINGLES
1 May 70, CBS, Nashville? Dylan w/George
    CLASS3
16 Apr 73, *James Paul McCartney*
    FCK, MYLO
1 Nov 75, Wings, Perth
    FLY
13 Nov 75, Wings, Melbourne
    FLY, 9MM, ONEH
15 May 76, Wings, Largo
    GEAR
19 May 76, Wings, Atlanta
    ATLAN
10 Jun 76, Wings, Seattle?
    FORTW
23 Jun 76, Wings, L.A. Forum
    LASER, WINGS
16 Nov 76, George (*SNL* rehearsal)
    ROUGH, UTOPIA
Oct 77, Melvin Bragg interview
    SUN
25 Nov 79, Wings, Liverpool
    TOKYO
7 Dec 79, Wings, Wembley
    WEMB
29 Dec 79, Hammersmith

    KAMP
You Can't Catch Me
John, 73 **R&R** sessions
    LOST6
You Can't Do That
25 Feb 64, EMI; take 9 (cv)
    SPLHCB
30 Mar 64, BBC
    BEEB9
4 Apr 64, BBC
    BEEB10
27 Apr 64, *Ready Steady Go!*
    RSG!
18 May 64, BBC
    BEEB10
16 Jun 64, Melbourne
    BEEB11, CANDLE, FANS, HOTW, SINGLES, TOUR
17 Jun 64, Melbourne
    MELB
22 Aug 64, Vancouver
    VANC
23 Aug 64, Hollywood Bowl
    BACK, COMPL, 8ARMS, KNIGHT, ONLY, STONE, RAREST2, ROMA, TOP
2 Sep 64, Philadelphia?
    FLATS
Jan 69, **GB** sessions
    JOURN, MAGTR, TRAX3
You Gave Me The Answer
15 May 76, Wings, Largo
    GEAR
21 Jun 76, Wings, San Francisco
    ZOO
23 Jun 76, Wings, L.A. Forum
    WINGS
unknown, Paul home rehearsal
    HOME
You Got Me Going
Jan 69, **GB** sessions
    BLACK, COMMON, JOURN, WHISP
You Got The Message
Jan 69, **GB** sessions
    JOURN, Y'ORITE
You Gotta Get Back (improv)
Jan 69, **GB** session
    IHAD, JOURN, Y'ORITE
You Know I Will
Summer 79, **McII** home sessions
    RAVING
You Know It Makes Sense
86, Ringo, from Anti-Heroin project
    RIZZ
You Know It's True
unknown, Paul, home rehearsal
    HOME
You Know My Name
67? John composing on piano
    ARCH2, LOST3

67-69, EMI; from the 45
    ITEMS, MARY, REN4
You Must Write Every Day
  Spring 60, Quarry Men
    STU
You Never Give Me Your Money
  6 May, Olympic & 1/11 Jul 69, EMI; take
  30, extended
    B-ROAD, EXTEN, LOOKING, NO3,
    1234, RARER, RETURN, ROAD,
    TALKS
  6 May, Olympic & 1/11 Jul 69, EMI; take
  30, short
    ARW1
You Really Got A Hold On Me
  performance/LP edit (bogus)
    BEAT, CAVERN, THOSE, SUPER1
  4 Jun 63, BBC
    BEEB2, MONKEY, STUDIO, STUD1
  13 Aug 63, BBC
    BEEB5
  17 Sep 63, BBC
    BEEB6, WITHER
  24 Oct 63, Stockholm
    BUG, PETE, SILVER, STAGE, STOCK
  26 Jan 69, Apple (from *Let It Be*)
    BWORD, BYEBYE, CIRCUIT,
    HEARD, PLAY, SING, SUPER1
You Win Again
  Jan 69, **GB** sessions
    BLACK, JOURN, REVOLT, TWICK,
    WATCH, Y'ORITE
You'll Be Mine
  Spring 60, Quarry Men
    STU
You're Going To Lose That Girl
  19 Feb 65, EMI; take 3 (alternate mix,
  from acetate: no bongos, diff guitar)
    NOTG
  19 Feb 65, EMI; take 3 (cv)
    ELVIS
  Jan 69, **GB** sessions
    JOURN, Y'ORITE
You're My Girl
  12 Dec 69, Copenhagen; D&B
  w/George
    FALCON
You're Sixteen
  78, *Ringo* television special
    OGNIR
You've Got Me Thinking
  Jan 69, **GB** sessions
    IHAD, JOURN, REVOLT, Y'ORITE
You've Got To Hide Your Love Away
  9 Aug 65, Silkie (cv)
    REN4
Your Feets Too Big
  Dec 62, Star-Club, Hamburg (cv)
    B4TIME, REICH, STARS

Young Blood
  11 Jun 63, BBC
    BEAUT, BEEB2, BEEBCD, KNIGHT,
    MONKEY, 1234, WOND, YOUNG
Young Love
  John, Dakota; date unknown
    ARCH3, LOST4
Your Mother Should Know
  22 Aug 67, Chappell; take 8? the basic
  tracks
    EXTEN, 1967, NOT4, TRAGIC
  22/23 Aug, Chappell & 29 Sep 67, EMI;
  take 52 (cv)
    SPLHCB
Your True Love
  Jan 69, **GB** sessions
    COMMON, JOURN, REVOLT, TRAX3
  21 Nov 85, *Blue Suede Shoes*
    LOOK, ONOT
YULESVILLE (promo LP) — see
UTOPIA

Z

Zig Zag
  87 (cv, from UK 12-inch)
    UTOPIA
Zoo Gang
  Sep 73 (cv, from the 45)
    1970S, ORIENT, ZOO

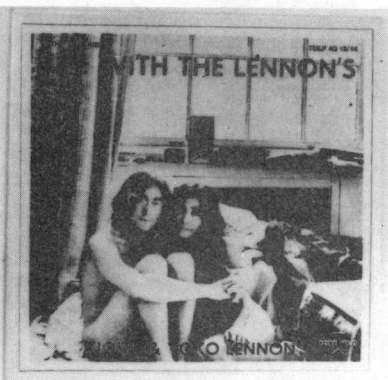

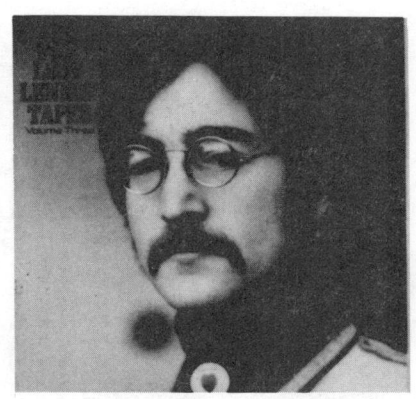

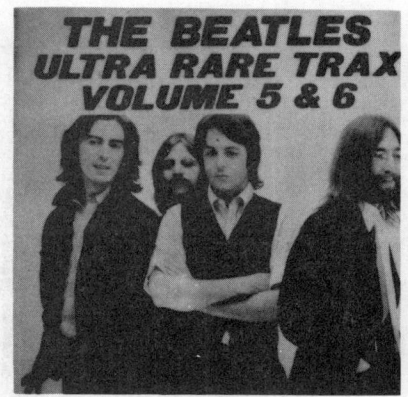

The Very Best of the
BEATLES' RAREST
Number Two

The Very Best of the
BEATLES' RAREST
Number Six

VIRGIN + THREE (Get Back Sessions II)

With love
from us
to you,
The Beatles

withered
beatles

mono